DATA ACQUISITION APPLICATIONS

Edited by **Zdravko Karakehayov**

Data Acquisition Applications
http://dx.doi.org/10.5772/2596
Edited by Zdravko Karakehayov

Contributors

Sohaib Majzoub, Hassan Diab, Wang Rui, Wang Tingfeng, Sun Tao, Chen Fei, Guo Jin, Troy C. Richards, Carlos Ricardo Soccol, Michele Rigon Spier, Luciana Porto de Souza Vandenberghe, Adriane Bianchi Pedroni Medeiros, Luiz Alberto Junior Letti, Wilerson Sturm, Paul Osaretin Otasowie, Chen Fan, José R. García Oya, Andrew Kwan, Fernando Muñoz Chavero, Fadhel M. Ghannouchi, Mohamed Helaoui, Fernando Márquez Lasso, Enrique López-Morillo, Antonio Torralba Silgado, Bogdan Marius Ciurea, Salah Sharieh, Franya Franek, Alexander Ferworn, Andrew Lang, Vijay Parthasarathy, Ameet Jain, V. González, D. Barrientos, J. M. Blasco, F. Carrió, X. Egea, E. Sanchis, Paulo R. Aguiar, Cesar H.R. Martins, Marcelo Marchi, Eduardo C. Bianchi, Feng Chen, Xiaofeng Zhao and Hong Ye

Published by InTech
Janeza Trdine 9, 51000 Rijeka, Croatia

Publishing Process Manager Tanja Skorupan
Technical Editor InTech Prepress, Novi Sad
Cover InTech Design team

Additional hard copies can be obtained from orders@intechopen.com

Data Acquisition Applications, Edited by Zdravko Karakehayov
p. cm.
ISBN 978-953-51-0713-2

For EU product safety concerns:
IN TECH d.o.o., Prolaz Marije Krucifikse Kozulić 3, 51000 Rijeka, Croatia,
info@intechopen.com or visit our website at intechopen.com.

Meet the editor

Dr Zdravko Karakehayov is an Associate Professor in the Department of Computer Systems at the Technical University of Sofia, Bulgaria. Formerly he was affiliated with the Technical University of Denmark, Lyngby and the University of Southern Denmark, Sønderborg. Dr Karakehayov received his Ph.D. and D. Sc. degrees in computer science from the Technical University of Sofia, Bulgaria. He is a senior member of the IEEE Computer Society and Computer Society Distinguish Visitors Program Speaker. He authored six books in the field of embedded systems and holds eight patents. His research field includes low-power design for embedded systems, low-power and secure routing for wireless sensor networks. Dr Karakehayov served as a reviewer for the Journal Transactions on Embedded Computing Systems and several international conferences.

Contents

Preface

Today, the data acquisition technology has found its way into virtually every segment of electronics. A digital signal processing (DSP) system accepts analog signals as input, converts those analog signals to numbers, performs computations using the numbers and eventually converts the results of the computations back into analog signals. Once converted to numbers, signals are unconditionally stable. Error detection and correction methods can be applied to store, transmit and reproduce numbers with no corruption. Signals stored digitally are really just large arrays of numbers. As such, they are immune to the physical limitations of analog signals. Furthermore, DSP can allow large bandwidth signals to be sent over narrow bandwidth channels. Finally, communications security can be significantly improved through DSP. Since numbers are traveling instead of signals, encryption and decryption can be easily done.

While traditionally the goal of data acquisition was to sense the environment, modern computing systems add another axis along which data acquisition is organized. Those systems are capable of measuring internal variables such as on-chip temperature or energy in the battery. Thus the environment to machine data flow frequently works in parallel with machine to machine data flow.

Data acquisition systems have numerous applications. This book has a total of 13 chapters and is divided into three sections: *Industrial applications, Medical applications* and *Scientific experiments*. The chapters are written by experts from around the world.

The targeted audience for this book includes professionals who are designers or researchers in the field of data acquisition systems. Faculty members and graduate students could also benefit from the book.

Many people have contributed to this book; first and foremost the authors who have contributed 13 chapters. These colleagues deserve our appreciation for taking the time out of their busy schedules to contribute to this book. I also owe a big word of thanks to the publishing process manager of this book, Tanja Skorupan. Tanja put in a great deal of effort organizing the interaction with the authors and the production team.

Zdravko Karakehayov
Department of Computer Systems, Technical University of Sofia,
Bulgaria

Section 1

Industrial Applications

Chapter 1

Reconfigurable Systems for Cryptography and Multimedia Applications

Sohaib Majzoub and Hassan Diab

Additional information is available at the end of the chapter

http://dx.doi.org/10.5772/10.5772/30186

1. Introduction

The area of reconfigurable computing has received considerable interest in both its forms: fine-grained (represented in FPGA) and coarse-grained architectures. Both architecture styles attempt to combine two of the important traits of General Purpose Processors (GPPs) and Application-Specific Integrated Circuits (ASICs): flexibility and speed (Hartenstein, 2001). It provides performance close to application-specific hardware and yet preserves, to a certain degree, the flexibility of general-purpose processors. In this chapter, we explore, evaluate, and analyze the performance of a reconfigurable hardware, namely MorphoSys, considering certain key applications targeted for such hardware (Hauck, 1998).

MorphoSys is a reconfigurable architecture designed for multimedia applications, digital signal and image processing, cryptographic algorithms, and networking protocols (Singh et al., 1998). In this chapter, we discuss application mapping, identify potential limitations and key improvements and compare the results with other reconfigurable, GPP, and ASIC architectures. In cryptography, we present the mapping and performance analysis of the Advanced Encryption Standard, namely Rijndael, (Daemen & Rijmen, 2002), along with another cryptography algorithm, namely Twofish, (Schneier et al., 1998). In image processing, we present linear filtering, and 2D and 3D computer graphics algorithms, (Diab & Majzoub, 2003), (Damaj et al, 2002). We present the mapping with detailed analysis, highlighting bottlenecks, proposing possible improvements, and comparing the results to other types of multimedia processing architectures (Maestre et al., 1999), (Mei et al, 2003), (Tessier & Burleson, 2001).

2. Reconfigurable computing

General-purpose processor (GPP) is a confined hardware system that computes any task using existing instructions and registers. Thus, GPP is used to compute diverse range of applications. Application-Specific Integrated Circuits (ASIC), on the other hand, are used to implement a single fixed function. Therefore, ASICs have no flexibility and they can only execute a very limited type of the targeted applications known beforehand (Singh et al., 1998), (Kozyrakis, 1998), (Möller et al., 2006).

Combining the two main traits of the two design styles, namely GPPs and ASICs, reconfigurable systems stand halfway between traditional computing systems and application specific hardware (Kozyrakis & Patterson, 1998). Thus, reconfigurable hardware is a name referred to a system that can be reconfigured and customized in post-fabrication to execute a specific algorithm. MorphoSys, with its customizable logic and routing resources, can be configured, and customized during runtime. This feature provides the ability to compute a wide variety of applications. It shares characteristics of microprocessors, it can be programmed in post-fabrication, and of specific hardware, it can employ a specific algorithm or function to gain the speed (Hartenstein, 2001), (Ferrandi et al, 2005).

Reconfigurable computing is the hardware capability to adapt, configure, and customize itself to provide the best performance for a specific application. It is shifting some of the software complexity to the hardware itself. Fine-grain reconfigurable platforms have bitwise reconfigurable logic, for instance FPGAs. Coarse-grain reconfigurable platforms have more than one bit granularity. Coarse-grain reconfigurable platforms have the advantage of less power consumption and area over the fine-grain at expense of lower flexibility (Galanis et al, 2004), (Eguro & Hauck, 2003). For the multimedia applications, the foreseen potential of the reconfigurable computing in general and coarse-grain reconfigurable platforms in particular is well recognized. The goal of reconfigurable platforms, whether fine-grain or coarse-grain, is to provide high performance, close to ASIC and high flexibility close to general-purpose processors. As such, reconfigurable computing is seen as a major shift in the processor design and research (Hartenstein, 2001).

The parallelism feature of most of the coarse-grain platforms adds a distinctive yet essential advantage to such hardware. Recent work in mesh-based coarse-grain reconfigurable architectures includes GARP (UC Berkeley) (Hauser & Wawrzynek, 1997), MATRIX (CalTech) (Mirsky & DeHon, 1996), REMARC (Stanford) (Miyamori & Olukotun, 1998), and MorphoSys (UC Irvine) (Singh et al., 1998).

In view of all that, performance and hardware analysis should be investigated to identify all the bottlenecks and provide a realistic feedback in order to propose future improvements. Targeted applications, such as multimedia, cryptographic, and communication, should be mapped to determine the hardware behaviour. The analysis is intended to provide feedback on the hardware capability and highlight potential modifications and enhancements (Bosi, Bois, & Savaria, 1999). Unfortunately, most of the coarse-grain reconfigurable platforms, except the FPGA based platforms, lack-easy-to-use compiler and mapping tools to map such applications on the hardware under examination. Therefore, the mapping of the targeted applications for such hardware evaluation must be carried out manually. This hand-mapping process can provide valuable information to prospective compilers that eventually will emerge out of the implementation of wide range of applications (Majzoub & Diab, 2003), (Majzoub & Diab, 2006), (Majzoub et al, 2006), (Itani & Diab, 2004),(Bagherzadeh, Kamalizad & Koohi, 2003).

3. MorphoSys design

MorphoSys is one of the few coarse-grain reconfigurable platforms. Fig. 1 shows the block diagram and internal structure of MorphoSys M1 chip and the logic block for each reconfigurable cell. MorphoSys consists of two main blocks: a RISC processor, TinyRISC, and the Reconfigurable Cell (RC) Array. The other supporting blocks are: the RC context memory, the frame buffer, and the DMA controller. The frame buffer as well as the context memory provides the data and instructions, respectively, in parallel fashion to the RC Array (Lee et al., 2000).

The computing power of the MorphoSys hardware lies in the reconfigurable device. It is divided into four quadrants. Fig. 2 shows the internal interconnectivity of the RC system (Lee et al., 2000). As shown, three hierarchical levels define the interconnection meshwork. The first is a layer that connects each cell to its adjacent cell, i.e. upper, lower, and left cells. The second is an intra-quadrant connection that connects the RCs in the same row or column within the same quadrant. The third level of connectivity is an inter-quadrant connection that links any two cells in different quadrant but in the same column or in the same row. Fig. 1 also shows the RC block diagram. It consists of multiplexers, ALU, four registers, variable shifter, and output register. The inputs for every RC are from the frame buffer, other RCs, and internal Registers (Singh et al., 1998).

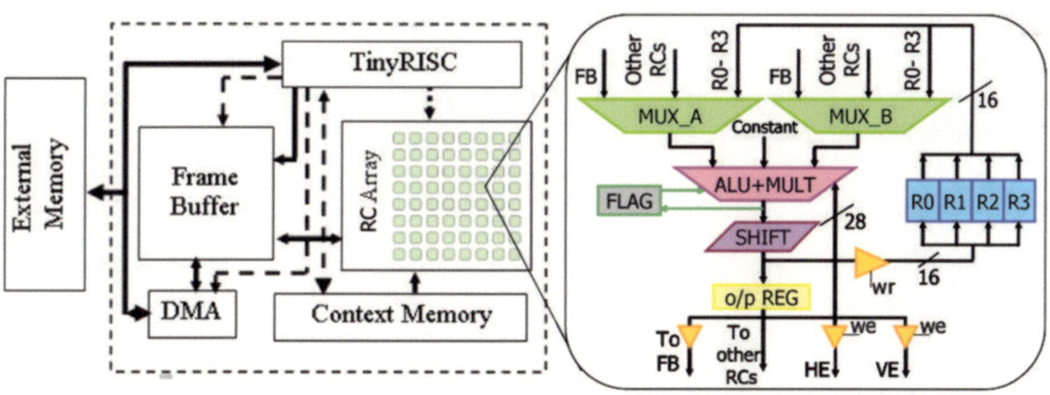

Figure 1. MorphoSys Block Diagram and RC Logic Digaram

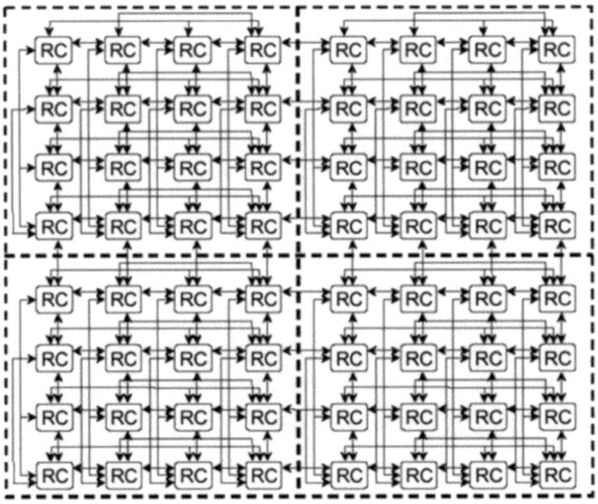

Figure 2. RC Array Communication Buses

4. Cryptographic algorithms mapping onto MorphoSys

Cryptography has grown to be a fundamental element to handle authenticity, integrity, confidentiality and non-reputability of private data flows through public networks. With the increasing demand for high performance hardware, and high level of security, better ciphers are making their way to replace aging algorithms that have proven to be too weak or too slow for the current applications (Schneier, 1996). In this section, we discuss the mapping of the Rijndeal and Twofish encryption algorithms.

4.1. Rijndael encryption algorithm

The Advanced Encryption Standard, AES, is a block cipher adopted as an encryption standard by the National Institute of Standards and Technology, NIST, in November 2001 after a five-year standardization process. The block diagram of the Rijndael algorithm is shown in Fig. 3. The figure shows the steps for both encryption and decryption cases (Daemen & Rijmen, 2002).

4.1.1. Rijndael rounds

First, the input bits are arranged according to the length of the plain text to be encrypted. In the case of 128 bit length, the bits are arranged as 4×4 matrix of bytes; for 192, it will be 4×6 matrix of bytes; and for 256, it will be 4×8 matrix of bytes. The numbers 4, 6, and 8 are called the block width, N_b. The keys of the cipher are also arranged in the same fashion (Daemen & Rijmen, 2002).

Rijndael has three different types of Rounds; as shown in Fig. 3:

i. The first is the **Initial Round**. It is, as shown in equation (1), performed by XORing the input Plain Text matrix with a predefined Key. This process called *Add-Round-Key*.

$$B = A \oplus K \tag{1}$$

where B (size 4 by N_b) is the output byte matrix, A (size 4 by N_b) is the input byte matrix and K (size 4 by N_b) is the Key byte matrix.

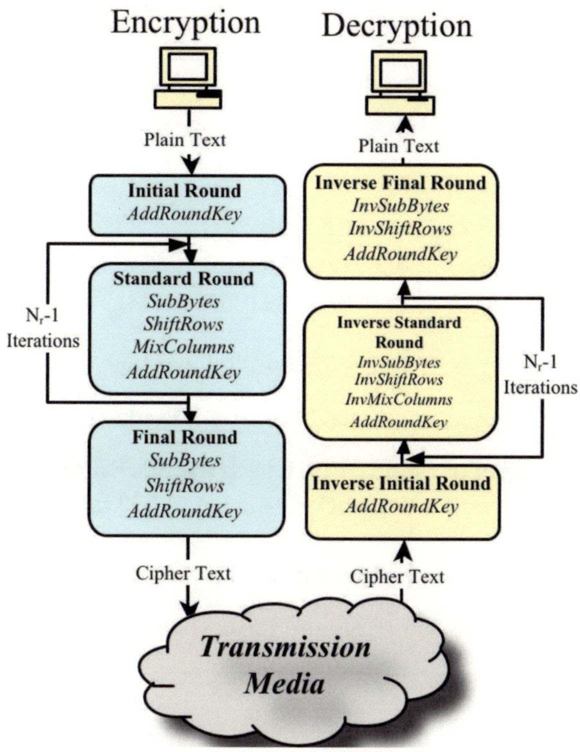

Figure 3. The Rijndael Algorithm (Daemen & Rijmen, 2002).

ii. The second is the **Standard Round**. In the Standard Round four different steps are performed:

a. *Sub-Bytes*: this is a simple byte substitution using a predefined lookup table. Two tables are used, one for encryption and another for decryption.

b. *Shift-Row:* this step is performed through shifting and rotating the bytes in each row of the input matrix in a predefined manner. The shifting offset is defined according to the block width N_b. The bytes will be shifted, then, rotated repeatedly.

c. *Mix-Column:* the columns are mixed through a matrix multiplication of the plain text by a predefined matrix, given by the authors of the Rijndael algorithm (Daemen & Rijmen, 2002), over Galois Field with an irreducible polynomial 100011011. In the decryption case, this step is referred to as Inverse Mix-Column or *InvMix-Column*.

Some mathematical simplification is carried out in order to reduce the multiplication computation. In the encryption case the multiplication is performed as shown in equation (2). Note that the multiplication operator is shown as ⊗ to indicate that the multiplication is over Galois Field (Daemen & Rijmen, 2002).

$$\begin{bmatrix} B_{00}\cdots B_{07} \\ B_{10}\cdots B_{17} \\ B_{20}\cdots B_{27} \\ B_{30}\cdots B_{37} \end{bmatrix} = \begin{bmatrix} 02 & 03 & 01 & 01 \\ 01 & 02 & 03 & 01 \\ 01 & 01 & 02 & 03 \\ 03 & 01 & 01 & 02 \end{bmatrix} \otimes \begin{bmatrix} A_{00}\cdots A_{07} \\ A_{10}\cdots A_{17} \\ A_{20}\cdots A_{27} \\ A_{30}\cdots A_{37} \end{bmatrix} \quad (2)$$

The matrix used in the multiplication during the Inverse Mix-Column (*InvMix-Column*) step is shown in equation (3). This multiplication is also carried over Galois Field with the irreducible polynomial 100011011 (Daemen & Rijmen, 2002).

$$\begin{bmatrix} B_{00}\cdots B_{07} \\ B_{10}\cdots B_{17} \\ B_{20}\cdots B_{27} \\ B_{30}\cdots B_{37} \end{bmatrix} = \begin{bmatrix} 0E & 0B & 0D & 09 \\ 09 & 0E & 0B & 0D \\ 0D & 09 & 0E & 0B \\ 0B & 0D & 09 & 0E \end{bmatrix} \otimes \begin{bmatrix} A_{00}\cdots A_{07} \\ A_{10}\cdots A_{17} \\ A_{20}\cdots A_{27} \\ A_{30}\cdots A_{37} \end{bmatrix} \quad (3)$$

a. *Add-Round-key:* is XORing each byte with a predefined key.

Rijndael has a variable number of iterations, N_i, for the **Standard Round**:

- $N_i = 9$, where N_r = Number of rounds = 10, if both the block and the key are 128 bits long.
- $N_i = 11$, where $N_r = 12$, if either the block or the key is 192 bits long, and neither of them is longer than that.
- $N_i = 13$, where $N_r = 14$, if either the block or the key is 256 bits long.

Table 1. shows the key size, block width N_b and the corresponding N_r.

	Key Size		
	128	192	256
N_b	4	6	8
N_r	9	11	13

Table 1. Key Size, Block Width N_b and Round Number N_r, (Daemen & Rijmen, 2002)

i. The third type of round is called the **Final Round**. In the Final Round only three of the four steps, mentioned in the Standard Round, are performed excluding the Mix-Column step.

During decryption, all the steps are preformed in reversed order (Daemen & Rijmen, 2002).

4.1.2. The key schedule for Rijndael

The Round-Keys are derived from the original Cipher Key by means of the **Key Schedule**. The algorithm to generate the key is shown in Fig. 4. The original key provided is 128, 192 or 256 bits. The key should be arranged in a $4\times N_b$ Matrix. As discussed in the previous section, the Add-Round-Key step is performed once in the First Round, N_r-1 times in the Standard Round, and once again in the Final Round. In total, N_r+1 Round-Key matrices are needed to cover all the rounds.

The first Round-Key is given, as shown in equation (4), however, the remaining, N_r, Round-Key matrices are generated (Daemen & Rijmen, 2002). For example, for a block length of 128 bits, 10 Round-Keys matrices are needed: 9 for the Standard Rounds and 1 for the Final Round. For block length of 192 bits, 12 Round-Keys are needed and for 256 bits length 14 are needed.

$$K = \begin{bmatrix} k_{00} \cdots k_{0N_b-1} \\ k_{10} \cdots k_{1N_b-1} \\ k_{20} \cdots k_{2N_b-1} \\ k_{30} \cdots k_{3N_b-1} \end{bmatrix} ;\ K_0 = \begin{bmatrix} k_{00} \\ k_{10} \\ k_{20} \\ k_{30} \end{bmatrix} \cdots\ K_{N_b-1} = \begin{bmatrix} k_{0N_b-1} \\ k_{1N_b-1} \\ k_{2N_b-1} \\ k_{3N_b-1} \end{bmatrix} \quad (4)$$

if $N_b \leq 6$ **then**

for $i = N_b + 1$ **to** $N_b \times (N_r + 1)$ **do**

$$K_i = \begin{cases} K_{i-N_b} \oplus SubByte(S_1(K_{i-1})) \oplus rcon(\frac{i}{N_b}) & if\ \ i \mod N_b = 0 \\ K_{i-N_b} \oplus K_{i-1} & if\ \ i \mod N_b \neq 0 \end{cases}$$

end

elseif $N_b > 6$ **then**

for $i = N_b + 1$ **to** $N_b \times (N_r + 1)$ **do**

$$K_i = \begin{cases} K_{i-N_b} \oplus SubByte(S_1(K_{i-1})) \oplus rcon(\frac{i}{N_b}) & if\ \ i \mod N_b = 0 \\ K_{i-N_b} \oplus SubByte(K_{i-1}) & if\ \ i \mod N_b = 4 \\ K_{i-N_b} \oplus K_{i-1} & elsewhere \end{cases}$$

end

end

Figure 4. Generating key schedule for Rijndael (Daemen & Rijmen, 2002).

Then the remaining keys are generated (Daemen & Rijmen, 2002). Fig. 4 shows the key schedule algorithm, where i denotes the column number, iterating from 0 to N_b-1. The function $S_1(K_{i-1})$ is a cyclic shift of the elements in K_{i-1}. For example, if K_{i-1} column is [k_{0x}, k_{1x}, k_{2x}, k_{3x}], then $S_1(K_{i-1})$ is [k_{1x}, k_{2x}, k_{3x}, k_{0x}].

The *rcon* function is a round-dependent constant XORed to the first byte of each column (Daemen & Rijmen, 2002). These round constants are calculated offline. It is the successive powers of 2 in the representation of GF(2^8) (Daemen & Rijmen, 2002). The Key is saved in the memory to be XORed during the encryption or decryption.

4.1.3. Rijndeal performance analysis

In this section, the performance results are presented. Some of the bottleneck problems are discussed, and possible solutions are proposed (Majzoub et al., 2006). Fig. 5(a) shows the time cost of the four steps done in one iteration of the Standard Round. The figure shows the encryption and the decryption costs for all the key length cases. Clearly, the Sub-Bytes step, or the lookup table step, is dominating the computation time. The Sub-Bytes step is taking 83% of the total Round cost in the best case and 97% in the worst case. The next bottleneck is the Mix-Column and InvMix-Column step. Both InvMix-Column and Mix-Column steps are taking 2% in the best case and 16% in the worst case.

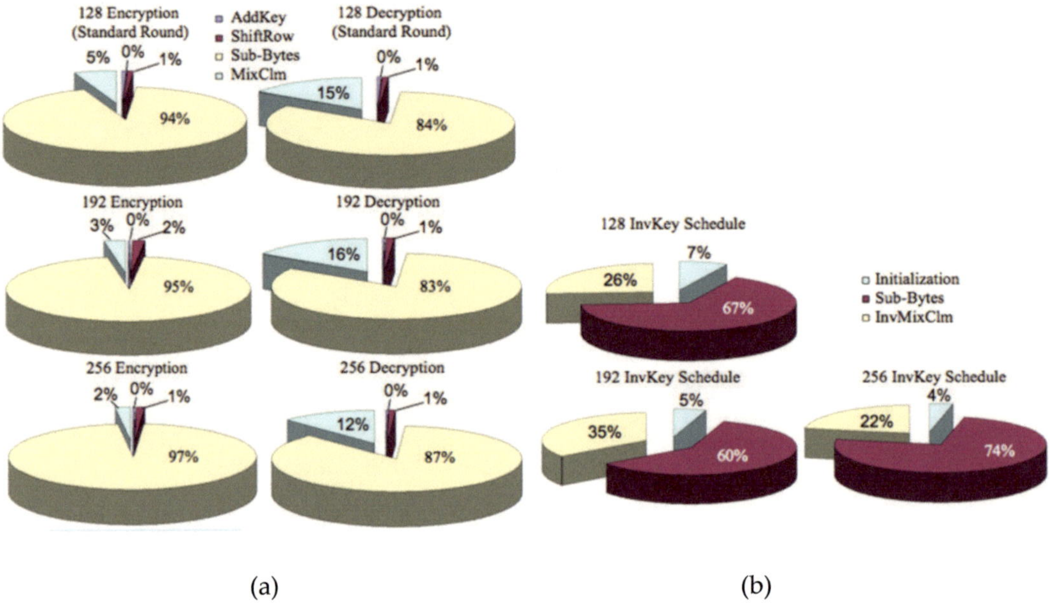

Figure 5. Time cost breakdown, (a) Encryption and Decryption, and (b) Inverse-Key (Inv-Key) Schedule.

Fig. 5(b) shows the time cost of the Inverse Key Schedule performance results. Again, the Sub-Bytes and the InvMix-Column are the major bottlenecks. The Sub-Bytes is taking 60% in the best case and 74% in the worst case. The InvMix-Column is taking 22% in the best case and 35% in the worst case.

Fig. 6 shows the RC Utilization during the encryption and decryption respectively. The figure shows the RC utilization for one iteration of the Standard Round. It is clear the 8×8 RC Array is fully utilized during the lookup table and partially utilized, but with high rate, during the Mix-Column and InvMix-Column.

As shown in Fig. 6, there are 4 lookups in case of 256 covering the 4 rows. In the 192 case, there are 3 lookups to cover the 3 rows and in the case of 128 there are 2. During every lookup there is a full utilization and then a small stall when switching from one row to another. At the end of lookup step, the Mix-Column step starts. The Mix-Column utilizes half the RC Array in the 192 and 256 cases and quarter of the RC Array in the 128 case. The InvMix-Column almost utilizes the whole RC. In the utilization image, seem the lookup table and the InvMix-Column still dominates the major bottlenecks.

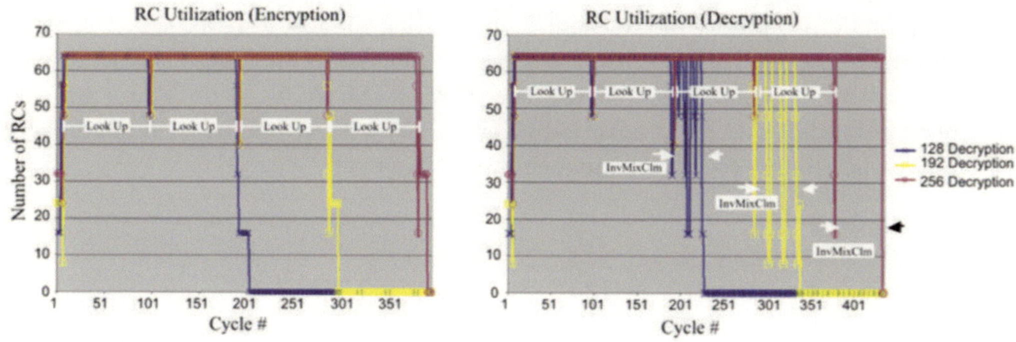

Figure 6. RC Utilization, Encryption and Decryption (Standard Round)

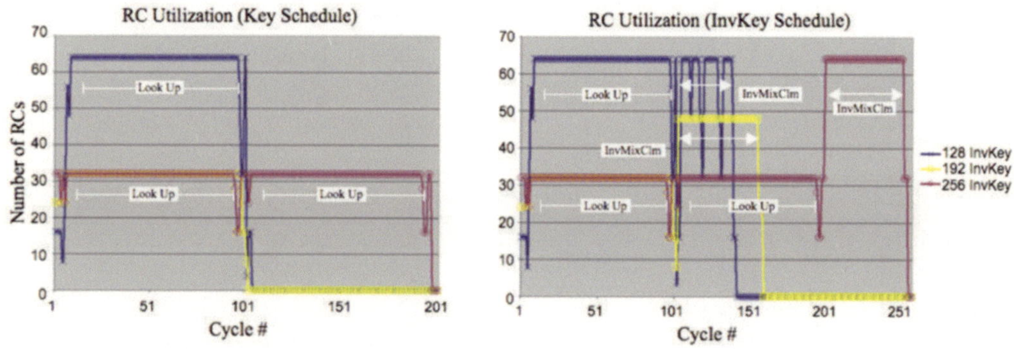

Figure 7. RC Utilization, Key and Inverse Key Schedule (One Round-Key)

Fig. 7 shows the RC Utilization during the Key Schedule. The lookup table steps are utilizing half of the RC Array in the 256 and 192 cases. However, it utilizes the whole RC Array in the case of 128, this is because it is doing a redundant lookup on the other half to save few cycles. This can be changed to be like the 192 and 256 cases, especially if two keys need to be processed at a time. This way we can double the throughput in the cost of few cycles, which is better implementation anyway. The Inverse key shows the same results the key with the addition of the InvMix-Column. In the InvMix-Column case the utilization is a bit high. This is because the column mixing should be done for all the columns not for one like the case of the lookup.

As all the figures and analysis showed, the lookup table is the major bottleneck in terms of both RC utilization and time consuming. In order to improve the Rijndael on MorphoSys, the first idea to think of is implanting a lookup table. A good implementation of a lookup table in the system can improve the Rijndael performance tremendously. Although the InvMix-Column is of specific nature, there are still some improvements that can be proposed. Further work could be by implementing new bit wise instructions. Moreover, better results can be achieved also by implementing a second level of RC-Instruction level parallelism.

Fig. 8 shows the RC instruction utilization. These results are for one iteration of the Standard Round for the three cases: 128, 192 and 256. The CMULBADD instruction is basically multiplying MUX_A input by the constant C and adding the result to MUX_B. The SR and SL are shifting to the right and left respectively. The analysis in these figures can clarify the importance of some of the instructions. The XOR, BTM, ADD, and SR are the most instructions utilized during the process (Singh et al., 1998). Note that the BTM instruction is a bit-wise instruction that counts the number of ones in a byte.

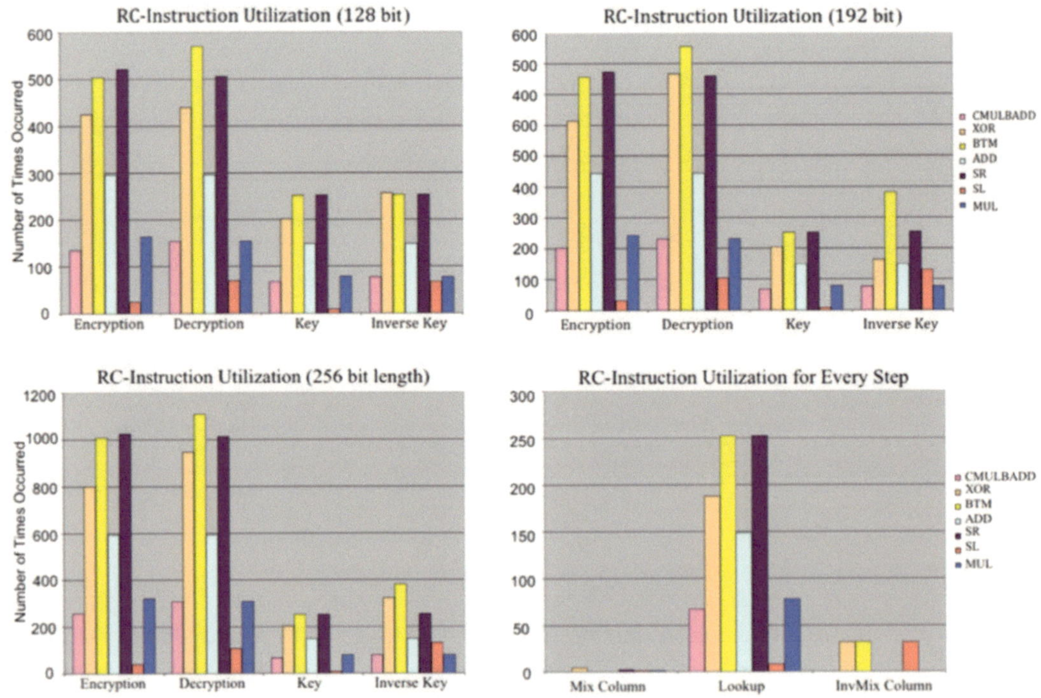

Figure 8. RC-Instruction Utilization, 128 and 192, and 256 cases (One Round)

It should be mentioned here that if the lookup table, the most extensive operation, is replaced by other means then this figure might change dramatically. One improvement could be by adding a parallelism at the RC instruction level. For instance, The XORing will have three operands instead of two. This reduces the XORing utilization by one third. Similar improvements can be done in the same fashion for the other instructions.

The fourth plot in Fig. 8 shows the RC instruction utilization in the major steps. This figure clearly shows that if there is any further investigation, it should be in the lookup table and the InvMix-Column. Better implementation of the BTM instruction improves the results (Singh et al., 1998). For instance, implementing a similar BTM instruction but with XORing all the output instead of counting all the ones eliminates 8 cycles of the computation of every byte. We will elaborate on this issue later.

Fig. 9 shows the final performance results for both the encryption and the decryption for the three plain text length cases. It shows also the performance results of the Key Schedule for the three plain text length cases.

Tables 2 and 3 show the performance results of the MorphoSys compared to the platforms submitted with the Rijndael proposal to the NIST (Daemen & Rijmen, 2002).

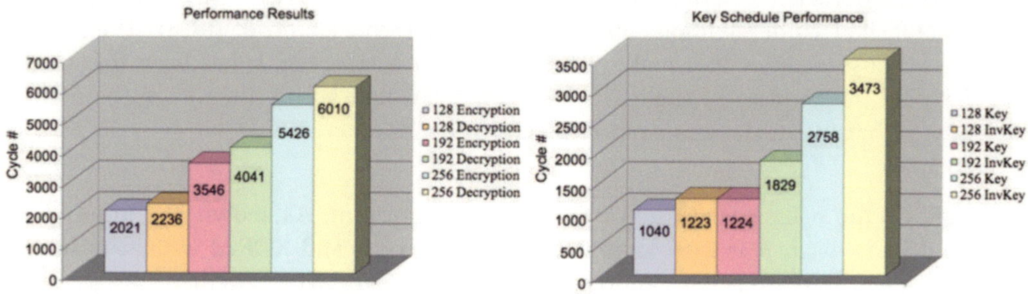

Figure 9. Rijndeal Performance Results

Key Size	AES CD (ANSI C)		Brain Gladman (VC++)		MorphoSys	
	Key	InvKey	Key	InvKey	Key	InvKey
128	2100	2900	305	1389	1040	1223
192	2600	3600	277	1595	1224	1829
256	2800	3800	374	1960	2758	3473

Table 2. Key Schedule compared to other platforms showing number of cycles, (Daemen & Rijmen, 2002).

Key Size	Intel 8051	Motorola 68HC08	AES CD (ANSI C)	Brain Gladman (VC++)	Java	MorphoSys En/Dc
128	4065	8390	950	363	23000	2021/2236
192	4512	10780	1125	432	27600	3546/4041
256	5221	12490	1295	500	32300	5426/6010

Table 3. Performance results for Encryption/Decryption compared to other platforms, showing number of cycles, (Daemen & Rijmen, 2002).

The MorphoSys shows acceptable results compared these platforms. However, and since the proposal submission, there were many implementations on FPGAs and ASIC platforms (Sklaos & Koufopavlou, 2002). These implementations showed a throughput that MorphoSys cannot compete with. For instance, the throughput ranged from 248 up to 3650 MBps which is very high throughput compared to our results. In contrast, the MorphoSys platform is much more flexible than the ASIC or FPGA. A wide range of applications can be implemented on MorphoSys, taking advantage of the fact that MorphoSys is a low power consumption platform (Majzoub & Diab, 2006). Saying all this, still the MorphoSys can and should be improved in order to compete with other platforms.

4.2. Twofish encryption algorithm

In this section, the Twofish cipher, one of the five finalists considered in the advanced encryption standard (AES) competition is implemented on MorphoSys. Twofish is a 128-bit cipher that supports keys with length of 128-, 192- or 256-bits. It is the successor of Blowfish, a well-established cipher without any known flaws (Schneier et al., 1998). The Twofish cipher has many qualities that make it interesting for a research. It has been designed to offer different possibilities of trade-offs between space and speed, thus it can be mapped efficiently to hardware devices such as FPGAs, SmartCards and RCs (Majzoub & Diab, 2003), (Schneier 1996).

Fig. 10 shows the overall structure of the Twofish algorithm. As shown, the input is first latched into a register. It is then separated into four words and XORed with four subkeys K_0,K_1,K_2 and K_3. This step is referred to as the input whitening. The data then goes through a F-function module where various rotations, transformations and permutations are applied. The F-function is made of two g-functions containing key-dependant S-boxes, a Maximum Distance Separable (MDS), (Schneier et al., 1998), matrices and a Pseudo-Hadamard Transform (PHT), (Schneier et al., 1998); all of which will be described later. After performing 16 rounds of the F-function, the four data words are once again XORed with another four subkeys K_4, K_5, K_6 and K_7 to produce the cipher text. This step is called the output whitening (Schneier et al., 1998).

4.2.1. *Twofish phases*

In this section, we explain the mapping details of the Twofish algorithm on MorphoSys platform. The computationally expensive operations, such as the S-box, MDS and PHT, are performed in the reconfigurable part of the MorphoSys. While the other operations, for instance data loading and saving operations are executed in the TinyRISC processor. Fig. 10 shows the overall steps of the Twofish algorithm.

The Twofish steps are as following:

a. *Input Whitening*: the plain text input, P_0,P_1,P_2, and P_3, are XORed with the whitening keys i.e.: $P_0 \oplus K_0$; $P_1 \oplus K_1$; $P_2 \oplus K_2$; and $P_3 \oplus K_3$.
b. *S-Box Computations*: The S-box is a phase in which a lookup table is used. The inputs are substituted by data with the same number of bits from a predefined lookup table.
c. *MDS Matrix Multiplication*: the input data is multiplied by a predefined matrix over Galois field with irreducible polynomial 101101001.
d. *PHT Computations*: The PHT, (Pseudo-Hadamard Transforms), as stated before, is the calculation of the following equations:

$$P_0' = P_0 + P_1 \mod 2^{32}; \ P_1' = P_0 + 2P_1 \mod 2^{32} \tag{5}$$

where P_0 and P_1 are 32 bit each, the first one in the first four columns and the second is in the second four columns of the RC Array. P_0' and P_1' are the expected results of these two equations.

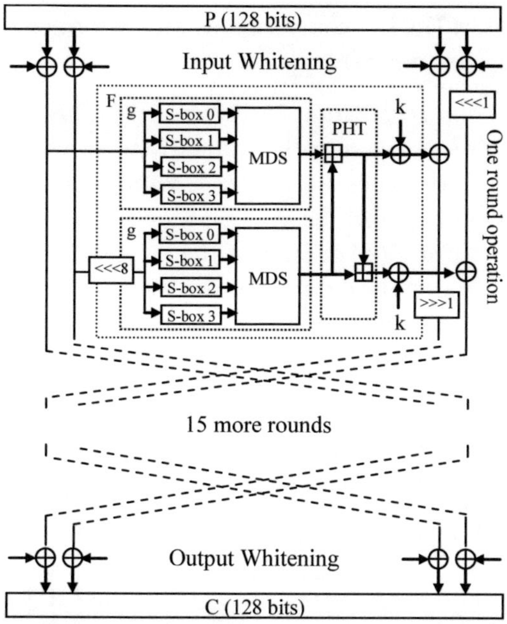

Figure 10. Overall Structure of Twofish Algorithm

a. *XOR with k-Subkeys*: This operation can be done either by adding or XORing. In our implementation, we used XORing as it is faster.

b. *XORing with P_2 and P_3*: the result should be XORed with P_2 and P_3. Then, a rotation to the left or to the right by one bit is performed after or before the XORing. The first block, i.e. P_0, is XORed with P_2 and then rotated by one bit to the right. The next one, i.e. P_1, is XORed with P_3, and then rotated by one bit to the left.

c. *Output Whitening*: This phase is exactly the same as the input-whitening step, which is basically XORing with output subkeys.

4.2.2. The key schedule for Twofish

The key schedule has to provide 40 words of expanded key K_0 ,…, K_{39}. Twofish is defined for keys of length N = 128, N = 192, and N = 256. A constant k is defined as k = N/64. Key generation begins by deriving three key vectors each half the length of the original key (Schneier et al., 1998). The first two are formed by splitting the key into 32-bit parts. These parts are numbered starting from zero, the even-numbered are M_e, and the odd-numbered are M_o. This can be expressed by equation (6).

$$M_i = \sum_{j=0}^{3} m_{(4i+j)} . 2^{8j} \quad i = 0,...,2k-1 \tag{6}$$

The first two vectors are M_e=(M_0,M_2,…,M_{2k-2}) and M_o=(M_1,M_3,…,M_{2k-1}). The calculation of the vectors M_o and M_e are straightforward. We just have to separate the odd bytes from the even ones. Afterwards the expanded key words should be derived from M_e and M_o and stored in the memory to be used later. The key computations are performed offline and then stored in main memory to be used later in the encryption.

The key scheduling operation is shown in Fig. 11. Initially, 2i and 2i+1 words are passed to the S-Boxes so that the M vector is initially XORed with values represent S(2i) or S(2i+1). This is because the 2i and 2i+1 values are predefined and do not change with different key values. For each expanded key word the vector M_e or M_o is XORed with a number taken from the frame buffer represents S(2i) or S(2i+1). The RC instructions used to calculate the h-function in the context memory are the same ones used to calculate F function with some modifications. Some additional planes in context memory are used to resolve the difference in the h- and g-functions. Before the PHT step, the word k_{2i+1} is rotated 8 bits to the left.

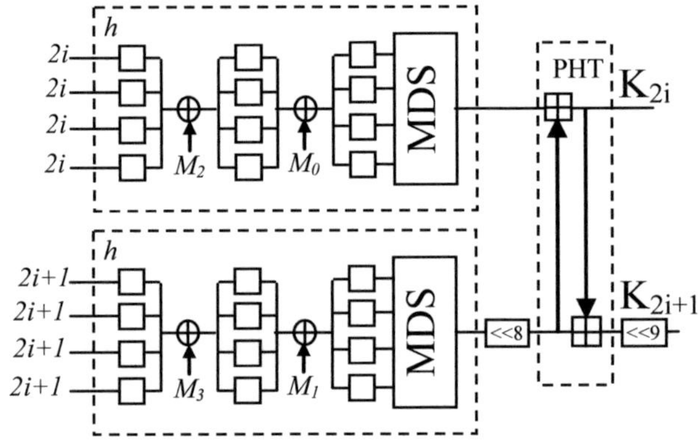

Figure 11. Key Schedule for Twofish

Afterwards, the PHT is performed. Then, the last four bytes are rotated by nine bits. The final result is transferred to the cell in the first row. The content is then loaded from this cell to the registers in the TinyRISC using RCRISC instruction.

In the case of 256 bits, there are eight bytes. In the case of the 192 bits, there are three bytes in each vector. Finally, in the case of the 128, there are 2 bytes in each vector. As stated before, the odd bytes should be separated from the even ones. Each vector has four bytes. On the other hand, the S vector is derived through multiplying the Key K (256, 192, or 128 bits) by the RS matrix. The key K is divided into 8 bytes groups and multiplied by the RS matrix as shown in equation (7).

$$\begin{pmatrix} s_{i,0} \\ s_{i,1} \\ s_{i,2} \\ s_{i,3} \end{pmatrix} = \begin{pmatrix} 01 & A4 & 55 & 87 & 5A & 58 & DB & 9E \\ A4 & 56 & 82 & F3 & 1E & C6 & 68 & E5 \\ 02 & A1 & FC & C1 & 47 & AE & 3D & 19 \\ A4 & 55 & 87 & 5A & 58 & DB & 9E & 03 \end{pmatrix} \cdot \begin{pmatrix} m_{8i} \\ m_{8i+1} \\ m_{8i+2} \\ m_{8i+3} \\ m_{8i+4} \\ m_{8i+5} \\ m_{8i+6} \\ m_{8i+7} \end{pmatrix} \tag{7}$$

Similar to the MDS matrix the multiplication should take place over Galois field with irreducible polynomial, 101101001.

4.2.3. *Twofish performance analysis*

The performance analysis of the Twofish algorithm is shown in Table 4. . Fig. 12 shows the performance results with key lengths of 128, 192 and 256 respectively compared to other platforms. Twofish has been tested in different architectures, for instance Pentium Pro, Pentium II, UltraSPARC, PowerPC 750, and 68040 smart card (Majzoub & Diab, 2003), (Majzoub & Diab, 2010).

Table 5. shows the speedup achieved by the MorphoSys system. As shown, as far as encryption, MorphoSys shows better results than 68040 processor only. However, in terms of the key-schedule the MorphoSys architecture provides a minimum of 3.8 speedup ratio compared to Pentium Pro. The overall speed up shows that MorphoSys is 1.86 times faster than Pentium Pro.

Architecture	Cycles to Encrypt	Cycles to Key (256)	Overall Cycles
MorphoSys	3541	3557	7098
Pentium Pro	315	13500	13815
Pentium II	315	16000	16315
UltraSPARC	750	24900	25650
PowerPC 750	590	22200	22790
68040	3500	96700	100200
Architecture	Cycles to Encrypt	Cycles to Key (192)	Overall Cycles
MorphoSys	2884	2797	5681
Pentium Pro	315	10700	11015
Pentium II	315	14100	14415
UltraSPARC	750	21600	22350
PowerPC 750	590	17100	17690
68040	3500	63500	67000
Architecture	Cycles to Encrypt	Cycles to Key (128)	Overall Cycles
MorphoSys	2324	2037	4361
Pentium Pro	315	7800	8115
Pentium II	315	8200	8515
UltraSPARC	750	16600	17350
PowerPC 750	590	12200	12790
68040	3500	53000	56500

Table 4. Performance Analysis compared to other architectures (128 key)

Architecture	Encrypt	Key (128)	Overall
MorphoSys	1	1	1
Pentium Pro	0.13	3.8	1.86
Pentium II	0.13	4	1.95
UltraSPARC	0.32	8.14	3.97
PowerPC 750	0.25	6	2.93
68040	1.5	26	13

Table 5. Speedup normalized to MorphoSys

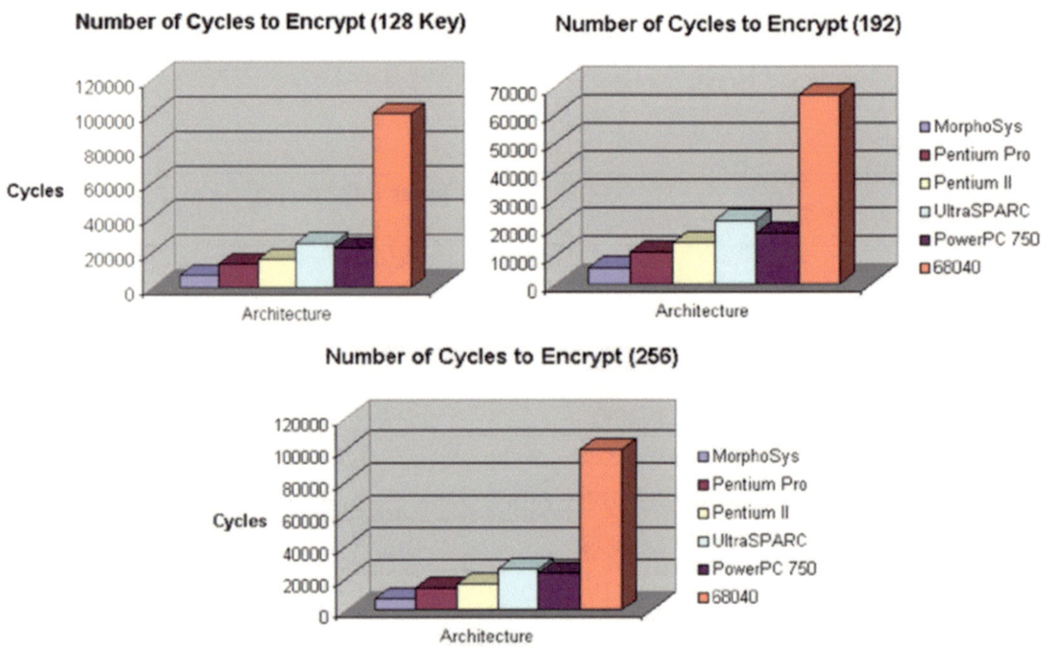

Figure 12. Twofish Performance Results

The implementation of the Twofish on MorphoSys clarifies some of the pros and cons of the system. The encryption process takes more time than the keying process. This is due to the fact that the encryption process involves more sequential operations. There are 16 repeated rounds that should finish considering 128 bits input and output each round. This can be done using an 8-bit bus only, that is available at the RC level. Accordingly, the 16 rounds cannot be parallelized further. On the other hand, there are a lot more that can be parallelized in key scheduling. The expensive matrix multiplication and the hash tables are converted and mapped into parallel and simpler mathematical operations that can benefit from the MorphoSys architectural attributes.

5. Image processing algorithms on MorphoSys

In this section, we discuss two image manipulation algorithms, namely linear filtering and computer graphics transformation.

5.1. Linear filtering algorithm

Filtering is a technique for amending or enhancing an image. Images can be of low quality due to a poor image contrast or, more usually, from an improper usage of the available range of possible brightness and darkness levels. In performing image enhancement, we compute an enhanced version of the original image. The most basic methods of image enhancement involve point operations, in which the value of any given pixel in the output image is determined by applying an algorithm to the values of the pixels in the neighborhood of the corresponding input pixel. A pixel's neighborhood is some set of pixels, defined by their locations relative to that pixel. The most common point operation is the linear contrast stretching operation, which seeks to maximally utilize the available gray-scale range. In other words, in linear filtering, the value of an output pixel is a linear combination of the values of the pixels in the input pixel's neighborhood (Diab & Majzoub, 2003). Linear filters are useful for image enhancement, which includes noise-smoothing, sharpening or simply emphasizing certain features and removing others. Usually, an image is dimmed because of improper exposure setting. Images are also blurred by motion in the scene or by inherent optical problems. The benefactor of image enhancement either may be a human observer or a computer vision program performing some kind of higher-level image analysis, such as target detection or scene understanding.

5.1.1. Two-dimensional convolution

Multi-dimensional convolution is a common operation in signal and image processing with applications to digital filtering and video processing (Diab & Majzoub, 2003). Thus, many approaches have been suggested to achieve high-speed processing for linear convolution, and to design efficient convolution architectures.

Linear filtering can be implemented through the two-dimensional convolution. In 2D convolution, the value of the output pixel is computed by multiplying elements of two matrices and summing the results. One of these matrices represents the image itself, while the other matrix is the filter kernel or the computational molecule (Diab & Majzoub, 2003).

The sliding window, filter kernel, centers on each pixel in an input image and generates new output pixels. The new pixel value is computed by multiplying each pixel value in the neighborhood with the corresponding weight in the convolution kernel and summing these products. This is placed step by step over the image, at each step creating a new window in the image the same size of kernel, and then associating with each element in the kernel a corresponding pixel in the image.

This operation is shown in Fig. 13, which is the general case of the convolution operation. The image size is M×N pixels and the kernel is R×S elements.

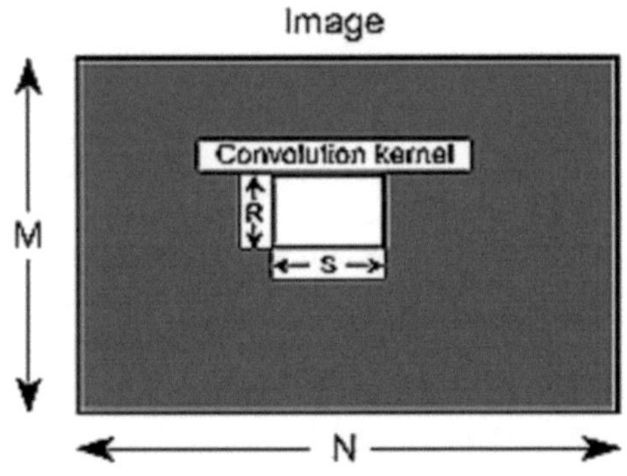

Figure 13. An M×N image processed using an R×S convolution kernel

This "shift, add, multiply" operation is termed the "convolution" of the kernel with the image. If the kernel is an odd-sized $(2r_x + 1)\times(2r_y + 1) \equiv R\times S$ kernel and $I_1(x,y)$ is the image, then the convolution of K with I1 is written as:

$$I_2(x,y) = \sum_{m=-r_x}^{r_x} \sum_{n=-r_y}^{r_y} K(r_x + 1 - m, r_y + 1 - n) \times I_1(x+m, y+n) \quad (8)$$

5.1.2. *Algorithm steps*

The 2D convolution operation can be summarized by the following steps:

a. Rotate the convolution kernel 180 degrees to produce a computational molecule.
b. Determine the centre pixel of the computational molecule.
c. Apply the computational molecule to each pixel in the input image.

This can be expressed by equation (9). If the kernel size is 3×3 and $I_1(x,y)$ is an 8×8 pixel image, then:

$$k = \begin{bmatrix} k_1 & k_2 & k_3 \\ k_4 & k_5 & k_6 \\ k_7 & k_8 & k_9 \end{bmatrix}; I_1 = \begin{bmatrix} a_{11} & \cdot & \cdot & a_{18} \\ \cdot & & & \cdot \\ \cdot & & & \cdot \\ a_{81} & \cdot & \cdot & a_{88} \end{bmatrix} \quad (9)$$

The value of any given pixel in I_2 is determined by applying the computational molecule k to the corresponding pixel in I_1. This can be visualized by overlying k on I_1, with the center pixel of k over the pixel of interest in I_2. Then each element of k must be multiplied by the corresponding pixel in I_1, and sum the results. For example, to determine the value of the pixel (4,5) in I_2, overlay k on I_1, with the center pixel of k covering the pixel (4,5) in I_1 as shown in Fig. 14.

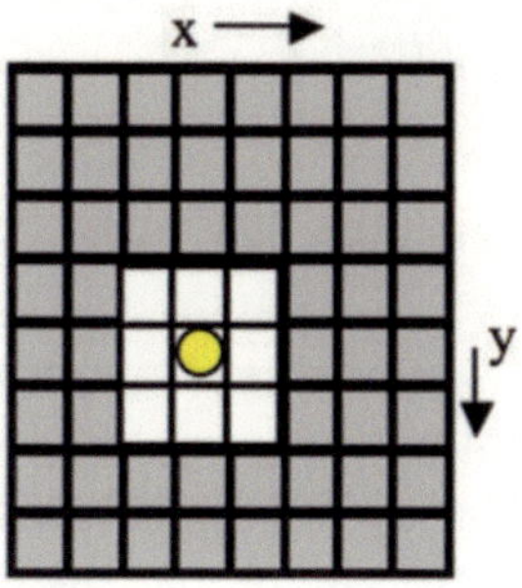

Figure 14. The 8×8 pixels image and the computational molecule at pixel (4,5)

$$I_2(4,5) = k_1 \times a_{43} + k_2 \times a_{44} + k_3 \times a_{45} + k_4 \times a_{53} + \\ k_5 \times a_{54} + k_6 \times a_{55} + k_7 \times a_{63} + k_8 \times a_{64} + k_9 \times a_{65} \quad (10)$$

Perform this procedure for each pixel in I_1 to determine the value of each corresponding pixel in I_2.

STAGE	PROCESS	No OF CYCLES
1	MM to FB	28 cycles (4 insts + 25 NOPs)
	MM to CM	74 cycles (1 inst + 73 NOPs)
2	2D convolution operation	24 cycles
	RC to FB	8 cycles
3	F to MM	28 cycles (2 insts and 26 NOPs)

Table 6. Performance results of the three stages of overall operation on MorphoSys.

	Total number of cycles	Cycles per Pixel
Case (1)	162	2.5
Case (2)	32	0.5

Table 7. Performance results on MorphoSys.

	Number of cycles per pixel
MorphoSys	0.5
C40 coprocessor	2

Table 8. MorphoSys Case(2) compared to C40.

Some of the elements of the computational molecule may not overlap actual image pixels at the borders of an image. In order to compute output values for the border pixels, a special technique should be used in this algorithm. This technique pads the image matrix with zeroes. In other words, the output values are computed by assuming that the input image is padded on the edges with additional rows and columns of zeros.

5.1.3. Performance analysis of linear filtering

The execution speed of the algorithm is used to evaluate the performance of the MorphoSys system with an operational frequency of 100 MHz, as a platform to demonstrate the implementation of 2D convolution on RC systems. For this mapping of the 2D convolution operation, the time of the whole operation can be divided into three categories as shown in Table 6: the loading from main memory to the context memory (CM) and frame buffer, the 2D convolution operation then RC Array to Frame Buffer, and the loading from the Frame Buffer (FB) to the Main Memory. As a result of this, the performance can be calculated with (Case (1)) or without (Case (2)) the loading from and saving to memory. For each case, the corresponding performance results are shown in Table 7. The performance results compared to an FPGA-based 2D convolution coprocessor for the TMS320C40 DSP microprocessor (C40) from Texas Instruments (TI). The comparison is shown in Table 8 (Diab & Majzoub, 2003).

5.2. Geometrical transformations in computer graphics

Transformations are a fundamental part of computer graphics. Transformations are used to position, shape, and change viewing positions of objects, as well as change how they are viewed (e.g. the type of perspective that is used) (Damaj et al, 2002).

There are many types of transformations used in computer graphics, such as translation, scaling, rotation, shear, and composite transformations. These transformations can also be combined to obtain more complex transformations. The purpose of composing transformations is to increase the efficiency by applying a single composed transformation, rather than applying a series of transformations, one after the other.

Transformation can be as simple as a matrix multiplication operation. Multiplying a matrix A with matrix B would mean multiplying one row of A with one column of B and then adding their results yielding (c_{11}) of the result matrix C. Matrices A, B, and C are considered to be dense matrices. The matrix-matrix multiplication involves $O(n^3)$ operations on a single processing plat form, since for each element C_{ij} of C, we must compute

$$C_{ij} = \sum_{k=0}^{N-1} A_{ik} B_{kj} \tag{11}$$

Considering translation, scaling, and rotation, the following matrices are used to perform the overall operation:

- Translation:

$$T = \begin{bmatrix} 1 & 0 & 0 & d_x \\ 0 & 1 & 0 & d_y \\ 0 & 0 & 1 & d_z \\ 0 & 0 & 0 & 1 \end{bmatrix} \tag{12}$$

- Scaling:

$$S = \begin{bmatrix} S_x & 0 & 0 & 0 \\ 0 & S_y & 0 & 0 \\ 0 & 0 & S_z & 0 \\ 0 & 0 & 0 & 1 \end{bmatrix} \tag{13}$$

- Rotation, in our case we took the rotation angle to be 90 around the z-axis:

$$R_z(\theta) = \begin{bmatrix} \cos\theta & -\sin\theta & 0 & 0 \\ \sin\theta & \cos\theta & 0 & 0 \\ 0 & 0 & 1 & 0 \\ 0 & 0 & 0 & 1 \end{bmatrix} \tag{14}$$

The resultant transformation will be:

$$W = T \times S \times R \tag{15}$$

To get the results: matrix W should be multiplied by the coordinate vectors of the points to be translated. With MorphoSys capabilities, the transformation can be done for eight elements at once. Translated Points Matrix:

$$\begin{bmatrix} 0 & -w_2 & 0 & w_4 \\ w_1 & 0 & 0 & w_5 \\ 0 & 0 & w_3 & w_6 \\ 0 & 0 & 0 & 1 \end{bmatrix} \times \begin{bmatrix} x_1 & x_2 & x_3 & x_4 & x_5 & x_6 & x_7 & x_8 \\ y_1 & y_2 & y_3 & y_4 & y_5 & y_6 & y_7 & y_8 \\ z_1 & z_2 & z_3 & z_4 & z_5 & z_7 & z_7 & z_8 \\ 1 & 1 & 1 & 1 & 1 & 1 & 1 & 1 \end{bmatrix} \tag{16}$$

5.2.1. *Performance analysis of 3D geometric transforms*

The performance is based on the execution speed of the algorithms. The MorphoSys system is considered to be operational at a frequency of 100 MHz. The algorithm takes 70 cycles in order to terminate. The cycle time for the MorphoSys is 1/100 MHz i.e. the cycle time is equal to 10 nsec. Thus the speed in matrix elements per cycle is equal to 4.38 cycles for each element. Accordingly, the time for the algorithm to terminate is equal to 2.56 µsec (Damaj et al, 2002).

After presenting the obtained results of the mapped algorithm, a comparison is done with the same algorithms mapped onto some Intel micro-processing systems. In this research the chosen processors are the Intel 80486 and Pentium. Note that the instructions used are upward compatible with newer Intel processors. Note that the chosen systems have comparable frequencies of 100 ~ 133 MHz.

The above mapped matrix-matrix multiplication algorithm, has its direct positive effect on fast computations for graphics geometrical transformations. Especially, that a matrix is a general enough representation to implement any geometrical transformation: Translation, Rotation, Scaling, Shear, or any composition of these. Performance analysis is compared with other reconfigurable systems, such as FPGAs with one prototype chosen from this field: RC-1000 from CELOXICA as shown in Table 10.

Algorithm	System	N# of Cycles	Speedup
General Composite Algorithm Using Matrix Algorithm "16 Elements".	Morphosys	70	1
	Pentium	1328	18.97
	80486	3354	47.91
General Composite Algorithm Using Matrix Algorithm "64-Elements".	MorphoSys	45	1
	Pentium	2551	56.67
	80486	6773	150.5

Table 9. Comparisons with other systems.

Algorithm	System	N# of Cycles	Speedup of the RC-1000 over MorphoSys
General Composite Algorithm Using Matrix Algorithm "16 Elements".	MorphoSys	70	
	RC-1000	12	5.8
General Composite Algorithm Using Matrix Algorithm "64-Elements".	MorphoSys	45	
	RC-1000	12	3.7

Table 10. Comparisons with RC-1000 FPGA.

6. Discussions and analysis

In this section we discuss some of the bottlenecks and problems we faced during the implementation of the Rijndael (Daemen & Rijmen, 2002), Twofish (Schneier et al., 1998), 2D convolution (Diab & Majzoub, 2003), and 3D transformation (Damaj et al, 2002) algorithms on MorphoSys (Singh et al., 1998). First, the lookup table should be considered to improve the performance, with an appropriate tradeoff of area and power. Second, the BTM instruction should be improved so that it can produce the result in one cycle.

The implementation of the lookup table can follow two approaches: local versus global lookup table. A local approach would implement a lookup table for every RC. These lookup tables can be accessed through one of the RC internal Multiplexers. Filling these lookup tables can follow the same Frame-Buffer-Data-Distribution scheme, which means same Row/Column would have the same data or completely unshared data are sent to every one. Whether the lookup table is place on or off the RC, the drawback of this method is that it increases the RC size greatly, and thus, the area of the whole chip, which make the system hard to scale. Moreover, it puts a heavy load on the buses in loading the data to the tables to fill the 64 RCs tables. The advantage of this method is that it speeds the lookup access. So this method is the optimal in terms of speed but it is the worst in terms of area. In this option the size of the lookup table should be small and scaling up the RC Array size to more than 8×8 would be difficult.

A more global approach is to put one lookup table outside the RC Array that all the RCs can access. This option requires less area. It is feasible to increase the size of the lookup table here into the size of the frame buffer itself. The cost of loading data into the lookup table is then the same as the Frame Buffer. This global lookup table could be placed between the Frame Buffer and the RC Array. The data coming from the Frame Buffer to RC Array is multiplexed to the address bus of this lookup table and the needed data are passed to the RCs from this table. The distribution of the data on the RCs follows the same Frame-Buffer-Data-Distribution scheme. The disadvantage of this method is that all the RCs have the same lookup table. If another lookup table is needed then it should be reloaded. Another disadvantage is that it takes more time to access it by the RCs. The time is at least double the time accessing the Frame Buffer. This method will have lower performance.

A middle solution between the two methods is to have 8 lookup tables, where each one would cover one Row/Column. This way the access time is fast, because every lookup table is covering only one Row or Column. More over it will be reasonable in terms of area, because instead of 64 lookup tables only 8 are needed in this approach. Ideally, the speed up in case of lookup hardware implementation will be 96% in the best case and 82% in the worst per one round in the case of the Rijndeal algorithm. This improvement puts the MorphoSys into high competitive level with other platforms.

On the other hand, to improve the fine-grain capabilities in MorphoSys, the BTM instruction should be changed. For instance, it should be ANDing MUX_A and MUX_B and then XORing the bits of the output result instead of counting the 1's. For instance, this implementation will save several cycles in the Mix and InvMix- Column. Other schemes could be implemented as well, so that the MorphoSys can handle fine-grain operations with a very good performance.

Instruction Mnemonic	Description
BWAX	ANDing MUX_A and MUX_B, then XORing all the output bits in the result
BWRA	ORing MUX_A with MUX_B, then ANDing all the bits in the output result
BWRP	XORing MUX_A with MUX_C, then ORing the result with MUX B, then ANDing all the bits in the output result
CNCT	Concatenate the lower 8 bits from both MUX_A and MUX_B.
ORALL	ORing MUX_A, MUX_B, and MUX_C
ANDALL	ANDing MUX_A, MUX_B, and MUX_C
XORALL	XORing MUX_A, MUX_B, and MUX_C

Table 11. The proposed new RC-Instructions

In order to improve the bit wise operations some new instructions should be implemented. Table 7 shows the proposed RC-instructions. Also, it is very useful to introduce another MUX_C to the RC. MUX_C can be identical to MUX_A. As the bus overhead to the RC itself already paid, it is useful to increase the use of these buses.

The first instruction, BWAX, is a bit wise XOR of input coming from MUX_A. The second instruction is calculating terms in Modulo-2 algebra. This instruction can help implementing new Modulo-2 compiler. The third instruction is to calculate Boolean terms. This instruction will help implementing a Boolean algebra compiler. These instructions are very useful in the Mix-Column and its inverse (InvMix-Column) in Rijndael as well as the MDS in Twofish.

The concatenate instruction is necessary to exploit the 16 bus width. Since the frame buffer bus is only 8 bits, the other 8 bits of the RC Array are useless most of the time, the RC bus width is 16 bits. So it is better either to reduce the RC bus width to 12, or may be 8, or to implement new instructions that can make use of the 16 bits. The other three instructions are to implement another level of parallelism on the RC level. These logical instructions are very easy to implement and can greatly help the performance. Since most of the cryptographic applications, as well as multimedia type of applications requires iterative and repetitive operations on different data.

7. Conclusion

In this chapter we implemented a number of multimedia applications, namely Rijndael, Twofish, image filtering and computer graphics algorithms. This implementation was carried out on a coarse grained reconfigurable architecture, MorphoSys, designed and implemented at UC Irvine. Furthermore, we presented the results of such implementations along with analyses and highlights of the current bottlenecks and problems. Solutions and possible workarounds are suggested to improve the performance results and further improve the MorphoSys hardware as a viable solution for multimedia applications.

Author details

Sohaib Majzoub
American University in Dubai, Dubai, UAE

Hassan Diab
American University of Beirut, Beirut, Lebanon

8. References

Bagherzadeh, N., Kamalizad, A. H., & Koohi, A. (n.d.). Design and analysis of a programmable single-chip architecture for DVB-T base-band receiver. *2003 Design, Automation and Test in Europe Conference and Exhibition* (pp. 468-473). IEEE Comput. Soc. doi:10.1109/DATE.2003.1253653

Bosi, B., Bois, G., & Savaria, Y. (1999). Reconfigurable Pipelined 2D Convolvers for Fast Digital Signal Processing. IEEE Trans. On Very Large Scale Integration (VLSI) Systems. Retrieved from http://citeseerx.ist.psu.edu/viewdoc/summary?doi=10.1.1.42.124

Christoforos E. Kozyrakis, D. A. P. (n.d.). A New Direction for Computer Architecture Research. Retrieved from http://citeseer.ist.psu.edu/viewdoc/summary?doi=10.1.1.146.743

Daemen, J., & Rijmen, V. (2002). *The Design of RijndaeL: AES - The Advanced Encryption Standard (Information Security and Cryptography)* (p. 255). Springer. Retrieved from http://www.amazon.com/Design-RijndaeL-Encryption-Information-Cryptography/dp/3540425802

Damaj, I., Majzoub, Sohaib, & Diab, Hassan. (2002). 2D and 3D Computer Graphics Algorithms under MORPHOSYS, 1076-1079. Retrieved from http://portal.acm.org/citation.cfm?id=647929.740227

Diab, H., & Majzoub, S. (n.d.). Linear filtering using reconfigurable computing. *ACS/IEEE International Conference on Computer Systems and Applications, 2003. Book of Abstracts.* (p. 15). IEEE. doi:10.1109/AICCSA.2003.1227452

Eguro, K., & Hauck, S. (n.d.). Issues and Approaches to Coarse-Grain Reconfigurable Architecture Development. Retrieved from http://citeseerx.ist.psu.edu/viewdoc/summary?doi=10.1.1.15.3501

Ferrandi, F., Santambrogio, M. D., & Sciuto, D. (n.d.). A Design Methodology for Dynamic Reconfiguration: The Caronte Architecture. *19th IEEE International Parallel and Distributed Processing Symposium* (p. 163b-163b). IEEE. doi:10.1109/IPDPS.2005.17

Galanis, M. D., Theodoridis, G., Tragoudas, S., Soudris, D., & Goutis, C. E. (2004). A novel coarse-grain reconfigurable data-path for accelerating DSP kernels. *Proceeding of the 2004 ACM/SIGDA 12th international symposium on Field programmable gate arrays - FPGA '04* (p. 252). New York, New York, USA: ACM Press. doi:10.1145/968280.968337

Hartenstein, R. (2001, March 13). A Decade of Reconfigurable Computing: A Visionary Retrospective. Published by the IEEE Computer Society. Retrieved from: www.computer.org/portal/web/csdl/doi/10.1109/DATE.2001.915091

Hauck, S. (1998). The Future of Reconfigurable Systems. in 5th Canadian Conference on Field Programmable Devices. Retrieved from http://citeseerx.ist.psu.edu/viewdoc/summary?doi=10.1.1.37.5820

Hauser, J. R., & Wawrzynek, J. (n.d.). Garp: a MIPS processor with a reconfigurable coprocessor. *Proceedings. The 5th Annual IEEE Symposium on Field-Programmable Custom Computing Machines Cat. No.97TB100186)* (pp. 12-21). IEEE Comput. Soc. doi:10.1109/FPGA.1997.624600

Itani, M., & Diab, Hassan. (2004). Reconfigurable Computing for RC6 Cryptography. *Proceedings of the The IEEE/ACS International Conference on Pervasive Services* (pp. 121–127). Washington: IEEE Computer Society. doi:10.1109/ICPS.2004.25

Lee, M.-hau, Singh, Hartej, Lu, G., Bagherzadeh, Nader, Kurdahi, Fadi J., Fadi, & Kurdahi, J. (2000). Design and Implementation of the MorphoSys Reconfigurable Computing Processor. Journal of VLSI and Signal Processing-Systems for Signal, Image and Video Technology. Retrieved from http://citeseerx.ist.psu.edu/viewdoc/summary?doi=10.1.1.37.3761

Maestre, R., Kurdahi, F.J., Bagherzadeh, N., Singh, H., Hermida, R., & Fernandez, M. (n.d.). Kernel scheduling in reconfigurable computing. *Design, Automation and Test in Europe*

Conference and Exhibition, 1999. Proceedings (Cat. No. PR00078) (pp. 90-96). IEEE Comput. Soc. doi:10.1109/DATE.1999.761102

Majzoub, S., & Diab, H. (n.d.). Mapping and performance analysis of the Twofish algorithm on MorphoSys. *ACS/IEEE International Conference on Computer Systems and Applications, 2003. Book of Abstracts.* (p. 9). IEEE. doi:10.1109/AICCSA.2003.1227446

Majzoub, Sohaib, & Diab, Hassan. (2006). Instruction-Set Extension for Cryptographic Applications on Reconfigurable Platform. *2006 6th International Workshop on System on Chip for Real Time Applications* (pp. 173-178). IEEE. doi:10.1109/IWSOC.2006.348231

Majzoub, Sohaib, & Diab, Hassan. (2010). MorphoSys reconfigurable hardware for cryptography: the twofish case. *The Journal of Supercomputing*, 1-20-20. Springer Netherlands. doi:10.1007/s11227-010-0413-3

Majzoub, Sohaib, Saleh, R., & Diab, Hassan. (2006). Reconfigurable Platform Evaluation Through Application Mapping And Performance Analysis. *2006 IEEE International Symposium on Signal Processing and Information Technology* (pp. 496-501). IEEE. doi:10.1109/ISSPIT.2006.270852

Mei, B., Vernalde, S., Verkest, D., De Man, H., & Lauwereins, R. (2003). *Field Programmable Logic and Application.* (P. Cheung & G. A. Constantinides, Eds.)*Lecture Notes in Computer Science* (Vol. 2778, pp. 61-70). Berlin, Heidelberg: Springer Berlin Heidelberg. doi:10.1007/b12007

Mirsky, E., & DeHon, A. (1996). MATRIX: a reconfigurable computing architecture with configurable instruction distribution and deployable resources. *Proceedings IEEE Symposium on FPGAs for Custom Computing Machines FPGA-96* (pp. 157-166). IEEE. doi:10.1109/FPGA.1996.564808

Miyamori, T., & Olukotun, K. (1998). REMARC: Reconfigurable Multimedia Array Coprocessor. IEICE Transactions on Information and Systems E82-D. Retrieved from http://citeseerx.ist.psu.edu/viewdoc/summary?doi=10.1.1.56.607

Möller, L., Soares, R., Carvalho, E., Grehs, I., Calazans, N., & Moraes, F. (2006). Infrastructure for dynamic reconfigurable systems. *Proceedings of the 19th annual symposium on Integrated circuits and systems design - SBCCI '06* (p. 44). New York, New York, USA: ACM Press. doi:10.1145/1150343.1150360

Schneier, B. (1996). *Applied Cryptography: Protocols, Algorithms, and Source Code in C, Second Edition* (p. 758). Wiley. Retrieved from http://www.amazon.com/Applied-Cryptography-Protocols-Algorithms-Source/dp/0471117099

Schneier, B., Kelsey, J., Whiting, D., Wagner, D., Hall, C., & Ferguson, N. (1998). Twofish: A 128-Bit Block Cipher. in First Advanced Encryption Standard (AES) Conference. Retrieved from http://citeseerx.ist.psu.edu/viewdoc/summary?doi=10.1.1.35.1273

Singh, H., Kurdahi, F.J., Bagherzadeh, N., & Filho, E. M. C. (n.d.). MorphoSys: a reconfigurable architecture for multimedia applications. *Proceedings. XI Brazilian Symposium on Integrated Circuit Design (Cat. No.98EX216)* (pp. 134-139). IEEE Comput. Soc. doi:10.1109/SBCCI.1998.715427

Sklaos, N., & Koufopavlou, O. (2002). Architectures and VLSI implementations of the AES-Proposal Rijndael. *IEEE Transactions on Computers, 51*(12), 1454-1459. doi:10.1109/TC.2002.1146712

Tessier, R., & Burleson, W. (2001). Reconfigurable Computing for Digital Signal Processing: A Survey. *Journal of VLSI Signal Processing Systems, 28*(1/2), 7-27. doi:10.1023/A:1008155020711

Chapter 2

High Accuracy Calibration Technology of UV Standard Detector

Wang Rui, Wang Tingfeng, Sun Tao, Chen Fei and Guo Jin

Additional information is available at the end of the chapter

http://dx.doi.org/10.5772/48344

1. Introduction

Nowadays, with the development of the technology, Ultraviolet optics has showed great implication prospect in the fields of space science, material, biophysics and plasma physics. Recently, with the development of the space remote sensing, the UV remote sensing technology has been re-known. The atmosphere is not only the main carrier and activity stage of earth climate and environment, but also is the main element of the space circumstance. So, realizing the global uniform sensing, always has been the common object of earth and space science community.

UV remote sensing is a necessary method of knowing the vertical structure and change of the atmosphere intensity [1], Ozone, gasoloid, and monitoring the state and turbulence of the middle layer atmosphere. It has a great science meaning in knowing the interacting procedure between the upper and lower atmosphere, establishing and proving the dynamic atmosphere model, and understanding the relationship between the sun activity and the climate of the space and earth.

With the developing of the quantization remote sensing researching, and the increasing of the test accuracy. All kinds of sensors have to be calibrated by the high accuracy standard at UV wavelength, and the testing accuracy, long-time stability and the date comparative of the sensors have to be evaluated. In theory, there are two way in realizing the absolute radiation calibration, the first one is standard light calibration method, and the second one is standard detector calibration method. The standard light calibration method is so easy to realizing the standard transmitting in the whole wavelength, but some uncertainty factor has also been introduced, it makes the calibration accuracy increasing so hardly. Because the uncertainty of the standard source is so low(1.2%), and some method has been using in removing a lot of uncertainty factor, the standard detector calibration method would been a effective way in increasing the calibration accuracy at UV wavelength. This section will have a discussion about the UV detector calibration method, analyzing the calibration theory, establishing the experiment system, and finally gives a complete high accuracy UV standard detector calibration method.

2. UV detector standard and standard transmission

2.1. Present status and development of the cryogenic radiometer

First of all, the source of the UV detector standard will be introduced. Nowadays, the cryogenic radiometer had been used as the UV absolute standard detector in the world. The cryogenic radiometer is developed on the basic of the cold radiometer. The cold radiometer is the earliest detector which applying as the radiation measurement reference. There is a layer of black material with high absorptance on the receive area of the cold radiometer, the receive area would have a temperature rising when receiving the light. Using the equivalence between the electric heating and the light heating to testing the radiation power is the working principle of the cold radiometer. The cold radiometer has went through several generation development, until the 1980s, the uncertainty of using the cold radiometer to test the radiation power is about 0.1%. Because the cold radiometer working at the normal temperature, and affecting by the material and environment. the testing uncertainty can't been reduced.

In the middle of the 1980s, J.Martin made the fist cryogenic radiometer [2]. It has the same working principle with the cold radiometer. Because working at the liquid temperature, the cryogenic radiometer gets rid of the limitation of the environment and material. The uncertainty had been reduced by an order. So the great performance displayed by the cryogenic radiometer brought the researching on the cryogenic radiometer technology by the measurement organization in the industry development countries. The cryogenic radiometer technology is also hot point and focal point in the field of the radiation measurement now. In 1996, the international measurement organization made a cryogenic radiometer comparison. There are 16 nation measurement organizations joining the comparison. The comparison result indicated that the testing uniformity of each country was about 3x104.This is the best comparison result of the international comparing. So the cryogenic radiometer has been the highest accuracy radiation measurement method in the world.

2.2. The system structure and working principle of the cryogenic radiometer

The system structure and working principle of the US.NIST (National Institute of Standards and Technology) HARC (high-accuracy cryogenic radiometer) would be introduced as an example. Cryogenic radiometers provide an absolute basis for optical power (flux) measurements at the lowest possible uncertainties. They are used as primary standards for optical power at many other national laboratories as well [3-8]. A cryogenic radiometer is an electrical substitution radiometer (ESR) that operates by comparing the temperature rise induced by optical power absorbed in a black receiving cavity to the electrical power needed to cause the same temperature rise by resistive (ohmic) heating. Thus the measurement of optical power is determined in terms of electrical power, watt, via voltage and resistance standards maintained by NIST. There are several advantages to operating at cryogenic temperatures (≈ 5 K) instead of room temperature. The heat capacity of copper is reduced by a factor of 1000, thus allowing the use of a relatively large cavity. Also the thermal radiation emitted by the cavity or absorbed from the surroundings is reduced by a factor of $\approx 10^{7}$, which eliminates radiative effects on the equilibrium temperature of the cavity. Finally, the cryogenic temperature allows the use of superconducting wires to the heater, thereby removing the nonequivalence of optical and electrical heating resulting from heat dissipated in the wires. Consequently, most electrical substitution radiometers, including NIST-maintained ESRs, operate at cryogenic temperatures.

The Optical Technology Division within NIST presently has two cryogenic radiometers that provide the basis for the spectral radiant power responsivity scale: the NIST-designed POWR (Figure 1), and the L-1 ACR [9] (Figure 2). The POWR is the primary U.S. national standard for the unit of optical power. It has the capability to optimize its configuration for measurements in different spectral regions and for different input laser power levels. For optimized noise performance, it can operate at temperatures as low as 1.7 K for extended periods. The L-1 ACR is also an absolute radiometer, but one whose operation is optimized for the μW to mW power levels in the UV to NIR spectral region. In comparison with POWR, the L-1 ACR is compact and mobile, which makes it a convenient instrument to use for scale transfers. The relative combined standard uncertainty of the NIST cryogenic radiometer measurements range is from 0.01 % to 0.02 % in the visible region of the spectrum [10]. The largest components of the uncertainty are those due to the systematic correction for the Brewster angle window transmittance and the nonequivalence between electrical and optical heating. A comparison between POWR and the L-1 ACR showed that these two standards agreed to within 0.02 %, which is within their combined uncertainties as shown in Figure 3 [9].

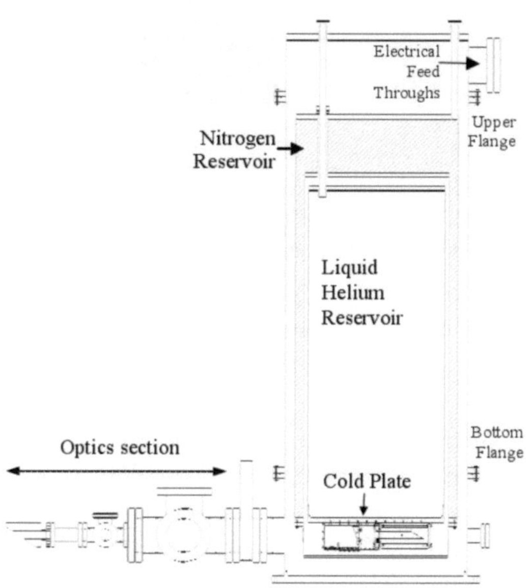

Figure 1. The construction of the NIST Primary Optical Watt Radiometer(POWR)

Figure 2. The NIST L-1 ACR used in Spectral Irradiance and Radiance Responsivity Calibrations using Uniform Sources (SIRCUS)

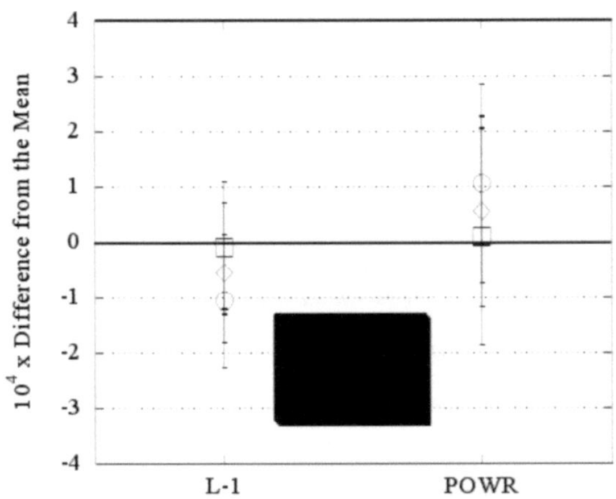

Figure 3. Comparison of POWR and the L-1 ACR measurements showing the agreement between the ACRs. The error bars are the measurement uncertainty

2.3. The procedure of the detector standard transmitting

2.3.1. Calibration of transfer standards with a cryogenic radiometer

The NIST detector standard transmitting procedure will be discussed as an example. The cryogenic radiometers described above use lasers as their source and a variety of transfer detectors to disseminate the spectral power responsivity scale. Historically, the scale was realized using the High Accuracy Cryogenic Radiometer (HACR) [11] at nine discrete laser lines in the visible wavelength range. A physical model was developed to interpolate the responsivity of silicon trap detectors over the spectral range from 405 nm to 920 nm [12].

Outside of this spectral range, the detector responsivity scale was based on pyroelectric detector with a spectrally flat responsivity [13]. While the pyroelectric detector had a spectrally flat responsivity, its absolute responsivity value was low. While it could extend the scale, its noise performance dramatically increased the uncertainties in the UV and the NIR spectral regions because of the low flux available on the comparator facilities (see the 1998 version of this document [14] for more information). The UV responsivity scale uncertainty was improved by calibrating the UV WS (UV working standard) at the NIST Synchrotron Ultraviolet Radiation Facility (SURF III) with an ACR-monochromator system [15, 16].

2.3.2. *Calibration of the working standards*

Two UV working standards (UV WS) were calibrated from 200 nm to 400 nm by a series of measurements at the Ultraviolet Spectral Comparator Facility (UV SCF), Visible to Near-Infrared Spectral Comparator Facility(Vis/NIR SCF), and SURF with various Si photodiode UV transfer standards and trap detectors. The UV WS were calibrated with a Vis Trap at the Vis/NIR SCF from 405 nm to 500 nm. The combination of the UV transfer standards and the Vis Trap provides the lowest uncertainties over the entire UV WS calibration range. The calibration chain for the UV working standards is shown in Figure 4.

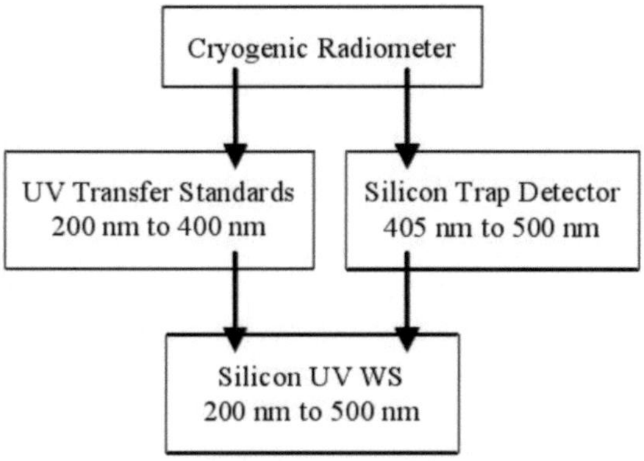

Figure 4. The calibration chain for the ultraviolet working standards (UV WS)

The responsivity of the UV WS was determined by an average of 3 independent scans against each UV TS and Vis Trap. As with the Vis WS, each UV WS was removed from the SCF and realigned between each scan. The resulting data from the transfer standards were combined to create a single scale from 200 nm to 500 nm for the UV WS.

2.3.3. *Ultraviolet Spectral Comparator (UV SCF)*

The UV SCF is a monochromator-based system that measures the uniformity and spectral power responsivity of photodetectors in the 200 nm to 500 nm spectral region. The UV SCF is very similar in configuration and operation to the Vis/NIR SCF. Only the differences between the two will be described. A diagram of the UV SCF is shown in Fig. 5

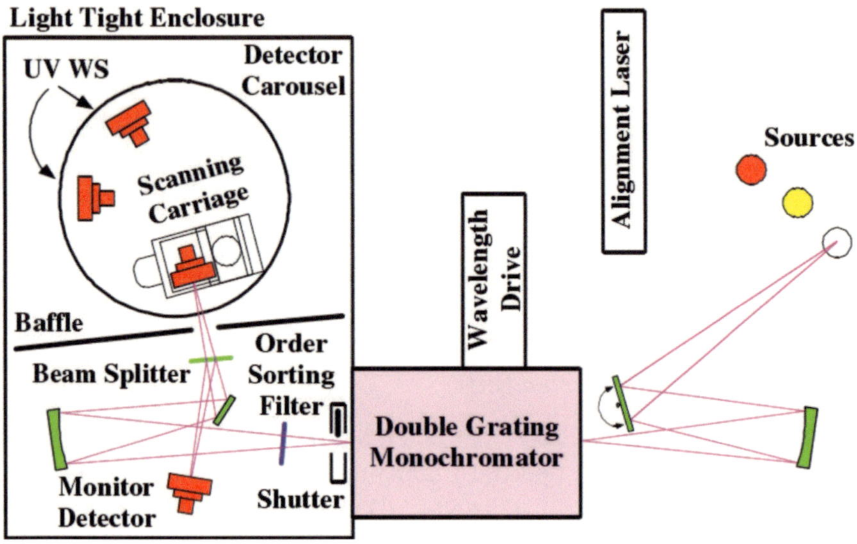

Figure 5. Ultraviolet Spectral Comparator Facility (UV SCF)

UV enhanced silicon photodiodes serve as the working standards for the UV SCF. A rotary stage is used in the UV SCF; currently only one test detector at a time can be measured. The test and working standard detectors are fixed onto optical mounts that rotate and tilt. Motorized translation stages position the test detector in the horizontal and vertical planes while the working standards are positioned manually.

3. High Accuracy UV Standard Radiometer (HAUVSR)

As the main radiation testing facility, the radiometer has a important position in the radiation field. But the radiometer using in the practical application doesn't have responsivity standard, needs to be calibrated by the standard source. Because of the error introducing in the calibration procedure, the radiometer uncertainty will reduce. So the radiometer doesn't have a good performance in the radiation application [17].

For solving the problem discussing above, the HAUVSR had been established using the NIST working standards detector as a core element. A series of capability testing had been made to confirm its stability. And the HAUVSR responsivity standard had been deduced at the basic of the NIST detector standard. The uncertainty analyzing also had been done. Finally, there is a radiometer with high stability, high accuracy and self- responsivity standard that would have a great performance in the calibrating application.

3.1. Establishmen of the HAUVSR

3.1.1. System construction

The design concept of the HAUVSR is compact structure, easy to carrying on, simple interior constitution and stability performance. And there is no other optical element in the HAUVSR. So the responsivity standard can be deduced with high accuracy.

For satisfying the requirement listing above, The HAUVSR has been established using the NIST working standards detector as a core element, and adding the light filter splitting system, motor driving system and date acquisition system. The structure of the whole facility is shown in Fig.6

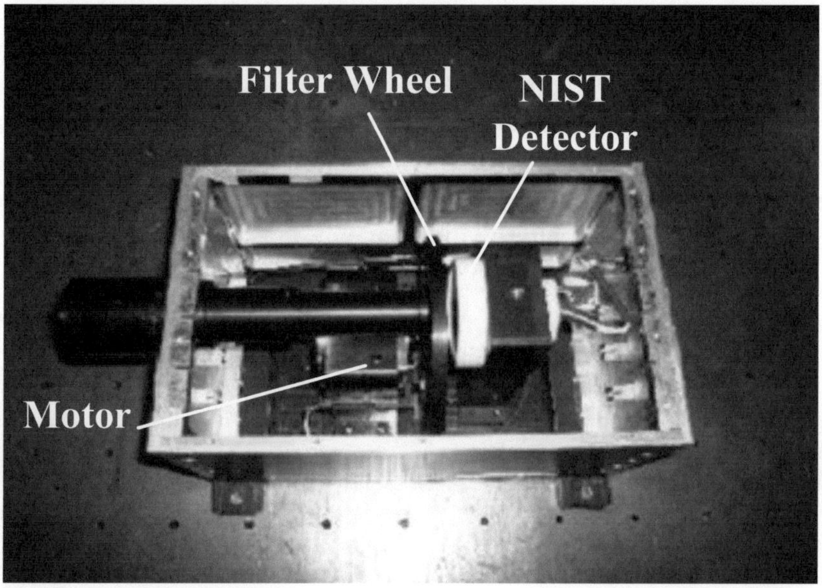

Figure 6. The structure of the HAUVSR

The incident light pass through the lightproof canister, filter, and arrives at the receive area of the detector. There is three UV filter with different wavelength fitting on the filter wheel. The three wavelengths are 313nm, 352nm, 365nm. The filter wheel is controlled by the motor driving to make sure different wavelength light passing through. The data acquisition system collects the detector signal and saves it on the computer. According to the responsivity standard of the HAUVSR, the incident optical radiation can be calculated with the data.

3.1.2. Detector selection

As the core element of the HAUVSR, The detector's performances will effect the accuracy and stability of the HAUVSR. So the detector choosing is very important. According to the design requirement of the HAUVSR, a detector with good stability, great linearity, compacting structure, wide response wavelength range and self-responsivity will be used standard. After considering all the factor, the NIST working standard detector S2281 will be the best choice. The advantage of the NIST detector will display obviously in a series of testing results by comparing with the HAMAMATSU detector.

a. Space Uniformity Testing of Detector Receive Area

Space uniformity is a very important character of Si detector. In theory, the detector would have great space uniformity, it means that the output signal will be sameness, when incident optical radiation illuminate on the difference zone of the detector receive area. But the uniformity actually is restricted by the photo surface material, making technique and the little speck on the photo surface. And the detector receive area heterogeneity will effect the testing accuracy.

The detector space uniformity testing system is shown in Fig.7.At first, the untested detector would be fitted on the detector rotary table which can move at X and Y direction. The moving distance is 50mm.Two-direction repeatable accuracy< 2μm. There are a φ 1mm apertures stop and two lens before the detector. A φ 1mm optical speckle on the receive area can be acquired by secondary imaging. The responsivity with different coordinate can be tested by varying the detector position. The testing wavelength is 350nmn.The scanning area is 10mmx10mm with 1mm interval. And the delay time is 5 second.

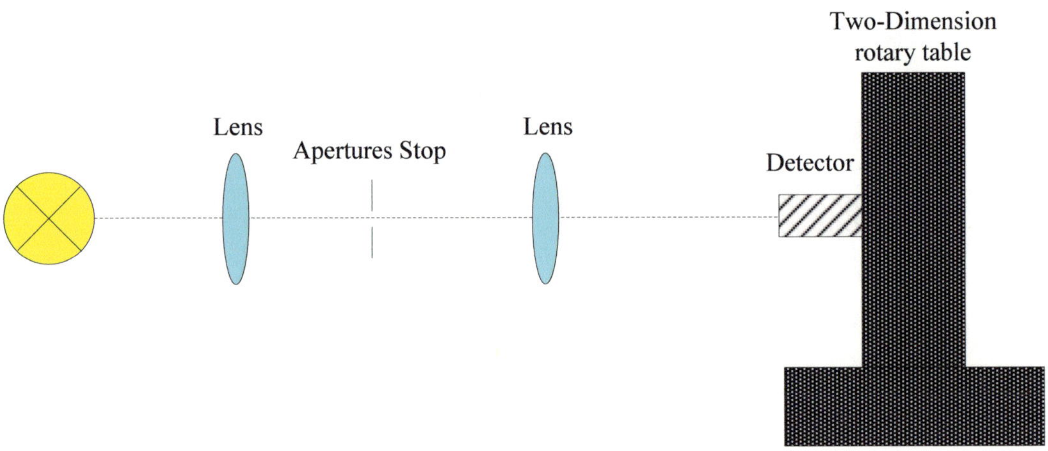

Figure 7. Detector Space Uniformity testing system

Three detectors had been tested(NIST S2281 detector and two HAMAMATSU detectors).The testing result (different position responsivity) had been normalized. And the 3D figure had been drawn using the MatLab software.Fig.7 displays the responsivity space uniformity of the three detectors.

Just like shows in Fig.8, the space uniformity of the NIST detector has a great advantage comparing with the two HAMAMATSU detectors. The three detector's space uniformity also can be calculated. The result is shown in Table.1.

Detector	Space Uniformity
The Space Uniformity of NIST S2281 detector	≤1.5%
The Space Uniformity of HAMAMATSU detector 1	≤2.7%
The Space Uniformity of HAMAMATSU detector 2	≤2.4%

Table 1. The Space Uniformity of the three Detectors

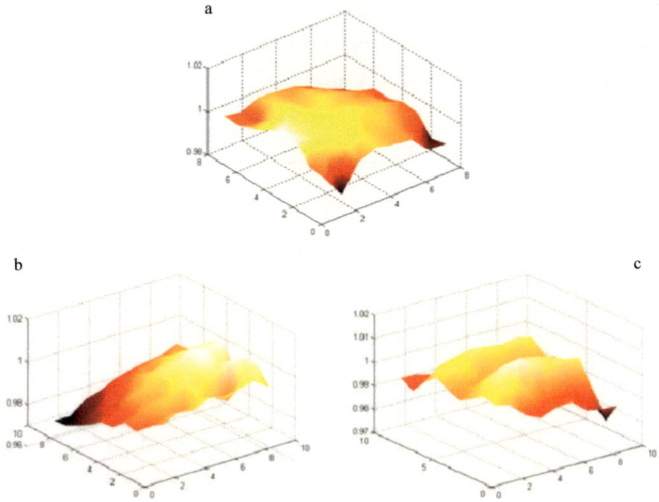

Figure 8. Detector Space uniformity curved
(a.NIST S2281 detector; b. HAMAMATSU detector1; c. HAMAMATSU detector2)

b. Detector linearity

Linearity is a basic feature of detector. In theory, the detector responsivity is stationary[18]. The responsivity won't change when the incident optical power varies.

There are a lot of methods for detector linearity testing, just like inverse ratio method of distance square, polarizing film method and so on. Neutral weakener and double optical stops method with high accuracy had been adopted in this section.

Fig.9 shows the linearity testing facility. The standard light F08 had been used. The detector had been putted into a light-tight box to eliminating the stray light. The neutral weakener was fitted on the filter wheel, and putted before the detector. Double light stop is laid between the light and the weakener. Different neutral weakener was moved into the light path by controlling the filter wheel to realize the incident optical energy varying. The weakener gradient is 0.01%, 0.1%, 1%, 10%, 31.62%, 50.12%, 79.43%, 100%. And the signal with different optical stop would be saved.

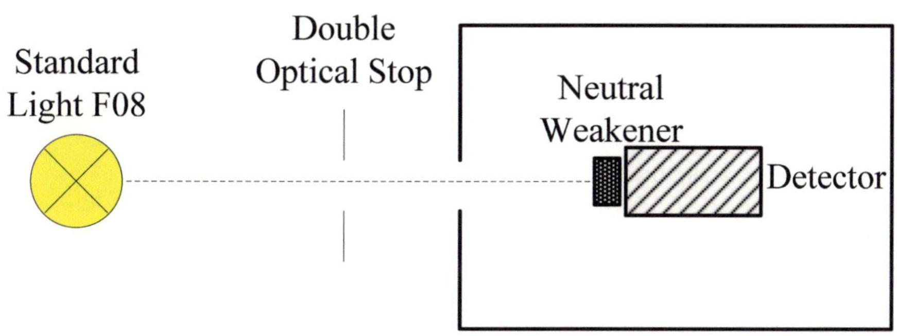

Figure 9. Detector Linearity testing facility

The testing results shows that the NIST detector linearity is about 0.6% in the 10^4 dynamic ranges, and the HAMAMATSU linearity is about 0.7%. So the NIST detector linearity can satisfy the design requirement of the HAUVSR.

3.1.3. The filter stability and uniformity testing

According to the design requirement of the HAUVSR, the filter needs to own some characteristic listing below:

1. Narrow band width：Narrow band width is propitious to calculate the self-responsivity of the HAUVSR.
2. High stability: The stability of the filter will effect the HAUVSR performance.
3. Great uniformity: The filter's transmittance uniformity will have a influence on the HAUCSR testing accuracy.

So some filters which produced by different manufactory had been tested. Finally, some filter which could satisfy the requirement had been selected.

The filter stability had been tested for 1 year. The test result is shown in Table.2

Filter	Central Wavelength		
	2008.6	2009.6	changes
280.000	280.150	280.250	0.100
313.000	314.300	314.450	0.150
352.000	353.500	353.350	0.015
365.000	364.950	364.750	0.020
Filter	Band Width		
	2008.6	2009.6	changes
280.000	25.500	24.300	1.200
313.000	10.600	9.800	1.100
352.000	10.100	8.900	1.200
365.000	11.400	10.400	1.000
Filter	Peak Transmittance		
	2008.6	2009.6	changes
280.000	0.277	0.271	0.006
313.000	0.648	0.643	0.002
352.000	0.551	0.549	0.002
365.000	0.438	0.432	0.006

Table 2. Filter Long Time Stability Testing

The testing result showed that the central wavelength, band width, peak transmittance of the filter had so little change in a year to satisfy the design requirement.

For limiting by the facture technics the filter transmittance uniformity had a discrepancy. The filter uniformity had been tested with the testing facility introduced in the section 3.1.2.

There are 9 points being selected to do the test. The diameter of the optical speckle is 1mm. Just like shows in Fig.10.

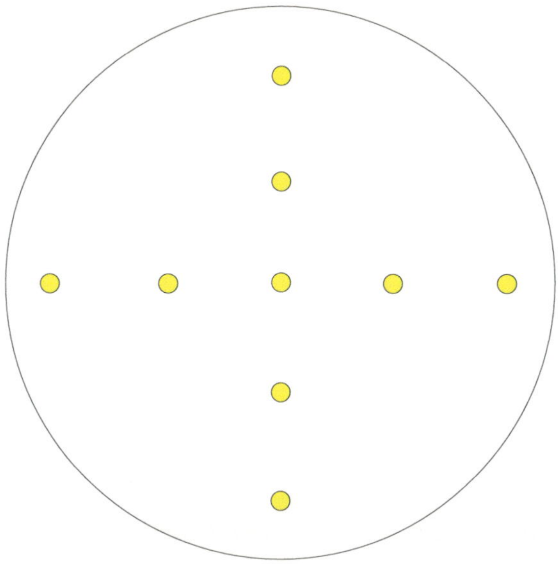

Figure 10. Filter Transmittance Uniformity Testing

The testing result shows in Table.3

Filter	Nonuniformity
280.000	0.06%
313.000	0.05%
352.000	0.07%
365.000	0.04%

Table 3. The Testing Result of the Filter Transmittance Uniformity

The testing result displays that the filter transmittance uniformity is so great that its influence on the HAUVSR could be ignored.

3.2. High Accuracy UV Standard Radiometer performance testing

The whole HAUVSR system had been tested on the basic of performance evaluation of the core elements.

The output signal from the HAUVSR would effect the testing accuracy. So it is so necessary to test the HAUVSR signal repeatability [19].

Using the standard light F08 with stable output, the signal form HAUVSR had been tested for 20 times at 3 wavelengths in 3 months. After standard deviation calculate with the data. The signal repeatability result is shown in Fig.11. The signal standard deviation is less than 0.6% at three wavelengths.

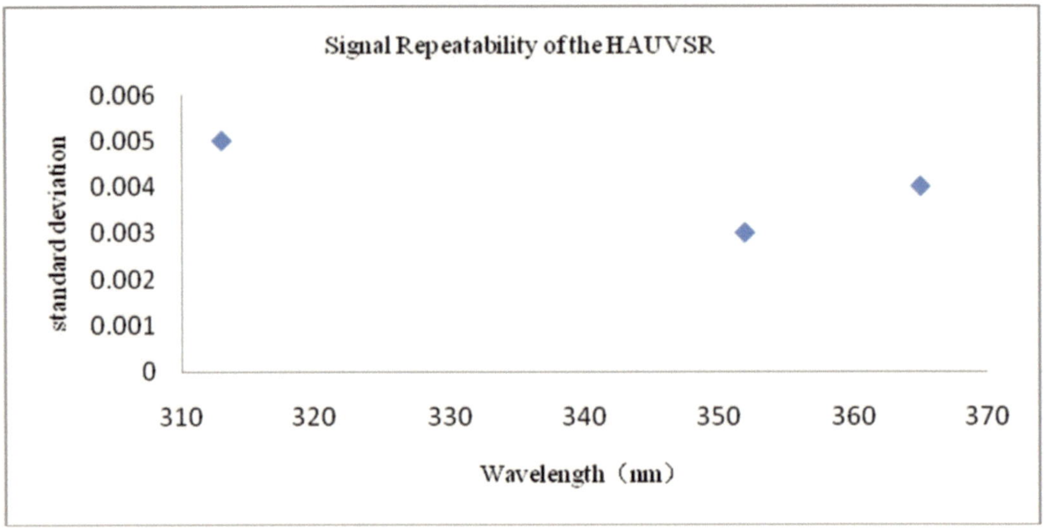

Figure 11. Signal Repeatability of the HAUVSR

The signal repeatability had also been tested in different temperature. The varying range of the temperature is 15ºC-32ºC. The testing result shows in Fig.12. The testing result had proved the great stability of the HAUVSR.

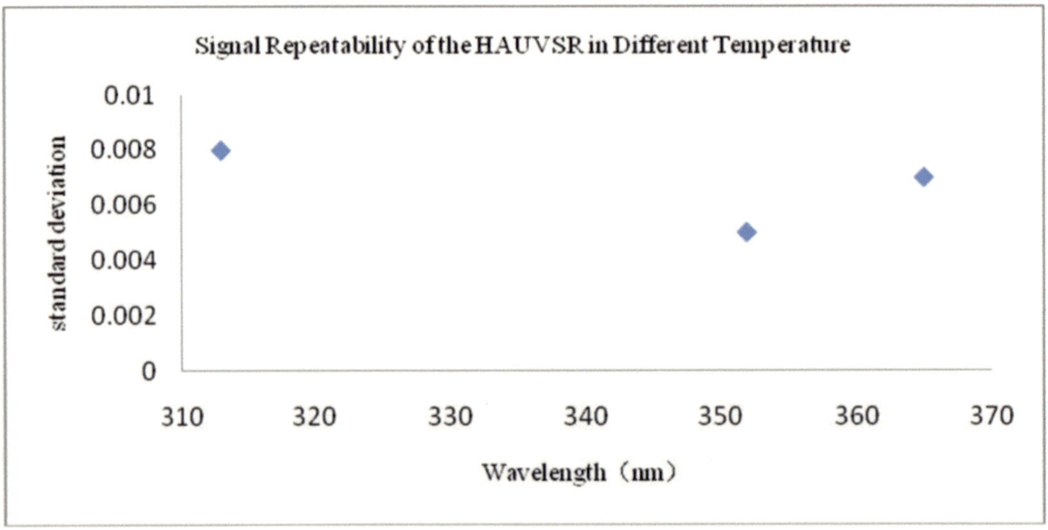

Figure 12. Signal Repeatability of the HAUVSR in Different Temperature

3.3. The responsivity deducing of the high accuracy UV radiometer

As the core element of the HAUVSR, the NIST working standards detector's spectral responsivity had been calibrated in NIST. The calibration procedure had been introduced in the section 2.3.But the calibration result is the radiant flux responsivity, and the irradiance and radiance responsivity always are used in application. So the HAUVSR irradiance and radiance responsivity had to be deduced in this section.

3.3.1. Irradiance and radiance responsvity deducing of the HAUVSR

First of all, the definition of the radiant flux, irradiance and radiance is given.

The radiant flux Φ is given by:

$$\varnothing = \frac{dQ}{dt} \tag{1}$$

dQ is the transmission and receiving radiation energy in the time of dt

The irradiance that is the illuminated radiant flux at unit surface can be written as:

$$\mathrm{E} = \frac{\mathrm{d}\varnothing}{\mathrm{dA}} \tag{2}$$

And the radiance L can be written as:

$$L = \frac{d\varnothing}{d\Omega dA cos\theta} \tag{3}$$

dA is the unit radiant surface, $d\Omega$ is the unit spatial angle, θ is the separation angle between the radiant direction and the surface normal direction.

The responsivity R defines as the electric signal generating by the unit radiant quantity.

1. Radiant flux responsivity

$$\mathrm{R}_{\phi} = \mathrm{S} / \phi \tag{4}$$

2. Irradiance responsivity

$$\mathrm{R_E} = \mathrm{S} / \mathrm{E} \tag{5}$$

3. Radiance responsivity

$$\mathrm{R_L} = \mathrm{S} / \mathrm{L} \tag{6}$$

S is the system output signal, E is the irradiance receiving by the system, and L is the radiance receiving by the system.

According to the Ep.(2) and Ep.(5), the R_E also can be written as :

$$R_E = R_{\phi} \cdot dA \tag{7}$$

So the irradiance responsivity is given as Ep.(8) according to the Ep.(3) and Ep.(6),

$$R_L = R_\phi \cdot d\Omega \cdot dA \cdot \cos\theta \tag{8}$$

3.3.2. *Radiant energy proportionality coefficient deducing in the filter band width*

There are three filters in the HAUVSR. The band width and peak transmittance of the filters will effect the spectral responsivity of the HAUVSR. So the filter modifying factor has to be added in the responsivity deducing procedure.

The band width of the filters being used are 10.6nm, 10.1nm and 11.4nm. But the calibration data band width of the NIST working standards detector is 1nm after interpolation calculating. The radiant energy transmission proportionality coefficient in narrow band width will be deduced in this section.

At first, the transmissivity of the filters has to be tested with spectrometer Lamda950. The wavelength interval is 0.5nm. $T_{(\lambda)}$ is the transmissivity at different wavelength. $I_{(\lambda)}$ is the incident radiant energy. $R_{(\lambda)}$ is the detector responsivity. So the optical radiation receiving by the detector can be written in general:

$$I_d = \int_{\lambda_1}^{\lambda_2} I_{(\lambda)} \cdot T_{(\lambda)} \tag{9}$$

The detector output signal S_d is:

$$S_d = \int_{\lambda_1}^{\lambda_2} I_{(\lambda)} \bullet T_{(\lambda)} \cdot R_{(\lambda)} \tag{10}$$

S_m is the signal at central wavelength, it can be written as:

$$S_m = I_{(\lambda m)} \cdot T_{(\lambda m)} \cdot R_{(\lambda m)} \tag{11}$$

So the proportionality coefficient in narrow band width f can be obtained through divding Ep.(11) by Ep.(10):

$$f = \frac{S_m}{S_d} = \frac{I_{(\lambda m)} \cdot T_{(\lambda m)} \cdot R_{(\lambda m)}}{\int_{\lambda_1}^{\lambda_2} I_{(\lambda)} \cdot T_{(\lambda)} \cdot R_{(\lambda)}} \tag{12}$$

3.3.3. *The correction factor deducing of detecor uniformity*

As the optical radiation receving instrument, the detector uniformity will effect the HAUVSR testing accuracy. So the correction factor of detector uniformity has to be added in the process of the HAUVSR responsivity deducing.

According to the detector uniformity testing result in the section 3.1.3, the detector nonuniformity normalization value B_i can be obtained. The nonuniformity correction factor can be written as:

$$\gamma = \frac{\int_1^m B_i R}{mR} = \frac{\int_1^m B_i}{m} \tag{13}$$

3.3.4. *The HAUVSR responsivity deducing result*

According to the correction factors discussing above, the HAUVSR spectral responsivity is:

1. HAUVSR irradiance responsivity :

$$R_E = \frac{R_\phi \cdot \gamma \cdot A \cdot \tau}{f} \tag{14}$$

2. HAUVSR radiance responsivity :

$$R_L = \frac{R_\phi \cdot \Omega \cdot \gamma \cdot A \cdot \tau}{f} \tag{15}$$

3.3.5. *The uncertainty of the HAUVSR*

According to the Ep.(14) and Ep.(15) , the uncertainty of the HAUVSR can be written as:

$$\frac{\Delta R_s(\lambda)}{R_s(\lambda)} = \left\{ \left| \frac{\Delta R_\phi(\lambda)}{R_\phi(\lambda)} \right|^2 + \left| \frac{\Delta \gamma(\lambda)}{\gamma(\lambda)} \right|^2 + \left| \frac{\Delta f(\lambda)}{f(\lambda)} \right|^2 + \left| \frac{\Delta \tau(\lambda)}{\tau(\lambda)} \right|^2 \right\}^{1/2} \tag{16}$$

The uncertainty item are listed in the Table.4

Uncertainty Source	value
The NIST detector uncertainty	1.1%
The testing and calculating error of the correction factor γ	0.5%
The testing and calculating error of the correction factor f	0.5%
The testing correction of filter transmissivity τ	0.5%
The stray light uncertainty	0.3%
Total uncertainty	1.3%

Table 4. The uncertainty of the HAUVSR

1. The NIST standard detector uncertainty 1.1% is given by NIST calibration result.
2. The uncertainty of the detector uniformity correction factor γ is decided by the number of the testing point and the instrument accuracy. The uncertainty value is 0.3%

3. The uncertainty of the correction factor f is also decided by the testing and calculating error. The value is 0.3%.
4. The uncertainty of the filter transmissivity τ is effected by the Lamda950 testing error. The value is 0.5%.

4. The untested spectrometer responsivity calibrated with standard detector calibration method

After a series of deducing in the section 3.3, the HAUVSR had self- responsivity standard. So the HAUVSR can be used to calibrate the untested sensor with standard detector calibration method. The basic theory of standard detector calibration method is that the responsivity of untested sensor can be acquired when the two device receive the same incident optical radiation. Because the responsivity of standard detector is known, the untested sensor calibration result can be obtained easily with substitution method [20].

In this section, The HAUVSR system will be used as a standard detector to calibrate the untested spectrometer with standard detector calibration method.

4.1. Irradiance responsivity calibration with standard detector calibration method

The calibration instrument is shown in Fig.13. A quartz tungsten-halogen lamp with great stability is used. The HAUVSR and untested spectrometer are putted on the experiment table. The distance between the HAUVSR and the lamp is 650mm[21]. The lamp center and the optical stop center of the HAUVSR are fitted at the same horizontal line. The system has to be preheated for 40 minutes before the signal acquisition. There are 3 wavelengths (313nm, 352nm, 365nm) being tested. The signal has to be acquired for 3 times, and calculate an average value to eliminate the random error. Then, the untested spectrometer is moved into the optical path. Keeping the distance of 650mm, the signal is acquired at the same 3 wavelength.

The spectral irradiance receiving by the HAUVSR and the untested spectrometer comes from the same lamp. If the distance between the lamp and sensor is fixed, and the lamp has a great stability, the Ep. (17) can be obtained. E_{F08} is the spectral irradiance of the quartz tungsten-halogen lamp at the distance of 650mm. S_{ES}, S_{ED} are the signal value of the HAUVSR and the untested spectrometer. R_{ES}, R_{ED} are the irradiance responsivity of the HAUSR and the untested spectrometer.

$$E_{F08} = \frac{S_{ES}}{R_{ES}} = \frac{S_{ED}}{R_{ED}} \tag{17}$$

Because the irradiance responsivity is known, the irradiance responsivity of the untested spectrometer is [22]:

$$R_{ED} = \frac{S_{ED} \cdot R_{ES}}{S_{ES}} \tag{18}$$

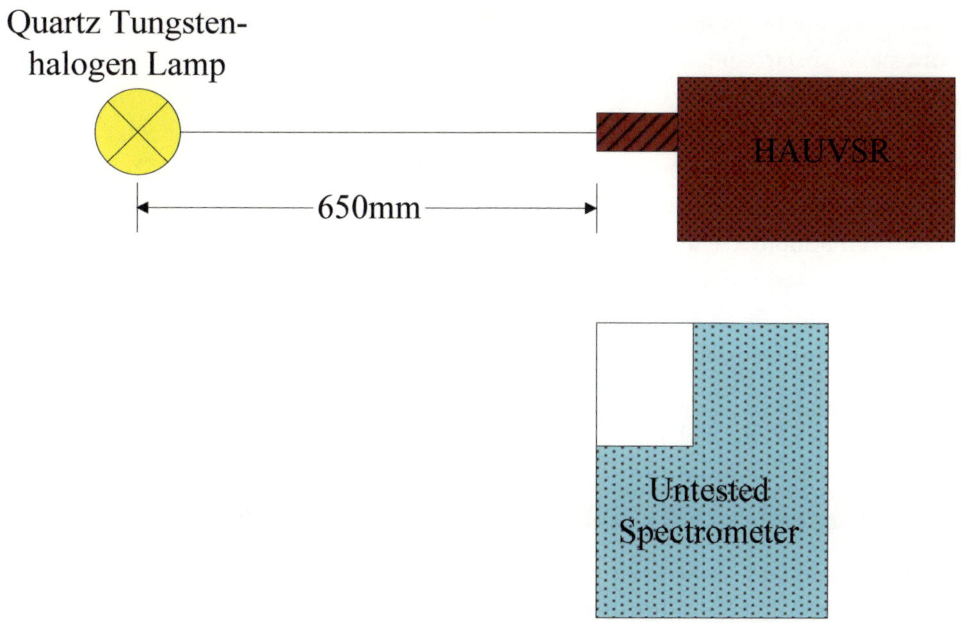

Figure 13. The Irradiance responsivity calibration instrument using standard detector calibration method

Substituting the signal measurement into the Ep. (18), the irradiance responsivity of the untested spectrometer R_{ED} can be acquired.

The uncertainty analyzing can be done with the Ep. (18).

$$\frac{\Delta R_{ED}(\lambda)}{R_{ED}(\lambda)} = \left[\left| \frac{\Delta S_{ED}(\lambda)}{S_{ED}(\lambda)} \right|^2 + \left| \frac{\Delta R_{ES}(\lambda)}{R_{ES}(\lambda)} \right|^2 + \left| \frac{2\Delta h}{h} \right|^2 \right]^{1/2} \tag{19}$$

The uncertainty item is shown in Table.5

Uncertainty source	Value
The HAUVSR self- responsivity uncertainty	1.3%
The testing error of the distance between the lamp and the instrument	1.2%
The uncertainty generated by the instrument position deviation	0.5%
The wavelength accuracy and repeatability of the untested spectrometer	0.6%
The detecting system excursion and linearly of the untested spectrometer	0.5%
The stray light uncertainty	0.3%
Total uncertainty	1.9 %

Table 5. The uncertainty of the standard detector irradiance calibration method

1. The uncertainty of the HAUVSR self- responsivity is 1.3% .(in sec.3.3.5)
2. The testing error of the distance between the lamp and the instrument is about 3mm. using Ep.(19),the uncertainty can be calculated. The value is 1.2%
3. The instrument position deviation will change the separation angle between the untested spectrometer diffused plate and the lamp, and effects the bi-directional reflectivity. The value is 0.5%.
4. The detecting system excursion and linearly of the untested spectrometer is effected by the performance of the amplifier of the detector. The value is about 0.5%.
5. The stray light effect is an assignable factor in the process of calibration. Some measures had been adopted. The experiment table had been masked with black cloth. So there is no obstacle and reflect light around the lamp. The HAUVSR and untested spectrometer has been made black finish. Their surface emissivity is about 0.8%. The measures listing above can minimize the stray light error to 0.3%.

So the uncertainty of the HAUVSR calibrating the untested spectrometer with standard detector method is 1.9%.

4.2. Irradiance responsivity calibration standard light calibration method

Using NIST standard light F528 to calibrate the irradiance responsivity of the untested spectrometer with standard light calibration method is also been done.

The standard light is used to illuminate the center of the diffused plate of the untested spectrometer. The distance between them is 650mm. The calibration instrument is shown in Fig.14.Because the irradiance of the lamp is known, the irradiance responsivity of the untested spectrometer can be obtain easily after getting the output signal. E_{F528} is the irradiance of the standard light F528.

$$R_{ED} = \frac{S_{ED}}{E_{F528}} \tag{20}$$

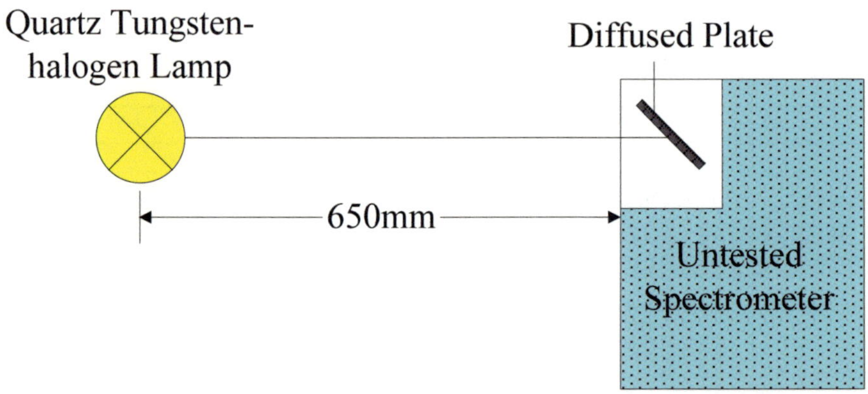

Figure 14. The Irradiance responsivity calibration instrument using standard light calibration method

According to the Ep. (20), the uncertainty becomes:

$$\frac{\Delta R_E(\lambda)}{R_E(\lambda)} = \left[\left| \frac{\Delta S_{ED}(\lambda)}{S_{ED}(\lambda)} \right|^2 + \left| \frac{\Delta E_{F528}(\lambda)}{E_{F528}(\lambda)} \right|^2 + \left| \frac{2\Delta h}{h} \right|^2 \right]^{1/2} \tag{21}$$

The uncertainty item is listed in the Table.6

Uncertainty source	Value
The irradiance uncertainty of the standard light F528	2%
The testing error of the distance *h* between the lamp and the instrument	1.2%
The uncertainty generated by the instrument position deviation	0.5%
The wavelength accuracy and repeatability of the untested spectrometer	0.6%
The detecting system excursion and linearly of the untested spectrometer	0.5%
The stray light uncertainty	0.3%
Total uncertainty	2.6 %

Table 6. The uncertainty of the standard light irradiance calibration method

The irradiance uncertainty of the standard light F528 is provided by the NIST calibration report.

So the uncertainty of the lamp F528 calibrating the untested spectrometer with standard light method is 2.6%.

4.3. Two methods comparison

The irradiance responsivity of the untested spectrometer had been calibrated by the two methods. The calibration result is listed in the Table.7. Form the result we can see that the Standard detector calibration method has a higher accuracy comparing with the standard lamp calibration method. The calibration result comparison also approves the effectivity of the standard detector calibration method.

Wavelength	Irradiance response calibration of the untested spectrometer		Uncertainty comparison of the two calibration methods	
	Standard detector calibration result	Standard lamp calibration result	Standard detector calibration method	Standard lamp calibration method
nm	$V.uw^{-1}.cm^2.nm$	$V.uw^{-1}.cm^2.nm$		
313	4.80E+00	4.73E+00	1.90%	2.60%
352	5.67E+00	5.58E+00		
365	5.82E+00	5.72E+00		

Table 7. Irradiance response calibration result comparison between the two calibration methods

5. Conclusion

This paper introduces the standard detector calibration method. The detector standard source and standard transmission process is also discussed. And the HAUVSR is established using NIST standard detector. After a series of testing, the performance of the HAUVSR has been proved. We also deduce the responsivity standard of the HAUVSR, and its uncertainty is so high (1.3%).Using the HAUVSR, we calibrate the untested spectrometer with standard detector method. The calibration result is compared with the standard light calibration method. The comparison date indicates that the standard detector method can increase the calibration accuracy. The uncertainty of the standard detector calibration method (1.9%) is higher than the standard light calibration method (2.6%). Using this method, we can provide a untested sensor calibration result with higher accuracy. So our research on the standard calibration method is very important for the developing of the radiant calibration field.

Author details

Wang Rui, Wang Tingfeng, Sun Tao, Chen Fei and Guo Jin
Changchun Institute of Optics, Fine Mechanics and Physics, Chinese Academy of Sciences, State Key Laboratory of Laser Interaction with Matter, China

6. References

[1] D. F. Heath, A. J. Krueger, H. A. Roeder and B. D. Henderson. The Solar Backscatter Ultraviolet and Total Ozone Mapping Spectrometer (SBUV/TOMS) for NIMBUSG [J]. Optical Engineering, 1975, 14(4):323-331.

[2] T.J.Quinn. Primary methods of measurement an primary standards [J].Metrologia.1997,20: 34-63.

[3] F. Lei and J. Fischer, Characterization of Photodiodes in the UV and Visible Spectral Region-Based on Cryogenic Radiometry, Metrologia 30 (4), 297-303 (1993).

[4] R. Goebel, R. Pello, R. Kohler, P. Haycocks, and N. P. Fox, Comparison of the BIPM Cryogenic radiometer with a mechanically cooled cryogenic radiometer from the NPL, Metrologia 33 (2), 177-179 (1996).

[5] R. Kohler, R. Goebel, R. Pello, O. Touayar, and J. Bastie, First results of measurements with the BIPM cryogenic radiometer and comparison with the INM cryogenic radiometer, Metrologia 32 (6), 551-555 (1996).

[6] R. Goebel, R. Pello, K. D. Stock, and H. Hofer, Direct comparison of cryogenic radiometers from the BIPM and the PTB, Metrologia 34 (3), 257-259 (1997).

[7] J. E. Martin, N. P. Fox, and P. J. Key, A cryogenic radiometer for absolute radiometric measurements, Metrologia 21 147-155 (1985).

[8] L. P. Boivin and K. Gibb, Monochromator-based cryogenic radiometry at the NRC, Metrologia 32 (6), 565-570 (1996).

[9] J. M. Houston and J. P. Rice, NIST reference cryogenic radiometer designed for versatile performance, Metrologia 43 (2), S31-S35 (2006).

[10] S. W. Brown, G. P. Eppeldauer, and K. R. Lykke, Facility for spectral irradiance and radiance responsivity calibrations using uniform sources, Applied Optics 45 (32), 8218-8237 (2006).

[11] T. C. Larason, S. S. Bruce, and C. L. Cromer, The NIST high accuracy scale for absolute spectral response from 406 nm to 920 nm, Journal of Research of the National Institute of Standards and Technology 101 (2), 133-140 (1996).

[12] T. R. Gentile, J. M. Houston, and C. L. Cromer, Realization of a scale of absolute spectral response using the national institute of standards and technology high-accuracy cryogenic radiometer, Applied Optics 35 (22), 4392-4403 (1996).

[13] A. C. Parr, A National Measurement System for Radiometry, Photometry, and Pyrometry Based Upon Absolute Detectors, NIST Technical Note 1421 (1996).

[14] T. C. Larason, S. S. Bruce, and A. C. Parr, Spectroradiometric detector measurements: part 1-ultraviolet detectors and part II-visible to near-infrared detectors, NIST Special Publications 250-41, U.S. Government Printing Office, Washington, DC (1998).

[15] P. S. Shaw, K. R. Lykke, R. Gupta, T. R. O'brian, U. Arp, H. H. White, T. B. Lucatorto, J. L. Dehmer, and A. C. Parr, Ultraviolet radiometry with synchrotron radiation and cryogenic radiometry, Applied Optics 38 (1), 18-28 (1999).

[16] P. S. Shaw, T. C. Larason, R. Gupta, S. W. Brown, R. E. Vest, and K. R. Lykke, The new ultraviolet spectral responsivity scale based on cryogenic radiometry at Synchrotron Ultraviolet Radiation Facility III, Review of Scientific Instruments 72 (5), 2242-2247 (2001).

[17] Donald.F.Heath, Zongying Wei, et al. Calibration and characterization of remote sensing instruments using ultra stable interference filters[J]. SPIE, 1997, 3221:300-308.

[18] D.F. Heath, E. Hilsenrath, and S. Janz, Characterization of a 'hardened' ultra-stable UV linear variable filter and recent results on the radiometric stability of narrow band interference filters subjected to temperature/humidity, thermal/vacuum and ionizing radiation environments [J],.SPIE, 1998, 3501: 410-421.

[19] M.Durak,F.Samadov. Realization of a filter radiometer-based irradiance scale with high accuracy in the region from 286nm to 901nm[J].Metrologia,2004,41:401-406.

[20] T.R.Gentile, J.M.Houston, J.E.Hardis, C.L.Cromer, A.C.Parr. National Institute of Standards and Technology high-accuracy cryogenic radiometer [J]. Appl.Opt, 1996, 35(7): 1056-1068.

[21] Donald F,Heath, Zia Ahmad, Multipurpose spectrotadiometer for satellite instrument calibration and zenith sky remote sensing measurements[J],.SPIE,2001, 4150(45):115-123.

[22] D.Einfield, D.stuck and B.Wende. Calibration of radiometric transfer standards in the UV and VUV by electron synchrotron radiation using a normal incidence radiometer [J], Metrologia 1978, 14: 111-122.

Chapter 3

Dynamic Testing of Data Acquisition Channels Using the Multiple Coherence Function

Troy C. Richards

Additional information is available at the end of the chapter

http://dx.doi.org/10.5772/48539

1. Introduction

The use of the Fast Fourier Transform (FFT) has revolutionized digital signal processing in many ways; and one of its principle uses continues to be the calculation of power spectral densities that are then used to estimate system transfer functions. When performing transfer function measurements, best practise dictates that the coherence between the input and output also be computed to provide a measure of the confidence in the measurement.

Many researchers, however, have turned the FFT based calculation of system transfer functions into a means to identify and remove coherent noise present in sensor measurements. Based on power spectral densities calculated using the FFT, the coherent noise between signals can be determined and then subtracted to reduce the noise floor of the sensor data acquisition channel.

To achieve good coherence between the input and output signals at all frequencies of interest it is necessary to ensure that those frequencies are present in the input signal. Poor coherence between the input and output can identify frequencies where external signals are being picked up, or it can indicate that the input or output signals are reduced or not present. Good coherence at all frequencies of interest can only be achieved with the use of white or wideband input noise signals.

When the dynamic range of the device under test exceeds that of the measuring device, over the frequency range of interest, maintaining good coherence becomes increasingly difficult. In these cases, it becomes necessary to use band-limited inputs, or sine wave inputs, where the signal gains can be optimized to improve the dynamic range and the coherence.

Manufacturers and end-users alike require methods to characterize the performance or quality of the data acquisition channels they either produce or use. The study of quality, however, is actually devoted to understanding the noise of the devices under test. Often manufacturers report zero-input noise levels for their devices, however, those levels may not be achieved when the device is performing during actual use. The coherent removal procedure, to be presented, provides a method to dynamically test amplifiers, filters, or analog-to-digital (A/D) converters, and to compute their noise levels when using typical input signals.

The idea of inputting a white noise signal into two A/D converters and computing the residual spectra from the ordinary coherence function, in order to characterize the noise of the devices was first reported in [19], and that concept was extended to testing multiple A/D converters using the multiple coherence function in [20]. In this chapter, those methods are expanded to encompass the entire data acquisition channel, so that dynamic testing of multiple amplifiers, filters or A/D converters can be performed.

1.1. Preface

Bendat and Piersol's texts [1, 2] provide much of the theoretical background to the work to be presented here. Their treatment of the subject matter walks the reader through power spectral density estimation with discrete Fourier transforms and introduces data windowing and averaging periodograms, to arrive at estimates of the auto power spectral density based on the method popularized by Welch [21]. The foundation for both single-input single-output systems, as well as multiple-input single-output systems is also established, as is the concept of the coherent estimate of the output signal, and the residual spectrum.

The removal of coherent background signals is particularly effective at improving detection ranges of electromagnetic (EM) sensing systems, where incoming background micro-pulsation EM signals arrive virtually instantaneously on remote sensors (known as reference sensors), and can be (coherently) subtracted from signals monitoring areas of interest [6, 10, 17]. The removal of coherent background signals lowers the noise floor and therefore increases the detection range of the EM sensing system.

In the early efforts of using the multiple coherent removal procedure to enhance array performance, the number of reference sensors was limited to two or three channels and the required equations were solved for the given case. Recognizing that the system of equations for the optimum system transfer functions gave rise to a positive definite matrix which could be solved using the Cholesky algorithm was first reported in [20]. (Although, the conditioned spectral densities discussed by Bendat and Piersol bare close resemblance to the Cholesky decomposition into a lower triangle matrix, known as the square root of the matrix, followed by the back substitution procedure to yield the solution.) This approach then allowed any number of channels to be easily and efficiently programmed and solved. In that same work, the level of the residual spectrum was interpreted in terms of the noise of the individual A/D converters and a procedure was given to compute the individual A/D converter noise levels.

The IEEE has recently approved a standard [8] on the terminology and testing of A/D converters to provide a framework on the reporting on the dynamic testing of A/D converters. All of the principle methods discussed; the frequency domain method, the curve-fit method and the histogram method, use sine waves for their input signal. As the quality of the devices under test has improved, so too have the requirements for the spectral purity of the sine wave and the requirement to synchronize the sine wave frequency with the sampling rate. The frequency domain method has emerged as the most commonly used technique, however with the increasing resolution of A/D converters this approach will be limited by spectral leakage even for the best data windows. For end users who wish to verify the advertised specifications of high quality devices, the requirements of the test signal can be difficult and expensive to attain, in that, a standard off-the-shelf function generator is insufficient to perform the testing.

The relationship between coherence and time delay has been extensively studied, and the selected IEEE reprint volume [5] is an excellent reference on the subject (the single-input single-output treatment given here parallels page 1 of that work very closely). One of the most significant results in the volume is provided by Carter [4] where it is shown that the coherence function, as calculated using the FFT, has a bias error proportional to the delay between the signals.

It is, precisely the reason, that the coherence function as estimated using the FFT method, is biased by the time delay between those signals, which results in rather poor performance when attempting to remove coherent background acoustic signals. Sound waves travel much slower then EM waves and, therefore, there can be appreciable delay between the arrival of background acoustic signals.

The coherent removal technique is, however, well suited to testing multiple data acquisition channels because, generally, it is a simple matter to synchronize signals under user control. Simultaneously sampling the inputs is one of the basic principles behind the success of FFT-based spectrum analyzers.

1.2. Chapter overview

The chapter begins with a brief review of Welch's procedure for estimating the auto and cross power spectral densities of signals, and introduces the concept of determining the root mean square (rms) level of a signal in the frequency domain. Next the single-input single-output system and optimum system transfer function is introduced, and the concept of the coherent output and residual spectrum is explained. These results are then generalized for the multiple-input single-output system. Procedures for computing the cross spectral densities of a general number of signals are then discussed and the solution of the optimum system transfer functions using the Cholesky decomposition is presented, to establish the background theoretical material for the remainder of the chapter.

Next a general model for a data acquisition channel is introduced, which includes both amplifier and A/D converter noise sources, along with an noiseless gain and filter stage. To interpret the residual spectrum where any number of channels are tested, each channel of a multiple-input single-output system is represented by the data acquisition channel model, and the optimum system transfer functions and residual spectrum are determined in terms of the data acquisition model parameters. These results are then generalized, to allow any of the channels to be the output and the remaining channels the inputs. Assuming the input signal is large and the channel characteristics are matched leads to simple expressions for the optimum system transfer functions and the residual spectra, in terms of the data acquisition channel model parameters. It is then demonstrated how to test for either the amplifier noise or the A/D converter noise of the acquisition channel by adjusting the channel gain.

Measurement examples are then given demonstrating the technique with a set of analog amplifiers and filters, measured with simultaneously-sampled, 24-bit, sigma-delta ($\Delta\Sigma$) A/D converters, as well as a 16-bit, multiplexed, successive approximation register (SAR) A/D converter, with a constant inter channel delay between channel samples.

Firstly, the well-accepted procedure of using the FFT to compute the (single-input single-output) transfer functions is demonstrated by computing the transfer functions for each of the amplifiers and filters under test. Next, the multiple coherent removal procedure is used to calculate the noise of the high resolution ΔΣ A/D converters, and then the SAR-based A/D converter, using a wideband noise source, and then a narrower band noise source. Results are then presented for the noise of the amplifiers under test using the same inputs. The final measurement examines the implications of using a sine wave as the test signal, and the effect of data windowing is examined. Lastly, a brief summary of the presented work, highlighting areas of interest, is given.

2. Basic definitions of coherent removal

2.1. Calculation of the power spectral density

Generalizing the procedure made popular by Welch [21] for computing the power spectral density of one signal, the cross spectral density of two signals can be estimated by averaging the product of the FFT of segments of the two signals. If x and y represent the two data streams, and X_k and Y_k are the FFT of the k-th segment of data, which is possibly overlapped and windowed (to enhance its spectral content), the cross spectral density can be estimated as the average of K segments and is given as

$$S_{xy} = \frac{1}{KU} \sum_{k=1}^{K} X_k^* Y_k, \tag{1}$$

where * denotes the complex conjugate, and the quantity

$$U = f_s \sum_{n=1}^{M} w(n)^2 \tag{2}$$

is a constant which accounts for the spectral weighting of the data window $w(n)$ and, assuming the input is measured in volts, properly scales the power spectral density to have units of a volts squared per hertz (V^2/Hz). The segment length, which is also equivalent to the window length is defined as M, and the FFT size is defined as P, which is typically a power of 2 and is greater than M.

The auto (or self) spectral density, can be determine by setting $x = y$ to arrive at

$$S_{xx} = \frac{1}{KU} \sum_{k=1}^{K} |X_k|^2 . \tag{3}$$

As is evident by the above expressions the auto spectral densities are real valued, whereas, cross spectral densities are complex-valued functions.

Using Parseval's theorem, the root mean square (rms) level of the signal x, defined as σ_x, can be estimated as

$$\sigma_x^2 = \frac{f_s}{P} \sum S_{xx}, \tag{4}$$

where f_s is the sampling rate. The rms level calculated by Equation (4) is an averaged quantity and will be approximately equal to the variance of the (entire) signal computed in the time domain. (For each individual segment the computation of the rms level in the time and frequency domains are precisely equal, as required by Parseval's theorem.)

Some references explicitly define both a one-sided and two-sided spectral density, while the definitions used here are not specific to either definition, when plotting spectral densities we shall use the accepted practise of plotting the one-sided spectral density, so that the spectral density values are doubled and one side of the spectra plotted. By this approach, summing the $P/2$ values of the one-sided spectral of density, will yield the rms level of x as defined in Equation (4). It is helpful to consider the operation as a numeric integration of the spectral density, so that S_{xx} is summed over all frequency bins and then multiplied by the integration width fs/P, to obtain the square of the rms level σ_x^2.

The use of the Welch FFT-based method for computing spectral densities is well documented in the literature, the texts by Kay [9] and Marple [11], and their review paper [12], as well as the text by Oppenheim and Schafer [16], all have sections devoted to the Welch method. In MATLAB, the Signal Processing Toolbox includes the functions `pwelch` and `cpsd` for calculating auto and cross spectral densities [14]. In Section 2.5 of this chapter the Welch procedure is generalized for any number of signals.

2.2. Single-input single-output systems

A common use of spectral densities estimated by the Welch method is to compute the transfer function of an amplifier or filter under test. Digitally recorded representations of the input signal x and output signal y of a device can be segmented, possibly overlapped, windowed to improve spectral content, and the spectral densities S_{xx}, S_{yy} and S_{xy} calculated. The optimum system transfer function, in terms of its expected value or minimizing the error between y and the output of the filter, is given as

$$H_{xy} = \frac{S_{xy}}{S_{xx}}. \tag{5}$$

The coherence between the two signals, is defined as

$$C_{xy} = \gamma_{xy}^2 = \frac{|S_{xy}|^2}{S_{xx} S_{yy}} \tag{6}$$

and is a measure of how well the two signals are linearly related to each other. The coherence function is normalized such that $0 \leq C_{xy} \leq 1$. Good coherence, $C_{xy} \approx 1$, is essential to accepting the calculation of H_{xy} as the true transfer function of the device under test. The coherence function between just two channels, is sometimes referred to as the *ordinary coherence function*. The calculation of frequency domain transfer functions based on Welch's procedure and ultimately the FFT, forms the computational basis of many two-channel spectrum analyzers.

2.3. Concept of coherent removal

To understand the concept of coherent removal it is useful to refer to the single-input, single-output model in Fig. 1, and to define v as the signal at the output of H_{xy}. Since the optimum system transfer function, in terms of its expected value or minimizing the square

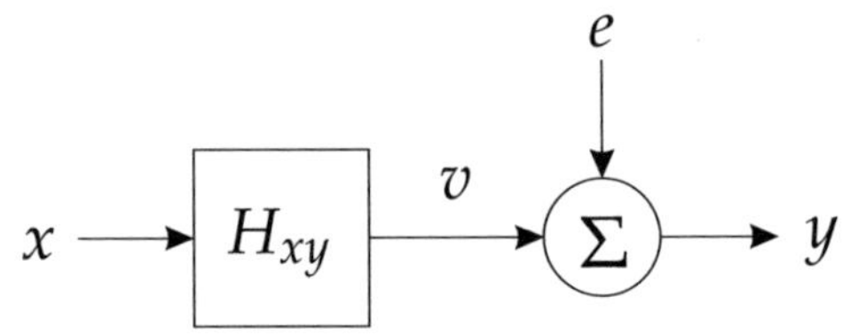

Figure 1. Single-input single-output system where H_{xy} is the optimum transfer functions which linearly relate the input x to the system system output y.

of the error signal e, is given by Equation (5), the spectral density of v can be equivalently expressed as

$$S_{vv} = \left|H_{xy}\right|^2 S_{xx} = H_{xy}^* S_{xy} = C_{xy} S_{yy} \tag{7}$$

and is recognized as the portion of y, which can be linearly accounted for by the input x.

Also, as a consequence of the optimization procedure, the error signal is uncorrelated with S_{vv}, and therefore, the power spectral density of the output can be written as

$$S_{yy} = S_{vv} + S_{ee}. \tag{8}$$

The error, or residual spectral density, is then given as

$$S_{ee} = S_{yy} - S_{vv} = S_{yy}\left(1 - C_{xy}\right), \tag{9}$$

and represents the portion of y, which is not linearly accounted for by the input x. In practise, since the spectral density of the error signal, S_{ee}, is always greater than zero, S_{vv} is always less than S_{yy}.

On rearrangement of Equation (9), the signal to residual noise ratio can be determined as

$$\frac{S_{yy}}{S_{ee}} = \frac{1}{1 - C_{xy}}. \tag{10}$$

This ratio is often termed the degree of cancellation and for coherent removal applications provides a useful measure of the coherence and is an important indicator of the quality of the measurement. Since larger input signals, increase the value of the signal to residual noise ratio, it should be quoted along with the input signal level. For the spectral density plots presented later, one can easily estimate the degree of cancellation in dB by subtracting the level of the input signal from the residual spectrum.

The residual spectrum is computed directly from the recorded data and can always be calculated regardless of the data set. In a worse case scenario, where the input signal is completely uncorrelated with the output, the residual spectra would be equal to the output spectrum and S_{vv} would be zero. Conversely, perfect coherence of unity is only achieved when the signals are identical and then Equation (10) approaches infinity. To avoid this possibility, it is sometimes advantageous to add random noise to each channel at a level sufficient to ensure that the inputs are not equal but small enough not to impact the results. Such measures are ordinarily not required as there is usually sufficient difference in the signals being processed.

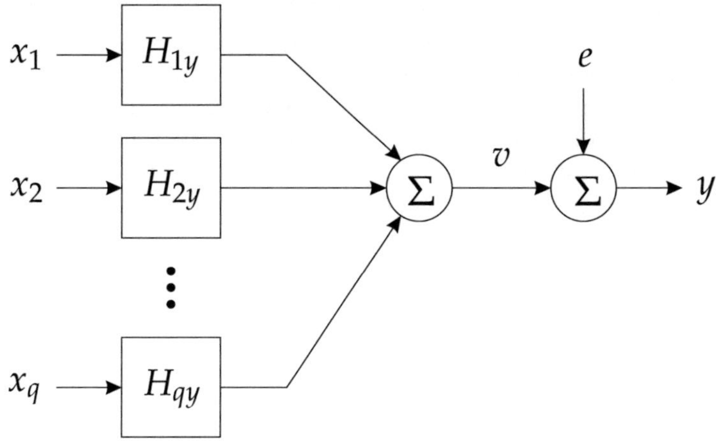

Figure 2. Multiple-input single-output system where $\{H_{iy}, i = 1 \ldots q\}$ are the optimum system transfer functions which linearly relate the inputs $\{x_i, i = 1 \ldots q\}$ to the system system output y.

2.4. Multiple-input single-output systems

To expand the single channel coherent removal concept to the multiple channel case, consider the system shown in Fig. 2, where the q inputs $\{x_i,\ i = 1, \ldots, q\}$ and the output signal y, are measured signals and the goal is to determine the optimum transfer functions $\{H_{iy},\ i = 1, \ldots, q\}$ which best relate the inputs to the output. Representing the $\mathcal{Z}$-transform of a signal by its upper case, the operations depicted in Fig. 2 can be described as

$$Y = V + E = \sum_{i=1}^{q} H_{iy} X_i + E, \tag{11}$$

where v is the optimum estimate of y, and e is the error between the two signals.

The optimum system transfer functions which minimize the error, can be determined in a least squares or an expected value sense, and are given by the solution of the following equations [2, Eq.(8.12)],

$$S_{iy} = \sum_{j=1}^{q} H_{jy} S_{ij} \quad \text{for} \quad i = 1, \ldots, q, \tag{12}$$

where $S_{ij} = S_{x_i x_j}$, represents the cross spectral density of x_i and x_j, and $S_{iy} = S_{x_i y}$ is the cross spectral density of x_i and the output y. To appreciate the structure of these equations it is useful to express them in matrix form as:

$$\begin{bmatrix} S_{1y} \\ S_{2y} \\ \vdots \\ S_{qy} \end{bmatrix} = \begin{bmatrix} S_{11} & S_{12} & \cdots & S_{1q} \\ S_{21} & S_{22} & \cdots & S_{2q} \\ \vdots & \vdots & \ddots & \vdots \\ S_{q1} & S_{q2} & \cdots & S_{qq} \end{bmatrix} \begin{bmatrix} H_{1y} \\ H_{2y} \\ \vdots \\ H_{qy} \end{bmatrix}. \tag{13}$$

Noting that $S_{ij} = S_{ji}^*$, the square matrix in Equation (13) is recognized as being positive definite, and therefore, the equations can be efficiently solved using the Cholesky decomposition.

The Cholesky decomposition separates a positive definite matrix into the product of a lower triangle matrix and its conjugate transpose. The resulting lower triangle matrix is sometimes referred to as the square root of the matrix, and once determined allows the equations to be solved using the back substitution method. Numerical procedures for the Cholesky decomposition are discussed in [18]. With an FFT size of P, the optimum system transfer functions will require the solution of $P/2$ sets of q simultaneous equations. Using the Cholesky decomposition for each set of these equations provides the most efficient, as well as accurate solution.

Once the optimum transfer functions are determined, the power spectral density of the best linear predictor due to the q inputs can be calculated from [2, Eq.(8.36)] as

$$S_{vv} = \sum_{i=1}^{q} H_{iy}^{*} S_{iy} \tag{14}$$

$$= H_{1y}^{*} S_{1y} + H_{2y}^{*} S_{2y} + \cdots + H_{qy}^{*} S_{qy}. \tag{15}$$

Similar to the single input case, the error spectral density is given as

$$S_{ee} = S_{yy} - S_{vv} = S_{yy}\left(1 - C_{\mathbf{x}:y}\right), \tag{16}$$

and represents the portion of y, which is not linearly accounted for by the multiple inputs, in this case. And, here, the multiple coherence function has been introduced, and is defined as

$$C_{\mathbf{x}:y} = \frac{S_{vv}}{S_{yy}}. \tag{17}$$

For the dynamic testing of acquisition channels, the primary interest is actually the residual spectrum, and therefore the multiple coherence function often remains uncalculated.

2.5. Calculation of the cross power spectral density for multiple channels

To obtain the required cross spectral densities used to calculate the optimum system transfer functions, and ultimately the residual spectrum, the Welch spectral estimates must be computed for all auto and cross spectral densities of the inputs and the output.

To accomplish this task, each time segment of the q input channels and the output channel can be arranged into a matrix defined as

$$\boldsymbol{x}_k = \left(\begin{bmatrix} \\ x_1 \\ \\ \end{bmatrix}_k \begin{bmatrix} \\ x_2 \\ \\ \end{bmatrix}_k \cdots \begin{bmatrix} \\ x_q \\ \\ \end{bmatrix}_k \begin{bmatrix} \\ y \\ \\ \end{bmatrix}_k \right) \tag{18}$$

where $[x_i]_k$ is a column vector of the k-th time segment of the i-th channel. Performing the FFT on each column of the $\boldsymbol{x}_k$ matrix produces the FFT matrix of $\boldsymbol{x}_k$ defined as

$$\boldsymbol{X}_k = \left(\begin{bmatrix} \\ X_1 \\ \\ \end{bmatrix}_k \begin{bmatrix} \\ X_2 \\ \\ \end{bmatrix}_k \cdots \begin{bmatrix} \\ X_q \\ \\ \end{bmatrix}_k \begin{bmatrix} \\ Y \\ \\ \end{bmatrix}_k \right). \tag{19}$$

To construct the cross, and auto, spectra of all channels, each row of $\boldsymbol{X}_k$ can be extracted and multiplied by its conjugate transpose, in an operation often referred to as the outer product.

To explicitly recognize the frequency dependence each row of $\boldsymbol{X}_k$ can be identified as $\boldsymbol{X}_k(f)$, then, to obtain the cross spectral densities, the outer products are averaged for each of the K data segments, to yield the cross spectral density matrix, which can now be expressed as

$$\boldsymbol{S}_{ij}(f) = \frac{1}{KU} \sum_{k=1}^{K} \boldsymbol{X}_k^H(f)\,\boldsymbol{X}_k(f) \tag{20}$$

$$= \begin{bmatrix} S_{11} & S_{12} & \cdots & S_{1q} & S_{1y} \\ S_{21} & S_{22} & \cdots & S_{2q} & S_{2y} \\ \vdots & \vdots & \ddots & \vdots & \vdots \\ S_{q1} & S_{q2} & \cdots & S_{qq} & S_{qy} \\ S_{y1} & S_{y2} & \cdots & S_{yq} & S_{yy} \end{bmatrix}. \tag{21}$$

Where ^{H} represents the conjugate transpose, and the explicit reference to the frequency dependence of the cross spectral densities has been omitted. The matrix $\boldsymbol{S}_{ij}$, now contains all the elements required to calculate the optimum system transfer functions in Equation (13), the optimum predictor S_{vv} given in Equation (15), and the residual spectrum S_{ee} in Equation (16).

3. Applying coherent removal to testing acquisition channels

With the ability to remove the coherent or linear portion of a signal, it is now possible to suppress coherent noise signals, and this is how the technique is used to improve the detection ranges of EM sensing systems. It is also possible to use the procedure to dynamically test sensors, amplifiers and A/D converters by applying the same signal to multiple devices under test and remove the coherent portion based on multiple channel recordings. The difficulty arises in interpreting what the residual error means in terms of the noise of the devices under test. To answer this question, one must first define a noise model for a single data acquisition channel, and then determine the optimum system transfer functions and residual spectrum, in terms of the data acquisition model parameters of each channel.

3.1. Data acquisition channel noise model

In the study of noise in electronic components, it is usual to lump together all noise sources into equivalent noise sources for the whole device [15]. Assuming that multiple acquisition channels are operating, Fig. 3 considers the i-th channel which is sampling some input signal u_i and the system output x_i is a digital representation of u_i. The additive input noise m_i is met to represent the amplifier noise, while the additive output noise source n_i represents the quantization noise or A/D converter noise. The channel transfer function G_i relates u_i to x_i and takes into account gain and anti-aliasing requirements of the data acquisition channel.

Assuming that m_i and n_i are uncorrelated with each other and the input u_i, we can write the auto spectral density of x_i as

$$S_{ii} = |G_i|^2 \left(S_{u_iu_i} + S_{m_im_i}\right) + S_{n_in_i}. \tag{22}$$

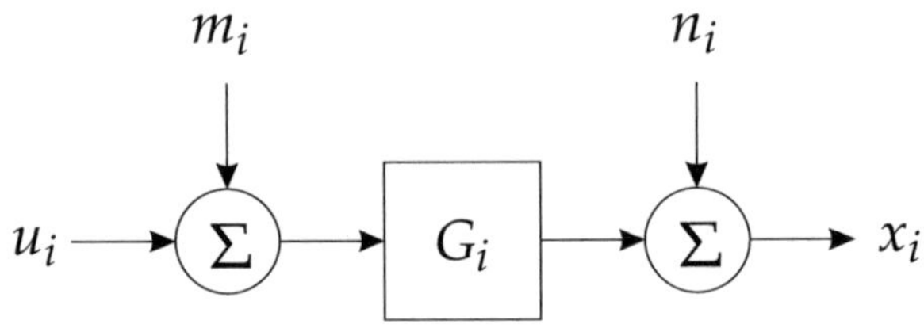

Figure 3. Equivalent noise model of a data acquisition channel, where x_i is the digitally recorded representation of the true input signal u_i. The additive noise sources, m_i and n_i represent the amplifier noise and converter noise, respectively, and the ideal linear transfer function G_i takes into account gain and anti-aliasing requirements.

If we now consider a second channel x_j and assume that its noise sources m_j and n_j are uncorrelated with each other and the inputs x_i and x_j, we can write for the cross spectral density of x_i and x_j, that

$$S_{ij} = G_i^* G_j \left(S_{u_i u_j} + S_{m_i m_j} \right) + S_{n_i n_j}. \tag{23}$$

3.1.1. Zero-input noise level

When the input signal is zero, the auto spectral density of the output becomes the zero-input noise level and is given as

$$S_{ii} = |G_i|^2 S_{m_i m_i} + S_{n_i n_i}. \tag{24}$$

This term represents all the noise present in the acquisition channel and is sometimes referred to as the combined noise. As a rule, when performing noise measurements the gain of the channel is adjusted to test for the noise of the amplifier or the converter, separately.

3.2. Interpretation of the residual spectrum

In [20] the residual spectrum was interpreted for the case where the A/D converter noise is dominate over the gained amplifier noise. To determine a more general result, in terms of both the amplifier and converter noise sources, we can substitute the expressions given in Equations (22) and (23) into Equation (12), to obtain the following general expression for the optimum system transfer functions

$$G_i^* G_{q+1} \left(S_{u_i u_{q+1}} + S_{m_i m_{q+1}} \right) + S_{n_i n_{q+1}} = \sum_{j=1}^{q} H_{jy} \left(G_i^* G_j \left(S_{u_i u_j} + S_{m_i m_j} \right) + S_{n_i n_j} \right), \tag{25}$$

where the output channel y, is identified as the $q+1$ data acquisition channel. To this point, the only assumption made is that the true signals u_i are uncorrelated with the noise sources n_i and m_i. These equations allow for individual amplifier and converter noise levels, for correlation to exist between the noise sources, and include the effects of the gain and anti-aliasing filters.

3.2.1. Uncorrelated noise approximation

Electronic devices which are manufactured and packaged together will have similar noise characteristics. Nevertheless, when physically isolated from one another or when operating independent of each other, no linear relationship will exist between the instantaneous noise values and therefore, the noise, although similar, will be uncorrelated. When multiple data acquisition channels are used in a common operating environment some correlation will undoubtedly exist between the equivalent noise sources, however, very often it is possible to assume with little error, that the noise sources under consideration are uncorrelated [15, p.24].

Applying this basic underlying assumption of the study of noise to our example, if the noise sources are uncorrelated with each other then $S_{m_i m_j} = 0$ and $S_{n_i n_j} = 0$ for $i \neq j$, and Equation (25) will simplify to

$$G_i^* G_{q+1} S_{u_i u_{q+1}} = H_{iy} \left(|G_i|^2 S_{m_i m_i} + S_{n_i n_i} \right) + \sum_{j=1}^{q} H_{jy}\, G_i^* G_j S_{u_i u_j}. \tag{26}$$

To proceed, it becomes necessary at this point to enforce that all the inputs are the same signal, so that $u = u_i = u_{q+1}$, which allows us to divide through by S_{uu}, to arrive at

$$G_i^* G_{q+1} = H_{iy} \frac{|G_i|^2 S_{m_i m_i} + S_{n_i n_i}}{S_{uu}} + \sum_{j=1}^{q} H_{jy}\, G_i^* G_j. \tag{27}$$

The structure of these equations is, perhaps, better demonstrated in matrix notation as:

$$\begin{bmatrix} G_1^* \\ \vdots \\ G_q^* \end{bmatrix} G_{q+1} = \left(\begin{bmatrix} \frac{|G_1|^2 S_{m_1 m_1} + S_{n_1 n_1}}{S_{uu}} & 0 & 0 \\ 0 & \ddots & 0 \\ 0 & 0 & \frac{|G_q|^2 S_{m_q m_q} + S_{n_q n_q}}{S_{uu}} \end{bmatrix} + \begin{bmatrix} G_1^* \\ \vdots \\ G_q^* \end{bmatrix} \begin{bmatrix} G_1 & \cdots & G_q \end{bmatrix} \right) \begin{bmatrix} H_{1y} \\ \vdots \\ H_{qy} \end{bmatrix}, \tag{28}$$

where it is now observed that the solution requires the inversion of a matrix which is the sum of a diagonal matrix and an outer product.[1] Computing the inverse of this matrix, one arrives at the solution for the optimum system transfer functions in terms of the data acquisition channel parameters, given as

$$H_{iy} = \frac{G_i^* G_{q+1} S_{uu}}{|G_i|^2 S_{m_i m_i} + S_{n_i n_i}} \left(1 + \sum_{k=1}^{q} \frac{|G_k|^2 S_{uu}}{|G_k|^2 S_{m_k m_k} + S_{n_k n_k}} \right)^{-1}. \tag{29}$$

Substitution of this result into Equation (15), and then into Equation (16), leads to an expression for the residual error in terms of the data acquisition channel parameters, which is given as

$$S_{ee} = |G_{q+1}|^2 S_{m_{q+1} m_{q+1}} + S_{n_{q+1} n_{q+1}} + |G_{q+1}|^2 S_{uu} \left(1 + \sum_{k=1}^{q} \frac{|G_k|^2 S_{uu}}{|G_k|^2 S_{m_k m_k} + S_{n_k n_k}} \right)^{-1}. \tag{30}$$

[1] From [3], if $\mathbf{A}$ and $\mathbf{B}$ are square matrices and $\mathbf{u}$ and $\mathbf{v}$ are column vectors, and $\mathbf{A} = \mathbf{B} + \mathbf{u}\mathbf{v}'$ then $\mathbf{A}^{-1} = \mathbf{B}^{-1} - \lambda \mathbf{y}\mathbf{z}'$, where $\mathbf{y} = \mathbf{B}^{-1}\mathbf{u}, \mathbf{z}' = \mathbf{v}'\mathbf{B}^{-1}$ and $\lambda = (1 + \mathbf{z}'\mathbf{u})^{-1}$.

3.2.2. Generalizing the output channel

Since any of the $q+1$ channels under consideration can be selected as the output channel, the results above can be generalized to let any of the channels be the output and the remaining channels form the inputs. If the output channel is defined as x_j, and the q input channels as $\{x_i,\, i \in \mathbf{i}\}$, where $\mathbf{i} = \{1, \ldots, q+1, i \neq j\}$, the results for the optimum transfer functions in Equation (29) can be written as

$$H_{ij} = \frac{G_i^* G_j S_{uu}}{|G_i|^2 S_{m_i m_i} + S_{n_i n_i}} \left(1 + \sum_{k \in \mathbf{i}} \frac{|G_k|^2 S_{uu}}{|G_k|^2 S_{m_k m_k} + S_{n_k n_k}} \right)^{-1} . \tag{31}$$

Similarly, the residual spectra in Equation (30) now becomes the residual of the j channel, and is defined as

$$S_{ee:j} = |G_j|^2 S_{m_j m_j} + S_{n_j n_j} + |G_j|^2 S_{uu} \left(1 + \sum_{k \in \mathbf{i}} \frac{|G_k|^2 S_{uu}}{|G_k|^2 S_{m_k m_k} + S_{n_k n_k}} \right)^{-1} . \tag{32}$$

Since each channel can be selected as the output $j \in \mathbf{j}$, where $\mathbf{j} = \{1, \ldots, q+1\}$, and for each value of j, the optimum system transfer functions and residual spectra can be computed. Note that H_{ij} is defined on $i \in \mathbf{i}$, which are the channels which form the inputs.

3.2.3. Matched channel characteristics approximation

If the anti-aliasing filters are well matched (or can be calibrated to be so) then $G_i = G_j = G$, and the optimum system transfer functions and the residual error expressions will simplify to

$$H_{ij} = \frac{1}{|G|^2 S_{m_i m_i} + S_{n_i n_i}} \left(\frac{1}{|G|^2 S_{uu}} + \sum_{k \in \mathbf{i}} \frac{1}{|G|^2 S_{m_k m_k} + S_{n_k n_k}} \right)^{-1} \tag{33}$$

and

$$S_{ee:j} = |G|^2 S_{m_j m_j} + S_{n_j n_j} + \left(\frac{1}{|G|^2 S_{uu}} + \sum_{k \in \mathbf{i}} \frac{1}{|G|^2 S_{m_k m_k} + S_{n_k n_k}} \right)^{-1} \tag{34}$$

respectively.

3.2.4. Large signal approximation

Since the applied signal u is under user control it should be possible to ensure that the spectral density of the applied signal is much larger than all noise sources, such that $S_{uu} \gg |G|^2 S_{m_i m_i}$ and $S_{uu} \gg S_{n_i n_i}$. Under this assumption the optimum system transfer functions further simplify to

$$H_{ij} = \frac{1}{|G|^2 S_{m_i m_i} + S_{n_i n_i}} \left(\sum_{k \in \mathbf{i}} \frac{1}{|G|^2 S_{m_k m_k} + S_{n_k n_k}} \right)^{-1} , \tag{35}$$

from which it is observed that the optimum system transfer function for each channel is inversely proportional to the combined noise of that channel. Similarly, the residual noise expression now becomes

$$S_{ee:j} = |G|^2 S_{m_j m_j} + S_{n_j n_j} + \left(\sum_{k \in \mathbf{i}} \frac{1}{|G|^2 S_{m_k m_k} + S_{n_k n_k}} \right)^{-1} , \tag{36}$$

from which it is seen that the residual error is the noise of the output channel, plus the parallel combination of the noise of the input channels.

Note that the residual spectrum is always greater than the noise of the present output channel, and that, since the optimum system transfer function for each input channel is inversely proportional to the noise of that input channel, nosier channels are suppressed in the prediction of the output channel, while quieter channels are enhanced.

3.2.5. *Amplifier testing with large gain*

If the acquisition channel gain is large, such that $|G|^2 S_{m_i m_i} \gg S_{n_i n_i}$, then

$$H_{ij} = \frac{1}{S_{m_i m_i}} \left(\sum_{k \in \mathbf{i}} \frac{1}{S_{m_k m_k}} \right)^{-1} \tag{37}$$

and

$$S_{ee:j} = |G|^2 \left[S_{m_j m_j} + \left(\sum_{k \in \mathbf{i}} \frac{1}{S_{m_k m_k}} \right)^{-1} \right], \tag{38}$$

and the amplifier noise sources are dominate in the optimum system transfer function and residual expressions.

3.2.6. *A/D converter testing with small gain*

Conversely, if the acquisition channel gain is small, so that $|G|^2 S_{m_i m_i} \ll S_{n_i n_i}$, then

$$H_{ij} = \frac{1}{S_{n_i n_i}} \left(\sum_{k \in \mathbf{i}} \frac{1}{S_{n_k n_k}} \right)^{-1} \tag{39}$$

and

$$S_{ee:j} = S_{n_j n_j} + \left(\sum_{k \in \mathbf{i}} \frac{1}{S_{n_k n_k}} \right)^{-1}, \tag{40}$$

and the converter noise dominates in the optimum system transfer function and residual expressions.

3.3. Determining the channel noise sources from the residual spectra

To determine the individual converter noise of each channel in terms of the directly measurable residual error signals a solution to Equation (36) is required. Assuming that the residual spectrum of each channel has been calculated, with the remaining channels composing the inputs, it is possible to establish a set of nonlinear equations which can be solved for the individual channel noise using a constrained nonlinear least squares optimization procedure.

To demonstrate the situation, consider the case where the gain is small and the converter noise is dominate and four A/D converters sample the same signal, so that $q = 3$ in the above expressions. (This discussion could be performed equally well with combined noise or the amplifier noise.) Using the coherent removal technique the residual spectrum for each channel can be determined, such that the quantities ($S_{ee:1}$,$S_{ee:2}$,$S_{ee:3}$,$S_{ee:4}$) are known. Applying the approximation given in Equation (40), the residual error spectra of each channel can be expressed in terms of the individual converter noise for each channel as:

$$\begin{bmatrix} S_{ee:1} \\ S_{ee:2} \\ S_{ee:3} \\ S_{ee:4} \end{bmatrix} = \begin{bmatrix} S_{n_1n_1} + \left(\frac{1}{S_{n_2n_2}} + \frac{1}{S_{n_3n_3}} + \frac{1}{S_{n_4n_4}} \right)^{-1} \\ S_{n_2n_2} + \left(\frac{1}{S_{n_1n_1}} + \frac{1}{S_{n_3n_3}} + \frac{1}{S_{n_4n_4}} \right)^{-1} \\ S_{n_3n_3} + \left(\frac{1}{S_{n_1n_1}} + \frac{1}{S_{n_2n_2}} + \frac{1}{S_{n_4n_4}} \right)^{-1} \\ S_{n_4n_4} + \left(\frac{1}{S_{n_1n_1}} + \frac{1}{S_{n_2n_2}} + \frac{1}{S_{n_3n_3}} \right)^{-1} \end{bmatrix} . \quad (41)$$

This nonlinear set of equations can be iteratively solved to determine ($S_{n_1n_1}$,$S_{n_2n_2}$,$S_{n_3n_3}$,$S_{n_4n_4}$). It is noted that the residual spectra can be used as the initial estimate for the converter noise and that the solutions are constrained such that $S_{II} < S_{n_jn_j} < S_{ee:j}$, where S_{II} is the spectrum of the ideal converter. For $q \geq 2$ this procedure was observed to converge quickly. It should be noted that the matrix does become singular for $q = 1$, which represents the single-input single-output case, which was examined separately in [19].

3.4. Effective number of bits

The most intuitive measure of the quality of an A/D converter is the effective number of bits (ENOB). An A/D converter may provide N digitized bits but the number of bits which are actually *good*, is what is of interest. For an N-bit A/D converter with a voltage range of V_R the device's achievable resolution is $Q = V_R/2^N$. The effective number of bits is defined as

$$\text{ENOB} = N - \log_2 \left(\frac{\sigma_n^T}{\sigma_I} \right) \quad \text{(bits)}, \quad (42)$$

where σ_n^T is the rms value of the total noise of the device under test and σ_I is the rms level of the ideal quantization noise. Inspecting Equation (42), it can be seen that ENOB is a ratio comparing the noise of the device under test to that of an ideal device. Since the ideal quantization noise is well approximated to be a uniformly distributed random variable, its rms level is given as

$$\sigma_I = \frac{Q}{\sqrt{12}} \quad \text{(V)}. \quad (43)$$

Determining σ_n^T (the single unknown in Equation (42)), for various operating conditions, forms the basis of nearly all A/D converter testing procedures. For a given sampling rate f_s, the one-sided spectral density of the ideal converter is constant with a value given as

$$S_{II} = \frac{2}{f_s}\sigma_I^2 = \frac{Q^2}{6f_s}. \quad (44)$$

When the multiple channel coherent removal method is applied to A/D converter testing, it is possible to calculate the residual spectra of each channel, compute the converter noise spectra using the approach described in Section 3.3, and then compute the rms level of the noise σ_n, by integrating the converter noise spectra using Parseval's theorem, such that

$$\sigma_n^2 = \frac{f_s}{P} \sum S_{nn}. \tag{45}$$

To avoid confusion with the ENOB definition, we shall define the number of coherent bits (for an A/D converter) as CB where

$$CB = N - \log_2 \left(\frac{\sigma_n}{\sigma_I} \right) \quad \text{(bits)}. \tag{46}$$

which is analogous to ENOB but based on the noise estimated using the coherent removal process.

4. Measurement examples

4.1. Multiple channel data acquisition setup

To investigate how the multiple coherence function can be used to dynamically test multiple amplifiers and A/D converters a 4-channel data acquisition system was created using two series of amplifiers as shown in Fig. 4. The Series A amplifiers provide 60 dB of gain and 0.1 Hz ac coupling, while the Series B amplifiers have unity gain, 0.1 Hz ac coupling and a 8-th order Chebyshev low pass filter with a 512 Hz corner frequency.

The amplifiers are a general purpose post amplifier known as the RPA designed (in the early 2000's) for measuring EM signals in the sub-Hertz to 1 kilo-Hertz frequency range. Each channel of the RPA has a differential input which is based on a standard three op-amp instrumentation amplifier design. The RPA is unique in that it uses LTC1150 [13] chopper-stabilized operational amplifiers (op-amps) to eliminate the $1/f$ noise associated with linear op-amps. By modulating the input signal up in frequency, quieter electronics can be used to amplify the signal and then demodulate the signal back to the baseband.

To dynamically test the system a pseudo-random noise source (PRNS) was connected to the input of each of the Series A amplifiers. The PRNS is based on the output of a Linear Feedback Shift Register (LFSR) as described by [7] which is then filtered with a programable raised cosine 10-th order low pass filter. The signal level, cycle rate and clock frequency can be adjusted.

The A/D converters under test are based on an National Instruments (NI) CompactRIO data acquisition system and include four NI 9239 4-channel DAQ modules and one NI 9205 32-channel DAQ module. The NI 9239 modules use 24-bit $\Delta\Sigma$ converters and simultaneously sample the inputs, while the NI 9205 module uses a 16-bit SAR based A/D converter with an inter-channel delay set to 8 μs. (The NI 9205 is capable of sampling up to 250 kHz, using a 4 μs inter-channel delay, but the bit noise increases from 2 LSB, at 8 μs, to 8 LSB.) Note that only eight of the NI 9205 32 channels are used in the following measurement examples.

The total of 24 channels, that are recorded for each measurement example, are arranged such that the first sixteen channels are recorded with the 4 NI 9239 modules and the last eight channels are from the NI 9205. Referring again to Fig. 4, the first NI 9239 module records the input signal (CH1) and three of the Series A amplifier outputs (CH2–CH4). The

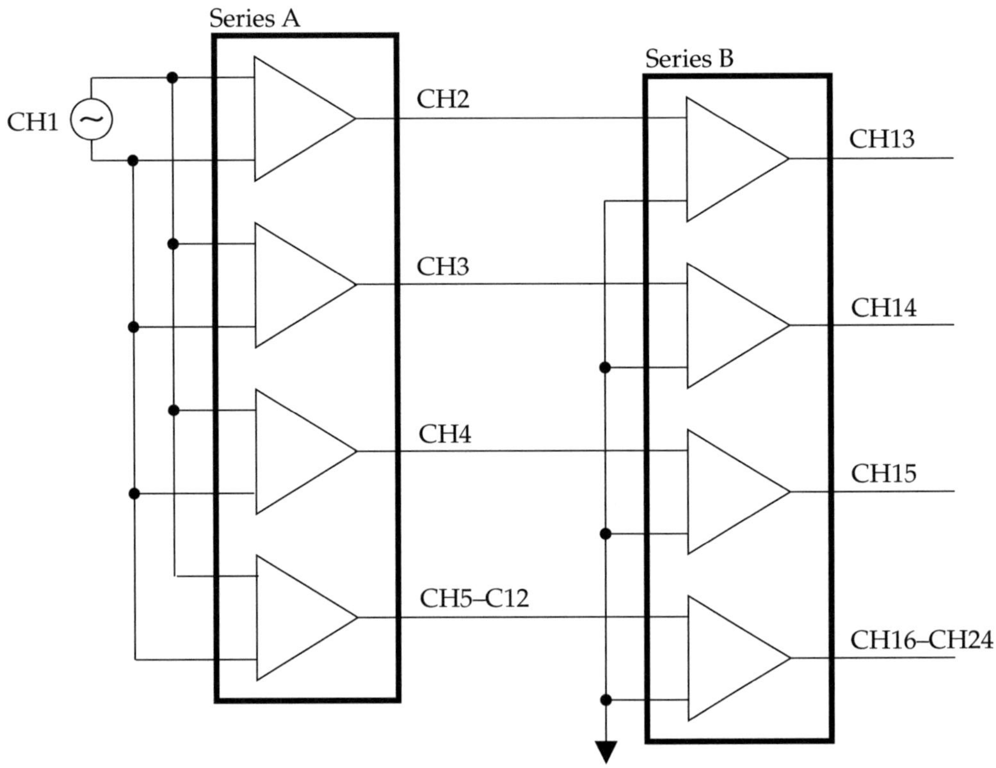

— Amplifiers / Filters —

Series	Gain	Filter
A	60 dB	0.1 Hz 1-st order high-pass
B	0 dB	0.1 Hz 1-st order high-pass and 512 Hz 8-th order low-pass

— A/D Converters —

Channel	Module	Chan.	A/D converter	Sample rate	Simult. sampling
CH1–CH4	NI9239	4	24-bit ΔΣ	50 kHz/ch	yes
CH5–CH8	NI9239	4	24-bit ΔΣ	50 kHz/ch	yes
CH9–CH12	NI9239	4	24-bit ΔΣ	50 kHz/ch	yes
CH13–CH16	NI9239	4	24-bit ΔΣ	50 kHz/ch	yes
CH17–CH24	NI9205	32	16-bit SAR	250 kHz	no

Figure 4. Amplifier configuration and channel assignment for the measurement examples.

next two NI 9239 modules (8 channels) record eight copies of the final Series A amplifier output (CH5–CH12). The fourth NI 9239 module records the four outputs of the Series B amplifiers (CH13–CH16), and the NI 9205 records eight copies of the final Series B amplifier (CH17–CH24). Note that the Series B amplifiers provide the anti-aliasing filtering required for the NI 9205 and that the NI 9239 use $\Delta\Sigma$ based A/D converters, which provide their own anti-aliasing.

The four NI 9239 modules share a common sampling clock and the inputs (even between modules) can be considered to be sampled simultaneously. The result of the $\Delta\Sigma$ A/D converter process, however, is not available until 38.4 samples plus 3 μs after the start of the acquisition. Conversely, The NI 9205 provides data from multiple channels asynchronously (i.e. when requested) at rates limited by the inter-channel delay. Coarse synchronization of the two technologies, to within a sample, is accomplished by ignoring an integer number of samples of the NI 9239 at startup. Finer synchronization can be achieved by using filters which delay the signal a fractional number of samples.

4.1.1. Measurement summary

The sampling rate for all the measurement examples is set to 10 kHz and, unless stated otherwise, the following parameters are used for the Welch cross spectral density estimates:

- segment size = 16384
- overlap = 50%
- averages = 256
- Hann data window.

To gain insight into the interpretation of the residual spectra given in Section 3, the 24 channels were recorded for the following three input signals:

1. 16 kHz noise, σ_u=1.6 mV
2. 500 Hz noise, σ_u=3.6 mV
3. 250 Hz sine wave, σ_u=5.3 mV

The precise level of the input signal is not specifically required for the coherent removal process and is given for information purposes. Note that once gained by the Series A amplifiers these mV levels will be V levels at the A/D converters (other than the raw input measurement of CH1). A sample of the data from each channel recorded with the 16 kHz input noise signal is shown in Fig. 5.

The first results to be presented are the transfer functions between the input signal and the output of the Series A and Series B amplifiers. These results are based on the single-input single-output relationships given in Section 2.2, calculated with the wide band noise data set, and include plots of the ordinary coherence function between the input and each of the outputs.

Next the coherent removal process is applied to CH5–CH12 and CH17–CH24 (separately) to calculate the residual spectra of the NI 9239 and the NI 9205 A/D converters; and ultimately the coherent number of bits of both devices. The process is repeated for both noise inputs to investigate how the two different input noise signals effect the two A/D converter types.

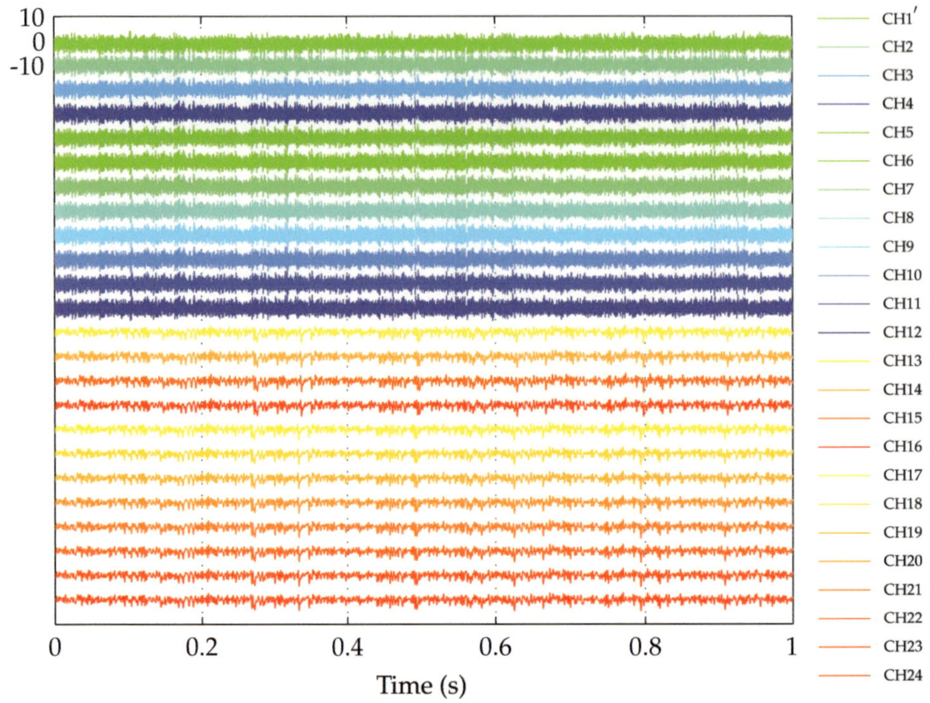

Figure 5. A one second snippet of the raw data recorded with the 16 kHz noise source. The prime on CH1 indicates it has been scaled by 1000, refer to Fig. 4 for channel details.

Next, to investigate the noise of the RPA amplifier the coherent removal process is applied to channels (CH2–CH5) and (CH13–CH16), again for both input noise signals in order to investigate the effect on the RPA amplifier noise (which is based on a chopper-stabilized instrumentation amplifier design).

The last results presented look at the coherent removal process of CH5–CH12 and CH17–CH24 with the sine wave data described above, processed with a Hann window and no window.

4.2. Transfer function measurements

To confirm that each of the amplifiers are operating as specified, transfer function measurements can be calculated using either of the listed noise inputs. The single-input single-output transfer functions of the four Series A amplifiers, namely $G_{1,2}$, $G_{1,3}$, $G_{1,4}$, and $G_{1,5}$, and the transfer functions for the Series B amplifiers, $G_{1,13}$, $G_{1,14}$, $G_{1,15}$, and $G_{1,16}$ were calculated for both input noise signals and little variation in the results were observed.

The magnitude and phase of each of the transfer functions along with the coherence is shown in Fig. 6 for the data collected with the 16 kHz input noise signal. From the transfer functions plots, the gain of the Series A amplifiers is confirmed to be 60 dB, and the 8-th order roll-off and phase response of the Series B Chebyshev filter is evident. As is the custom, γ_{xy} is plotted for the coherence function and it is observed that the coherence is very close to unity, indicating that the output is highly dependent on the input signal. The drop in coherence

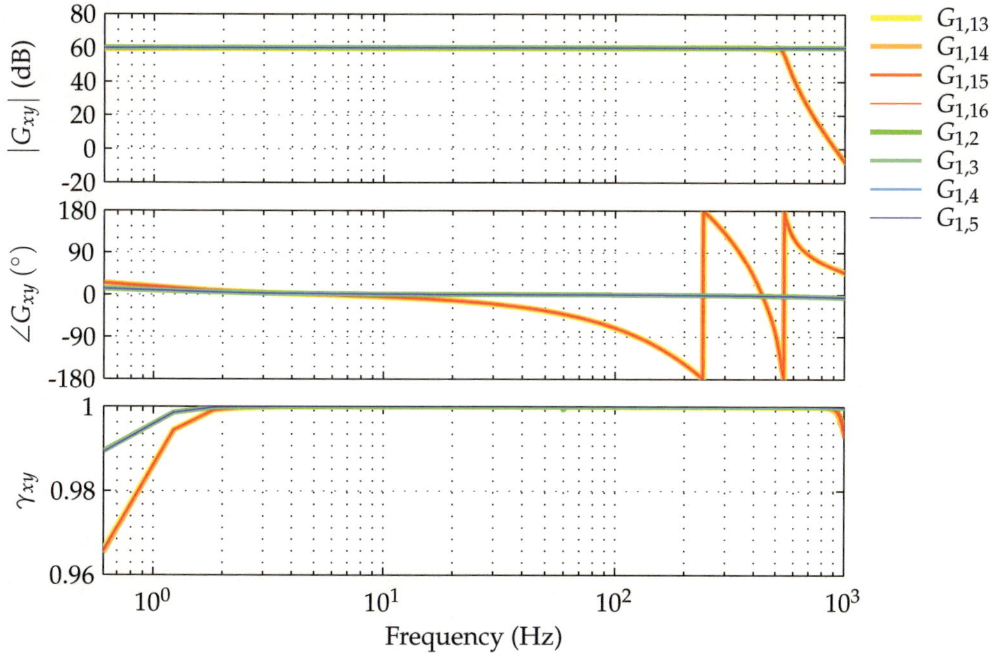

Figure 6. Measured transfer functions (magnitude and phase) and coherence.

below 1 Hz for both, and above 800 Hz for the Series B amplifiers, is due to attenuation of the output signal due to the filtering process. From the results given it is apparent that the amplifiers and filters are performing as specified, and the high level of coherence provides confidence in this assessment.

4.3. A/D converters tests with noise input

We begin the coherent removal examples looking at the residual spectra of CH5–CH12 and CH17–CH24 for the two input noise signals. Fig. 7 shows the input spectra and residual spectra for each channel with the 16 kHz input noise signal, while Fig. 8 shows the results for the 500 Hz input noise signal. For reference the noise floor of an ideal 24-bit and ideal 16-bit device are shown as dashed lines in both figures. We adopt the practice of plotting the input and residual spectra with the same line type and colour, and note that where the curves interact that the input spectra is always greater than the residual spectra.

To compute the individual converter noise spectral densities, the procedure discussed in Section 3.3 is implemented using MATLAB's `fmincon` subroutine, which allows the converter noise of each channel to be calculated at each frequency value. These results are then integrated to obtain the rms level of the converter noise (σ_n), and ultimately the coherent bits (CB), which are tabulated in Table 1.

4.3.1. NI 9239 noise input results

Turning the discussion first towards CH5–CH12, which are the two NI 9239 modules sampling the same Series A amplifier, we observe as expected that all eight input spectra are nearly

input	16 kHz noise σ_u=1.6 V			500 Hz noise σ_u=3.6 V			250 Hz sine wave Hann window			250 Hz sine wave no window		
Chan.	σ_e (μV)	σ_n (μV)	CB	σ_e (μV)	σ_n (μV)	CB	σ_e (μV)	σ_n (μV)	CB	σ_e (μV)	σ_n (μV)	CB
CH5	45.66	42.61	17.05	45.78	42.74	17.04	46.83	43.79	17.01	46.69	43.59	17.02
CH6	45.97	42.96	17.04	46.47	43.50	17.02	46.69	43.63	17.01	46.60	43.49	17.02
CH7	47.06	44.15	17.00	47.32	44.42	16.99	47.13	44.12	17.00	47.69	44.68	16.98
CH8	46.61	43.65	17.01	46.40	43.42	17.02	47.11	44.09	17.00	47.87	44.88	16.97
CH9	46.06	43.06	17.03	45.99	42.97	17.04	47.04	44.02	17.00	47.10	44.03	17.00
CH10	46.48	43.51	17.02	45.86	42.83	17.04	46.70	43.64	17.01	47.68	44.67	16.98
CH11	46.46	43.49	17.02	46.65	43.70	17.01	47.25	44.25	16.99	47.47	44.44	16.99
CH12	46.74	43.80	17.01	46.72	43.77	17.01	47.44	44.45	16.99	47.59	44.57	16.98
CH17	459.6	430.1	13.71	1003.0	940.0	12.58	459.4	429.9	13.71	711.6	679.3	13.05
CH18	460.4	431.1	13.71	993.4	929.6	12.60	459.1	429.6	13.71	631.2	593.3	13.25
CH19	458.7	429.2	13.72	988.5	924.3	12.61	458.7	429.2	13.72	589.9	548.2	13.36
CH20	458.1	428.5	13.72	986.8	922.4	12.61	460.2	430.8	13.71	561.3	516.4	13.45
CH21	457.5	427.9	13.72	991.0	927.0	12.60	460.2	430.7	13.71	568.5	524.5	13.43
CH22	458.8	429.3	13.72	981.0	916.1	12.62	458.0	428.3	13.72	592.9	551.5	13.35
CH23	458.1	428.5	13.72	994.0	930.3	12.60	457.8	428.1	13.72	620.6	581.9	13.28
CH24	459.6	430.2	13.71	1007.8	945.3	12.58	459.1	429.6	13.71	716.3	684.2	13.04

Table 1. Residual spectra levels, converter noise levels, and coherent bits for CH5–CH12 (8 NI 9239 channels) and CH17–CH24 (8 NI 9205 channels) for the three test signals.

identical and that the residual spectra of each channel are approximately equal. It is also noted that the residual spectra are virtually unchanged when the band width of the input noise is changed.

Consistent with the fact that the residuals are unchanged, we see for the 16 kHz input noise signal tabulated in columns 2–4, or the 500 Hz input noise signal tabulated in columns 5–7, nearly identical values for the rms level of the residual, the rms level of the converter noise and the coherent bits. From the table, the NI 9239 achieves about 17.0 coherent bits, at a sample rate of 10 kHz. The consistency of the coherent removal results, for a variety of inputs signals, are a good indicating of the dynamic range of the NI 9239, and its ability to reject signals beyond the Nyquist frequency.

4.3.2. Comments on the input noise spectrum

Closer inspection of the input signal spectrum reveal some interesting facts about the chopper-stabilized instrumentation amplifier design used in the RPA. In order to achieve its improved noise at ultra low frequencies the input signal is chopped (or modulated) at a fixed frequency, which in the case of the RPA is 2.048 kHz. Note that the modulation frequency and its first harmonic are clearly visible in the input spectral densities of Fig. 7.

The RPA design assumes that the input signal is band-limited such that Nyquist theory is satisfied. With the wideband noise source we are clearly violating this requirement, and the

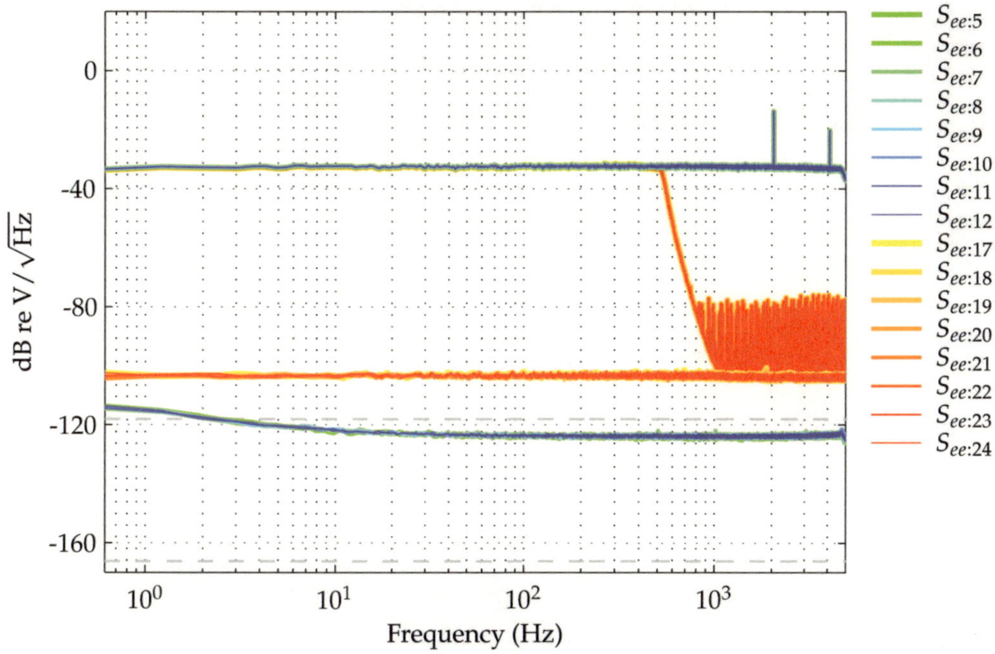

Figure 7. Input and residual spectra for CH5–CH12 and CH17–CH24 with the 16 kHz noise input.

input spectrum is an ensemble of frequencies mixing together due to the chopping process. This mixing is greatly exaggerated when the 16 kHz noise source is used. The net outcome, however, as seen in Fig. 7 is that the spectrum is still flat and harmonics are present at the chopping frequency. When the input noise bandwidth is reduced to 500 Hz, the noise floor of the RPA amplifier (after gain) is now visible for frequencies above ≈ 1 kHz as seen in Fig. 8.

In terms of the residual spectra computed for CH5–CH12, which are all measuring the same amplifier output, whatever input signal is used, the residual spectra is limited by the noise of the individual A/D converters and not the amplifier noise present in the signal. We will look at the coherent removal process with the amplifier outputs after discussing the results for the NI 9205, which uses a SAR A/D converter.

4.3.3. NI 9205 noise input results

The importance of using simultaneous sampling to maintain the phase relationship between channels is essential to the coherent removal process. In [19] the introduction of a delay in one of the channels was investigated and was shown to increase the residual spectrum, a result which was consistent with the finding in [4] that the coherence function (as calculated using FFT-based block data methods) has a bias error proportional to the delay between the signals.

How to process the NI 9205 channels presented a bit of dilemma, since absolute synchronization with the NI 9239 modules is achieved by applying a fractional sample delay filter to the NI 9205 channels in order to match the input delay of the $\Delta\Sigma$ A/D converters. And, the design of such a delay filter should in fact minimize the residual spectra of the two channels.

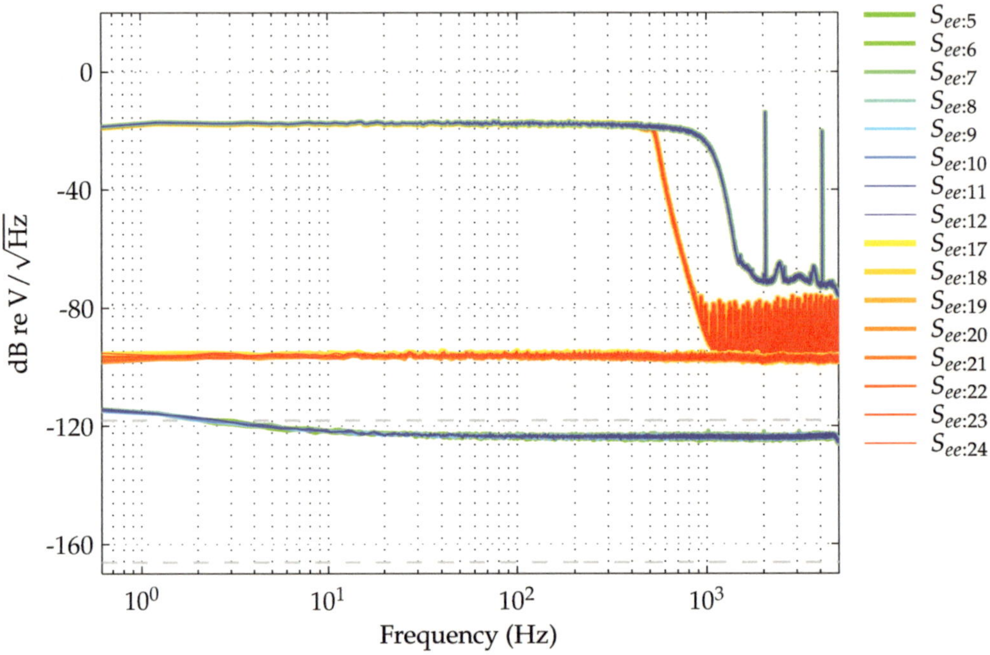

Figure 8. Input and residual spectra for CH5–CH12 and CH17–CH24 with the 500 Hz noise input.

Noting that the bias error in the coherence is proportional to the amount delay, and that the delay between any adjacent channel of the NI 9205 (based on 10 kHz sampling and an 8 μs inter channel delay) represents a delay of only 0.08 of a sample, the decision was made to process the eight NI9205 channels as a set. It is worth noting that tests done at lower sampling rates would exhibit less inter-channel delay bias.

To simultaneously sample the NI 9205 channels and yield residual spectra that are unbiased by the inter-channel delay, analog sample-hold circuitry could be developed to *sample* the signal and then *hold* the level until the SAR A/D converter is able to read the value. This is in fact how the early coherent removal systems, developed for EM sensing systems, were designed in order to maintain the phase.

Processing data channels CH17–CH24 as a set for the two input noise signals allows us to investigate the residual spectra of the NI 9205 channels for these two test cases. The spectra of the input signals as well as the residual spectra of each channel, are plotted in Fig. 7 and Fig. 8 for the 16 kHz and 500 Hz PRNS tests respectively (alongside the results for the NI 9239). The rms levels of the residuals and converter noise, and the coherent bit values are given in Table 1.

Firstly, it is evident that the residual spectra of the NI 9205 increases when the 500 Hz PRNS source is used. This increase is a result of the fact that the input signal with the narrower band source has a larger signal level resulting in more signal in both the pass band as well as the stop band. It is, however, the increase in the signal level in the stop band that is eventually aliased backed that results in the increase of the residual spectra noise floor. Part of the issue arises from the aliasing artifacts that occur in the input signal due to the chopping process of

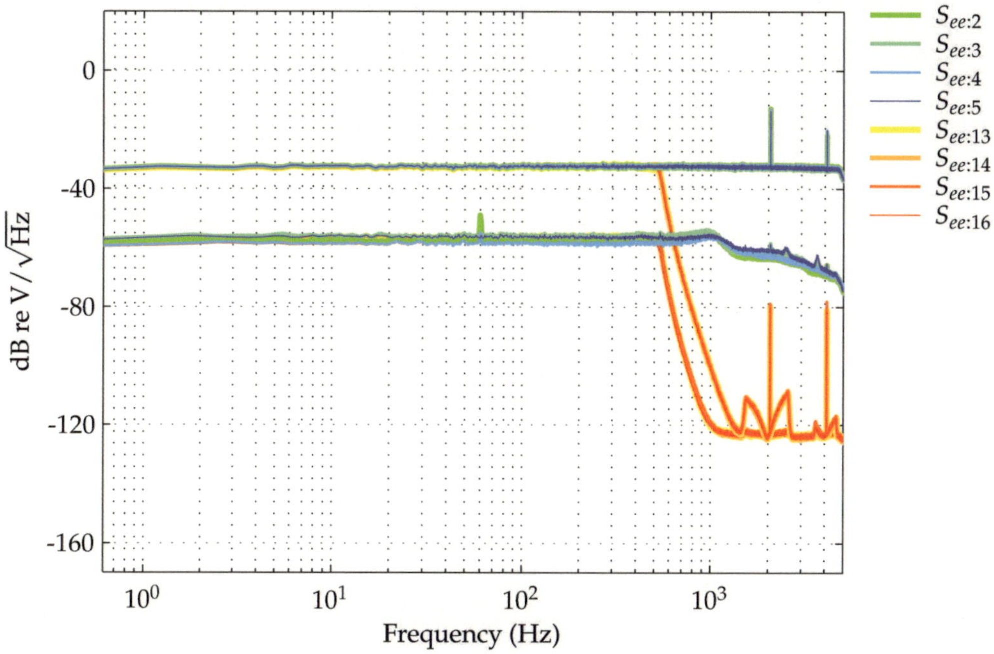

Figure 9. Input and residual spectra for CH2–CH5 and CH13–CH16 with the 16 kHz noise input.

the RPA, which are not adequately removed before the NI 9205 samples the signal. Also, note that the residual spectra of the NI 9205 is flat for frequencies above 1 kHz, indicating that the aliasing artifacts are coherent between channels and removed.

The coherent removal measurements presented here for the NI 9205 are some of the first for a SAR based A/D converter with inter-channel delay. While results are not considered definitive due to the inter-channel delay it does appear that the technique is at least viable as a means to assure a certain level of residual is being achieved. Increasing the number of channels would also help to reduce the residual spectra levels. It is of interest to observe that the first and last channels in the channel list (which are recorded first and last) have the highest residual spectra consistent with the fact that these channels are time-wise the furthest from the other channels.

4.4. Amplifier tests with noise input

To test the coherent removal procedure with amplifier signals we processed channels CH2–CH5 and channels CH13–CH16 each as a separate channel set, for both the input noise signals listed above. Recall that these channels are recorded using the NI 9239 modules and are therefore simultaneously sampled.

The results for each channel set, with the 16 kHz input noise source is shown in Fig. 9. For both of the channel sets, we observe that the noise floor is significantly above the noise level expected for the RPA. The cause is that the chopping process of the RPA is folding incoherent noise back into the frequencies of interest.

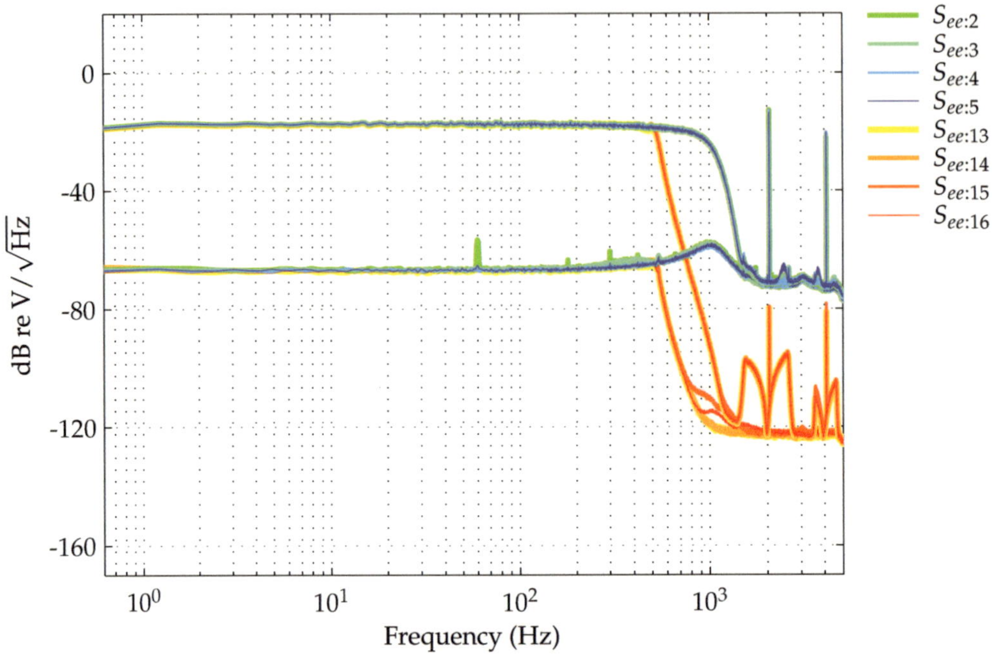

Figure 10. Input and residual spectra for CH2–CH5 and CH13–CH16 with the 500 Hz noise input.

When the 500 Hz input noise signal is used, the input spectrum contains much less out-of-band signal and the RPA residual, as seen in Fig. 10, is closer to the expected level for the RPA.

While the RPA chopping process has complicated the analysis of the amplifier testing presented here, if linear amplifiers had been used, far less variation in the residual spectrum would have been observed with changes in the input signal level and spectrum content.

Similar to the process used to determine the individual converter noise sources, the individual amplifier noise can also be calculated from the residual spectra and if desired the rms level computed. As these are some of the first examples presented for the testing of amplifiers, we conclude the discussion at the calculation of the residual spectra.

In terms of the residual spectra at the output of the Series A amplifiers and the Series B amplifiers the spectra levels are consisted with the operation of the amplifiers and filters for those devices. As an interesting note on the performance improvement with the NI 9239, compare the aliasing artifacts that arose in CH17–CH24, to the spectra for CH13–CH16 which clearly show the chopping harmonics still present in the stop band.

4.5. Sine wave input test

As sine wave inputs are often the test signal of choice for many dynamic testing procedures, it is of interest to test the coherent removal process with a sine wave input and to investigate how changing the data window effects the results. The input and residual spectra for CH5–CH12 and CH17–CH24 with the sine wave signal listed above are shown in Fig. 11, for

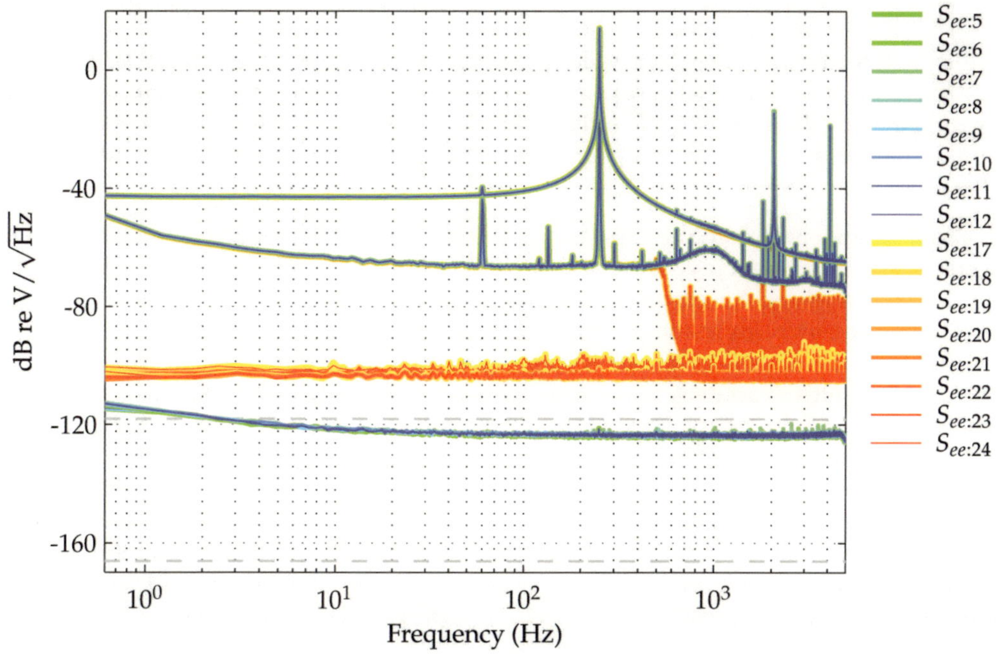

Figure 11. Input and residual spectra for CH5–CH12 and CH17–CH24 with the 250 Hz sine wave input signal processed with no window and the Hann window.

both the Hann window and no window case, and the rms levels of the residual and converter noise, and the coherent bits are given in Table 1.

For the NI 9239 we observe once again that the residual spectra is unchanged from the white noise case, and changing the data window has little effect on this result. For the NI 9205 channels the residual spectra increase slightly when no data window is used, and this is reflected in a 0.7 bit decrease in coherent bits. Why the results are better with the Hann window are not entirely clear, but it appears related to the aliasing artifacts that have been introduced due to the RPA chopping process. Exactly how the window shapes the residual spectra also appears to be influencing the residual calculation.

The sine wave used for this test was of poor quality and with the Hann data window the spectrum of the sine wave can be seen to be contaminated with the noise of the RPA amplifier. This noise accounts for some spectral energy in the input throughout the frequency band and assures the coherent removal process is successful. When there is no (or close to no) signal present in a given frequency band the calculation of the coherence can become numerically unstable. This is, in fact, the case for an ultra pure sine wave processed with a data window to highly suppress the sidelobe energy. In this case, applying no data window actually helps to ensure that signal input is present throughout the frequency band because applying no window causes the spectrum to leak significantly into the sidelobes.

Using sine waves to measure the residual spectrum is somewhat analogous to using a single sine wave to measure the entire transfer function frequency response. As with transfer function measurements, the user should use wideband noise signals to try to maximize the coherence between the signals under test for all frequencies of interest.

4.6. Summary

To implement the measurement examples presented, a LabVIEW application was developed to record and analyze the data in real-time. One of the reasons for implementing the entire processing in LabVIEW was to carry out the calculations using extended precision arithmetic. For the results presented, all of the spectral processing was implemented using MATLAB in double precision arithmetic.

Earlier simulations had suggested the use of extended precision would be necessary when using the coherent removal procedure with large channel counts. These same simulations also showed loss of numerical accuracy when the optimum system transfer functions equations are solved using matrix inversion procedures other than the Cholesky decomposition. While this result is still true, under closer scrutiny, and taking care to simulate bit noise with uniformly distributed variables and the amplifier noise sources with gaussian distributed variables, it was in fact possible to simulate results for as many as thirty-two 24-bit channels with 1 bit of noise using double precision arithmetic. Another important aspect, in order to match simulation results, was to use a large number of spectral averages. While extensive simulations have not been performed, a good rule of thumb is to use about ten times the number of channels, for the number of the averages. For the measurement examples presented no more than eight channels are actually processed using the coherent removal process at one time, so the use of double precision arithmetic and 256 averages is sufficient.

One of the perhaps overlooked aspects of the residual spectra interpretation is that the analysis verifies the practise of paralleling acquisition channels to improve noise performance. When the noise of each of the channels are approximately equal, the residual spectral density will simplify to $S_{ee} = S_{nn} + S_{nn}/q$. The second term in the sum, is actually the noise of the best linear predictor v and has q times lower noise than that of an individual channel.

The ability of modern $\Delta\Sigma$ A/D converters, such as those used in the NI 9239, to provide both simultaneous sampling and brick-wall anti-aliasing filtering, are the principle reasons why, the multiple coherent removal technique works so well for this device. Results with the NI 9205 were hampered, by its inability to simultaneously sample the inputs, and difficulties with aliasing of the input spectrum. The results presented with the NI 9205 make it clear the coherent removal process must take account of the anti-aliasing requirements of the devices under test, by filtering the input signal, or by avoiding inputting signal energy beyond the Nyquist frequency.

The material presented here is derived from well-accepted procedures for computing cross power spectral densities, the optimum system transfer functions, and the residual spectrum. For any combination of channel data, the residual spectra can always be calculated, and from this perspective presentation of the residual spectra is provided similar to that of any other accepted measurement, such as the transfer function or the power spectral density. The approach taken here has been not to present the individual channel noise spectra as these quantities are derived from the residuals and are based on interpretation, certainly, however, the temptation exists to do so, because results become specific to a single device, and this is desirable for marketing purposes.

The use of the multiple coherence function for the dynamic testing of data acquisition channels greatly simplifies the setup, and test signal requirements for dynamic testing of data acquisition channels because any input signal can be used, and depending on the gain, testing can be performed to measure either the amplifier or the A/D converter noise.

Author details

Troy C. Richards
Defence Research and Development Canada – Atlantic, Canada

5. References

[1] Bendat, J. S. & Piersol, A. G. [1971]. *Random Data: Anlysis and Measurement Procedures*, 1 edn, John Wiley and Sons, New York, NY.
[2] Bendat, J. S. & Piersol, A. G. [1980]. *Engineering Applications of Correlation and Spectral Analysis*, 1 edn, John Wiley and Sons, New York, NY.
[3] Beyer, W. H. (ed.) [1982]. *CRC Standard Mathematical Tables*, 26 edn, CRC Press Inc., Boca Raton, FL.
[4] Carter, G. C. [1980]. Bias in magnitude-squared coherence estimation due to misalignment, *IEEE Transactions on Acoustics, Speech, and Signal Processing* ASSP-28(1): 97–99.
[5] Carter, G. C. (ed.) [1993]. *Coherence and Time Delay Estimation*, 1 edn, IEEE Press, New York, NY.
[6] Holtham, P. M. & McAskill, B. [1987]. The spatial coherence of schumann activity in the polar cap, *Journal of Atmospheric and Terrestrial Physics* 50(2): 83–92.
[7] Horowitz, P. & Hill, W. [1989]. *The Art of Electronics*, 2 edn, Cambridge University Press, Cambridge, UK.
[8] *IEEE Standard for Terminology and Test Methods for Analog-to-Digital Converters* [2000].
[9] Kay, S. M. [1993]. *Fundamentals of Statistical Signal Processing: Estimation Theory*, Prentice Hall, Englewood Cliffs, NJ.
[10] Kuwahara, R. H. [1975]. Examples of DREP magnetics group involvement with coherence-function interpretation and analysis, *DREP Technical Memorandum* (75-7).
[11] Marple, S. L. [1987]. *Digital Spectral Analysis with Applications*, Prentice Hall, Englewood Cliffs, NJ.
[12] Marple, S. L. & Kay, S. M. [1981]. Spectral analysis - a modern perspective, 69: 1380–1419.
[13] LINEAR© [2012]. *LTC1150 Zero-Drift Operational Amplifier*, LINEAR Technology, Milpitas, California.
URL: *www.linear.com*
[14] MATLAB © [2011]. *Signal Processing Toolbox - Help Manaul*, The MathWorks, Inc, Natick, Massachusetts.
URL: *www.mathworks.com*
[15] Motchenbacher, C. D. & Connelly, J. A. [1993]. *Low-Noise Electronic System Design*, John Wiley and Sons,, New York, NY.
[16] Oppenheim, A. V. & Schafer, R. W. [1975]. *Digital Signal Processing*, 1 edn, Prentice Hall, Englewood Cliffs, NJ.
[17] Otnes, R., Lucas, C. & Holtham, P. [2006]. Noise suppression methods in underwater magnetic measurements, *Marelec Conference* .
[18] Press, W. H., Teukolsky, S. A., Vetterling, W. T. & Flannery, B. P. [1992]. *Numerical Recipes in FORTRAN 77*, 2 edn, Cambridge University Press, New York, NY.

[19] Richards, T. C. [2006]. Dynamic testing of A/D converters using the coherence function, *IEEE Transactions on Instrumentation and Measurement* 55: 2265–2274.

[20] Richards, T. C. [2008]. Dynamic testing of A/D converters using the multiple coherence function, *IEEE Transactions on Instrumentation and Measurement* 57: 2596–2607.

[21] Welch, P. D. [1967]. The use of fast fourier transform for the estimation of power spectra: A method based on time averaging over short, modified periodograms, *IEEE Transactions on Audio and Electroacoustics* AU-15: 70–73.

Chapter 4

Data Acquisition Systems in Bioprocesses

Carlos Ricardo Soccol, Michele Rigon Spier,
Luciana Porto de Souza Vandenberghe, Adriane Bianchi Pedroni Medeiros,
Luiz Alberto Junior Letti and Wilerson Sturm

Additional information is available at the end of the chapter

http://dx.doi.org/10.5772/48466

1. Introduction

Data acquisition systems in bioprocesses have distinct working specification. These processes normally involves microbial cells, vegetable cells, mammalian cells, microalgae cells or even enzymatic biochemical reactions, which implicates in time required for biochemical transformations and biomolecules production. Monitoring bioprocesses do not require real time monitor, because low times intervals (minutes or seconds) do not present significant differences on process parameters values. Bioprocesses are important area in the biotechnology and they are applied in many industries. It has many reaction routes available at any time, each one permitting a different distribution of biomolecules and products based on the conditions under which the fermentation process takes place. Control techniques are indicated to improve the productivity, yield and efficiency of the biotechnological processes. In the bioprocesses, it is very important to have a real time analysis of the process for creating a product with high speed, quality and economy. Knowing the parameters which affect biomolecule formation as well as the concentration of the nutrients, and develop or chose a cheap and simple system capable of on line measurements are required for bioprocesses control.

This chapter is separated into four parts for better understanding of the systems described. First, the data acquisition system $Fersol_1$ is described and its application in different bioprocesses are also presented. Second, the $Fersol_2$ system is also presented describing its functional components such as sensors, controllers, interface and the software and their functions in this system. Examples of application of $Fersol_2$ are described in the second item. Third part presents other systems already developed and the final part presents biosensors and its applications.

Data acquisition system as a source of information about the process behavior and further processing of generating the parameters allows a comparative analysis. Besides the main softsensors and biosensors in biotechnology and applicability to several processes and respective microorganisms, through the use of acquisition system data, sensors and computational tool is presented.

2. Data acquisition systems developed in DEBB

2.1. Fersol$_1$

Fersol$_1$ is a software that was developed in 1987, which runs only on DOS operational systems, using the methods described by [1]. It was developed and used to manipulate solid-state fermentation (SSF) parameters to solve the problem of difficult separation of biomass from the solid substrate and its heterogeneous characteristics [2]. SSF is characterized by the development of microorganisms in a low-water activity environment on a non-soluble material which is used as nutrient source and physical support [3].

Several authors used respirometry to follow the gas effluents from the bioreactor (CO_2 and O_2) in order to control fermentation and to evaluate different microorganisms' activities [4-13]. O_2 consumption and CO_2 production are the result of metabolic activity of microorganisms from which they obtain the necessary energy for growth and maintenance. Besides, the metabolic activity is associated to the growth and it can be employed for biomass biosynthesis estimation [2,3].

2.1.1. Biomass determination in a fermentation process

One of the most important factors in bioprocesses evaluation and control, both in laboratory and industrial scale, is the estimation of biomass. In a submerged fermentation process this is normally done through measurement of biomass at a particular time by the so-called direct methods. Such methods include direct cell counting, dry biomass determination or optical density determination [2,3].

Considering all the above facts, several methods have been developed for biomass determination that can be divided as direct or indirect measurements. Direct measurements are based on direct separation of biomass followed by normal standard procedures as established for submerged biomass determination (cell counting, etc.). The main problem with this method is the necessity of a whole extraction of biomass from the remained solid substrate. The employment of innocuous detergent in order to guarantee the whole extraction of the biomass from the sample was attempted. However, in the case of mycelium production, the method is not feasible due to the impossibility of a complete separation of biomass. Indirect measurements are based on the determination of a particular component of the cell, or the mycelium that is not present in the solid substrate [2,3,4,8].

It includes:

a. Glucosamine content determination: The method is based on the fact that glucosamine is a monomer component as acetylglucosamine of chitin. Chitin is an insoluble polymer present in the mycelium. The process consists in the depolymerisation of chitin, followed by the liberated glucosamine determination. Principal difficulties with this method are the lengthy analytical procedure, which takes about 24 hours and the sample adequacy as statistically representative.

b. Ergosterol method: The method is based as the former one due to the presence of ergosterol in the biomass but presents same difficulties such as time-consuming procedure as glucosamine content determination.
c. DNA determination: The basis of this method is the precise increase of the DNA content in the medium as the biomass develops due to the fact that DNA is a constant cellular component. The principal errors that could be made are related with sample adequacy and the possible consumption of cell DNA containing during the process. Another difficulty encountered is related with the DNA isolation and procedures with determination, which takes a long time.
d. Protein determination: This may be the most intended method for direct estimation of biomass. The principal problems of this determination are how exactly protein content is determined and which part of the protein present in the substrate are not consumed, or transformed. It seems that when the solid matrix has no or high protein content, the method could work reliable. For protein estimation, it is usual to determine the N content by the Kjeldahl determination, previous precipitation of the present protein, but a more accurate procedure could be obtained by using an amino acid analyzer.
e. Metabolic gas method Method: This method overcomes the sample adequacy, damage of biomass, or mycelium and is an on-line and fast delivery method. As a matter of fact, this method could be considered a direct measurement of the process kinetics. O_2 consumption and/or CO_2 involved during the process are linearly related with biomass synthesis in an aerobic system. But it is also an indirect method for biomass estimation. In an anaerobic process, CO_2 evolved is a direct indication of biomass synthesis and associated product formation as it occurs in the alcoholic fermentation. The method considers the determination of exhaust gas (exhaust air) composition determination from the fermenter during fermentation. The procedure implies a balance for O_2 and CO_2 considering the airflow through the fermenter.

As has been pointed out previously, all these methods are subject to an appropriate sampling. This is more significant at the initial stages of the process, or when the problems with gradients are not solved. Besides, in particular processes biomass, or mycelium could be damaged by sample acquirement [2].

However, current methods used in liquid fermentation cannot be applied in solid-state processes. This fact is due, for example, to partial or complete adhesion of filamentous fungus mycelium to the solid substrate/support in solid-state fermentation (SSF) system heterogeneity. This causes difficulty in the measurement of whole biomass. Besides, the heterogeneous character of the system demands a more precise acquirement of the samples, which is not faced in submerged or homogeneous fermentation processes [8].

Regarding the software solution, the O_2 consumed and/or CO_2 evolved seems to be more adequate because of on-line measurement possibility and fast results [8]. Besides this method could be considered as a direct measurement of process kinetics, although in true sense it is still an indirect measure of biomass synthesis.

2.1.2. *Application of respirometry analysis using Fersol[1]*

2.1.2.1. *Estimation of growth by respirometry analysis*

The respiratory metabolism of the microorganism can be evaluated by determining the O_2 consumption and CO_2 production. This indirect method is used to estimate the biomass biosynthesis by the fungal culture [8]. The exhausted saturated air from the bioreactors passes through silica gel column and then is analyzed by gas chromatography in order to determine the oxygen uptake rate and the CO_2 evolved during the process.

Biomass analytical determination is made by subtracting the quantity of protein in a certain time of the initial quantity of protein present in the substrate.

A mass balance is carried out for the estimation of oxygen uptake rate (OUR) and CO_2 evolved in terms of volumetric flow (L/h). If exhausted airflow (F_{out}) is known and the inlet airflow is F_{in}, the following equations are considered:

$$V_{O_2out} = \left(\frac{\%O_{2out}}{100}\right) \times F_{out}$$

$$V_{CO_2out} = \left(\frac{\%CO_{2out}}{100}\right) \times F_{out}$$

$$F_{out} = V_{O_2out} + V_{CO_2out} + V_{N_2out}$$

$$V_{N_2out} = \left(\frac{100 - \%O_{2out} - \%CO_{2out}}{100}\right) \times F_{out}$$

Considering the air composition (79% N_2 and 21% O_2), it can be written:

$$V_{N_2in} = \frac{79}{100} \times F_{in}$$

$$V_{N_2in} = V_{N_2out}$$

Then, the follow equation relates the inlet and the outlet airflow:

$$F_{in} = \frac{\left(100 - \%O_{2out} - \%CO_{2out}\right) \times F_{out}}{79}$$

The mass balance for oxygen is given in order to evaluate the volumetric flow of O_2 uptake rate:

$$V_{O_2uptake} = \left(\frac{21}{100}\right) \times F_{in} - \left(\frac{\%O_{2out}}{100}\right) \times F_{out}$$

For the estimation of OUR and CO_2 evolved in mass flow units (mol/h), it is considered that the air was an ideal gas at the respective volumetric flow ($V_{O_2 uptake}$ and $V_{CO_2 out}$) and the proper corrections for temperature conditions.

Considering the balance of OUR, the following equation is obtained [8]:

$$X_n = \left\langle Y_{X/O}\Delta t\left\{\frac{1}{2}\left[\left(\frac{dO_2}{dt}\right)_{t=0}+\left(\frac{dO_2}{dt}\right)_{t=n}\right]+\sum_{i=1}^{i=n-1}\left(\frac{dO_2}{dt}\right)_{t=i}\right\}+\left(1-\frac{a}{2}\right)X_0-a\sum_{i=1}^{i=n-1}X_i\right\rangle \Big/ \left(1+\frac{a}{2}\right)$$

Where:

$$a = m_X Y_{X/O}\Delta t$$

From the results of the OUR and CO_2 production, some bioprocess parameters are estimated. The estimation of biomass in a certain time (X_n) consists of assuming values for its yield based on oxygen consumption ($Y_{X/O}$) and biomass maintenance coefficient (m_X). Fersol$_1$ software [1] is then used in the calculations.

2.1.2.2. Acquisition and manipulation of fermentation data

A SSF system, developed by Raimbault and Alazard [14], can be employed in different bioprocesses for diverse biomolecules production [4-13, 15, 16]. This system composed by ten glass column bioreactors with 20 cm length, 4 cm diameter, work volume of 250 cm^3 (Fig. 1). The columns are closed at both ends with cotton plugs, connected to humidifiers and aerated according to the different processes (value set with the aid of a rotameter). The production of CO_2 and O_2 consumption by the cultures is generally measured through a GC (Shimadzu GC-8A, Shimadzu Co., Japan), which is linked to a program for chromatograph control and integration.

The software Chroma (Biosystèmes, Ltd., France) can be employed. There are also other programs that are available such as PeakSimple (SRI Instruments, USA), Base Line N2000 (BaseLine, China), PCChrom (H&A Scientific, USA) and others. The column used in the GC was a Porapak 80/100 at 60ºC, with 2 m length, with helium as carrier gas and a thermal conductivity detector.

Case 1: Respirometry analysis of biomass production during citric acid production by SSF

The relationship between citric acid production, an organic acid, by solid-state fermentation (SSF) of cassava bagasse and the respiration of *Aspergillus niger* LPB 21 was studied. SSF was employed using column fermenters at laboratory scale (Figure 1) and a horizontal drum (HD) bioreactor at semi-pilot scale (Fig. 2), which was coupled with the gas chromatography system to evaluate the release of CO_2 evolved and the O_2 consumption.

SSF was conducted in glass columns with 80 g of humid substrate (laboratory scale) and horizontal drum bioreactor (semi-pilot scale) with 10 kg of humid substrate. Treated and inoculated substrate was placed inside the fermenters. As shown in Fig. 2, the horizontal drum bioreactor consisted of a shovel coupled to a motor axis that rotated with controlled speed. During fermentation the material was revolved 3 to 4 times a day. After 20 hours of fermentation, saturated air was inserted continually into drum in order promote growth and to control substrate temperature and moisture [17].

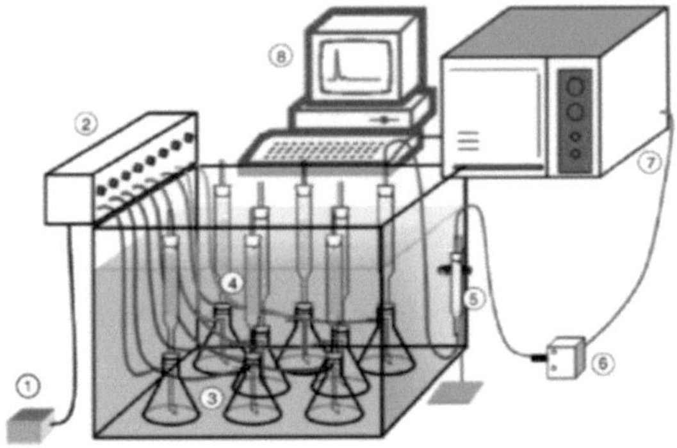

Figure 1. Column set-up for respirometry studies. (1) Air pump; (2) air distribution system; (3) humidifiers; (4) fermentation columns—these are immersed in a water bath with controlled temperature; (5) drying column attached to a column exit; (6) sampling valve; (7) gas chromatograph; (8) computer with data acquisition and control software. Source: [16].

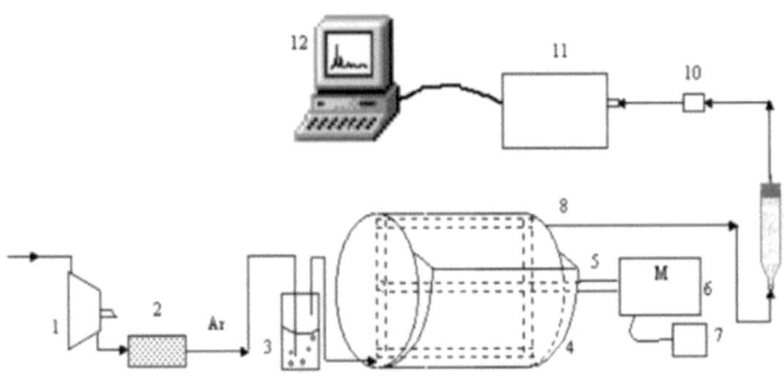

Figure 2. Outline of the horizontal drum bioreactor and auxiliary equipments: (1) compressor, (2) air filter, (3) humidifier, (4) horizontal drum bioreactor, (5) axis, (6) motor, (7) speed controller, (8) air discharge, (9) silica gel column, (10) automatic injector, (11) gaseous chromatograph, (12) computer. Source: [9]

Citric acid production and other characteristic parameters, such as substrate consumption, pH evolution and biomass, were followed during SSF of *A. niger* with CB as substrate. A higher citric acid production was reached in column fermenters (309.7 g/kg DM) than in HD bioreactor (268.94 g/kg DM), probably due to the influence of the fermentation temperature, which was not controlled in HD. Better results could have been attained if the system was adapted with temperature control. A novel prototype is being developed in our laboratory. For column bioreactors the temperature was controlled by a water bath at 30°C. The HD bioreactor worked at room temperature, which was approximately 25°C. It is also important to point out other factors that could affect the metabolism of the fungus and citric acid production such as heat and oxygen transfer that are the main scale-up problems of SSF [9].

Seven points of biomass were considered and analytically determined at 0, 24, 48, 72, 96, 120 and 144 h of fermentation. The system $Fersol_1$ determines the equation coefficients by successive approach. From the values of OUR and CO_2 production, obtained experimentally, the system determined a biomass yield ($Y_{X/O}$) of 4.37 g of biomass/g of consumed O_2 and a biomass maintenance coefficient (m_X) of 0.0162 g of consumed O_2/(g of biomass.h) for HD bioreactor. For column fermenters the biomass yield was 2.93 g of biomass /g of consumed O_2 and the maintenance coefficient was 0.0053 g of consumed O_2/ g of biomass h. Biomass yield was higher in HD bioreactor than in column fermenters due to the proportional higher levels of forced aeration rates [9].

Fig. 3 and Fig. 4 present the evolution of O_2 and CO_2 percentages during fermentation such as estimated biomass and analytical determined biomass for both types of bioreactor. The production of CO_2 did not exceed 0,4% and 2,2% for HD and column fermenters, respectively. This results show that in HD bioreactors the limitation of growth was excessive and, probably, the strategy of retarding aeration in 20 hours was not favorable to this system. This fact could also be shown by the biomass production during fermentation, which was only 0.87 g/100 g DM for HD bioreactor. However, in column fermenters biomass production reached 2.2 g/100 g DM.

In column fermenters, CO_2 production was detected after 24 hours, when biomass and citric acid concentrations started to raise. Maximal CO_2 production was observed at 36 hours of fermentation. Growth was associated with metabolite production. After 50 h of fermentation in HD bioreactor CO_2 production reached its maximum. At this point, citric acid production was about 30 g/kg DM. The difference between estimated and analytical determined biomass in HD bioreactor, mainly in 72 h of fermentation, was an indicative that indirect method of biomass determination, using on-line monitoring of CO_2 production, can probably correct the errors presented in biomass determination by analytical methods [9].

Case 2: Respirometry analysis of biomass production during biopigments production by SSF

Solid-state fermentation (SSF) was carried out to establish relation between growth, respirometric analysis and biopigments production from *Monascus* sp. in columns and in a drum-type bioreactor with forced air (Fig. 5 and Fig. 6). In these reactors, the best aeration rate for biopigment production was 1 ml of air, per gram of wet substrate, per minute. The outlet air composition was determined using gas chromatography (GC), while the pigments produced were measured by spectrophotometry after extraction with ethanol. An ergosterol-dosage method was used to estimate biomass production; in this method, the ergosterol was extracted and measured by liquid cromatography (HPLC). The results showed that although pigments were a secondary metabolite, its production was proportional to the biomass produced that was estimated by ergosterol analysis, and therefore could be used to estimate biomass formed in the natural support (rice). Specific velocities for pigment and biomass production were estimated by a sigmoid model applied to the data and also with the aid of $Fersol_1$. Under ideal conditions in column fermentation, a maximum specific growth velocity of 0.039 h^{-1} and a specific pigment production velocity of 27.5AU/g biomass h was obtained, at 140 h, with 500AU/g dry fermentate after 12 days.

The specific product formation velocity in the bioreactor was 4.7AU/g h, at 240 h fermentation, and the total pigment production was 108.7AU/g dry fermentate after 15 days [16].

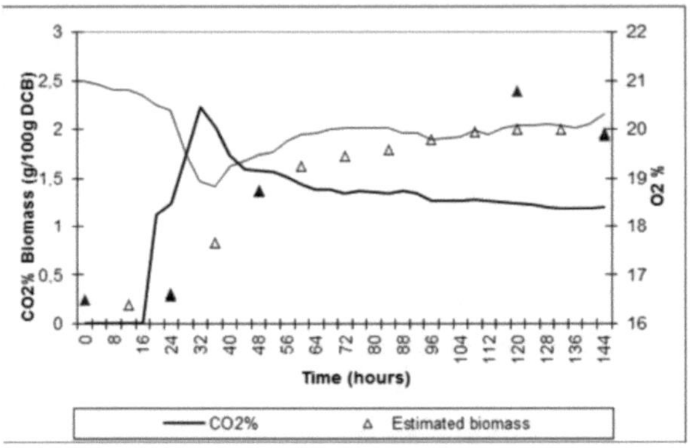

Figure 3. Evolution of kinetic parameters of citric acid production by SSF of cassava bagasse by *Aspergillus niger* LPB 21 in column bioreactor (CB). Source: [9]

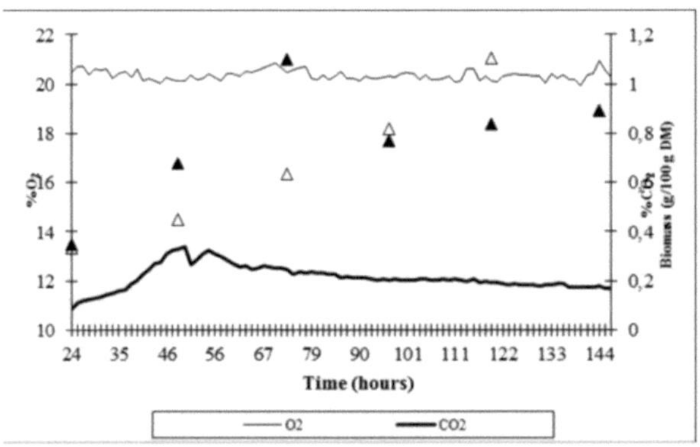

Figure 4. Evolution of kinetic parameters of citric acid production by SSF of cassava bagasse by *Aspergillus niger* LPB 21 in HD bioreactor. Source: [9]

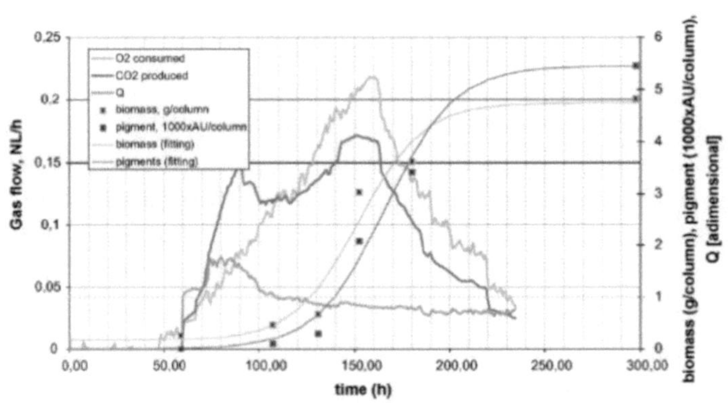

Figure 5. Results of the respirometric analysis in columns, using rice as substrate: O_2 consumption, production of CO_2, pigments (as SPABS), biomass and respiratory quotient *Q* in the course of time. Source: [16].

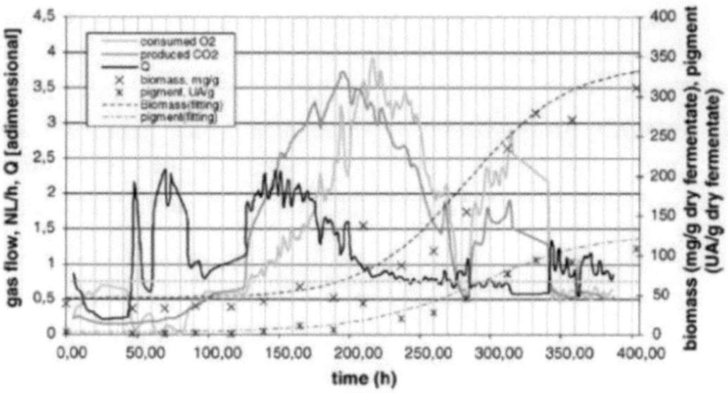

Figure 6. Results of the respirometric analysis in drum-type horizontal bioreactor using rice as substrate–oxygen uptake, CO2 and pigment production (as SPABS), biomass production and respiratory quotient in the course of time. Source: [16]

2.2. Fersol$_2$

2.2.1. Description of Fersol$_2$

The biomass synthesis is one of the most important patterns present in a fermentation bioprocess. In submerged fermentation process, this parameter can be normally measured through direct methods such as cell counting, dry biomass or optical density determination [18].

Fersol$_2$ was reported to monitor fermentation parameters and estimate biomass growth during solid state fermentation. In SSF, biomass growth kinetic behavior is very difficult to analyse because of the heterogeneous composition and the difficulty in separating the biomass from the solid substrate [19-21]. Regarding the software solution, the O_2 consumed and/or CO_2 produced seems to be more adequate because of on-line measurement possibility and fast results [21]. This method could be considered as a direct measurement of process kinetics, although in true sense it is still an indirect measure of biomass synthesis [22].

To monitor and control bioprocesses such as liquid cultures, submerged and solid state fermentations is necessary to measure the biomass, the mass of microorganism, as well as its evolution during the process. One way to measure is estimating the biomass by respirometry: measuring how much oxygen is being consumed and the carbon dioxide is being produced it is possible to estimate the mass of microorganisms. Until some years ago, our research group performed it through a gas chromatograph coupled to a data acquisition system (Fersol$_1$, described in 2.1) which made the process very expensive.

Fersol$_2$ system is a low cost alternative due the incorporation of current resources of informatics. The use of sensors for different variables detection such as temperature, flow, percentages of oxygen, and carbon dioxide, linked to a data acquisition system developed for monitoring, and subsequent, control these processes. With the measured data it is possible to use another software tool improved for the estimation of biomass growth and the determination of some kinetic parameters from process data. The parameters such as the specific growth rate, maintenance and production coefficients, which characterize the process, allowing a more thorough analysis of its performance. For validate $Fersol_2$ system, Sturm [23] reported some experiments carried out in different bioprocesses developed by our research group involving different microorganisms, in order to better embrace the possible processes. Monitoring processes with fungi, bacteria, algae and plant cells, allowed evaluating the possible validity of the system, facing the different behaviors of several microorganisms used in fermentation, both submerged and solid state fermentation and also in cell cultures.

The complete system $Fersol_2$ is a real time acquisition system to measure environmental variables of bioprocesses such as fermentation processes controlling these parameters and helping to monitor the process in real time. $Fersol_2$ was developed under C Sharp (Microsoft) in DotNet (Microsoft) platform, which works together with Laquis, for data acquisition. but it could be developed under another platform (software) commercially available. This system is capable to monitor bioprocesses environmental parameters such as O_2, CO_2, temperature, flow rate, humidity, pH depending on the sensors which will gather data and the controllers to adjust set points of the variables.

As a basis for the development of this system was taken the $Fersol_1$ software using the methodology reported by Rodriguez-León et al [1] described in the subitem 2.1 above.

As a basic requirement, this interface allows to analyze on a single screen all major parameters calculated, as well as an indication of any change to the parameters presented on the same screen. There is no information loss when the total number of reads exceeds a certain limit imposed on each screen line. On this same screen you can open, save, change and display properties of each file reads, file input and output can be saved as a text file or as a CSV (comma separated values) according to user needs, allowing the opening of data for analysis in other programs such as Microsoft Excel, for example.

As $Fersol_2$ used as a basis, $Fersol_1$, it had limitations on the generation of graphics, especially regarding the resolution and scale, hampering the analysis graphs generated by these and yet it was impossible to download these graphics to other external resources to the program. During the development of the $Fersol_2$ was researched new graphics library, besides the C language offered by C-Sharp®, because this also showed some limitations as to transfer to other external programs, which have been solved and are fully functional in the current version of program. The acquisition program is in development phase and has the possibility of calculation of gaseous masses, flow aeration, process temperatures and relative humidity. The decision to use an industrial network, Modbus, is due to the possibility of expanding the system, incorporating other sensors or actuators, improving automation in the same conditions [23, 25].

The project has been used in bioprocesses experiments such as phytases production by solid state fermentation (SSF) [26]. Also, a test conducted with data from submerged fermentation showed the methods used, resulting in very close values of the estimated and calculated by other means [23].

The decision to modify the structure of the system has brought increased speed, stability and proper use of resources of the lab computers, so that the change should bring more benefits than difficulties with regard to possible future work related to this system.

Part of the research work is related to the application process through sensors attached to the industrial network, quite immune to noise and wrong signals that could be captured, so the tables of values generated by the system should be more reliable, with minor discrepancies with compared to theoretical values or expected.

These new features in process instrumentation such as solid state fermentation (SSF) may generate input tables for processing samples with much larger numbers than in the past, because instead of collecting new sample every two hours, for example, may reap every second, or even fraction of seconds thereof. It is essential to update this software so you may handle this amount of data in reasonable time and without loss of information useful for subsequent monitoring and control of manufacturing a certain product.

The Fersol2 has the main interface design showed in Fig. 7. Using the graphics resources of the chosen programming language, the new program's main interface was designed.

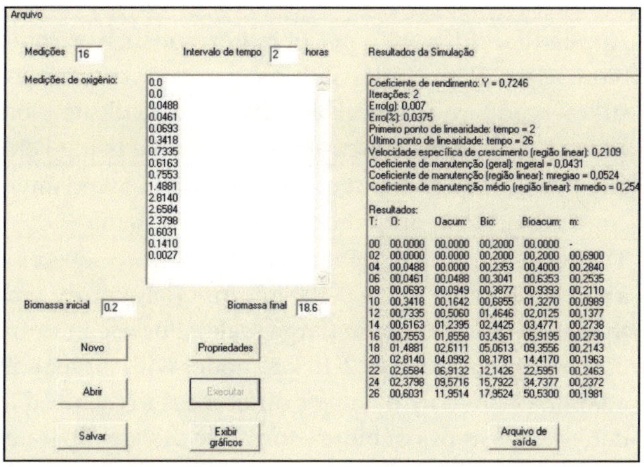

Figure 7. Fersol2 interface (*in portuguese*).

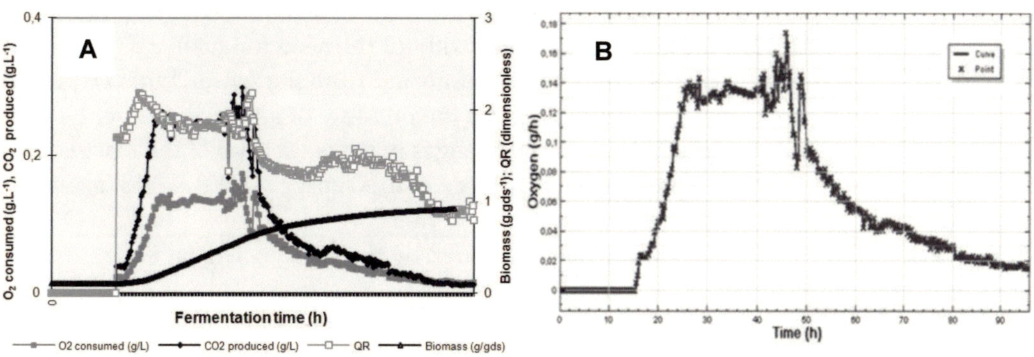

Figure 8. Example of graphs generated by the Fersol2 data acquisition system. (A) profile of O_2 consumption, CO_2 produced, biomass and respirometric quocient (QR) data transferred from Fersol2 to Microsoft® Office Excel and a graph plotted during a solid state fermentation by a fungal strain; (B) Oxygen consumption showed in Fersol2 software.

The Table 1 shows the components of $Fersol_2$ system and their descriptions.

Components	Description
PC with the software	The industrial network Modbus [18] was used and the platform of development Laquis® (LCDS Company) [24]
Air pump	Air supply when the bioprocess require O_2 (aerobic systems) or CO_2 (photosynthetic process)
Air distribution system	Air distribution in different bioreactors, when several experiments must be done simultaneously
Humidifiers	Air passes through flasks containing sterile water to keep moisture content of bioreactors and avoid drying during air distribution.
Water bath with controlled temperature	Normally used for keep Raimbault column or column-type bioreactors commonly used in solid state fermentation processes
Bioreactors	Applied for different types of bioreactor such as column-type bioreactors, Raimbault columns, tray-type bioreactor, drum bioreactor, submerged fermentation bioreactors, cell culture bioreactors are some examples of bioprocesses already reported using $Fersol_2$.
Filter	Air sterilization in input of bioreactor and avoid environmental air contamination in output of bioreactor systems
Flow sensor	The sensor model is Aalborg GFM [27]. Two sensors are used, one with a response in the range 0-100 mL/min (laboratory sacle) and the other in the range of 0-200 L/min (large scale). For use in drum-type reactors, both with a capacity of 2-10 kg, model with larger scale showed better adaptation, mainly by major differences in the need for aeration between the types of bioreactors. The sensors operate by the principle of thermal dispersion. To minimize errors due to pressure fluctuations, this sensor uses a method for disposing between two capillaries, where flow laminar, then calculating the value of actual flow, taking into account the law ideal gas and without the need for auxiliary measurements temperature before and from the sensor, which would be indispensable considering that the pressure of gas varies, either by pumping conditions, or by changes in pressure drop of the reactor itself during the process. The accuracy of this sensor is 1.5% at least against the full scale value.
Controllers display	Shows in real-time data measured by the sensors. Digital visor.
Cylindrical sensors base (Support)	The gas sensors and humidity are adjusted in a PVC tube where the air is applied through the flow sensor. Inside the tube is formed an "air" in the exhaust gases, where the respective sensors measure its concentration. For measurement or temperature control, the Pt100 has been adapted as directly as possible in touch with the process, in order to minimize possible errors.

Transmitter	A transmitter RHT-DM 4–20 mA 150 mm (Novus) measured relative air humidity (%) the outlet process temperature (ºC). This device works as a relative humidity probe. It is installed together with the cylindrical sensors base.
Thermistor sensor	A thermistor sensor is installed together with the cylindrical sensors base.
O_2 sensor	Two sensors are used for measuring gas percentage, in the process input, another installed in the output. The difference between the percentages of these sensors resulted in percentage consumed by microorganisms in the process. The sensors used are of the O_2-A2 model provided by Alpha Sense® [28]. Used in conjunction with an amplifier circuit, signal present between 4-20 mA signal industry standard. The signal varies according to the percentage of oxygen changes from 15% to 25% respectively. With the use of controllers for starting signal. Resolution was established in hundredths of a percentage. These sensors operate through a process called metal-air battery [29], where the oxidation reaction on a metal electrode generates an electrical signal proportional to the percentage of oxygen in the air.
CO_2 sensors	For later determination of the mass of CO_2, two sensors were used similar to those described above, one installed at the entrance and another at the output of the process. The model GMT 221 was provided by Vaisala [30] by interfering between two beams of infrared wavelengths slightly different. The result is generated by a signal output rate of 4-20 mA, with a range of activity between 0 and 20% CO_2. The resolution of this signal is of 0.006%, but the controller that this is connected has a resolution of 0.01%, thus limiting the latter value.
Humidity sensor	In order to monitor the change in relative humidity at the outlet of processes, we used a probe RHT-DM, supplied by the manufacturer Novus [31], with the measurement condition from 0 to 100%, with a signal 4-20mA output, the two wires, supporting a working temperature between -20ºC and 80°C. The basic operation of this sensor is a capacitive probe.
Temperature sensor	For the measurement of temperature and, in some processes its control was using a Pt100 sensor. This choice was based on a wide range of using this type of sensor, and its quick response associated with large linearity. In order to get a signal, this sensor is connected to a controller model N1100 [32], which allow the reading resolution of one-tenth of a degree Celsius, with a maximum error of 0.2% of measurement.

Source: Based on [23]

Table 1. Components and Descriptions of Fersol2 data acquisition system

2.2.2. Applications of Fersol2 system already reported

Several studies involving bioprocesses have been reported using the Fersol2 data acquisition system. Some examples are presented below:

Case 1: Relation of enzyme production and fungal growth in column-type bioreactor for SSF

Spier et al [26] reported the relation between phytase production and fungal growth during solid state fermentation in column-type bioreactor monitored by Fersol2 data acquisition system (Fig. 9). The biomass measured by indirect quantification by ergosterol concentration presented high correlation (R2=0.988) with the biomass estimated by the data generated by the Fersol2 system [23]. Fig. 9 shows a representative image of Fersol2 system connected to the column type bioreactor, including adaptation to sensors, controllers and computer system for data acquisition schematic form. Besides (B) shows digital display panel showing the parameters been monitored on-line.

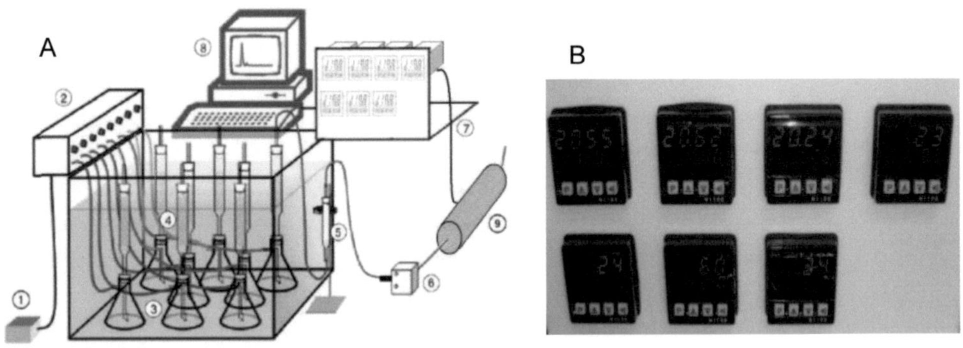

Figure 9. (A) Fersol2 system. Source: [26]; (B) Fersol2 control panel. Source: [23]

Case 2: Analysis of vegetable cell culture growth and respiration in a bubble immersion bioreactor

Fersol2 was applied for monitoring vegetable cells culture in a bubble immersion bioreactor (BIB) model for temporary immersion [33] showed the variation of the percentage of oxygen, considering the difference between input and output system, where it is possible to check the breathing cycle and photosynthesis. This cycle of respiration showed values of 10 hours 42 minutes and photosynthesis during 13 hours 4 minutes. The time for the supply of artificial light was 16 hours, which showed a small delay with respect to light exposure and it is associated in achieving reaction of photosynthesis. The application of Fersol2 system in this study was to assist in raising relevant information to determine a mathematical model of the reactor under study. The results were related to the flow of great use to design of the model, including showing some of the limitations of the real reactor [23].

Case 3: Microalgae growth

In study with microalgae there was observed one cycle determined in oxygen consumption and hence the gas production dioxide. Whereas microalgae perform photosynthesis, indicating a negative O_2 consumption can be interpreted as the production of gas, a constant rate. This shift in the signal O_2 consumption occurs in some periods, given the flow and mass of microalgae present in the process. In the same way, the behavior of production of carbon dioxide shows a cyclic behavior compared with oxygen, as determined by correlation between these elements in the metabolism of microalgae [23, 34].

2.3. Other systems already developed

2.3.1. Softsensors

The term "softsensor" is a combination of the words "software", once the models are usually computer programs, and "sensors", because the models are delivering similar information as their hardware counterparts. A softsensor enables bioprocess information acquisition in real time, such as data on the specific growth rate, the biomass concentration and/or the product concentration, via indirect measurements using software sensors. Considering the process control point of view, the biomass concentration is especially interesting to characterize the bioprocess [35]. A softsensor represents the association of hardware sensor(s) with an estimation algorithm, which is integrated into the monitoring, optimization and control systems. Its performance depends on the quality of the measured input data and the adequacy of the process description [36].

Softsensors can be distinguished in two different classes: model-driven and data-driven. The model-driven softsensors is most commonly based on First Principle Models. First Principle Models describe the physical and chemical background of the process. These models are developed primarily for the planning and design of the processing plants, and therefore usually focus on the description of the ideal steady-states of the processes which is only one of their drawbacks which makes it difficult to base softsensors on them.. On the other hand, data-driven softsensors are based on the data measured within the processing plants, and thus describe the real process conditions. Comparing to the model-driven softsensors, data-driven softsensors are more reality related and describe the true conditions of the process in a better way. According to Kadlec et al (2009) [37], the most popular modelling techniques applied to data-driven softsensors are the Principle Component Analysis (PCA) in a combination with a regression model, Partial Least Squares, Artificial Neural Networks, Neuro-Fuzzy Systems and Support Vector Machines (SVMs).

2.3.2. Some applications of softsensors in bioprocess

The automated control of bioprocess variables is difficult due to the complex nature of biotechnology processes, besides the lack of industrially viable sensors for online measurement of these variables.

The applications of fuzzy logic and artificial neural network approaches enable the optimization and control of small or large scale fermentation processes, especially where limited knowledge about the process is available. In recent years, the artificial neural network methodology has become one of the most important techniques applied for biomass estimation [35].

Arazo-Bravo et al [38] applied neuro-fuzzy FasArt and FasBack for the modelling and control of a penicillin production batch process. A softsensor for the prediction of the biomass, viscosity and penicillin production delivers the necessary information for the control mechanisms of the FasBack adaptive controller. The holistic control model is trained and evaluated using simulated process data. The trained model is then able to deliver satisfactory results for the real process control.

"Simple softsensors can also be based on titration techniques [39]." The consumption rates of base (or acid) were used as input for softsensors for substrate and biomass concentrations. The data acquisition and control software was written in LabVIEW 5.1 (National Instruments).The authors successfully demonstrated this titrimetric technique to: (a) Control of aerobic fermentation - estimation of biomass and substrate (phenol) concentrations; (b) Control of (anaerobic) acidification reactors - estimation of metabolite concentrations; (c) Control of (anaerobic) acidification reactors - estimation of inhibitory effects. The results show the versatility of software sensors based on titrimetric techniques and demonstrate the potential for process control in applications in which more sophisticated sensors are not available or affordable.

The use of a visual programming environment LabVIEW to program custom control functions for bioprocess research have already been presented [40]. The time taken for a bioprocess scientist to program new functions compared well with typical times expected for experienced programmers using conventional languages. Experienced LabVIEW programmers develop applications significantly faster. For the development of the system, three aspects of the study were carried out. First, the supervisory control program was written using LabVIEW to encode the feed control algorithm and drivers to communicate with equipment in the plant. A continuous culture was used to define the upper and lower limits to the range of specific growth rates which gave high growth yield from the carbon source as well to determine the value of the growth yield and the relationship between growth yield and specific growth rate in this range. The third aspect was the control system implemented for the production of yeast biomass at constant specific growth rate in a fed-batch bioprocess. The package described by the authors was flexible, easy to use and was ideally suited to developing new applications for control of bioprocesses. It was demonstrated with the development of a system to control specific growth rate in a fed-batch culture.

Knowledge based systems for supervision and control of a bioprocess was presented and applied to data of an industrial antibiotic fermentation [41]. In this paper an approach towards the automatic generation of fuzzy rules was generated describing the relationship between the kinetics of the preculture and the antibiotic yield of the main culture. The fuzzy-C-means algorithm was used for process classification (Software DataEngine, MIT GmbH, Aachen, Germany). For the selection of rules the software WINROSA (MIT GmbH) was applied. Fuzzy membership functions were tuned using the software tool FuzzyOpt (SEI GmbH, Ilmenau, Germany). In order to rate and select rules and finally to optimize parameters of membership functions of fuzzy variables different criteria are discussed in relation to the aim of the knowledge based control. Results are presented with respect to process monitoring. Genetic algorithms proved suitable for optimization procedures due to the existence of multiple local optima.

A system that can automatically select the moment when the feeding of inverted sucrose should start in the Cephalosporin C batch production process, was implemented using fuzzy methodology [42]. The quantities of sugars, cell mass and Cephalosporin C correspond to variables not monitored continually, but quantified through the analysis of samples taken periodically from the bioreactor. By monitoring the percentage of CO_2 in the outflow gases, it was possible to observe a point of maximum evolution when the microorganism growth phase finishes. Therefore, the moment when the feeding should begin was characterized by a transition from increasing (positive variations) to decreasing (negative variations) CO_2 evolution rates. A fuzzy controller was designed that operates on three reasoning levels, attention, action and protection. The corresponding algorithm was implemented in C language. The results obtained indicated that the algorithm is robust for the tested conditions, allowing a safe automatic operation.

The structure and the functions of the advanced knowledge-based BIOGENES© control system for the control of a fed-batch *S. cerevisiae* cultivation have been described [43]. The BIOGENES knowledge-based control system (KBCS) was built using the industrial control system programming tool GENESIS ™ for Windows, from ICONICS Inc., for creation of the basic control level, and the expert system shell Clips 6.04, from NASA'S Johnson Space center, for creation of the advanced KB-level. The KB-level of the BIOGENES© was able to identify the metabolic state of the yeast and supervisory process control for the fed-batch process. In addition, with the BIOGENES© KBCS, the authors also developed a softsensor for biomass concentration estimation.

Solid-state fermentation is a complex process, including a combination of chemical, biological and transport phenomena. The development of reliable, real-time, and high-performance systems to control the fermentation process is essential [44].

Jiang et al [45] demonstrates that Fourier transform near-infrared (FT-NIR) spectroscopy combined with support vector data description (SVDD) is an efficient method to develop one-class classification model for the rapid monitoring of SSF. The physical and chemical changes in solid-state fermentation (SSF) of crop straws were monitored without the need for chemical analysis. SVDD algorithm was employed to build a one class classification model, and some parameters of SVDD algorithm were optimized by cross-validation in calibrating model. All algorithms were implemented in Matlab 7.1 (Mathworks, USA) under Windows XP. Result Software (AntarisTM II System, Thermo Scientific Co., USA) was used in NIR spectral data acquisition. The SVDD algorithm in the work was developed by Tax et al. (1999) and the SVDD Matlab codes were downloaded from http://homepage.tudelft.nl/n9d04/dd_tools.html for free of charge. Others were developed by authors themselves which were the modification of the algorithm described by Tax et al [46].

Baeza, Gabriel and Lafuente [47] presented the development and implementation of a Real-Time Expert System (RTES) for the supervision and control of a wastewater treatment pilot plant with biological removal of organic matter and nutrients. The hardware architecture contains different supervision levels, including two autonomous process computers (plant control and analysers control) and a PLC, being the expert system the top supervisory level. The expert system has been developed using a commercial, industrially validated RTES-development software G2Ô (by Gensym Corp). It actuates as the master in a supervisory setpoint control scheme and it is based on a distributed architecture. This system has been running continuously for 600 days. The supervisory Expert System has shown an excellent performance to manage the pilot wastewater treatment plant. The system developed detects and controls all the wrong and special operations, for example pump failure, feeding problems, probes malfunction, equipment maintenance, analysers control and maintenance.

Flow Injection Analysis (FIA) systems with an integrated biosensor could indeed be important tools in bioprocess monitoring. To facilitate the optimal use of a FIA system, the prerequisites are stable, sensitive and robust hardware with features for data analysis and evaluation.

A versatile automated continuous flow system (VersAFlo) was developed [48] for bioanalytical applications, providing a platform to employ biosensors for continuous analysis of bioprocesses with precise control of flow, volume and defined events has been developed. The system was based on National Instruments LabVIEW and was verified for online analysis of IgG employing a heterogeneous immunoassay in a competitive flow-ELISA mode. Also, the production of recombinant protein is a growing field and the requirements on bioprocess monitoring and control in such processes are crucial.

Di Sciacio and Amicarelli [35] proposed a biomass concentration estimator for a biotechnological batch process based on Bayesian regression with Gaussian process. A real bioprocess was designed and exemplified for a *Bacillus thuringiensis* δ-endotoxins production process on the basis of experimental data from a set of various batch fermentations. The authors concluded that this Bayesian non-parametric framework is sufficiently flexible to represent a wide variety of bioprocess data, and makes possible interpreting the prior distribution, computing the posterior, and the full predictive distributions, as well as, the mean predictions and the predictive uncertainties.

In industrial applications, there are some softwares that only work like a HMI (human machine interface), collecting data and displaying on the computer screen only. These systems do not perform control over the process variables. The software called SCADA (supervisory control and data acquisition) does both, acquisition and control functions, acting on the variables directly and changing process values. Some examples of suppliers of these systems are LabVIEW, by National Instruments, Elipse SCADA, by Elipse, andHMI / SCADA Software, by Advantech. These systems may be accessed in the following website links: http://www.ni.com/labview/, http://www.elipse.com.br/ and http://www.advantech.com/products/automation-software/sub_1-2mlc9t.aspx, respectively.

2.4. Biosensors

2.4.1. Concept of biosensor

Biosensors are bioelectronic devices able to detect rapidly chemical species and/or biological (analyte), both qualitatively and quantitatively. This type of detector allows varied tasks such as: on-line control at industrial level; automation of biochemical and chemical plants; environmental analysis in real-time; in vivo analysis; detection and quantification of relevant biological substances and detection of chemical warfare, among other applications. Biosensors` devices can be of continuous use (most of them) or disposable (i.e: blood glucose meters).

Biosensors are composed essentially by: biological element; transducer; and electronics. The biological element or sensor element has the property of selective recognition and interaction with the interest analyte. The surface of the sensor element is usually covered with biological material, i.e: antibodies, nucleic acids, proteins, organelles, cells, among others. The interaction between the biological element and the analyte results in the modification of one or more physico-chemical properties (pH, electron transfer, mass transfer, heat transfer, the release of ions or gases) which are detected and measured by the transducer. The main objective is to produce an electronic signal. This signal must be proportional in magnitude and/or frequency to the concentration of a particular analyte or a group of analytes interacting with the biosensor. Finally, electronics consists of an amplifier of electrical signals and system data processing.

Therefore, a biosensor combines the specificity of an active biological component to an analyte of interest, with a sensitive transducer, which converts the biological signal into an electrical signal proportional to the concentration of the analyte, which can be further processed and interpreted [49].

2.4.2. Immobilization of biological material: The most important step of the development of a biosensor

The most important step in the development of the biosensor is the immobilization of the biological material, and this must be done in a way that the binding site to the molecule of interest becomes clear. There are several ways to perform the immobilization: occlusion; microencapsulation; physical adsorption; covalent binding; attachment with polyethylenimine (PEI); acrylamide membrane; protein A.

Some of the desired properties after immobilization are: physico-chemical and mechanical stability of the components; short time of response when interacting with analytes of interest; good selectivity and sensibility; low limit of detection (which means low concentrations of the analyte are able to promote a response from the biosensor) and accuracy [50].

2.4.3. Classification

Biosensors can be classified according to the type of biological material of its sensor, or according to the type of transducer employed.

2.4.3.1. According to the biological component

The biosensors can be classified as: chemoreceptors; enzymatic sensors; immunosensors; microbiological sensors.

Chemoreceptors use proteins as sensing elements. The interaction with the analyte leads to conformational changes of the proteins and depending on the degree of this event, a different signal will be generated, transduced and transmitted. However, this type of sensor has a difficult handling and connection to the transducer, and has a lower specificity when compared to other types of sensors, like enzymatic sensors or immunosensors.

Enzymatic biosensors use enzymes, usually immobilized, as biological component. Enzymes are biological catalysts of high specificity and sensitivity, therefore, this class of biosensor is of great importance in biological processes. However, they have relatively low stability, and thus, a strict control over the environment conditions such as pH, temperature and pressure is necessary for its employment.

Imunosensors use globular proteins of serum, the immunoglobulins, as biological element. These proteins are antibodies, which mean they bind to antigens with high affinity and specificity. However, their high molecular weight makes difficult the adaptation to the transducer. In addition, background reactions may occur. To avoid these undesirable reactions, secondary antibodies must be added and the base on which the antibody is attached must be blocked.

The microbial biosensor uses immobilized microorganisms, which specifically recognize an organic compound. Thus his metabolic activity is altered, and such change is detected by the transducer.

2.4.3.2. According to the transducer

After interacting with the biological element, the signal is detected and sent for processing. This role is performed by an element called transducer. The signals can assume several forms, since there is a great variety in the biological components used. The transducers are classified according to the type of physico-chemical stimulus received. The main types are electrochemical, optical, calorimetric, and piezoelectric.

The electrochemical transducers are based on the movement of electrons and diffusion of electroactive species. There are three different types: amperometric, potentiometric and conductimetric [51].

The amperometric transducers are based on the measurement of electric current, generated from reactions of oxidation and reduction of electroactive species. The system is composed typically by three electrodes: a working electrode, in which will occur the reaction of interest; a reference electrode, which sets the potential applied to the first electrode; and a counter electrode, which provides current to the working electrode. In practice, for some applications only the first two are sufficient. The two major drawbacks of this class of sensor: they are sensitive to background noise, and the relatively high potential required can oxidize other compounds than the interest analyte, and so, generating a higher electrical current, and a false result. Some innovations have attempted to overcome these problems, such as the use of diffusion limiting membranes to maintain the concentration of substrate below the degree of saturation of the enzyme and the use of mediators [52]. The construction of chemically modified electrodes by the development of immobilization techniques of both enzymes and mediators has opened a new amperometric class of transducers, in which mediators can be incorporated into electrodes by adsorption, occlusion in polymer films, covalent bonding or simply mixed in carbon slurry [53]. This type of biosensor is largely available today at the market, because they are based on REDOX enzymes (oxiredutases). These enzymes have a well established market, and can act on fatty acids, sugars, amino acids, aldehydes and phenols.

The potentiometric biosensor, in general, has a reference electrode (inert) and a working electrode (preferably ion-selective). Both electrodes are put in contact with the sample; a constant electric current is generated. If the sample is a broth in which will occur an enzymatic reaction, a difference of potential is developed between the electrodes, due to the production or consumption of strong polar ions by the enzymes during the catalysis. These reactive species are detected by the ion selective electrode, and then a quantifiable signal will be generated and transmitted [54]. The ion-selective electrodes are fast, sensitive, cheap and the measurement is simple, because only pH measurement is required.

In conductimetric biosensors, changes are observed in conductance measurements resulting from products of catalytic reactions. The operating principle involves a pair of micro-electrodes separated by an electrolyte solution containing the enzyme and the sample to be detected. The electric field is generated by applying a difference of potential between the microelectrodes, where there are variations in the concentrations of polarized species. Many enzymatic reactions produce a change in conductivity, but only a few provide a signal with stable magnitude. This type of transducer has not been widely used, due to the difficulty to perform measurements with simple devices. Also, the signal is very dependent from the temperature and usually the dilution of the sample is required.

The optical methods to transduce signals are: absorption, fluorescence, phosphorescence, and polarization interference, which can be used in solid state sensors. Optical transducers can be associated with an immobilized biological component in the presence or absence of an indicator. Its principle is based on the fact that some enzymatic reactions alter the optical property of certain substances and the light emitted by this element or its response to biological lighting can be conveniently transmitted via optic fibers and monitored in optical equipments [55].

Some biological reactions are accompanied by the release of energy enabling them to be quantified calorimetrically, relating the amount of heat generated with the amount of substrate consumed or with the amount product formed. The calorimetric biosensors allow this monitoring, but have some important disadvantages: high costs, complexity, low specificity to the analyte. Another problem: changes of enthalpy occur not only in the biochemical reactions, but also in the mixture, dilution and solvation of the components. Heat is also exchanged with the environment. All these factors may contribute to possible errors of analysis.

Some types of crystals (ie: anisotropic crystals, those lacking a center of symmetry) generate an electrical signal when subjected to mechanical stress. Similarly, if subjected to an electrical signal, they undergo mechanical deformation proportional to the signal. This is called the piezoelectric effect. Thus, with the applying of an oscillating electric potential, the crystal will vibrate. These vibrant cristals can be used as devices to generate electrical currents. The vibration frequency is affected by the mass of adsorbed material in its surface, which can be related to changes in a reaction. Piezoelectric materials that can be used in sensors include ceramic materials such as barium and plumb titanates, as well as "natural" materials such as quartz and tourmaline. Some organic polymers, such as polyvinylidene fluoride (PVDF), also form crystals with piezoelectrical properties.

Tables 2 and 3 summarize the classification of biosensors, its principle of operation, advantages and disadvantages, some of them already cited in the text:

Transductor type	**Principle of operation**	**Advantages**	**Disadvantages**
Chemoreceptors	Interaction between proteins and the analyte	Simpler and cheaper than other sensors	Difficult conection with the transducer; low specificity for a particular analyte
Enzymatic	Catalysis of the substrate (analyte) by immobilized enzymes	High specificity	Low stability
Immunosensors	Specific binding of the analyte to an antibody	High specificity and afinity	Difficult conection with the transducer; background reactions
Microbiological	Specific recognition of an analyte by an immobilized microrganism	Easy to isolate; less sensitive to pH and temperature variations	Higher response time; lower selectivity

Table 2. Biosensors′ classification – according to the biological component

Transducer type	Principle of operation	Advantages	Disadvantages
Amperometric	Generation of electric current	Wide range of application for REDOX enzymes	Background noise and low selectivity (except for modified designs)
Potentiometric	Generation of a diference of potential	High selectivity, low time of response	Less reliable than amperometric; more complex than conductimetric
Conductimetric	Generation of a condutance change	Very cheap and simple design	Low range of application; low reliability
Optical	Alteration of optical properties of the medium	Low cost; perspective for new uses in the future	Only applicable when optical changes occur
Calorimetric	Detection of generated heat	Wide range of application; high reliability	High cost; high complexity; low specificity
Piezoelectric	Generation of electric current due to mechanical stress	Very high time of response; low complexity	Low reliability

Table 3. Biosensors′ classification – according to the type of transducer

2.5. Applications of biosensors

The application of biosensors is very broad and diversified, being used in several areas:

- Food industry (the determination of glucose in instant coffee and sulfite in foods);
- Pharmaceutical Industry (determination of ascorbic acid, epinephrine and dopamine on drugs);
- Medicine (quantification of urea in urine and glucose in human serum);
- Environmental Engineering (environmental control and the determination of pesticides);
- Bioprocess Engineering (determination of substrates and products of fermentation processes, ie:pentoses, hexoses, organic acids, aminoacids, lipids, proteins; determination of gases concentrations, ie: oxigen and carbon dioxide and even quantification of celular concentration).

In general, biosensors are the first element of a data acquisition system in Bioprocesses, when the variables to be measured and controlled are concentrations of biomolecules. The detection of these analytes requires greater sensibility and/or specificity, but once they are properly detected, as shown at the last subsections, the processing of data is similar to processes used in other industries. Some particular examples of application are shown in the previous section, with the detailing of the data acquisition system in its whole scope.

3. Conclusions

When monitoring a process, the verification in real-time of determinant parameters for a proper functioning of this process is crucial for better understanding. If the process is still under study, or if the monitoring processes is well known, allowing evaluate smaller changes in their characteristics when occur any disorder or condition unfavorable. Data acquisition systems in bioprocesses present great importance for industrial, economical and scientific purposes.

In industrial applications high speed data acquisition systems are generally required, for example in manufacturing machines. This characteristic is necessary because of the high frequency in the variables changing, and to perform real time acquisition. In other words, the process variables change rapidly over time, such as the speed of an electric motor, or the pressure value in a duct, for instance.

In bioprocesses, although there are a large number of variables to be monitored or controlled, the speed of values changing is not so high. Thus, to make the data acquisition relating to changes in pH or respirometric values, such as oxygen consumed and carbon dioxide produced, for example, many recordings are not necessary per unit of time, as these variables are usually connected to the biomass growth, which does not change very quickly.

Many alternatives of systems are commercially available for laboratory and/or industrial control. Besides two examples of systems $Fersol_1$ and $Fersol_2$ were described, and biosensors are specified to help students, scientists and engineers to understand and to choose which type and specifications of real-time systems may be the most adequate for their necessities and applications.

Author details

Carlos Ricardo Soccol, Michele Rigon Spier*, Luciana Porto de Souza Vandenberghe,
Adriane Bianchi Pedroni Medeiros, Luiz Alberto Junior Letti and Wilerson Sturm
*Bioprocesses Engineering and Biotechnology Department, Federal University of Paraná,
Curitiba, Brazil*

Acknowledgement

Authors would like to thank Prof. PhD José Angel Rodríguez-León (Positivo University, Brazil), Prof. PhD Dario Eduardo Amaral Dergint (UTFPR, Brazil) for technical assistant. And also CNPq for finantial support.

4. References

[1] Rodriguez-León J A, Sastre L, Echevarria J, Delgado G, Bechstedt W. A Mathematical Approach for the Estimation of Biomass Production Rate in Solid State Fermentation. Acta Biotechnologica, 1988; (8) 307-310.

* Corresponding Author

[2] Sturm W, Soccol CR, Dergint DEA, Rodríguez-León JA, Magalhães DCNV, Pandey A. Informatic in Solid-State Fermentation. In: Pandey A, Soccol CR, Larroche C. (ed.) Current Developments in Solis-State Fermentation. New Delhi: Asiatech Publishers; 2007. p.169-180.

[3] Soccol CR, Vandenberghe LPS. Overview of Solid-State Fermentation in Brazil. Biochemical Engineering Journal, 2003, (13): 205-219.

[4] Raimbault M, Roussos S, Lonsane BK. Solid State Fermentation at ORSTOM: History, Evolution and Perspectives. In: Roussos S, Raimbault M, Lonsane BK. (ed.) Advances in Solid Substrate Fermentation. New York : Springer-Verlag; 2008. p.577-612.

[5] Saucedo-Castañeda G. Contrôle du Métabolisme *de Schwanniomyces castellii* Cultivé sur Support Solide. Thèse de Doctorat. Université Montpellier II, Montpellier, France; 1991.

[6] Soccol CR. Physiologie et Métabolisme de *Rhizopus* en Culture Solide et Submergée en Relation avec la Dégradation d'Amidon Cru et la Production d'Acide L(+) Lactique. PhD Thesis. University of Compiegne France; 1992.

[7] Stertz SC, Soccol CR, Raimbault M, Pandey A, Rodriguez-Léon J. Growth Kinetics of *Rhizopus formosa* MUCL 28422 on Raw Cassava Flour in Solid State Fermentation. Journal of Chemical Technology and Biotechnology 1999; 74 1-7.

[8] Pandey A, Soccol CR, Rodriguez-León JA, Nigam P. Production of Organic Acids by Solid-State Fermentation. In: Pandey A, Soccol CR, Rodriguez-Leon JA, Nigam P. (ed.) Solid-State Fermentation in Biotechnology – Fundamentals and Applications. New Delhi: Asiatech Publishers Inc.; 2001. p. 113-126.

[9] Prado FC, Soccol CR, Vandenberghe LPS, Lisboa C, Paca J, Pandey A. Relation Between Citric Acid Production and Respiration Rate of Aspergillus niger in Solid-State Fermentation in Flasks, Trays and Horizontal Drum Bioreactors Using Treated Cassava Bagasse. Engineering in Life Sciences 2004; 4(2):179-186.

[10] Soccol CR, Prado FC, Vandenberghe LPS, Pandey A. General Aspects In Citric Acid Production by Submerged and Solid-State Fermentation. In: Pandey A. (ed.) Concise Encyclopedia of Bioresource Technology. New York: Haworth Press: 2004. p. 617-628.

[11] Brand D, Pandey A, Rodríguez-León JA, Roussos S, Brand I, Soccol CR. Relation Between COffee Husk Caffeine Degradatin and Respiration of Aspergillus sp. in Solid State Fermentation. Applied Biochemistry and Biotechnology 2002; 102, p. 169-177.

[12] Vandenberghe LPS, Soccol CR, Pandey A, Lebeault JM. On-line monitoring of citric acid production using respirometry in solid state fermentation with cassava bagasse. In: More Quality of lLife by Means of Biotechnology: proceedings of International Symposium on the Bioconversion of Renewable Raw Materials, 2000, Hannover: Germany.

[13] Vandenberghe LPS. Développement d'un Procédé pour la Production d'Acide Citrique par Fermentation en Milieu Solide à partir de Résidus de l'Agro-Industrie du Manioc. PhD Thesis. Université de Technologie de Compiègne Compiègne; 2000.

[14] Raimbault M, Alazard D. Culture Method to Study Fungal Growth in Solid Fermentation. European Journal of Applied Microbiology and Biotechnology 1980; 9 199-209.

[15] Pintado J, Torrado A, González MP, Murado MA. Optimization of Nutrient Concentration for Citric Acid Production by Soilid-State Culture of Aspergillus niger on Polyurethane Foams. Enzyme Microbial and Technology, 1998; 23, p. 149-156.

[16] Carvalho JC, Pandey A, Oishi BO, Brand D, Rodriguez-León JA, Soccol CR. Relation Between Growth, Respirometric Analysis and Biopigments Production from Monacus by Solid-State Fermentation. Biochemical Engineering Journal 2006; 29, p. 262-269.

[17] Vandenberghe LPS, Soccol CR, Pandey A, Lebeault J-M. Solid-State Fermentation for the Synthesis of Citric Acid by *Aspergillus niger*. Bioresource Technology 2000; 74 175-178.

[18] Sturm W, Dergint DEA, Soccol CR, Pandey A. Instrumentation and Control in SSF. In: Pandey A; Soccol CR; Larroche C (ed.) Current Development in Solid-State Fermentation. v.1. New York: Springer Science + Business Media, 2008. p. 146-168.

[19] Singhania RR, Soccol CR, Pandey A. Recent advances in solid-state fermentation. Biochemical Engineering Journal 2008; 44(1):13–18.

[20] Pandey A, Soccol CR, Mitchell D. New developments in solid state fermentation: I bioprocesses and products. Process Biochemistry 2000; 35:1153–1169

[21] Pandey A, Soccol CR, Rodríguez-León JA, Nigam P. Solid state fermentation in biotechnology: fundamentals and applications. New Delhi: Asiatech Publishers Inc, 2001.

[22] Sturm W, Soccol CR, Dergint DEA, Rodríguez-León JA, Magalhães DCNV. Informatics in solid state fermentation. Chapter 8. In: Ed. Pandey, A.; Soccol, C.R.; Larroche, C. Current Development in Solid-State Fermentation. Delhi: Springer Asiatech Publishers, 2008. p.168-178.

[23] Sturm, W. Development of Software Tools for Acquisition of Data and Evaluation of Results in Fermentation Processes in Solid and Submerged and Cell Culture. PhD Thesis. Federal University of Paraná, Curitiba; 2009. 104p. (*In Portuguese*).

[24] LCDS Company. Leão Consultoria e Desenvolvimento de Sistemas LTDA (Lion Consultant and Systems Development, Brazil. http://www.lcds.com.br/ (accessed 21 April 2012).

[25] Sturm W. Industrial Sensors – Theorical Concepts and Practical Aplications. Rio de Janeiro: Papel Virtual Editora, 2004. (*In Portuguese*).

[26] Spier MR, Woiciechowski AL, Letti LAJ, Scheidt GN, Sturm W, Rodriguez-León JA, de Carvalho JC, Dergint DE, Soccol CR. Monitoring fermentation parameters during phytase production in column-type bioreactor using a new data acquisition system. Bioprocess Biosystems Enginering 2010; 33:1033-1041.

[27] Aalborg. Low Cost Mass Flow Meters. GFM Model Flow Sensor. http://www.aalgorg.com. (accessed: 10 May 2010).

[28] Alphasense. Technical Specification: Oxygen Sensor O2A2. Data Sheet. Disponível em: http://www.alphasense.com . Acesso 25 July 2009.

[29] Alphasense. How Oxygen Sensors Work. Alphasense Application Note AAN009. http://www.alphasense.com (accessed 05 May 2008).

[30] Vaisala. CO_2 Sensors model GMT221. Technical Data. Disponível em: http://www.vaisala.com . Acesso: 10/05/2006.

[31] Novus, Brazil. Products Catalog. http://www.novus.com.br (accessed 10 May 2008).

[32] Novus, 2008b. Operation Handbook N1100. http://www.novus.com.br. (accessed: 10 May 2008).

[33] Soccol CR, Scheidt GN, Mohan R. Biorreator do tipo imersão por bolhas para as técnicas de micropropagação vegetal. Universidade Federal do Paraná. Patente (DEPR. 01508000078); 2008.

[34] Sydney EB. Respirometric balance and analysis of four microalgaes: Dunnaliela tertiolecta, Chlorella vulgaris, Botryococcus braunii and Spirulina platensis. 2009. Dissertação (Mestrado em Master BIODEV) - Université de La Méditerranée Aix Marseille II, 2009.

[35] di Sciascio F, Amicarelli AN (2008). Biomass estimation in batch biotechnological processes by Bayesian Gaussian process regression, Computers and Chemical Engineering, 32, 3264–3273.

[36] Gjerkes H, Malensek J, Sitar A, Golobic I. (2011) Product identification in industrial batch fermentation using a variable forgetting factor , Control Engineering Practice,2001, 19 1208–1215

[37] Kadlec P, Gabrys B, Strandt S. Data-driven Soft Sensors in the process industry, Computers and Chemical Engineering, 2009 33 795–814.

[38] Arazo-Bravo MJ, Cano-Izquierdo JM, Gmez-Snchez E, Lpez-Nieto MJ, Dimitriadis YA, Lpez-Coronado J. (2004). Automatization of a penicillin production process with soft sensors and an adaptive controller based on neuro fuzzy systems. *Control Engineering Practice*, *12*(9), 1073–1090.

[39] Feitkenhauer H, Meyer U. (2004).Software sensors based on titrimetric techniques for the monitoring and control of aerobic and anaerobic bioreactors, Biochemical Engineering Journal, 17, 147–151

[40] Gregory ME, Keay PJ, Dean P, Bulmer M, Thornhill NF. A visual programming environment for bioprocess control..Journal of Biotechnology, 1994, 33 233-241.

[41] Guthke R, Schmidt-Heck W, Pfaff M. Knowledge acquisition and knowledge based control in bioprocess engineering, Journal of Biotechnology, 1998, 65, 37–46.

[42] Sousa JR, Almeida PIF. Design of a fuzzy system for the control of a biochemical reactor in fed-batch culture, Process Biochemistry 2001, 37 461–469.

[43] Hrnĉiřík P, Náhlík J, Vovsík J. The BIOGENES System for Knowledge-based Bioprocess Control, Expert Systems with Applications, 2002, 23 145-153.

[44] Ödman P, Johansen CL, Olsson L., Gernaey, K.V.; Lantz, A.E. (2009) On-line estimation of biomass, glucose and ethanol in Saccharomyces cerevisiae cultivations using in situ multi-wavelength fluorescence and software sensors, J. Biotechnol., 144 102–112.

[45] Jiang H, Liu G, Xiao X, Mei C, Ding Y, Yu S. Monitoring of Solid-state fermentation of wheat straw in a pilot scale using FT-NIR spectroscopy and support vector data description. Microchemical Journal, 2012, 102, 68–74.

[46] Tax DMJ, Duin RPW. Support vector domain description, Pattern Recogn. Letter, 1999, 20, 1191–1199.

[47] Baeza J, Gabriel D, Lafuente J. An expert supervisory system for a pilot WWTP Environmental Modelling & Software, 1999 14, 383–390.

[48] Kumar MA, Mazlomi MA, Hedström M, Mattiasson B. (2012) Versatile automated continuous flow system (VersAFlo) for bioanalysis and bioprocess control. Sensors and Actuators B, 161, 855– 861.

[49] Salgado AM. Desenvolvimento e Aplicação de Sensores e Sistemas de Monitoração de Biomassa, Etanol e de Substrato por Modelo. Tese de Doutorado, Universidade Federal do Rio de Janeiro, Rio de Janeiro, Brasil; 2001.

[50] Walker JM, Gingold EB. Biologia Molecular y Biotecnologia. 2ª Edição, Zaragoza; 1997.

[51] Thévenot DR, Toth K, Durst RA, Wilson GS. Electrochemical Biosensors: Recommended Definitions and Classification. Biosensors & Bioelectronics, v. 16, p. 121-131; 2001.

[52] Perez EF. Desenvolvimento de um Biosensor Amperométrico para Oxalato. Dissertação de Mestrado. Universidade Estadual de Campinas, Campinas, São Paulo; 2000.

[53] Romani A, Minunni M, Mulinacci N, Pinelli P, Vincieri FF. Comparison among Differential Pulse Voltammetry, Amperometric Biosensor, and HPLC/DAD Analysis for Polyphenol Determination. Journal Agriculture Food Chemistry, v.48, p. 1197-1203; 2000.

[54] Arya SK, Datta M, Malhotra BD. Recent Advances in Cholesterol Biosensor. Biosensors and Bioelectronics, v. 23, p.1083–1100, 2008.

[55] Hall EAH. Amperometric Biosensor. Open University Press, London, p.351; 1990.

Chapter 5

Microwave Antenna Performance Metrics

Paul Osaretin Otasowie

Additional information is available at the end of the chapter

http://dx.doi.org/10.5772/48517

1. Introduction

An antenna is a conductor or group of conductors used for radiating electromagnetic energy into space or collecting electromagnetic energy from space. When radio frequency signal has been generated in a transmitter, some means must be used to radiate this signal through space to a receiver. The device that does this job is the antenna. The transmitter signal energy is sent into space by a transmitting antenna and the radio frequency energy is then picked up from space by a receiving antenna. The radio frequency energy that is transmitted into space is in the form of an electromagnetic field. As the electromagnetic field arrives at the receiving antenna, a voltage is induced into the antenna. The radio frequency voltage induced into the receiving antenna is then passed into the receiver. There are many different types of antennas in use today but emphasis is on antennas that operate at microwave frequencies. This chapter discusses the two major types microwave antenna which are the horn-reflector and parabolic dish antennas. In order to satisfy antenna system requirements for microwave propagation and choose a suitable antenna system, microwave design engineers must evaluate properly these antenna properties in order to achieve optimum performance.

1.1. Definition of microwave and microwave transmission

Microwaves refer to radio waves with wavelength ranging from as long as one meter to as short as one millimeter or equivalently with frequencies between 300MHz (0.3GHz) and 300GHz.

Microwave transmission refers to the technology of transmitting information by the use of radio wave whose wavelength is conveniently measured in small numbers from one meter to one millimeter.

2. Microwave antenna

Microwave antenna is used for radiating microwave signal into space and receiving microwave signal from space. Microwave antenna acts as a transition region between free space and guiding structure like a transmission line in order to communicate between two or more locations. In microwave antennas, high gains with very narrow beam width in one or more planes are required. These can be achieved with antennas of reasonable size.

2.1. Types of microwave antenna

There are two main types of antenna that are used in microwave links. They are:

1. A horn-reflector antenna
2. A parabolic dish antenna

2.1.1. Horn-reflector antenna

A horn antenna is nothing more than a flared wave-guide as shown in Figure 1. The horn exhibits gain and directivity, however its performance is improved more by using it in combination with a parabolic reflector.[1]

An open-ended wave-guide is an inefficient radiator of energy due to the impedance mismatch at the mouth, it can be improved by simply flaring the end of the waveguide. Flaring of the wave-guide ends creates a horn antenna as shown in Figure 2.

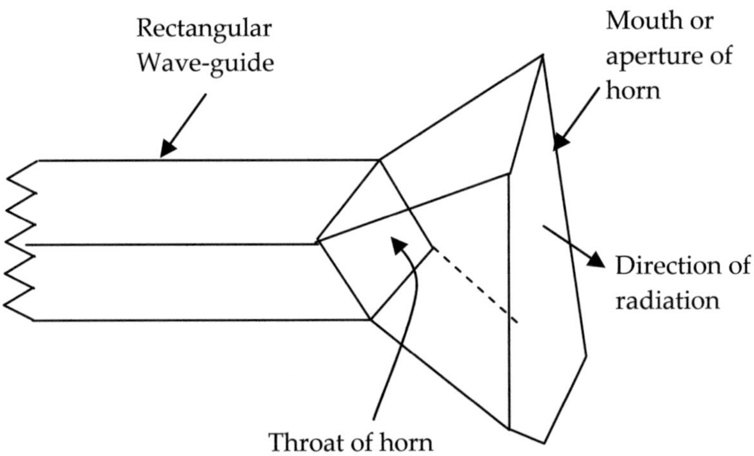

Figure 1. Basic horn antenna

Horn antennas have excellent gain and directivity. The longer the horn, the greater its gain and directivity. Different kinds of horn antennas can be created by flaring the end of the wave-guide in different ways for example flaring in one dimensions creates a sectoral horn e.g. horns flared in the E or H planes. Flaring the wave guide in both dimension produces a pyramidal horn e.g. horns flared in both E and H planes. If a circular wave-guide is used the flare produces a conical horn. These are shown in Figure 3.(a to d)

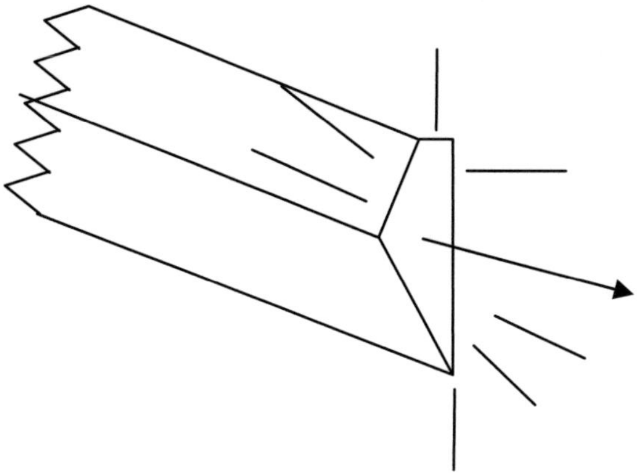

Figure 2. A wave-guide will act as an inefficient radiator

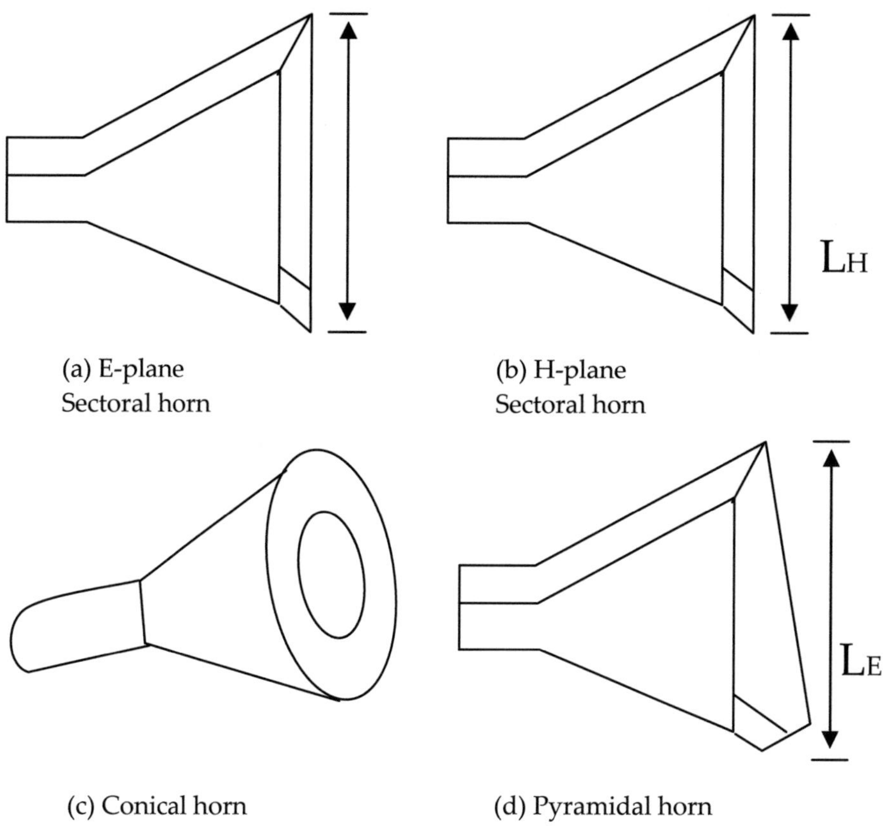

Figure 3. Types of horn Antenna

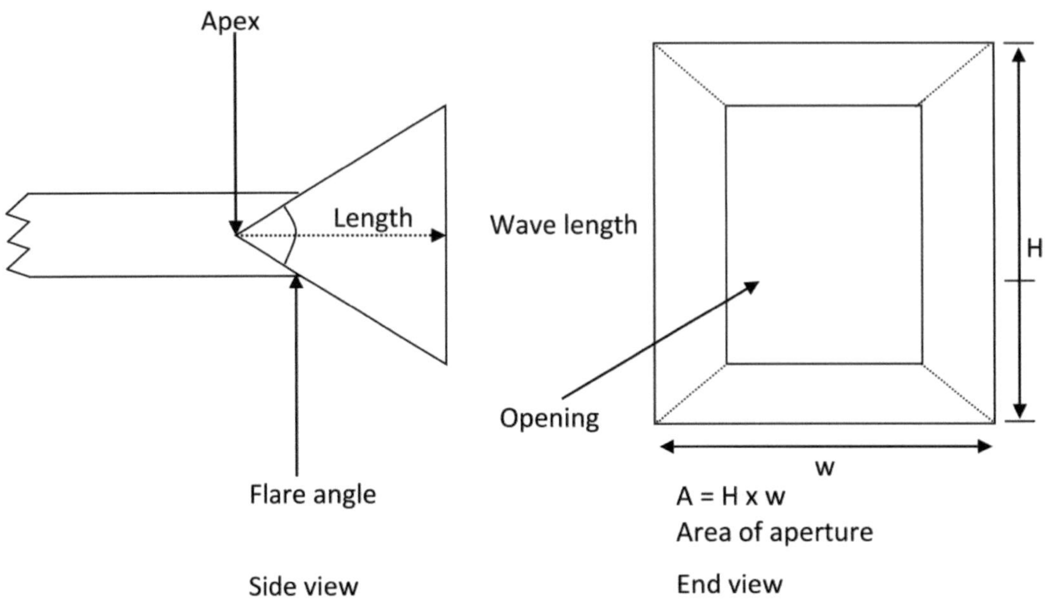

Figure 4. Dimensions of a horn

The important dimensions of the horn antenna are

i. Horn length
ii. Aperture area
iii. Flare angle

The length of a typical horn is usually 2 to 15 wavelengths at the operating frequency. The longer horns though more difficult to mount and work with provide higher gain and better directivity. The aperture area is the area of the rectangle formed by the opening of the horn and is simply the product of the height and width of the horn. The greater this area, the higher the gain and directivity.

The flare angle also affects gain and directivity. Typical flare angles vary from about 20^0 to 50^0. Increasing the flare angle increases the aperture area. For a given size of aperture area decreasing the length increases the flare angle as shown in Figure 4. Each of these dimensions is adjusted to achieve the desired design objective. An important aspect of a microwave antenna is its bandwidth. Most antennas have a narrow bandwidth because they are resonant at only a single frequency. Their dimensions determine the frequency of operation. Bandwidth is an important consideration at microwave frequencies because the spectrum transmitted on the microwave carrier is usually wide so that a considerable amount of information can be carried. Horn antennas have relatively large bandwidth. Horns are essentially non-resonant or periodic which means they will operate over a wide frequency range.

Horn antennas are used by themselves in many applications but many times higher gain and directivity is desirable. This can easily be obtained by using a horn in conjunction with a parabolic reflector.[1]

2.1.2. *Parabolic reflector*

The parabolic reflector antenna is one of the most wide spread of all the microwave antennas and is the type that normally comes to mind when thinking of microwaves systems. This type of antenna derives its operation from optics and is possible because microwaves are in transition region between ordinary radio waves and infrared/visible light. The parabolic reflector antenna (often called a dish antenna). The dish is not actually an antenna but serves a reflector. It must be driven by a radiating element at the focal length. This radiating element could be a dipole or a horn radiator. A parabola is a mathematical curve such that its reflection property causes an incoming beam of parallel rays to focus to one point. Conversely radiated waves from a point signal placed at the focal point are reflected by the surface to form parallel rays in the outgoing beam. Thus, a parabolic antenna can be employed as a transmitter and receiving device.

The parabolic reflector may take many forms. The larger the reflector with respect to the wave-length the narrower the beam width.

A typical dish antenna with a paraboloid shape is shown in Figure 5.

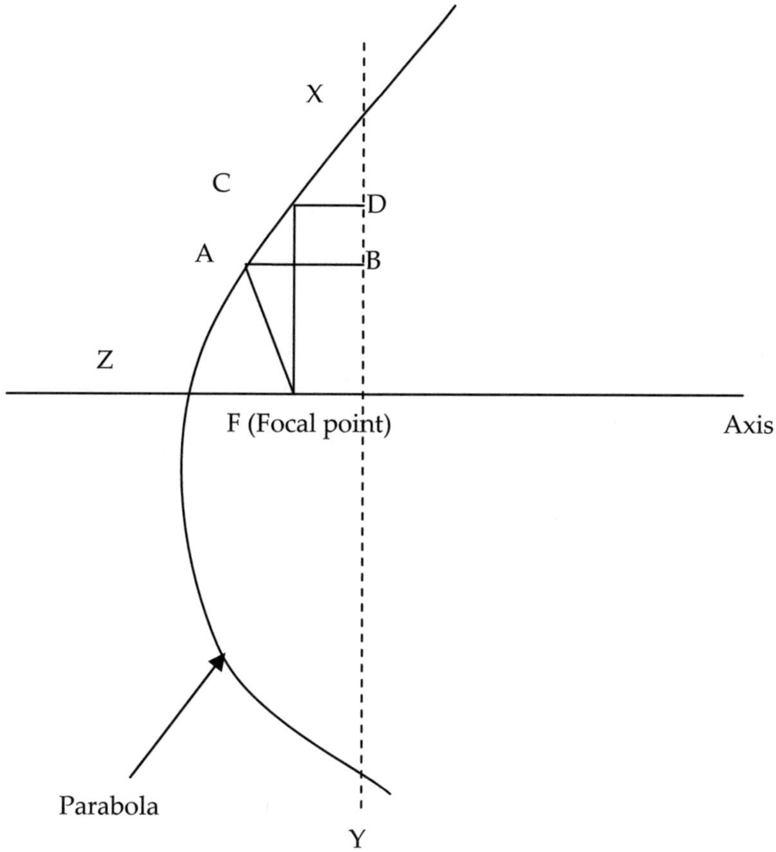

Figure 5. A Parabolic Dish

A key dimension of the parabola above is a line drawn from its center at point Z to a point on the axis labeled F which is the focal point. The ends of the parabola could extend outwardly for an infinite distance but usually they are limited. The limits are shown by the dashed vertical line with the end points labeled X and Y. The distance between the focal point and the parabola and the vertical dashed line is a constant value, for example in the Figure 5., the distance represented by the sum of the lines FA to AB and FC to CD are equal. This effect causes a parabolic shaped surface to collimate electromagnetic waves into a narrow beam of electrons. Placing an antenna at the focal point F will cause it to radiate waves from the parabola in parallel lines. If used as a receiver, the parabola will pick up the electromagnetic waves into a narrow beam of electrons. Placing an antenna at the focal point F will cause it to radiate waves from the parabola in parallel lines. If used as a receiver, the parabola will pick up the electromagnetic waves and reflect them to the antenna located at the focal length.

The gain of a parabolic antenna can be determined by:

$$G = K\left(\frac{\pi D}{\lambda}\right)^2$$

Where K is the reflection efficiency typically (0.4-0.7)
D = diameter of the dish (m),
λ = wave-length (m)
The reflection efficiency is 0.6 for most antennas

Thus gain can be approximated as:

The beam width (-3 d B) of a uniformity illuminated parabolic reflector antenna is approximated by $Bw = \frac{70\lambda}{D}$.

As stated before horn antenna can be used in conjunction with a parabolic reflector. The Figure 6. (a and b) shows how a parabolic reflector is used in conjunction with a horn antenna for both transmission and reception. The horn antenna is placed at the focal point. In transmitting the horn radiates the signal towards the reflector which bounces the waves off and collimates them into a narrow parallel beam, when used for receiving, the reflector picks up the electromagnetic signal and bounces the waves toward the antenna at the focal point. The result is an extremely high gain narrow beam width antenna.

The gain of the horn radiator is proportional to the area (A) of the flared open flange and inversely proportional to the square of the wave-length, $G = \frac{10}{\lambda^2}$

Where A = Flange area (m)
λ = Wave-length (m)

The -3 dB beam- width for vertical and horizontal extents can be approximated from the following:

1. Vertical $\varnothing v = \frac{51\lambda}{b}$
2. Horizontal $\varnothing v = \frac{70\lambda}{a}$

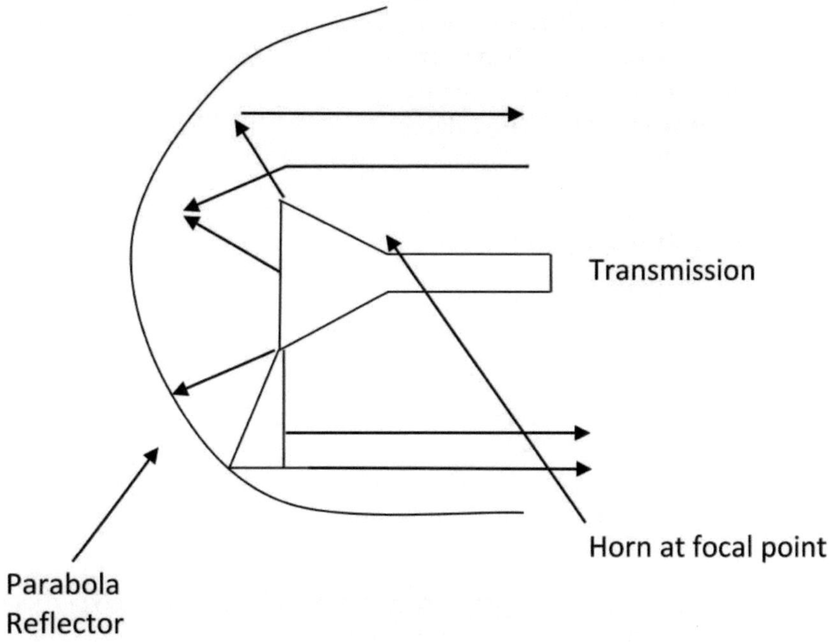

(a) Transmission

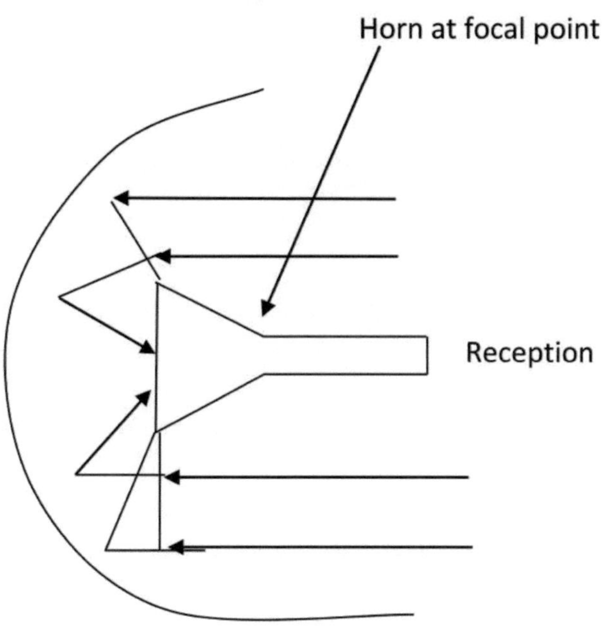

(b) Reception

Figure 6. (a and b) Parabolic reflector antenna used for Transmission and Reception

Where $\varnothing$ v = Vertical beam width in degrees
$\varnothing$ h = Horizontal beam width in degrees
b = Narrow dimension of the flared flange
a = Wide dimension of the flared flange
λ = Wave-length

2.2. Cassegrain feed system

A cassegrain reflector system is shown below

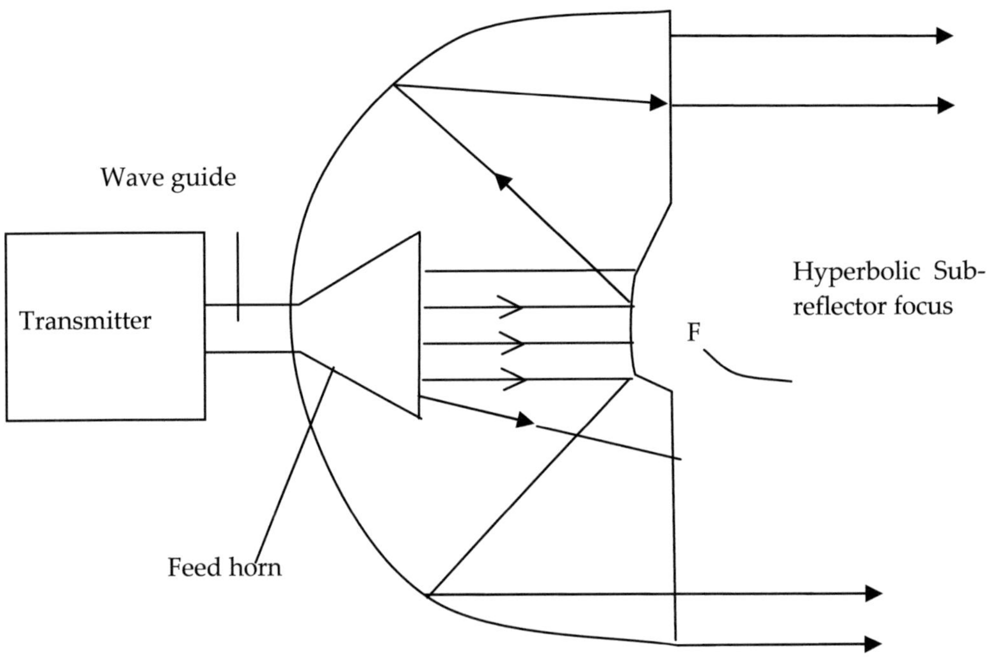

Figure 7. Cassegrain feed parabolic reflector

It consists of a feed horn, a hyperbolic sub reflector and the main parabolic reflector. Radiation from the feed horn illuminates the sub-reflector, which is placed at the focus of the main reflector. Energy scattered by the sub-reflector illuminates the main reflector and produces the secondary radiation pattern at the distant point. This construction leads to a low noise temperature for the antenna.[1]

2.3. Construction of parabolic reflectors

Parabolic reflectors are usually constructed of metal panels and the surface finish determines the maximum usable frequency. In many radar systems in order to reduce weight and wind loading and so increase mobility the surface consists of wire mesh. The spacing of the wires must be small compared to the wave-length used so as to reflect most of the incident radiation on the wire mesh.

Standard parabolic antennas are usually constructed of aluminum. They are manufactured by pressing a sheet of aluminum around a spinning parabola shaped chuck. The reflector themselves are not frequency dependent, but the higher the frequency, the greater the surface perfection required. In practice, the reflectors are therefore specified per frequency band. This antenna has standard parameters of gain, forward/backward ratio (F/B) ratio, beam width, and return loss (RL) if one wants an improvement in these parameters, certain changes to the antenna need to be made.

3. Antenna properties

The most important properties possessed by many antennas are polarization, radiation pattern. Directivity and power gain, radiation resistance, band width, effective aperture, power transfer and reciprocity.

1. **Polarization:** An electromagnetic wave launched from an antenna, may be vertically or horizontally polarized. The direction of the electric field specifies the polarization of the antenna. If the electric field is parallel to the earth electromagnetic wave is said to be horizontally polarized. If the electric field is perpendicular to the earth, the electromagnetic wave is said to be vertically polarized.

   Antennas that are horizontal to the earth produce horizontal polarization while antennas that are vertical in the earth produce vertical polarization. For optimum transmission and reception both the transmitting and receiving antennas must be of the same polarization.

   Electromagnetic waves are usually vertically polarized though other types of polarization may also be used for specific purposes. Vertical or horizontal polarization is also called linear polarization. Circular polarization refers to a combination of vertical and horizontal polarization.

   In a receiving system, the polarization of the antenna and incoming wave need to be matched for maximum response. If this is not the case there will be some signal loss, known as polarization loss. For example, if there is a vertically polarized wave incident on a horizontally polarized antenna, the induced voltage available across its terminal will be zero. In this case, the antenna is cross polarized with an incident wave. The square of the cosine of the angle between wave polarization and antenna polarization is a measure of the polarization loss. It can be determined by squaring the scalar product of unit vectors representing the two polarizations.[2]

2. **Radiation Pattern (polar pattern):** This is a graphical plot of the field strength radiated by the antenna in different angular directions. The plot may be obtained for the vertical or horizontal polar patterns respectively. A wide variety of polar patterns are possible such as:
   a. The omni-directional pattern in which energy is radiated equally in all directions
   b. The pencil beam pattern in which energy is concentrated mainly in one direction
   c. The multiple beam pattern in which energy is radiated in several adjacent beams.

The same polar patterns apply whether the antenna is transmitting or receiving radiation because of the principle of reciprocity.

3. **Directivity and Gain:** The directivity of an antenna is a measure of the ability to direct RF energy in a limited direction rather than in all (spherical) directions equally. The directivity of an antenna refers to the narrowness of the radiated beam. If the beam is narrow in either the horizontal or vertical plane, the antenna has a high degree of directivity in that plane. The power gain of an antenna increases as the degree of directivity increases because the power is concentrated into a narrow beam. The term gain implies that the antenna creates a higher power when it concentrates the power into a single direction. Directivity gain is the gain calculated assuming a loss less antenna in a preferred direction at maximum radiation.[3] Real antennas have losses and power gain is simply the directivity multiplied by the efficiency of the antenna G = D x Eff

Where G = Power gain
D = Directivity gain
Eff = Antenna efficiency

Power gain is the ratio of the output power of an antenna in a certain direction to that of an isotropic antenna. The gain of an antenna is a power ratio comparison between an isotropic and un-directional radiator. This ratio can be expressed as:

$$AdB = 10log_{10}\frac{P_2}{P_1}$$

Where AdB = Antenna gain in decibels
P_1 = Power of un-directional antenna
P_2 = Power reference antenna

4. **Radiation Resistance:** The radiation resistance is associated with the power radiated by the antenna. It is the portion of an antenna's input impedance that is due to power radiated into space. The power radiated by an antenna is I^2R Watts where I^2 is r.m.s antenna current and R, is a fictitious resistance termed the radiation resistance which is a resistance which if it carries the same terminal current as the antenna on transmission will dissipate the same amount of power as the one radiated. The power radiated by an antenna into space have losses in practical antennas, therefore the efficiency is less than 100%. This efficiency can be defined as $Eff = \frac{P_r}{P_T}$

Where P_r = Radiated power
P_T = Total power supplied to the antenna.
Recall; that $P = I^2R$ we have that $Eff = \frac{I^2R_r}{I^2R_T}$

$$Eff = \frac{R_r}{R_T}$$

Where R_r = Radiation resistance seen at the feed point

5. **Bandwidth:** Many antennas which operate at the higher radio frequencies do so over narrow bandwidths of about 10%, because the antennas are resonant at only a single frequency. In recent years attention has been given to designing wide band-width and frequency independent antennas. Wide bandwidths antennas are required to meet the growing demands of telecommunication today.[4,5]
6. **Effective Aperture:** The power received by an antenna can be associated with a collecting area. Every antenna may be considered to have such a collecting area which is called its effective aperture Ae. If P_d is the power density at the antenna and P_R is the received power available at the antenna terminals then

PR = Pd Ae watts

$$P_R = \frac{P_R}{P_d} m^2$$

It can also be shown that an antenna with power gain G has an effective aperture. Ae at the operating wave-length which is given by:

$$A_e = \frac{GA^2}{4\pi} m^2$$

7. **Power Transfer:** For the maximum transfer of power from a receiving antennal to a receiver, the impedance of the antenna should be matched to the input impedance of the receiver in accordance with the maximum power transfer theorem. The maximum power receiver, is given by:

P_R (max) = $\frac{V^2}{4_m}$ watts

Where V is the induced r.m.s

Voltage in an antenna connected to a receiver and R_i is the input resistance.

8. **Reciprocity:** The properties of a transmitting antenna are very similar to those of a receiving antenna because of the theorem of reciprocity which states that is an e.m.f is applied to the terminals of an antenna A and it produces a current i at the terminals of antenna B, then the same e.m.f applied to the terminals of antenna B, will produce an equal current i at the terminals
9. **side lobes:** Microwave antennas are intended to be directional. The maximum radiation is thus in the direction of propagation. In practice, it is impossible to shape all the energy in this direction. Some of it spills out off the side and back of the antenna. Due to the complex phases set up in an antenna pattern, lobes result. The main lobe is around the center of the antenna. Side lobes of lesser amplitude result around the rest of the antenna. The aim of a directional antenna is to maximize the energy in the main lobe by minimizing the energy in the side lobes. It is important to understand the radiation patterns when panning antennas to make sure that one does not pan the signal onto a side lobe.
10. **Front-to-back ratio:** It is not all energy that is radiated out in the front of the antenna. Some of the energy radiates out of the back lobe. The F/B ratio is defined as the ratio of the gain in

the desired forward direction to the gain in the opposite direction out of the back of the antenna. It is expressed in decibels. It is very important in microwave radio backbone systems to have antennas with a good F/B ratio to enable frequency re-use. Ratios as high as 70 dB may be required. When specifying the F/B ratio of an antenna, a wide angle at the back of the dish should be considered and not just the actual value at 180 degrees.[6]

11. **Beam-width:** The beam-width is an indication of how narrow the main lobe is. The half-power beam-width is the width of the main lobe at half power intensity (that is 2 dB below the bore sight gain): the higher the gain of the antenna, the narrower the beam-width. The reason has to do with the definition of antenna gain. Recall that as the gain is increased in one direction, the side lobes decrease in another. The beam-width of the antenna is usually decreased by increasing the size of the reflector. High-gain antennas not only improve the fade margin of a radio link but also result in reduced interference from signals off bore sight. One just has to be careful with very high gain antennas that the stability of the towers is sufficient to hold the weight of the large diameter antennas. Towers must also be rigid enough to avoid a power fade from tower twist. It is not uncommon to have microwave antennas with beam-width of less than one degree. With high-gain antennas where the beam-width is very narrow, angle-of-arrival fading can occur. This causes flat fading due to antenna discrimination. In practice, this limits the useful antenna gain especially on very high frequency links.

Beam-width refers to the angle of the radiation pattern over which a transmitter's energy is directed or received. The beam-width is measured on the antenna's radiation pattern. Figure 8. shows the horizontal radiation pattern of a typical directional antenna plotted on a polar coordinate graph.

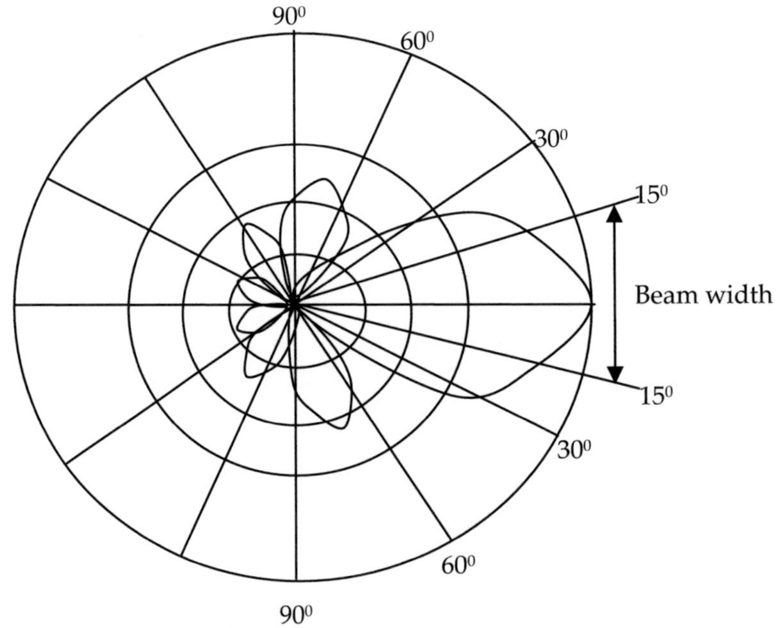

Figure 8. Beam- width

The antenna is assumed to be at the center of the graph. The concentric circles extending outward from the pattern indicate the relative strength of the single as it moves away from the antenna. The beam- width is measured between the points on the radiation curve that are -3dB from the maximum amplitude of the curve.

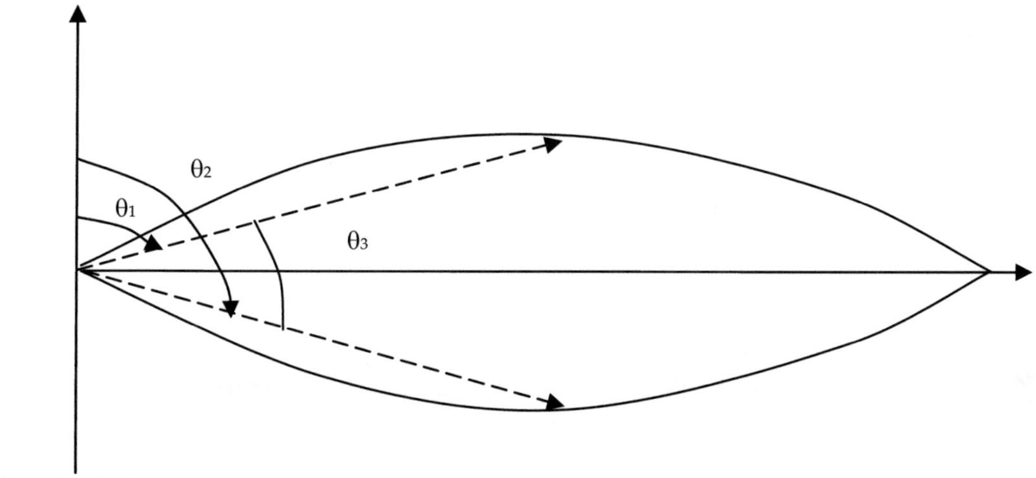

$\theta_3 = \theta_2 - \theta_1$

Figure 9. -3dB Beam-width

The beam-width -3dB is the angle subtended at the center of the polar diagram as shown in Figure 9.

12. Radomes

Special covers for antennas called radomes are available to protect the horn feed and reduce the wind loading the tower. These radomes vary in their construction depending on the type of antenna. For standard parabolic dishes the radomes are usually a conical shape constructed out of fibre glass. The radome must be constructed such that its insertion loss is minimized.

13. Voltage Standing Wave Ratio: An antenna presents a complex impedance to the feeder system which must be attached to it since the feeder system also represents a fixed impedance, there can be an impedance mismatch at the antenna connection. Not all the power is thus radiated out the antenna. Some power is reflected back down the feeder. This mismatch is quantified in terms of the voltage standing wave ratio (VSWR). In a real system there will always be some mismatch at both ends. A standing wave is therefore set up in the cable from the reflected waves that are reflected up and down the cable. The reflected wave sets up a standing wave with voltage minima and maxima every quarter wave-length. The voltage maxima coincide with points where the incident and reflected waves are in phase and the minima where they cancel in phase. The VSWR can thus be expressed as:[6]

$$VSWR = \frac{V_{max}}{V_{min}}$$

The VSWR value will always be greater than unity and the best VSWR is a value that approaches unity. Practically, a good match will result in a value of around 1.2.

A reflection coefficient (p) can be defined that expresses the ratio between the reflected and incident waves.

$$P = (VSWR - 1)/(VSWR + 1)$$

The most convenient way of expressing this mismatch is the return loss (RL), which is the decibel difference between the power incident on the mismatch and the power reflected from the mismatch. The RL in decibels is expressed in terms of reflection coefficient.

$$R_L dB = 20\, log\left(\frac{1}{P}\right)$$

The higher the value of the R_L, the better. Typically, this figure should be better than 20dB for microwave radio systems. To achieve this individual components should exceed 25dB.

4. Measurement of voltage standing wave ratio

The VSWR measurements per distance can be determined with the aid of an Anritsu site master instrument. Before the Anritsu site master is used, it has been calibrated as follows:

i. Turn on the site master by pressing the ON button
ii. Press the FREQ soft key from the main menu
iii. Press F1 Soft key from the main menu
iv. Enter the lower frequency limit in MHz for the antenna system by using the up/down arrow and press ENTER
v. Press the F2 soft key from frequency menu
vi. Enter the higher frequency limit in MHz or GHz for the antenna system by using the UP/down arrow and press ENTER
vii. Check that the FREQ (MHz) scale in the display area indicates the new frequency start and stop values.

The next stage in calibration is to perform the following.

i. Press the start key
ii. Choose calibration type and press ENTER
iii. Follow the instruction on the screen.

After the calibration, connect the site master to the transmission line as shown in Figure 10.

After calibration, the Anritsu site master can now be used for measurement of VSWR. A graph of VSWR versus distance can be plotted using Matlab software program. A VSWR model can be developed using the M-file environment of Matlab Software Program. The data obtained can be curve fitted with polynomial of nth order degree to give a prediction of VSWR per distance on a transmission line. This prediction is necessary for transmission planning purposes.

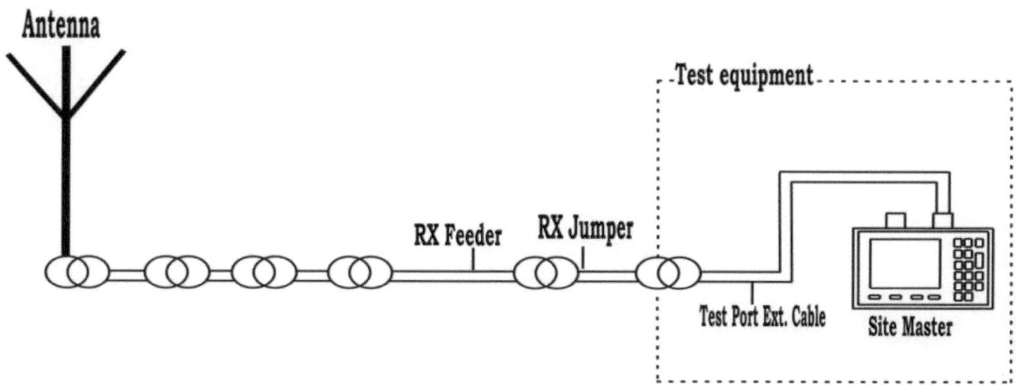

Figure 10. Measurement setup of Anritsu site master instrument

5. Conclusion

This chapter is on microwave antenna performance metrics. It describes vividly the types of two most commonly used microwave antennas. It also describes the properties of the antenna. This chapter will be very useful to microwave engineers and planners as a clear understanding of these properties will help in enhancing microwave antenna performance.

Author details

Paul Osaretin Otasowie
Department of Electrical/Electronic Engineering, University of Benin, Benin City, Nigeria

6. References

[1] Frenzel, L.E. (1996). Communication Electronics Macmillan/McGraw-Hill, New York.
[2] Misra, D.K. Radio frequencies and microwave communication circuits and design (2004). John Wiley and Sons Inc. Publication, New Jersey.
[3] Collin, R.E. Foundations of Microwave Engineering (2001) IEEE Press, U.S.A.

[4] Rappaport, T.S. (2006). Wireless Communication Principles and Practice. Prentice Hall, New Jersey.

[5] Juchen, H.S. (2005). Mobile Communication Addison Wesley Longman Publishing Company Massachusetts, U.S.A.

[6] Manning T.(1999) Microwave Radio Transmission Guide British Library Cataloguing in the Publications data. Uk

Chapter 6

The Data Acquisition in Smart Substation of China

Chen Fan

Additional information is available at the end of the chapter

http://dx.doi.org/10.5772/47853

1. Introduction

The construction of smart grid of China includes six segments which are power generation, transmission, transformation, distribution, utilization and dispatching, substation is one of the important parts belong to the transformation segment.. At present, the substation based on IEC61850 standard in China is called digital substation, new requirements are proposed by the construction of smart grid in China, and the combination resulted in the generation of smart substation. The smart substation is the use of advanced, reliable, integrated, low-carbon, environmentally friendly intelligent devices. Digital of all station information, network of communication platform and standardization of sharing information are the basic requirements to realize the automation of data acquisition, measurement, control, protection, metering, monitoring and other basic functions. The smart substation also supports the real-time automatic control, standardization, analytical decision-making online, collaborative interaction and other advanced functions·

The construction of secure and reliable smart substation is critical to the development of smart grid, the "Technical Guide for smart substation" is published by State Gird Corporation of China to guide the construction of smart substation in December, 2009. The data acquisition in electric power system is very important and includes a lot of areas such as substation. Smart substation is one of the key parts of smart grid and the network of process layer is an important foundation for smart substation which is related to the reliability and real-time of data acquisition and switch control. The type of message of process layer which include GOOSE (General Object-Oriented Substation Event), MSV (Multiple Sample Value) and synchronization with network will be the content of data acquisition in this chapter.

As the trend of development about the power system is along the large capacity, high voltage, extra-high voltage and the same about the device is along the small, smart and high-reliability, the electric transformer is widely used for its many advantages such as small size, light weight, good capability of anti-electromagnetic, wide dynamic range which is not easy to saturation, simple insulation structure and easy to the transmission of digital signal, etc. The merging unit is connected with the electric transformer and is used to transmit the sample value to the Intelligent Electronic Device(IED).It is not only useful to simplify the design and reduce the cable and area of substation but also can promote the development of digital substation and provide strong support to the construction of smart grid. With the construction of smart substation, the requirements about the merging unit are increased and the urgent need to develop a new type merging unit to meet the requirements of the smart substation is generated.

In the early period of the use of the electric transformer, the merging unit is mainly based on the standard IEC60044-7/8 and IEC61850-9-1(shortened as 9-1).In the digital substation stage, the 9-1 is widely used as it is easy to achieve, but it is conflict with the concept of IEC 61850 standard and has been abolished. Subsequently, the standard IEC61850-9-2(shortened as 9-2) has become the only standard of data acquisition. As this standard is based on model and multicast services, the requirements of the performance is greatly improved and is bound to involve the re-development of the product rather than a simple upgrade. At the same time, this standard also requires that the manufacture should have a more in-depth understanding about the IEC61850 standard. The two aspects resulted in that the merging unit based on 9-2 is few.

As the planning of smart grid released by the State Grid Corporation of China in 2009, the smart substation which is one of the important nodes of smart grid present new requirements about the data acquisition, especially the publication of Technical Specifications of Protection for Smart Substation by the State Grid Corporation of China. The data acquisition of relay protection based on the 9-2 process bus is cautious in this specification and it specify that the data acquisition of relay protection should use the direct connection way which is also called peer to peer based on the standard IEC60044-8.This present the new requirements of the merging unit, not only the transfer protocol is extended, but also the number of net port which is used to transmit sampling value has been greatly increased.

As the traditional way of cable connection is canceled by the digital sampling of smart substation. The function of bus voltage parallel and switching falls on the merging unit. This promotes a higher demand about the merging unit. As the realization of bus voltage parallel and switching needs the state information of bus circuit breaker and switcher, this requires that the merging unit should get the status information. In addition, the function of data cascade is proposed by the smart substation which is used to receive the sampling value of other interval and integrated with itself. The series of new requirements call for the development of a new type of merging unit with multifunction to meet the construction of smart substation.

2. The data acquisition

2.1. The data acquisition of merging unit

The most important data acquisition in substation is the sampling of the voltage and current which is realized through the merging unit. As the new requirements about the merging unit, the sampling mode, protocol and design of the device are discussed.

2.1.1. *The sampling model*

The standard of IEC61850 is used to guide the construction of substation. The model is used to realize the information normative. IEC61850-9-1 is firstly used in substation but has been abolished by the IEC because it does not fit the requirement of model of the IEC61850 standard, but in the early period of the application of the IEC61850, this way is easy to realize.

As the IEC61850-9-2 has been used, the model about the data acquisition is applied in the substation. Fig.1 is the data model of data acquisition device which called merging unit. In the device, there are a LPHD(Logical Physical Device), a LLN0(Logical Node 0) and some other voltage logical node TVTR and current logical node TCTR. In theory, the number of TVTR and TCTR logical is not limited and can add for real demand but this is not convenient in the project, so the IEC publish the IEC61850-9-2LE which is used to guide the application of IEC61850-9-2 to give some guide in the project. The obvious character is that the voltage and current logical node TVTR and TCTR is fixed which are both four as the fig.1. This model is based on IEC61850-9-2 which can realize the share of the data acquisition.

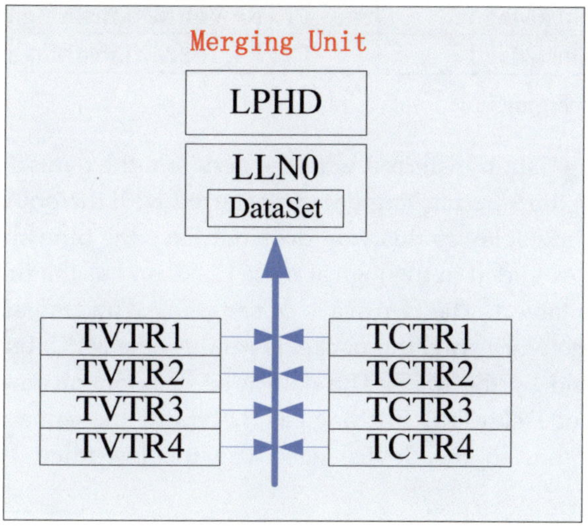

Figure 1. The structure of data model of merging unit

As the relay protect device in the smart substation of China is prudent to the sampling data getting from the network, the several segments of the communication add the risk to the relay protect device, so the new type model which called the extended IEC60044-8 standard is published by the state grid corporation of China to meet the sampling requirements of the relay protect device.

The extended IEC60044-8 standard still use the model of IEC61850-9-2, but add some new data attributes. In logical node LLN0, the logical device name(LDName) and nominal delay(DealyTRtg) is extended which used to meet the relay protect device and this way is called point-to-point.

The difference of configuration between 9-2 and IEC60044-8 is the configuration of dataset. The dataset in 9-2 not only includes the voltage and current , but also has the nominal time delay(DealyTRtg).In IEC60044-8 extend protocol, the header of packet include the nominal time delay(DealyTRtg) ,so it do not have to define it in the dataset. But the data attribute that logical device name(LDName) should be configured according the needs of project. So, the attribute LDName is expanded in the LLN0 to meet the actual demand and the value is 16-bit unsigned integer according to IEC60044-8.

The dataset of 9-2	The dataset of IEC60044-8
LLN0.DelayTRtg.instMag.i	None
TCTR1.Amp[MX].instMag.i	TCTR1.Amp[MX].instMag.i
TCTR2.Amp[MX].instMag.i	TCTR2.Amp[MX].instMag.i
TCTR3.Amp[MX].instMag.i	TCTR3.Amp[MX].instMag.i
TCTR4.Amp[MX].instMag.i	TCTR4.Amp[MX].instMag.i
TVTR1.Vol[MX].instMag.i	TVTR1.Vol[MX].instMag.i
TVTR2.Vol[MX].instMag.i	TVTR2.Vol[MX].instMag.i
TVTR3.Vol[MX].instMag.i	TVTR3.Vol[MX].instMag.i
TVTR4.Vol[MX].instMag.i	TVTR4.Vol[MX].instMag.i

Table 1. The dataset of merging unit

When the 9-2 sampling data transferred with the network, the dataset contains only voltage and current, But when the 9-2 sampling data transferred with the point to point way, it need contain the nominal time delay as this way does not have the time synchronization. So, the nominal time delay is extended in the logical node LLN0 and as the first data attribute in the dataset, as showed in table.1. The two ways of sampling data transmission are depend on the different chip, in network way, the packet is send by the MPC, but in the point-to-point way, the packet is send by the MCF. The data type of nominal time delay is SAV which meant that the type of DelayTRtg.instMag.i is 32-bit.But the same data transferred with IEC60044-8 is just 16-bit, so the device need use the low-rated 16-bit of the value of DelayTRtg.

Although the configuration of model is not real used while use the IEC60044-8 protocol to transfer sampling data to relay protection device through the point to point way, as it does not has the sample control block, but we can get the order of the sampling data through the model.

2.1.2. The transfer protocol

2.1.2.1. IEC61850-9-2

IEC61850-9-2 is the only protocol used in substation to realize the sampling data transfer. The table 2 is the control block which is part of the message.

The MsvCB is used to realized the sampling message control. But the message is as fig.2.

Element Name	MMS Type
MsvCBNam	ObjectName
MsvCBRef	ObjectRefrence
SvEna	Boolean
MsvID	Visible-string
DataSet	Object-Reference
ConfRev	Interger
SmpRate	Interger
OptFlds	
refresh-time	Boolean
sample-synchronized	Boolean
sample-rate	Boolean
Sample[1……n]	Struct

Table 2. The structure of MsvCB

1. The header MAC

   The destination address is defined in the standard of IEC61850-9-2 which is ranged from 01-0C-CD-04-00-00 to 01-0C-CD-04-01-FF.

   The source address is the MAC of the sending device.

2. Priority tagged

TPID (Tag Protocol Identifier) Field: Indicates the Ethernet Type assigned for 802.1Q Ethernet encoded frames. This value should be 0x8100.

TCI (Tag Control Information) Fields:

User Priority: BS3; User priority value shall be set by configuration to separate sampled values from low priority busload. If the priority is not configured then the default values of Table 7 shall be used.

CFI (Canonical Format Indicator): BS1 [0]; A single bit flag value. For this standard the CGI bit value shall be reset(value = 0).

VID: Virtual LAN support is optional. If this mechanism will be used, the VLAN Identifier (VID) shall be set by configuration, if it is not used, it shall be set to zero (0).

3. Ethernet-PDU

Ethernet Type: In this standard, the sampling type is defined 0x88BA.

APPID: application identifier. The APPID is used to select ISO/IEC 8802-3 frames containing sampled value messages and to distinguish the application association.The value of APPID is the combination of the APPID type, defined as the two most significant bits of the value (as defined in Table 8), and the actual ID. The reserved value range for sampled values is 0x4000 to 0x7FFF. If no APPID is configured, the default value shall be 0x4000. The default

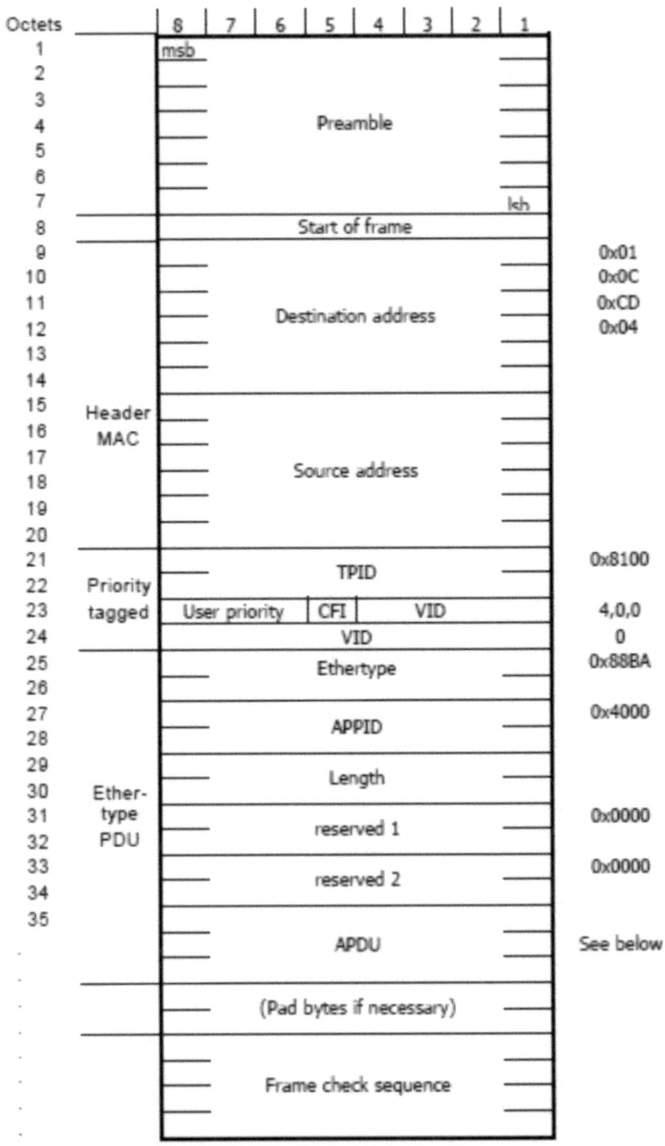

Figure 2. ISO/IEC 8802-3 frame format

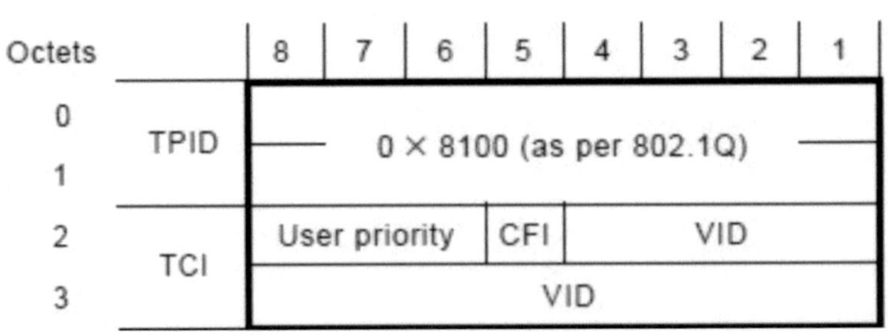

Figure 3. The structure of tag header

value is reserved to indicate lack of configuration. It is strongly recommended to have unique, source orientated SV APPID within a system, in order to enable a filter on link layer. The configuration of APPID should be enforced by the configuration system.

Length: Number of octets including the Ethertype PDU header starting at APPID, and the length of the APDU(Application Protocol Data Unit). Therefore, the value of Length shall be 8 + m, where m is the length of the APDU and m is less than 1492. Frames with inconsistent or invalid length field shall be discarded.

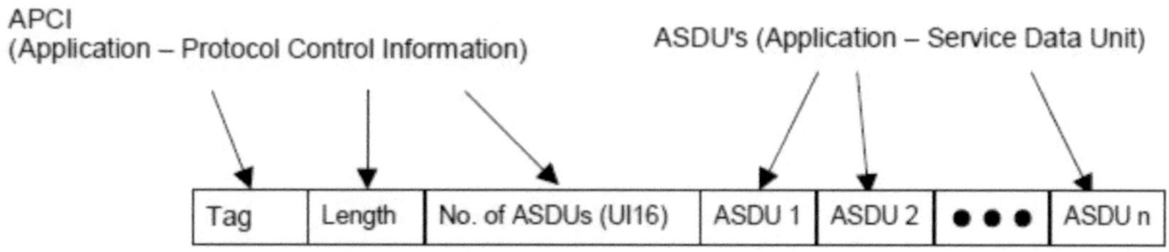

Figure 4. The structure of APDU.

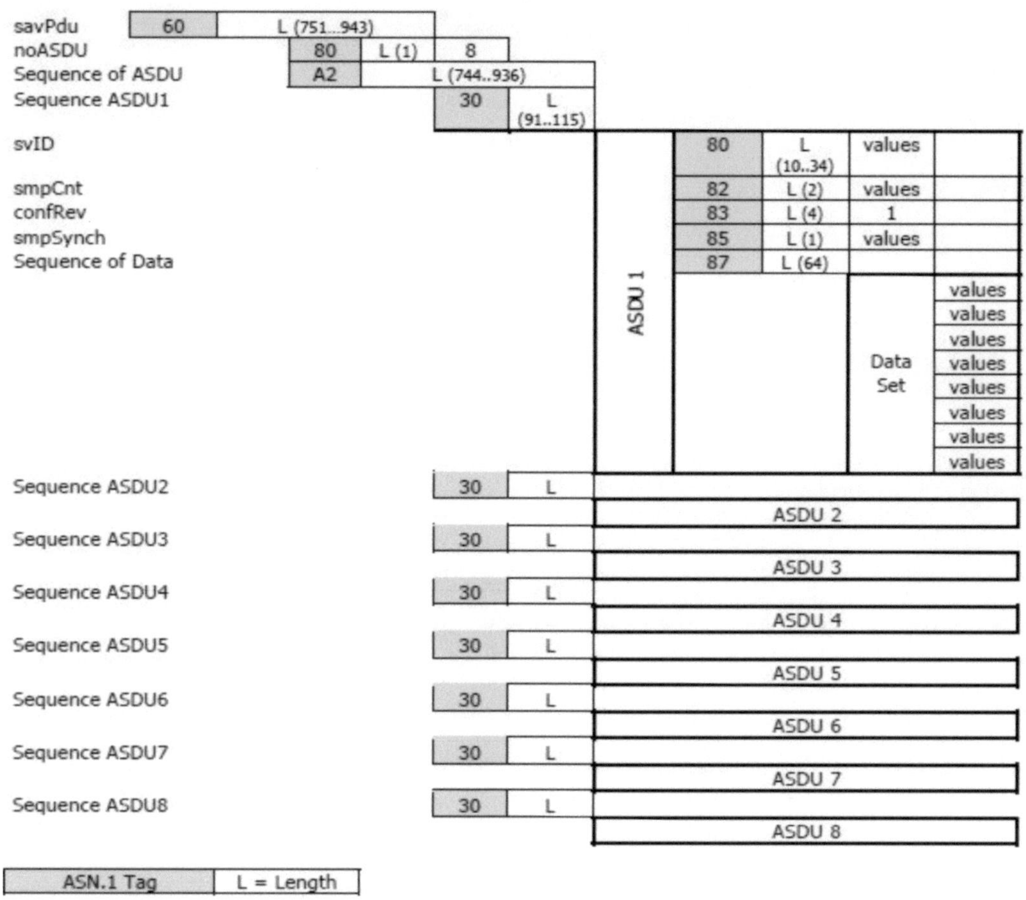

Figure 5. ASN.1 coded APDU frame structure

Reserved 1 and **Reserved 2**: This is used to extend in future, and now the value are 0x0000;

APDU: The structure is as fig.4, it can contain several ASDU.

As in fig.5, the APDU contain eight ASDU and the structure of every ASDU is the same. Every value will be coded with ASN.1 which is TLV type(Tag+Length+value).

In the figure above, the sample data is contained in the DataSet, the value can be struct or single. In Table 2-1, the model of sampling is only single value, the quality and time of the data can be send with the data. In real project, the value and quality are usually configured in the model , the time is not configured as all the time of the data in the same ASDU is same and can be get from the Frame. The fig.6 shows the parameter of quality.

```
.... .... .... ..00 = validity: good (0)
.... .... .... .0.. = overflow: Not Set
.... .... .... 0... = outOfRange: Not Set
.... .... ...0 .... = badReference: Not Set
.... .... ..0. .... = oscillatory: Not Set
.... .... .0.. .... = failure: Not Set
.... .... 0... .... = oldData: Not Set
.... ...0 .... .... = inconsistent: Not Set
.... ..0. .... .... = inaccurate: Not Set
.... .0.. .... .... = source: process
.... 0... .... .... = test: False
...0 .... .... .... = operatorBlocked: False
..1. .... .... .... = derived: True
```

Figure 6. The parameter of Quality

The quality of the sampling value is bit-string, in 9-2 there are only 13 bit, but in 9-2LE which is used to guide the application of 9-2 and published by IEC, one bit is added which is called derived. This bit used to show whether the data is original value or calculated value.

2.1.2.2. IEC60044-8

The IEC60044-8 is the standard for ECT/EVT to send the sampling value. In the smart substation of China, this standard is extended to meet the relay protection as the State dispatch center of China is prudent about the sampling through the network.

The extended frame of IEC60044-8 is consist of four data module and the length of every module is 16.The structure of the frame is as fig.7:

		2^7	2^6	2^5	2^4	2^3	2^2	2^1	2^0
字节 1	前导	msb	数据集长度（= 62 十进制）						
字节 2									lsb
字节 3	数据集	msb	LNName（=02）						lsb
字节 4		msb	DataSetName						lsb
字节 5		msb	LDName						
字节 6									lsb
字节 7		msb	额定相电流（PhsA.Artg）						
字节 8									lsb
字节 9		msb	额定中性点电流（Neut.Artg）						
字节 10									lsb
字节 11		msb	额定相电压（PhsA.Vrtg）						
字节 12									lsb
字节 13		msb	额定延迟时间（t_{dr}）						
字节 14									lsb
字节 15		msb	SmpCnt（样本计数器）						
字节 16									lsb

Data Module 1

字节 1	数据集	msb	DataChannel #1	
字节 2				lsb
字节 3		msb	DataChannel #2	
字节 4				lsb
字节 5		msb	DataChannel #3	
字节 6				lsb
字节 7		msb	DataChannel #4	
字节 8				lsb
字节 9		msb	DataChannel #5	
字节 10				lsb
字节 11		msb	DataChannel #6	
字节 12				lsb
字节 13		msb	DataChannel #7	
字节 14				lsb
字节 15		msb	DataChannel #8	
字节 16				lsb

Data Module 2

字节 1	数据集	msb	DataChannel #9	
字节 2				lsb
字节 3		msb	DataChannel #10	
字节 4				lsb
字节 5		msb	DataChannel #11	
字节 6				lsb
字节 7		msb	DataChannel #12	
字节 8				lsb
字节 9		msb	DataChannel #13	
字节 10				lsb
字节 11		msb	DataChannel #14	
字节 12				lsb
字节 13		msb	DataChannel #15	
字节 14				lsb
字节 15		msb	DataChannel #16	
字节 16				lsb

Data Module 3

字节 1	数据集	msb	DataChannel #17	
字节 2				lsb
字节 3		msb	DataChannel #18	
字节 4				lsb
字节 5		msb	DataChannel #19	
字节 6				lsb
字节 7		msb	DataChannel #20	
字节 8				lsb
字节 9		msb	DataChannel #21	
字节 10				lsb
字节 11		msb	DataChannel #22	
字节 12				lsb
字节 13		msb	StatusWord #1	
字节 14				lsb
字节 15		msb	StatusWord #2	
字节 16				lsb

Data Module 4

Figure 7. The frame of the extended IEC60044-8

In fig.7:

Length: The value is type of unsigned short and it is 62.

DataSetName: This type is ENUM8, The value is 1 or 0xFE.If the data channel is standard, the value is 1, else the value is 0xFE.

LDName: This type is unsigned short and the value is configured in the real project.

Nominal Phase Current(PhsA.Artg): The type is unsigned short.

Nominal Neutral Current(Neut.Artg): The type is unsigned short.

Nominal phase voltage and neutral voltage(PhsA.Vrtg): The nominal voltage is multiply with $1/(10 * \sqrt{3})$ kV, the nominal phase voltage and neutral voltage is multiply with $10\sqrt{3}$.

Nominal Delay(tdr): The type is unsigned short, the unit is us.

Sample Counter(SmpCtr): The type is unsigned short, The value will became zero(0) when receive the synchronization pulse, The value will invent if there is not synchronization. For example, if the sample rate is 4k/s, the range of SmpCtr is 0-3999

DataChanne#1 to DataChannel#22 : The type is short and the scale factor is different.

The scale factor of the phase current for relay protection is SCP, the scale factor of the neutral current is SCP, The scale factor of the measure current is SCM.The scale factor of the voltage is SV. The detail is as table 3:

	ECT for Measure (scale factor SCM)	ECT for protection (scale factor SCP)	EVT (scale factor SV)
nominal value(range-flag =0)	0x2D41H(11585)	0x01CFH(463)	0x2D41H(11585)
nominal value range mark (range-flag =1)	0x2D41H(11585)	0x00E7H(231)	0x2D41H(11585)
Reference:The ECT for protection should measure 50 multiple nominal current(0% offset)or 25 multiple nominal current(100% offset). The ECT and EVT should measure 2 multiple nominal value.			

Table 3. The scale factor and the nominal value

The status word#1 and status word#2 are used to show the status of every sampling channel, the detail is as table 4 and table 5

The two tables above show the status information from which we can know the status of every data channel.

2.1.3. The design of the merging unit

Considering the many requirements of smart substation about the multifunction merging unit, the mode that PowerPC+FPGA+MCF is designed as hardware architecture of the CPU board of the device.

Declaration			Comment
Bit 0	LPHD.PHHealth	0:goose; 1:warm	
Bit 1	LLN0.Mode	0:normal; 1:Test	
Bit 2	wake-up time indicatior	0:normal; 1: invalid	Should be set during the wake-up time
Bit 3	The synchronization way of merging unit	0:no interpolation 1: interpolation	
Bit 4	The different merging unit of synchronization	0:samle synchronization 1:invalid	
Bit 5	DataChannel#1	0:valid; 1:invalid	
Bit 6	DataChannel#2	0:valid; 1:invalid	
Bit 7	DataChannel#3	0:valid; 1:invalid	
Bit 8	DataChannel#4	0:valid; 1:invalid	
Bit 9	DataChannel#5	0:valid; 1:invalid	
Bit 10	DataChannel#6	0:valid; 1:invalid	
Bit 11	DataChannel#7	0:valid; 1:invalid	
Bit 12	The output type of ECT	0:i(t); 1: d(i(t)/dt)	
Bit 13	RangeFlag	0:SCP=0x01CFH; 1:SCP=0x00E7H	
Bit 14	for future		
Bit 15	for future		

Table 4. The statue word#1

Declaration			Comment
Bit 0	DataChannel#8	0:valid; 1:invalid	
Bit 1	DataChannel#9	0:valid; 1:invalid	
Bit 2	DataChannel#10	0:valid; 1:invalid	Should be set during the wake-up time
Bit 3	DataChannel#11	0:valid; 1:invalid	
Bit 4	DataChannel#12	0:valid; 1:invalid	
Bit 5	DataChannel#13	0:valid; 1:invalid	
Bit 6	DataChannel#14	0:valid; 1:invalid	
Bit 7	DataChannel#15	0:valid; 1:invalid	
Bit 8	DataChannel#16	0:valid; 1:invalid	
Bit 9	DataChannel#17	0:valid; 1:invalid	
Bit 10	DataChannel#18	0:valid; 1:invalid	
Bit 11	DataChannel#19	0:valid; 1:invalid	
Bit 12	DataChannel#20	0:valid; 1:invalid	
Bit 13	DataChannel#21	0:valid; 1:invalid	
Bit 14	DataChannel#21	0:valid; 1:invalid	
Bit 15	for future		

Table 5. The statue word#2

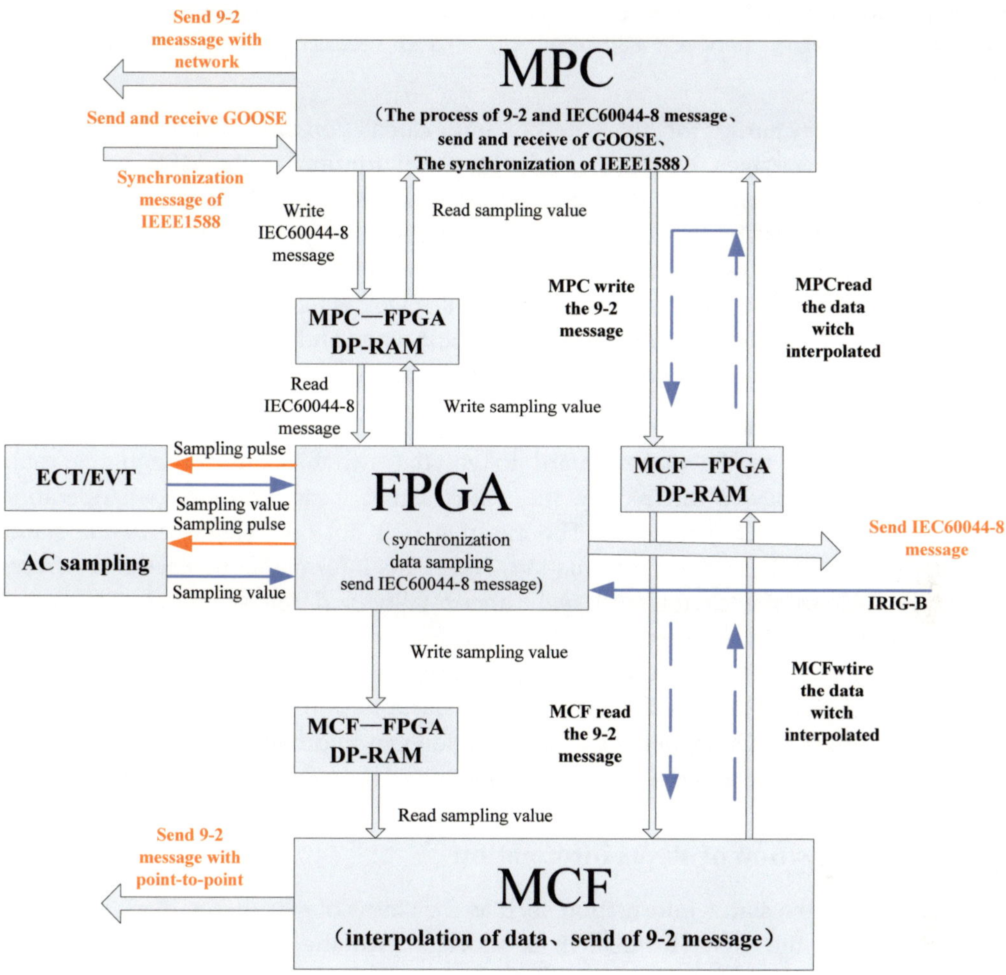

Figure 8. The hardware structure of the merging unit

The PowerPC is used to parse the model and realize the data processing which include that send the multicast sampling value packets, send and receive GOOSE message. The Freescale's MPC8313E chip which runs up to 333MHZ speed and 700MIPS performance is selected as the CPU chip. The most important factor is that this chip supports the synchronization of IEEE1588 and Gigabit Ethernet protocol for communication and these are very fit to the development of device.

The FPGA is used to send synchronous sampling pulse to electronic transformer and receive the data from the electronic transformer. In the signal processing and control system, the FPGA not only reduce the volume of circuit, improve the stability of circuit but also improve the signal process speed because it is based on the hardware circuit and the execution speed is nanosecond. The Spartan-3A devices of Xilinx Company which is based on the 90nm technology is used in FPGA module to realize the precise synchronization and timekeeping of merging unit. It can receive the second pulse of IEEE1588 and output the 5kHz to 10kHz high-speed synchronization sampling pulse and time scale. The time clock error is less than 1us and the time error between sampling pulse and second pulse just a few dozen nanoseconds.

MCF is designed primarily for the interpolation calculation and the point to point transmission of 9-2 messages. As the Vxworks system is running in the MPC, so the time delay of every packet is not fixed. The transmission time delay of 9-2 message through the network can be processed by the recipient, but while using the point to point transmission of 9-2 message, as there is no synchronization of the time, so the nominal transmission time delay should be stable. The time-interval of interrupt of DSP is fixed so it is most suitable to used to send the 9-2 packet through the point-to point way. And therefore, the MCF serial chip is selected under the consideration of performance and price of various chips.

As the merging unit may have the requirements that getting the status information. So the 16 channels are designed in the power board to get the switch status through the cable connection. Also, the device can receive the status signal from the intelligent operating terminal through the GOOSE network. The merging unit not only can receive the status signal, but also can send the alarm information. The status information of electronic current transfer(ECT) such as the circuit fault, A/D abnormality and the sampling data is not continuous can send with the sample data to merging unit, and this is part of the alarm information. Also, the internal fault of merging unit and the error during the data processing make up the other part of alarm information. These alarm information are transferred to the bay device through the GOOSE network. This function can improve the level of the station operation and maintenance and the safety and reliability of the substation effectively.

2.2. The data acquisition of status information

In smart substation, the status information such as the status of switch, the block signal are transferred through the GOOSE. GOOSE is shorted with the Generic Object Oriented Substation Event and is derived from the GSE(Generic Substation Event) which is defined in the standard of IEC61850.It is used to meet the requirements of fast transmission of the substation in IEC61850 and is based on the multicast communication through the Ethernet. In order to ensure the real-time and reliability of the transmission, the packet transmission do not require the receipt confirmation instead of using the order retransmission mechanism, so the performance of the network is critical to the reliability and real-time of GOOSE and has been widely used in substation.

GOOSE is used to trip in the digital substation which is based on IEC61850 standard. This technology and the associated network scheme have been tested in the worst-case condition and the GOOSE message can be able to send in real-time and ensure the reliability of the application of GOOSE in relay protection area. With the further application, the basic principles, the solution about the implementation and network have been researched. The research that the implementation of GOOSE, the structure of network and the double network control strategy are discussed in the reference which provide the technical guidance and promote the widely use of the GOOSE. The enable information of protection function and the change information of the switch position are transferred through GOOSE, then it is used in the block among the bays, even used in the area of bus protection and video monitoring which are all based on Ethernet .

During the construction of digital substation period, the merging unit do not has the function of the acquisition of status signal and the alarm information can not send to the bay device. But during the construction of smart substation, the project propose the requirements that the data acquisition of switch status and the monitoring information about the every section of the sample. At the same time, the merging unit used in smart substation should send the alarm information through the network and GOOSE(General Object-Oriented Substation Event)is used to meet this requirement.

2.2.1. The mechanism of the GOOSE

The generic substation event model provides the possibility for a fast and reliable system-wide distribution of input and output values and is based on the concept of an autonomous decentralization, providing an efficient method allowing the simultaneous delivery of the same generic substation event information to more than one physical device through the use of multicast/broadcast services.

GOOSE supports the exchange of a wide range of possible common data organized by a data-set. The information exchange is based on a publisher/subscriber mechanism. The publisher writes the values into a local buffer at the sending side; the subscriber reads the values from a local buffer at the receiving side. The communication system is responsible to update the local buffers of the subscribers. A generic substation event control class in the publisher is used to control the procedure.

Fig.9 gives an overview of the classes and services of the GOOSE model. The message exchange is based on the multicast application association. If the value of one or several DataAttributes of a specific functional constraint (for example ST) in the data-set changes, the transmission buffer of the publisher is updated with the local service "publish", and all values are transmitted with a GOOSE message. The data-set may have several members (numbered from 1 up – the numbers shall be called MemberOffset). Each member shall have a MemberReference referencing the DataAttribute with a specific functional constraint (FC). Mapping specific services of the communication network will update the content of the buffer in the subscribers. New values received in the reception buffer are signaled to the application.

The GOOSE messages contain information that allow the receiving device to know that a status has changed and the time of the last status change. The time of the last status change allows a receiving device to set local timers relating to a given event.

A newly activated device, upon power-up or reinstatement to service, shall send the current value of a data object (status) or values as the initial GOOSE message. Moreover, all devices sending GOOSE messages shall continue to send the message with a long cycle time, even if no status/value change has occurred. This ensures that devices that have been activated recently will know the current status values of their peer devices.

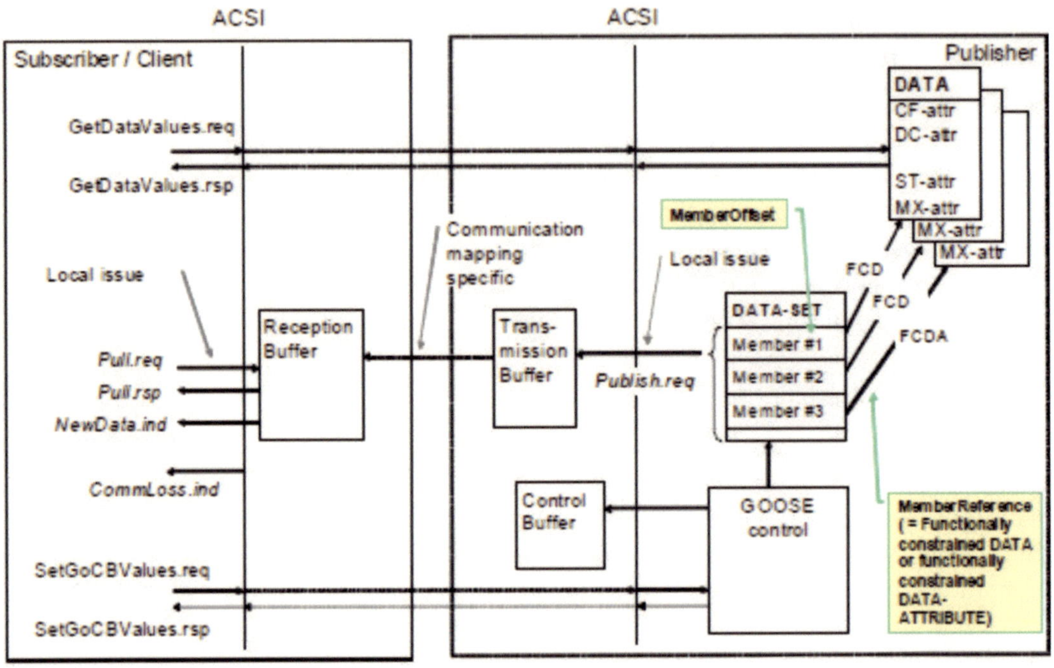

Figure 9. The model of GoCB

GoCB class			
Attribute name	**Attribute type**	**r/w**	**Value/value range/explanation**
GoCBName	ObjectName		Instance name of an instance of GoCB
GoCBRef	ObjectReference		Path-name of an instance of GoCB
GoEna	BOOLEAN	r/w	Enabled (TRUE) | disabled (FALSE)
GoID	VISIBLE STRING129	r/w	Attribute that allows a user to assign an identification for the GOOSE message
DatSet	ObjectReference	r/w	
ConfRev	INT32U	r	
NdsCom	BOOLEAN	r	
DstAddress	PHYCOMADDR	r	
Services SendGOOSEMessage GetGoReference GetGOOSEElementNumber GetGoCBValues SetGoCBValues			

Table 6. The GOOSE control block class definition

The table 6 shows the GOOSE control block which is the content of the GOOSE message. In order to make sure the GOOSE message can be transferred in real time, a special mechanism is defined. Fig.10 is the message of GOOSE captured in the project. We can be easy to understand the structure of the message of GOOSE.

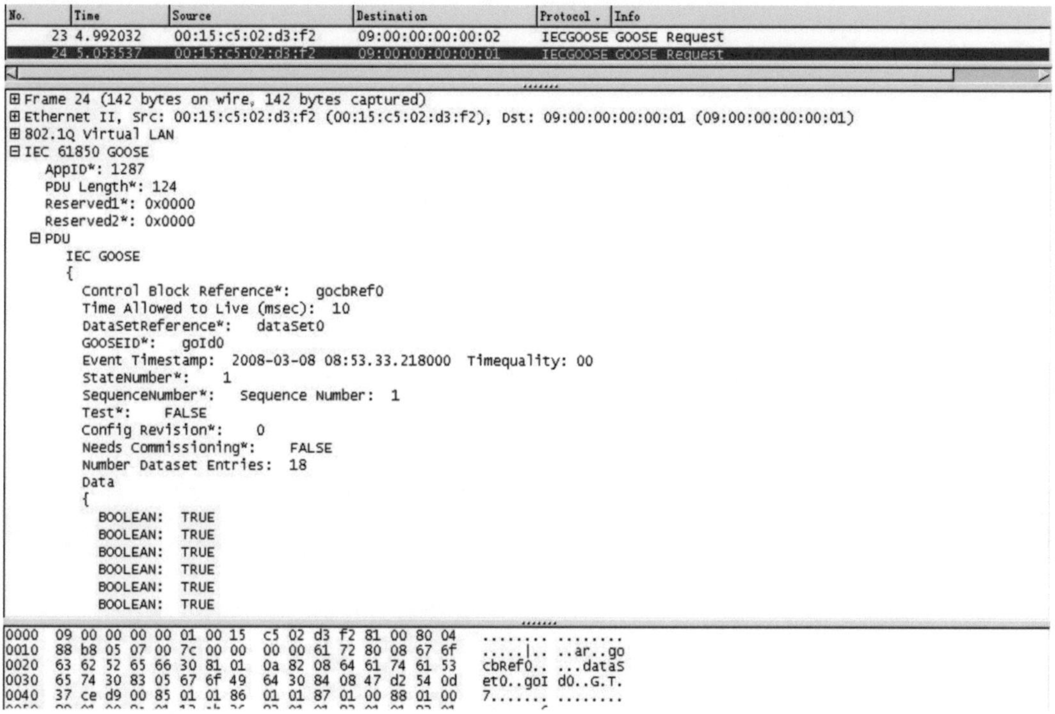

Figure 10. The message of GOOSE

2.2.2. *The configuration of GOOSE*

The key part of the application of GOOSE is the configuration which called the configuration of virtual terminal. As the GOOSE is the publish/subscribe model, so the message of the send is easier to realize. The different dataset should configure different GOOSE control block. But the subscriber should configure the terminal according the requirements. The sending data will be connected with the receiving data.

Fig.11 is one the project configuration view. The key part of configuration is the connection of virtual terminal. As the sender which is caller publisher does not know the requirements of receiver which is called subscriber, so the configuration is finished by the receiver. The receiver get the dataset which the publisher will send can choose the values needed and connect with the internal data. The fig.12 is the virtual connection of GOOSE . ExRef show that the data attribute which including iedName, ldInst, prefix, lnClass, lnInst, doName, daName come from the external device . The intAddr show that the value is internal of the receiver. The data attribute show be match and then the virtual terminal configuration is finished.

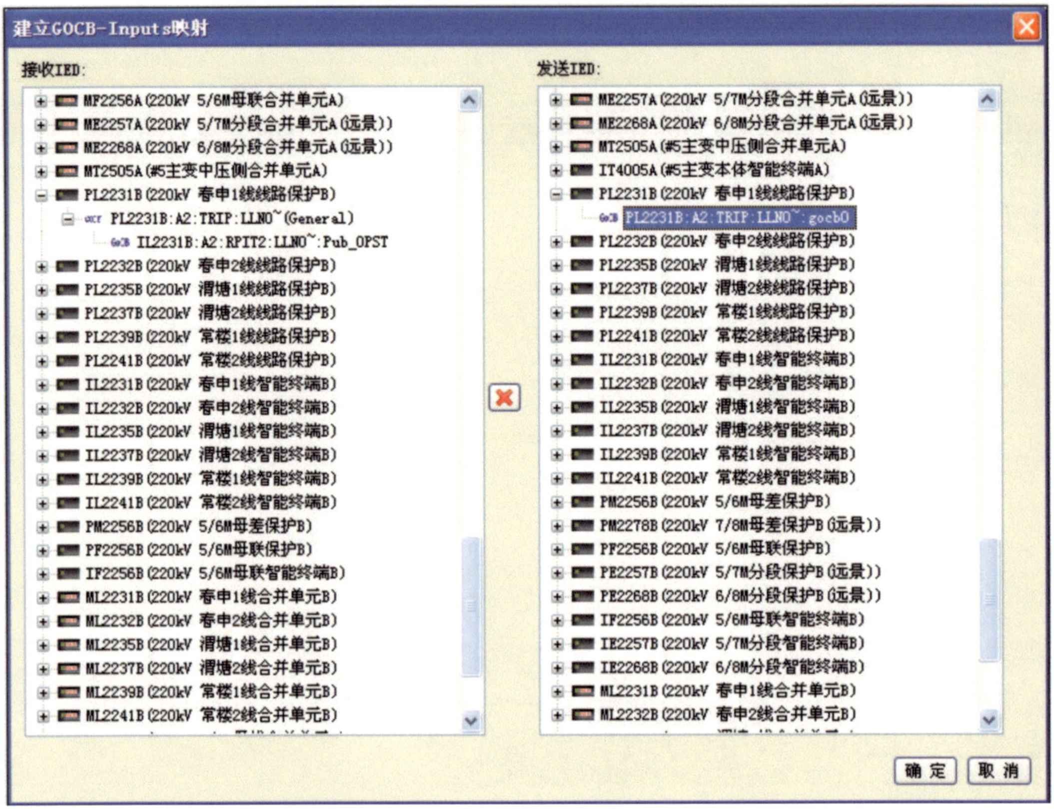

Figure 11. The configuration of the GOOSE

<ExtRef iedName="IT22097" ldInst="PI" prefix="GOOUT" lnClass="GGIO" lnInst="1" doName="Ind1" daName="stVal" ntAddr="GO/GOINGGIO0.Ind10.stVal" />.
<ExtRef iedName="IT22097" ldInst="PI" prefix="GOOUT" lnClass="GGIO" lnInst="1" doName="Ind2" daName="stVal" intAddr="GO/GOINGGIO0.Ind11.stVal" />.
<ExtRef iedName="IT22097" ldInst="PI" prefix="GOOUT" lnClass="GGIO" lnInst="1" doName="Ind3" daName="stVal" intAddr="GO/GOINGGIO0.Ind12.stVal" />.
<ExtRef iedName="IT22097" ldInst="PI" prefix="GOOUT" lnClass="GGIO" lnInst="1" doName="Ind4" daName="stVal" intAddr="GO/GOINGGIO0.Ind13.stVal" />.
<ExtRef iedName="IT22097" ldInst="PI" prefix="GOOUT" lnClass="GGIO" lnInst="1" doName="Ind5" daName="stVal" intAddr="GO/GOINGGIO0.Ind14.stVal" />.
<ExtRef iedName="IT22097" ldInst="PI" prefix="GOOUT" lnClass="GGIO" lnInst="1" doName="Ind6" daName="stVal" intAddr="GO/GOINGGIO0.Ind15.stVal" />.
<ExtRef iedName="IT22097" ldInst="PI" prefix="GOOUT" lnClass="GGIO" lnInst="1" doName="Ind7" daName="stVal" intAddr="GO/GOINGGIO0.Ind16.stVal" />.
<ExtRef iedName="IT22097" ldInst="PI" prefix="GOOUT" lnClass="GGIO" lnInst="1" doName="Ind8" daName="stVal" intAddr="GO/GOINGGIO0.Ind17.stVal" />.

Figure 12. The virtual connection of GOOSE

2.2.3. The application of GOOSE in relay protection

GOOSE can be used in all areas of substation in theory and is widely used through the network. But in the smart substation, the situation has changed, especially for the relay protection. Considering the special nature of the protection device, all protection devices are required to trip directly not with the network is defined in the "Technical specifications of relaying protection for Smart Substation". This can improve the performance of security and reliability but brought some new problems such as the increase of net port and the configuration of port which take the change about the application of GOOSE in smart substation.

2.2.3.1. The sending port of GOOSE

In the period of digital substation, the sending and receiving of GOOSE is realized through the network and the redundancy mode of double-network is widely used and there are only two network ports in maximum. The realization of the GOOSE is different from the different manufacturers. The sending port of GOOSE is fixed in some manufactures and the sending port can be configured according the requirement in other manufactures which mean that the mode of single network or double network is can be selected.

The requirements of the point-to-point way of the smart substation mean that the same protection device need to have more Ethernet port to trip. The direct connection mode generates the new problems, because there are many net ports, the ports witch the same GOOSE message will send must be configured with a flexible way to meet the complex engineering requirements. Take the smart terminal for example, this device may receive the trip command from several protection and send the status information of switch change to many protection devices. If the same message can be send from the multiple ports will be a good solution of the problem, the configuration of the net port can realize this function. Also, there is another way that does not need to support the configuration of the net port can solute the problem just through the creation of several datasets with the same data attributes. This way can meet the actual needs but have to increase the overhead of the device the workload of configuration. At the same time, the configuration of the net port is equipped with the hardware and do not impact the performance of the device, so it can improve the efficiency and flexibility of debugging and reduce the workload of the engineering application.

2.2.3.2. The receiving port of GOOSE

The receiving ports of the GOOSE messages are fixed in the mode of single network or double network. As the receiving port is limited and the receiving GOOSE messages have many types, the upper application program will extract the GOOSE message from the different net port. The content parsed from the message will be compared with the configuration of GoCB such as the APPID(Application Idenfication), Control Block Reference, DataSet Reference, GOOSE ID, only all the content are matched then the data from the message will be assigned to the associated data of the device. This way that compare the data attribute one by one will reduce the overall efficiency of the device, especially when the device have many number of GoCBs .

The receiving device has a lot of port in the direct connected mode of the smart substation. The port which the different packets will enter is uncertain. If the port is fixed, once the port is in trouble the device cannot receive the GOOSE message and must replace the board of the device and can not meet the actual needs of the project. If the port is optional, the device will extract the message and compare the content with configuration of every port which can avoid the compare with all the GoCB and save the overhead and improve the efficiency of the device.

2.2.3.3. The alarm about the GOOSE network

As the mechanism of GOOSE is based on the retransmission without the feedback through the network, the interruption of the network is detected by the receiving device. The alarm signal of the interruption will be generated by the receiving device when it can not receive the packet of GOOSE in twice the timetolive time. A device can receive many different GOOSE packets from one device or several other devices and the receiving port is the same. If one of the GoCB report the alarm of interruption while others not, the port is normal which can be sure, otherwise, the other GoCB will send the alarm of interruption also. So, the alarm of the interruption is identified with the GoCB in the network mode. Such as the fig.13, as the receiving port is fixed, the six GoCBs of the receiving device is matched with the external six GoCBs of different device according the configuration and can be adjusted also. So, once the alarm of interruption about GOOSE is generated, the GoCB should be identified with the configuration.

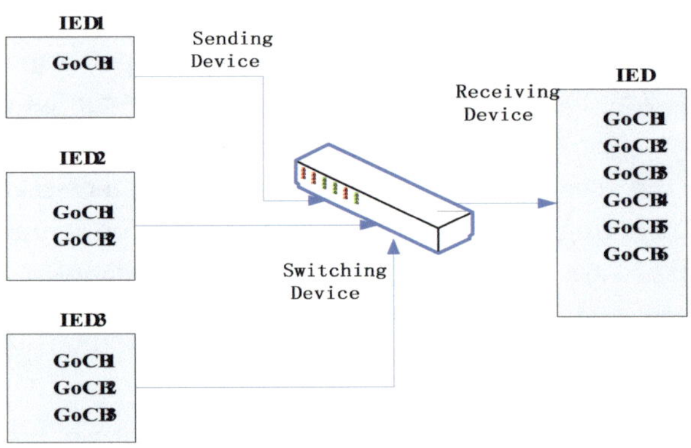

Figure 13. The mode of network about GOOSE interruption alarm.

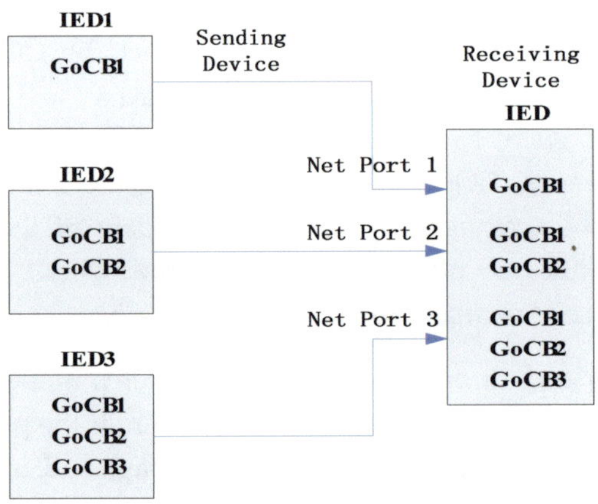

Figure 14. The mode of direct connection about GOOSE interruption alarm.

The principle of the direct connection mode of the smart substation is the same with the network mode, just the detection of the interruption distributed to each port. When the alarm of interruption is generated, the reason may not be the device which including the GoCB but the port of the receiving device, especially the sending device only has one GoCB. In fig.14, the sending devices are connected with the different port of the receiving devices, so there will be limitation if the alarm of interruption about GOOSE is judged with the GoCB, because the receiving port is different. So, when alarm of interruption about the GOOSE is generated, we need to find not only the device and the GoCB, but also the access port, because the abnormal of the port may be the reason of the alarm. So, if the detection of alarm is according to the GoCB is still possible but must based on the normal of the device, if we subdivide the GoCB further that the alarm is depend on the GoCB and the port number, the whole process will be more reasonable and compatible, this way is compatible with the old way which according to GoCB because the port is fixed in the old way. As the direct connection mode, each port is connected with the different device, so the port number is corresponded to the device, the alarm of the interruption become the "[IED name]+[GoCB number]", this alarm information is more detailed and is helpful to find the fault. This new way is corresponded with the configuration of receiving port, if the receiving port can be configured, this new way will be easily realized.

2.2.4. *The analysis of the further application of GOOSE*

As the application of GOOSE in project, the problems are growing generally. The mode of the data processing of the GOOSE , the isolation measures for the maintenance with GOOSE, the configuration and design of the project which have support the guide to the construction. The practical problems are not only these, some other problems about the application of GOOSE are analyzed in this paper.

2.2.4.1. *The define about the connection of virtual terminal*

The mechanism of the GOOSE is publish/subscription. The receiving device should be pre-configuration to realize the internal data associated with the external data. The current series of standards and specifications define how to configure data model and how to regulate the name, but not specific the data association and this will be discussed in this paper.

2.2.4.1.1. *The match of the sending and receiving data*

The data of GOOSE message are just fully meet the requirements of the receiving device which meant that all the data are matched. This mode is widely used in the most of the project and the system integrator need to coordinate the sending device and receiving device, in order to match fully, the workload of configuration of the both are very large, because they need to edit the sending data or receiving data.

2.2.4.1.2. *The mismatch of the sending and receiving data*

As the dataset can be flexibly defined, so the same device may send the GOOSE message to multiple devices. If the requirements of the data are the same, the sending device only needs to define one GoCB to meet the need. However, the project is complex and the requirements of the receiving device are not the same but only small differences in most case.

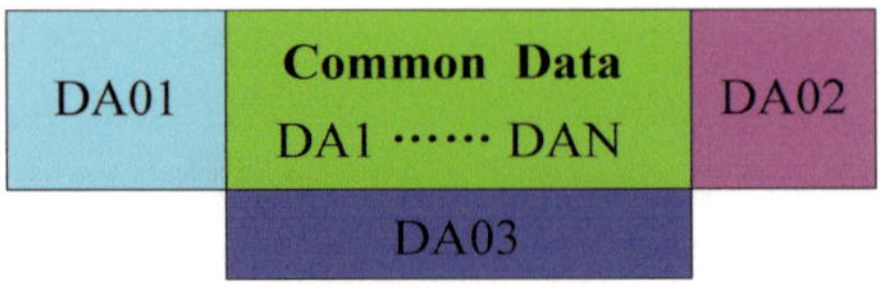

Figure 15. The define of dataset

In fig.15, DA1-DAN are defined as the Common Data,DA01, DA02 and DA03 are different data attribute used to meet the different requirement of different device. There are seven different datasets to meet the different requirements which are DA01+Commondata, DA02 + Common Data, DA03 + Common Data , DA01 + DA02 + Common Data, DA01 + DA03 + Common Data, DA02 + DA03 + Common Data, DA01 + DA02 + DA03 + Common Data and resulting the 7 associated GoCBs. This is not only increase the load of the device, more importantly, it increases the workload of configuration of the field especially in the case of small amount data. So, we suggest that the dataset should be one with DA01+DA02+ DA03+Common Data and the sending device only have one GoCB in case of the difference of data requirements of the device is little, the receiving device only get the needed data to associated with internal data, the small account data can be associated to the data of the device which are not used. This way is the indirect application of the mode of matching discussed above and can meet the requirements of the project and reduce the workload and complexity of configuration.

2.2.4.1.3. Differential receiving

The two modes above are directly or indirectly using the match mode which the sending data just meet the requirements of the receiving device. There is another mode called differential receiving which have more compatibility. In this mode, the sending data do not need to meet the requirements of the receiving device and the receiving device can recognize their own need data from the message of GOOSE according to the configuration of virtual terminal. This mode is more complex but can meet all the requirements of the project flexibly.

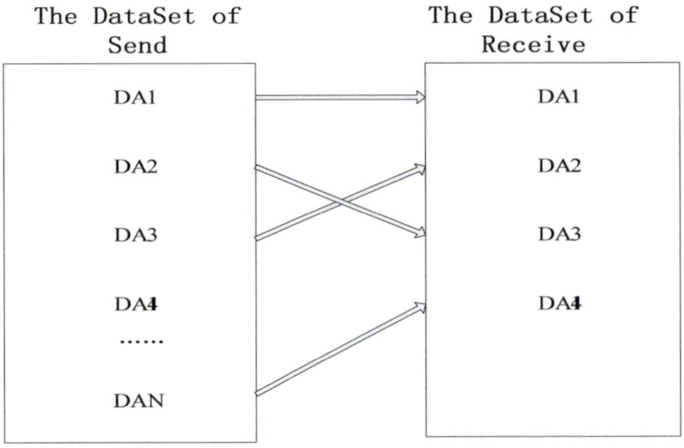

Figure 16. The configuration about virtual terminal

As the fig.16 shows, the sending data do not just match the requirements of the receiving device. The receiving device just need to choose the data needed from the receiving message which the other devices send. The other data which do not need are not be treated. This way can meet the requirements of the project and reduce the workload of configuration. The chart above is just for a sending device associated with multiple receiving devices. If multiple sending devices associated with one receiving device, the advantage of this mode is more obvious because it can avoid the sending device to send the data which must just match the requirements of the receiving device and the modification of the datasets and related GoCB. This mode is compatible with the two mode discussed above and is more intelligent.

2.2.4.2. The check of virtual terminal

The configuration of GOOSE is finished by the system integrator which has powerful system configuration tool and is responsible for the configuration of the station, including the configuration of GOOSE virtual terminal in current pilot project of smart substation. As the performance of different system configuration tool is different and the final configuration file is not be tested rigorously, so the device often generate the alarm of the configuration error after the configuration file is downloaded to the device which increase the difficulty of debugging. If the GOOSE virtual terminal can be checked immediately when the configuration is finished, the configuration error will be detected and modified which can improve the efficiency of the test of the project.

2.2.4.2.1. The check about the data attribute

In the configuration of the virtual terminal, the engineer may be careless to result the error of association of virtual terminal, especially in the configuration of IntAddr, the logical node number is easy to make mistake and resulting the Boolean type data of the sending device is associated with the int type or doubling point type data of the receiving device. These errors can be easily detected according to the model validation and comparison of data attribute and modified in time.

2.2.4.2.2. The check about the configuration of GoCB

The error is easily to generate in the virtual terminal configuration about GoCB such as the APPID and multicast address. Take the configuration of multicast address for example, the range of GOOSE multicast address is from 01-0C-CD-01-00-00 to 01-0C-CD-01-01-FF while the range of MSV multicast address is from 01-0C-CD-04-00-00 to 01-0C-CD-04-01-FF. These two type multicast address are often confused by the engineer of the project which is responsible for the configuration. This type of error is often find by the tester who analysis the message grabbed from the sending device and it slows the progress of test. If the configuration tool has the function of check, this type of error will be corrected quickly.

2.2.4.2.3. The check about the association of virtual terminal

The table and the wire splice are used in the association of virtual terminal and the way of wire splice is more convenient and is popular with the designer. It is easy to generate mistake when there are many virtual terminal need to be associated such as the virtual terminal of the receiving device is not connected or the same terminal is connected will several sending data. This type of error is hard to find only when the device cannot receive the need data and there are many reasons to result in it, the omission of the check of the virtual terminal increases the complexity of the test. If the configuration tool can check the configuration file and give the warning in time, it can effectively ensure the correction of the virtual terminal association and avoid this type error.

2.2.4.3. The test about the virtual terminal

Most of the configuration tool is off-line, the configuration file generated by the configuration tool is downloaded to the device and is tested by the external sending device or simulation testing device. These two modes are widely used in smart substation to test the correction of the configuration file but they are not comfortable. In former mode , although the message is send by the device but the data of the packet is generated by the external device which mean that the sending device need the external input signal to realize the data send. This way is inconvenient and less efficient. The other mode do not need the external device to generate the signal and can simulate the data flexible, but it need finish the configuration of GoCB and the datasets, this increase the workload of the test. If the configuration tool can send GOOSE message directly which mean that it can get the GoCB from the model of the device, it will avoid the configuration of the GoCB and dataset, if the data can be set according to the configuration tool, it will be comfortable to sending GOOSE message to realize the check of the configuration file about the association of the virtual terminal and improve the efficiency of debugging greatly.

In addition, most of the data in the GOOSE message are Boolean or double-point status information, if the configuration tool can set the time interval to control the every data change of the dataset automatically, it will be reduce the workload of the test and truly reflect the intelligent character. Some manufactures have developed this type configuration tool and have been used in pilot project of smart substation which improve the efficiency and realize the automatic test.

2.3. The synchronization with IEEE1588

IEEE1588 is a precision time protocol (PTP) standard for the networked measurement and control systems, the synchronization accuracy can reach sub-microsecond range. The application of IEEE1588 in the merging unit based on IEC61850-9-2 will be presented. The type of clock and the core algorithms of IEEE1588 will be introduced. The principle of high precision clock synchronization will be analyzed. The strategy of synchronization for process layer devices will be discussed. At last, The implement of GMRP protocol is analyzed.

The electronic transformer is connected through optical fiber with merging unit. The merging unit based on IEC61850-9-2 can realize the data sharing.. but this way has a key problem to solve which is synchronization especially to the cross-interval data sharing.. The bus protection will face this problem in project. There are two important type information transmission on the process lay which are sampling and the trip command. The sampling is realized through the merging unit and the trip command is realized through GOOSE. There are three levels synchronization accuracy in the standard of IEC61850 which are T3, T4 and T5. The T3 grade requirements for 25us used in the distribution of the line protection. T4 grade requirements for 4us used in transmission line protection. T5 grade requirements is 1us which is used in metering. It can be seen that, the synchronization with GPS can not meet the requirement of T5 because the accuracy only reach 1ms. At the same time, This way need additional wiring which increase the cost and reduce the reliability of the whole substation. Considering the IEEE1588 can reach 1us accuracy and is synchronized with network, so the application of IEEE1588 in merging unit is researched which can improve the reliability and sampling precision.

2.3.1. The principle of IEEE1588

The mode of the synchronization of IEEE1588 is master-slave which defines four multicast clock packets:(1)synchronization packet, shorted Sync;(2)following packet, shorted Follow_UP;(3)delay request packet, shorted Dealy_Req ;(4) response packet, shorted Dealay_Resp., the detailed is as follow:

During the synchronization, the master clock will send synchronization message periodically (typically 2 seconds). All the PTP terminal equipments which are in the same network with master clock will receive the Sync message and record the receiving time. The Sync message contain the timestamp which describes the expected sending time. As the expected time of the Sync message is not the real sending time, so the master clock will send the Follow_Up message after the Sync message which record the accuracy sending time of the Sync message. So the slave PTP terminal can calculate the the time offset between the master clock and slave clock through the return time in Follow_up message and the receive time in Sync message. As the transmission delay of the master clock and slave clock is unknown in the initialization stage, so the offset contain the network transmission dealy. Subsequently, the slave clock will send Dealy_Req message to master clock and record the the accurate sending time. The master clokc will record the accuracy arrival time of the Dealy_Req message and send the Dealay_Resp message to the slave clock which contain the accuracy arrival time of the Dealy_Req message.. The time offset between master clock and slave clock and the network transmission delay can be calculated through this "Ping-Pong" way.

In Fig.17, when the time is t1 in master clock , the relative time of slave clock is T1 which can be seen that the time offset need to be compensated. However, as the calculation of slaver terminal is based on the local clock, so the return time of the Follow_up message is the send time of the Sync message but is stand on the view of the slave clock. So

$$t2 - t1 = Delay + Offset \tag{1}$$

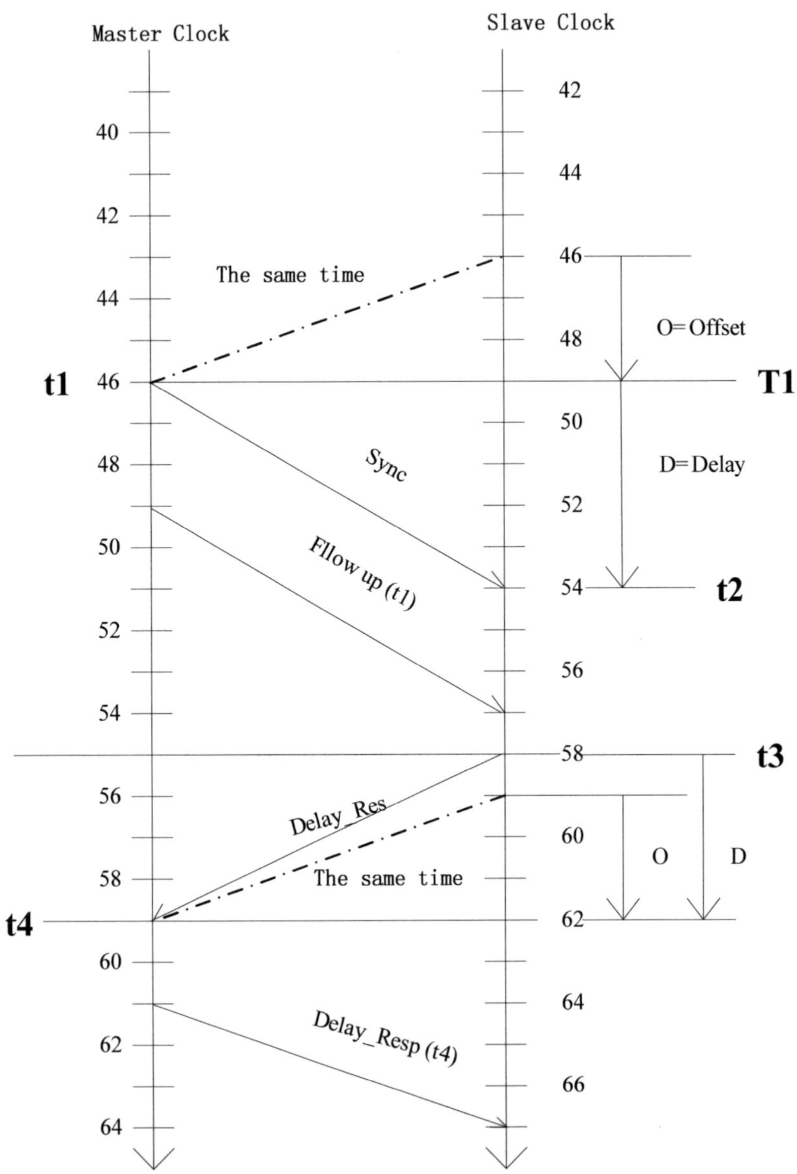

Figure 17. Synchronized principle of IEEE1588

The time offset between master and slave clock and the network transmission delay can not be calculated rom the equation (1) . so, the slaver terminal will send the Dealy_Req message after receive Sync message. The slave terminal will record the the accuracy sending time of the Dealy_Req. The master clock will record the accuracy arrival time of the Dealy_Req and send the Delay_Resp message to the slave termila. So,

$$t4 - t3 = Delay - Offset \tag{2}$$

According to the equation (1)and (2),we can calculate the time offset and network transmission delay, as equation (3)and (4):

$$\text{Delay} = ((t2\text{-}t1)+(t4\text{-}t3))/2 \tag{3}$$

$$\text{Offset} = ((t2\text{-}t1)-(t4\text{-}t3))/2 \tag{4}$$

2.3.2. *The realization of synchronization of IEEE1588*

Considering the synchronizaiton with IEEE1588 can reuse the communication network of substation and simple the stuucture, also the synchronization accuracy can reach 10ns-100ns which not only can meet the requirements of samling but also can meet all the requirements of automation system of substation. The IEEE1588 used in the merging unit which is to make sure the high accuracy of data acquisition is discussed.

2.3.2.1. The design of the hardware

As the synchonization of IEEE1588 is based on the MAC layer which should marked the timestamp so this way propose the higer requirements to the haredware.The Freescale's MPC8313E is choosed as the CPU of the merging unit which can up to 333MHz and 700 MIPS performance. The most important character of this chip is that it can support IEEE188 prototol and gigabit ethernet network which is very useful to the development of the merging unit. In order to send high precise sampling pulse the FPGA is implemented. In signal processing and control of the entrie system, FPGA can not only reduce the size of the circuirt to improve the stability and the logic based on lookup table structure and the parellel processing way can improve the signal processing speed, as the realization is based on the hardware circuit essentially, so the speed of execution is nanosecond. The FPGA module choose the Xilinx's Spartan-3A device which is based on 90nm technology to realized the synchronization and timekeeping. The FPGA receive the IEEE1588 second pulse and output 5kHz and 10kHz high speed synchronization sampling pulse and mark the timestamp. Ther time error is less than 1us and the time errror between the sampling pulse and second pulse is only a few nanosecondes.

2.3.2.2. The realization of the software

The time offset and delay calculated in the principle of IEEE1588 is based on the round-time dealy are the same.(ie, the dealy that the packet from the master clock to the slave ternimal and the packet from the slave ternimal to the master clock is the same), in fact, theser two delay time is different to exactly to the same. Considering the network traffic is relatively fixed in real project, so the time are considering being equal.The realizaiton is as follows:

In fig.18, the master clock send the synchronization message every two seconds while the merging unit send the delay request message every ten seconds, the specific time can be configured according the project. This way is based on the relatively fixed network time delay which is not changed and can reduce the network traffic.

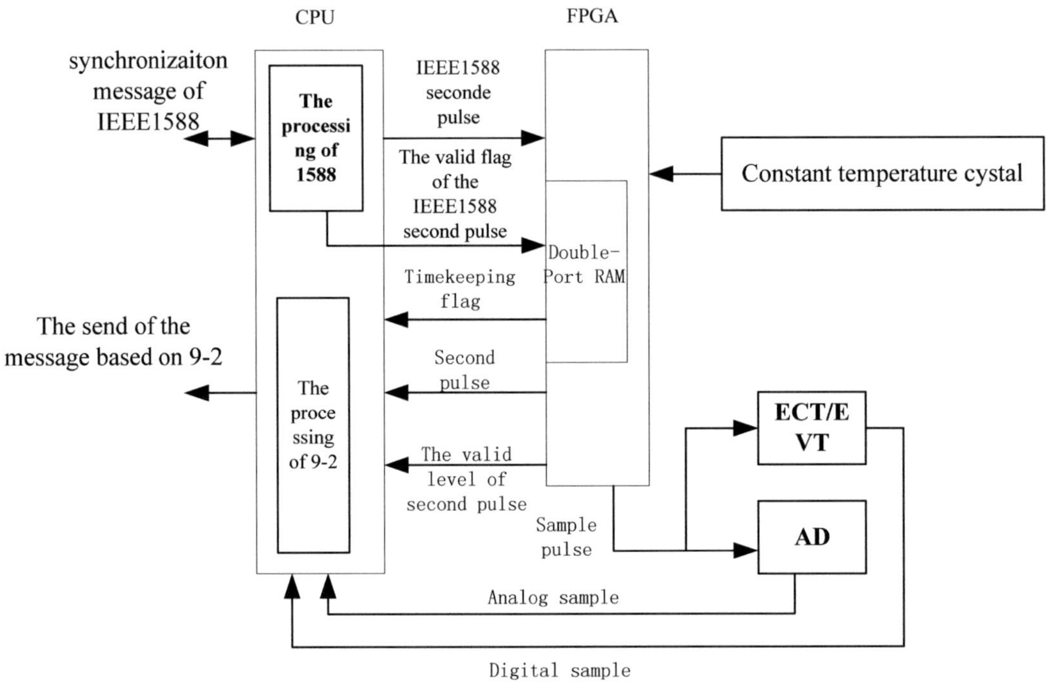

Figure 18. The process of IEEE1588

When the merging unit receives the synchronization message first time, the synchronization started. The process of synchronization need many times in order to reduce the time error less than 1us. If the merging unit calculates the time deviation within 1us in five continuous time then the device can be considered be synchronizated with the master clock . The merging unit send the second pulse to FPGA through the I/O pin and write the 1588 second pulse valid flag to the double-port of FPGA. When the FPGA detects the flag it will inform the processing of sampling and then the smpSynch will be set to True in the sampling message which is based on the 9-2.

The FPGA will be into punctual stage when the 1588 second pulse valid flag be detected for continuously for 32 seconds and then the FPGA will adjust the clock time of the device and write the 1588 punctuality flag in the double-port RAM. In the punctuality stage ,the FPGA always adjust the clock time according the 1588 second pulse in last 32 seconds. In this stage, the merging unit can make sure the accuracy of 1us even the FPGA detect the 1588 second pulse is invalid, so the smpSynch flag is still ture in sampling message of 9-2. The time of timekeeping can be tested and the device we developed can sustain 2 hours and the real time can be set according to the project. In fact, the substation which use the IEEE1588 synchronization often has two main clock or the slave clock will become the main clock once the main clock is failed. In the other time, once the failure of network of IEEE1588 is detected, the substation will alarm immedeliatly, the operator on duty will solve the problem. Once the timekeeping time exceed the set value the smpSynch flag will be set false.

When the time deviation between master clock and slave clock exceed 1us,the FPGA will write the 1588 second pulse invalid flag to the double-port RAM and then the smpSynch flag of 9-2 message will become false.

2.3.3. *The network of the IEEE1588*

As most of the device in substation can not support the IEEE1588 which have the higher requirements of the hardware, so the synchronization of IEEE1588 is used in process layer device such as merging unit. But in the pilot project of smart substation, the device of bay layer also support IEEE1588, the structure of the network is as follow:

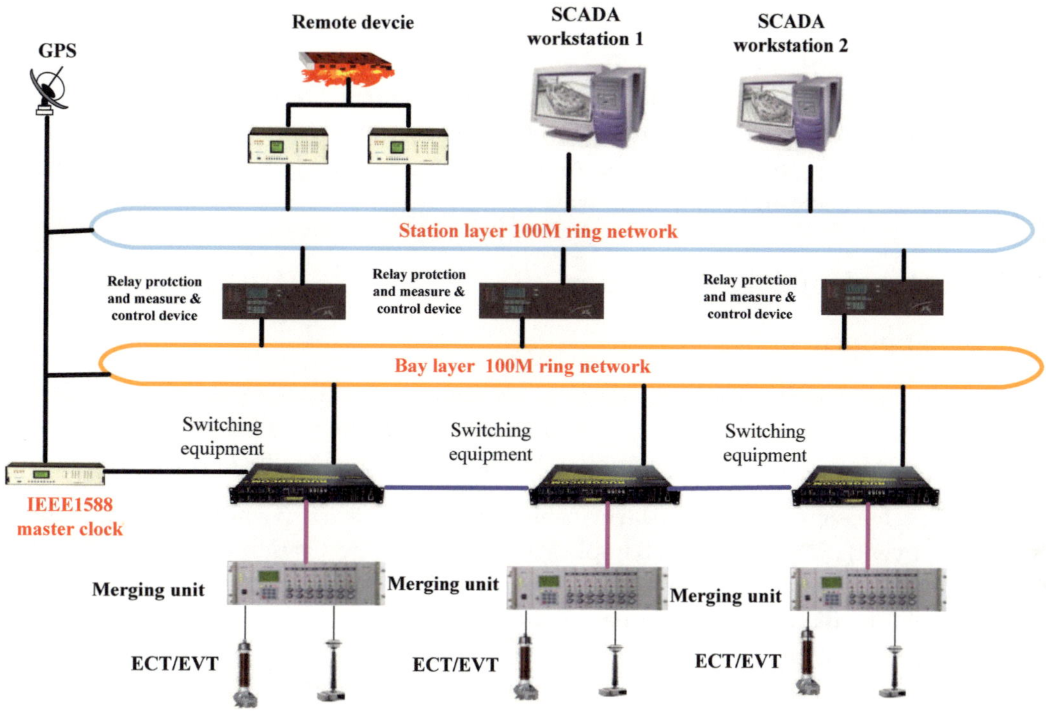

Figure 19. The structure of IEEE1588 network

The fig.19 is network of IEEE1588 of a 500kV substation. The voltage measurement of 500kV is still using the traditional electromagnetic voltage transformer but the current measurements using the optical-electrical transformer. The merging unit is based on 9-2 and the sampling frequency is 80 point per cycle which means 4kHz/s. The main clock of IEEE1588 is increased in the process layer which is used to send the synchronization message. The process layer switching equipment using the RUOGGECOM 2288 as the boundary clock which not only can be as the slave clock of the main clock but also can send synchronization message as the main clock of the merging unit. The merging unit receive the synchronization as the ordinary clock. The intelligent operation terminal which is used to close or open the switch through the GOOSE is also the process layer device, but as it does not have the requirement of high accuracy of synchronization so it does not include in the figure. According to the trend of IEEE1588, the process layer network will realize the IEEE1588, 9-2 sampling message and GOOSE in the same network. Although the IEEE1588 used in bay layer device is not suitable so the bay layer device have a large quality and overall cost of investment about the update is very high, it may be the direction of development. Now, the SNTP time network can be able to meet the bay layer an station layer requirement, so it can be a good way to solve the synchronization at this stage.

The fig.19 is the simple structure, the real project is more complex. In smart substation, the relay protection require the sampling using the point-to-point way. The synchronization structure is the same as the fig 19 above because every merging unit still retain the network port which is used to send 9-2 message and this port can be used receive the synchronization of IEEE1588.

Therefore, whether process layer network is a ring structure or bus structure, whether it is digital substation or smart substation, the scheme of synchronization is basically the same which through adding the master clock. All the merging unit are as the boundary clock and this is the most reliable and economical way.

3. The network of data acquisition

3.1. The introduction

The process layer involves data transmission and control of primary equipment such as data sampling and trip of protection. The research about the scheme of network structure of process layer is important and it determines the stability and reliability of smart substation.

The type of message of process layer which include GOOSE (General Object-Oriented Substation Event) , MSV (Multiple Sample Value) and synchronization with network will be generalized. The scheme of process layer network with different combination of the GOOSE and MSV will be discussed. The unite scheme of GOOSE, MSV and synchronization with IEEE1588 is researched, the scheme of hybrid mode which fits the requirements of relay protection of smart substation will be presented in detailed. The VLAN and GMRP technology which is used to divide the network of process layer to reduce the load of network will be proposed.

3.2. The message in process layer

The devices of process layer in smart substation include electronic (optical) transformer, merging unit, intelligent operation device (intelligent switch).The typical messages are GOOSE, MSV (multiple sample value) and synchronization with IEEE1588 may be included.

The sampling message in substation mainly based on the standard of IEC60044-8/7, IEC61850-9-1 (shortened with 9-1) ,IEC61850-9-2 (shortened with 9-2).The digital substations constructed earlier are mainly based on 9-1 which is abolished now. The 9-2 which is flexible and convenient to meet the requirements of the project but need the higher performance of the device becomes the unique standard of the sampling in process layer. The IEC60044-7 / 8 standard is also in use, primarily in accordance with the "Technical Specifications of Relaying Protection for Smart Substation" which require the transition of sampling data from the merging unit to protection device through the direct connect which like point to point .

The tripping network in smart substation is GOOSE. The principle and implementation are the same with the digital substation. The difference is that the transition of GOOSE is through direct connection not the network which is used to meet the requirements of standard of "Technical specifications of relaying protection for Smart Substation".

The network of IEEE1588 is included when the synchronization with IEEE1588 is used. This network can be attached to the network of GOOSE or MSV and need no additional electrical connections. The only requirement is that the switch should support the standard of IEE1588 and the master clock should be provided separately.

The topology of process layer network is the same with the bay layer which can divide three types such as star network, ring network and bus network. Among these three types, the reliability and cost of the bus network is the lowest but the delay is large. The delay of star network is the lowest and the reliability and cost is medium. The cost and reliability of ring network is the highest and the delay is very large also. According to the pilot project of digital substation in China, most of them choose the star network as the topology of process layer to achieve the optimization of performance and cost. The star network is also used in most high voltage substation.

3.3. The scheme of the process layer network

The communication of process layer include the digital sampling which involves the use of electric transformer and merging unit and the network of GOOSE which involves the use of intelligent operation device or smart switch. The process layer network which concerns the data source and the control of switch play a important part in the stable operation of substation. There is a need of the research of process layer network to choose the most safe, stable and economical scheme to make sure the security and stability of the substation. The main scheme is discussed in detailed:

3.3.1. The direct connection of MSV and GOOSE

The direct connection of MSV and GOOSE (also known as point to pint) is similar to the cable connection in traditional substation. The difference is that the cable is replaced by the fiber. The principles of MSV and GOOSE are remaining the same and the switching equipments are saved. The specific of fig.20 is as follow:

The scheme of fig.20 can ensure the reliability of data transmission but the sample value can not be shared. The direct connection needs the IED provide more network ports or optical ports and more fiber, the cost is very high. If the merging unit or intelligent operation device are installed beside the primary device, this scheme is suitable, but if the devices are centralized in the supervision room, this scheme is not suitable. At present, this scheme is not used in the project.

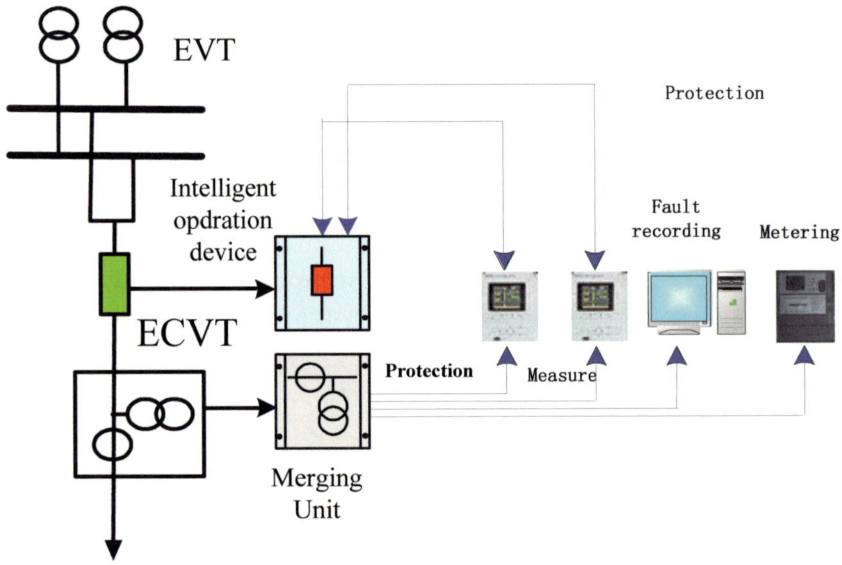

Figure 20. The structure of direct connection of GOOSE and MSV

3.3.1.1. Direct connection of MSV and network of GOOSE

This scheme has higher degree of automation than the scheme of fig.21. The discussion is followed:

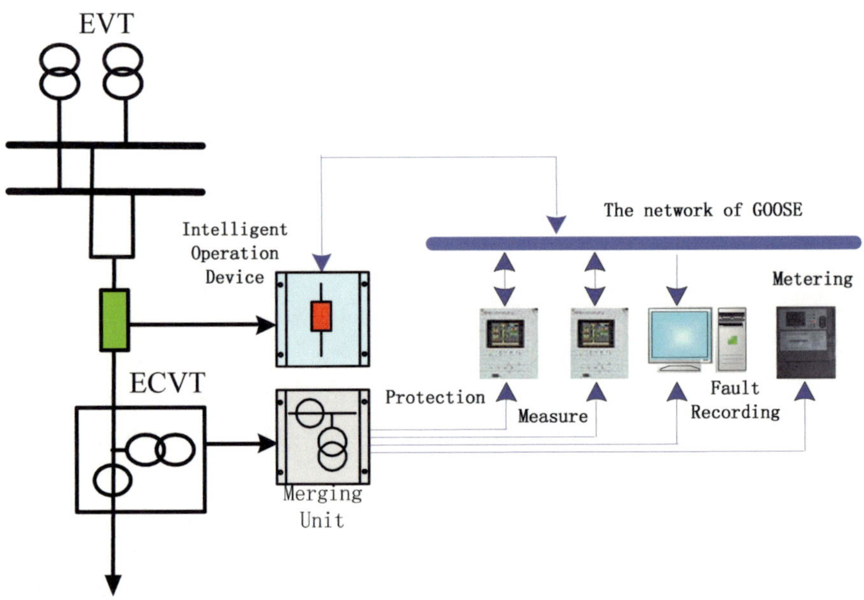

Figure 21. The structure of GOOSE network and MSV direct connect

The scheme cannot realize the sharing of sample data but can reduce the use of fiber as the trip is realized through the network of GOOSE. It meets the requirements of the standard of IEC61850 and the trend that the trip of intelligent switch through the network of GOOSE. It reflects the commonality and expandability of the standard of IEC61850.This scheme is widely used in the digital substation constructed earlier especially the substation of 220kV. The practical test show that the trip through the network of GOOSE can meet the requirements of real-time even in the heavy load.

3.3.1.2. The network of MSV and direct connection of GOOSE

This scheme only focuses on the network of sampling and can realize the share of sampling value.

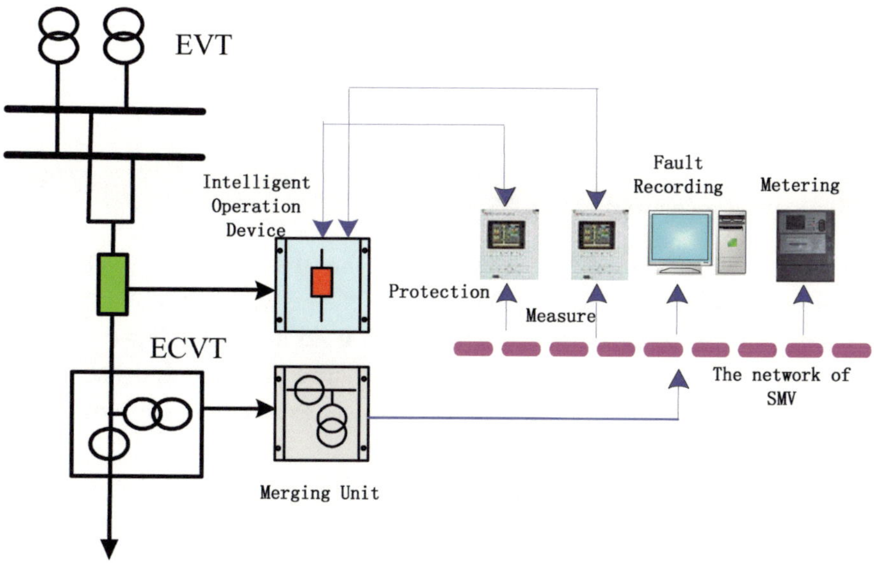

Figure 22. The structure of network of MSV and direct connection of GOOSE

This scheme is widely used in the digital substation constructed in early stage because of the GOOSE is not widely promoted as the performance and reliability of GOOSE is not tested by the project. In early stage, the focus is on the application the electronic transformer. Now, during the construction of smart substation, this scheme will be used in the upgrade of traditional substation.

3.3.1.3. The network of MSV and GOOSE

The scheme of the network of sampling data and GOOSE meets the requirements of process layer communication in the standard of IEC61850.

The network of sampling which can realize the sharing of data and the network of GOOSE which can realize the trip through the network can meet the development of substation automation and the requirements of process layer of smart substation. The structure of this scheme is complicated and the number of switch required is large especial the network is

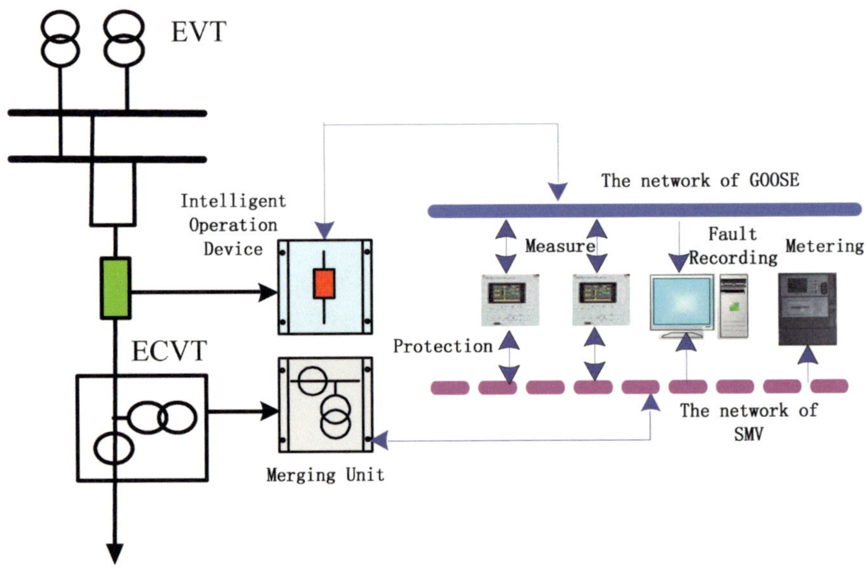

Figure 23. The structure of network of GOOSE and MSV

redundant which will increase the investment. The type of switch which meets the requirements of the standard of IEC61850 is few and the networks of MSV and GOOSE have the higher requirements of performance. The switch used in process layer is expensive and this is the reason that the cost of digital substation is large. At present, the scheme is widely used in digital substation and there is a lot of practical experience. The synchronization of IRIG-B is used in this type of substation.

3.3.1.4. The unite network of MSV, GOOSE and IEEE1588

This scheme is similar with the scheme of fig.23 except the synchronization. The accuracy of synchronization with IEEE1588 is less than 1 us and can meet all the requirements of substation. The realization of synchronization with IEEE1588 through the network has no requirements of additional connections which can reduce the cost. The type of synchronization with IEEE1588 is promoted and will be the trend of synchronization in smart substation.

This scheme has the higher requirements of performance of switch equipment which should support the function of IEEE1588 and process layer device which should have the higher processing power and support the synchronization of IEEE1588.The bandwidth of 100M can not meet the requirement of this scheme and the gigabit Ethernet will be the best choice. The implementation of this scheme needs the process layer device to be updated and the type of switch which fit the requirements is few, the product which is more expensive is new produced and the stability and reliability need verification in project. This scheme is already used in substation of 110kV of DaLv in ZheJiang province and substation of 220kV of MaShan in LiaoNing province.

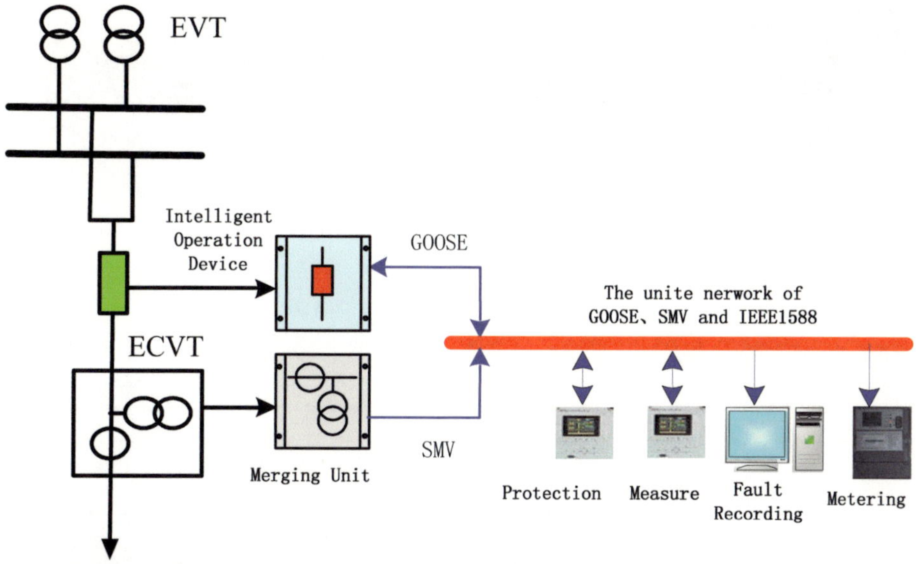

Figure 24. The structure of unite network of GOOSE, MSV and IEEE1588

3.3.1.5. The hybrid mode network

This scheme which the sampling and trip used for protection through the direct connection and the other implementation such as measure and metering through network is a hybrid of schemes discussed above and is generated according to the practical implementation of project.

This scheme is mainly on the consideration of the requirements of security and reliability of protection to avid the failure of protection caused by the network and is also defined in the "Technical specifications of protection for smart substation" published by State Grid Corporation of China. This method has the high requirements of devices in process layer and bay layer. The merging unit and intelligent operation device should add a lot of net ports to meet the requirements of direct connection. At present, the fiber ports need eight at least and the other devices such as bus protection need more. The devices which meet the requirement of process layer and bay layer are in developed and have not used in the project. But the first batch of smart substation is designed according this scheme.

This method which meets the requirements of standard of State Gird Corporation of China and the basis of digital information, standardization and network while improving the security and reliability of protection will be the major scheme in future.

3.3.2. The implementation of packets filter

The communication in process layer which includes the transmission of sampling value of current and voltage, the status information of primary device and the signal of protection

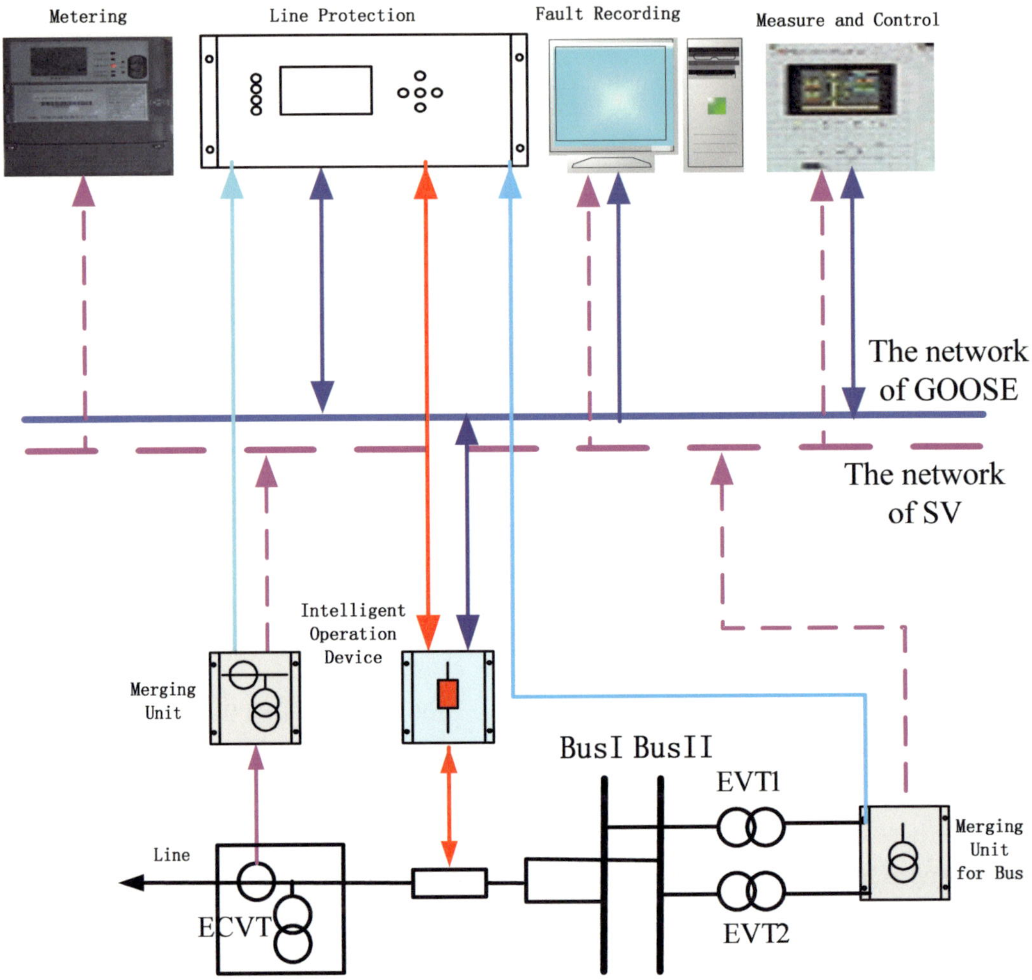

Figure 25. The structure of hybrid mode network in smart substation

and control device is real-time and has large information. In order to reduce the load of switch, to improve the security of network and increase the flexibility of management, convenience of maintenance and the expansion of substation, the virtual LAN should be implemented to filter the packets of the port which are not needed. The VLAN (virtual local area network) and GMRP (Group Multicast Registration Protocol) are the two methods widely used.

3.3.2.1. The implement of Virtual LAN

The load of the network of sampling value is very heavy especial when the sample rate is high, in order to reduce the number of packets retransmitted by the switch and to improve the reliability of the network, the devices in process layer should be divided into several virtual LAN. The unite network of MSV, GOOSE and IEEE1588 is also need to be divided in order to avoid the master clock receiving the other messages which are not synchronization message of IEEE1588.

The technology of VLAN is widely used to filter packets in digital substation but the configuration of switch is complicated which increase the complexity of construction and maintenance. Once the structure of network changed such as reduce or add device the virtual LAN should be configured again.

3.3.2.2. The implement of GMRP

GMRP is a multicast registered protocol based on GARP (Generic Attribute Registration Protocol) which is used to maintain the multicast registration information of switch. The basic principle is: when a host wants to join the multicast group. It will send the join information. The switch receives the message and joins the port to the multicast group and sends broadcasting to the group of VLAN and then the multicast source will know the existence of new member. All the switches which support the GMRP can receive the register information from the other switches to update the local register information dynamically and can send the local register information to other switcher also [6-8]. This kind of mechanism about information exchange can make sure the consistency of register information of the devices which support the GMRP in the same network. It suitable to the sampling based on the mechanism of publish/subscribe and IEC61850-9-2 and the transmission of GOOSE. Compared with the VLAN, the implement of GMRP do not need the configuration of switch but the switch should support the GMRP. This method is more flexible compared with VLAN and can reduce the difficulty of construction and maintenance.

Generally, the realization of VLAN which only need the configuration of switch is easy, but once the structure of network changed the VLAN should be divided again and the maintenance is complicated. Although the realization of GMRP involves the device and switch which should support the GMRP, it is more flexible and convenient to the construction and maintenance.

4. The introduction of the application in project

The construction of smart grid of China includes six segments which are power generation, transmission, transformation, distribution, utilization and dispatching, substation is one of the important parts. At present, the substation based on IEC61850 standard in China is called digital substation, new requirements are proposed by the construction of smart grid in China, and the combination resulted in the generation of smart substation. The smart substation is the use of advanced, reliable, integrated, low-carbon, environmentally friendly intelligent devices. Digital of all station information, network of communication platform and standardization of sharing information are the basic requirements to realize the automation of data acquisition, measurement, control, protection, metering, monitoring and other basic functions. The smart substation also supports the real-time automatic control, standardization, analytical decision-making online, collaborative interaction and other advanced functions.

The construction of secure and reliable smart substation is critical to the development of smart grid, the "Technical Guide for smart substation" is published by State Gird Corporation of China(shorted as SGCC) to guide the construction of smart gird in December, 2009. As there is not experience about the construction of the smart substation, the SGCC select different areas and different voltage level substation as the pilot. The data acquisition of the four smart substation of the pilot projects are introduced..

4.1. Shan-xi 750kV Yan-an substation

This substation is the highest voltage level substation in all the smart substations. The data acquisition is using the typical way which the data acquisition is through the network and the sampling network(SMV)and GOOSE network are separate. The detail is as fig.26:

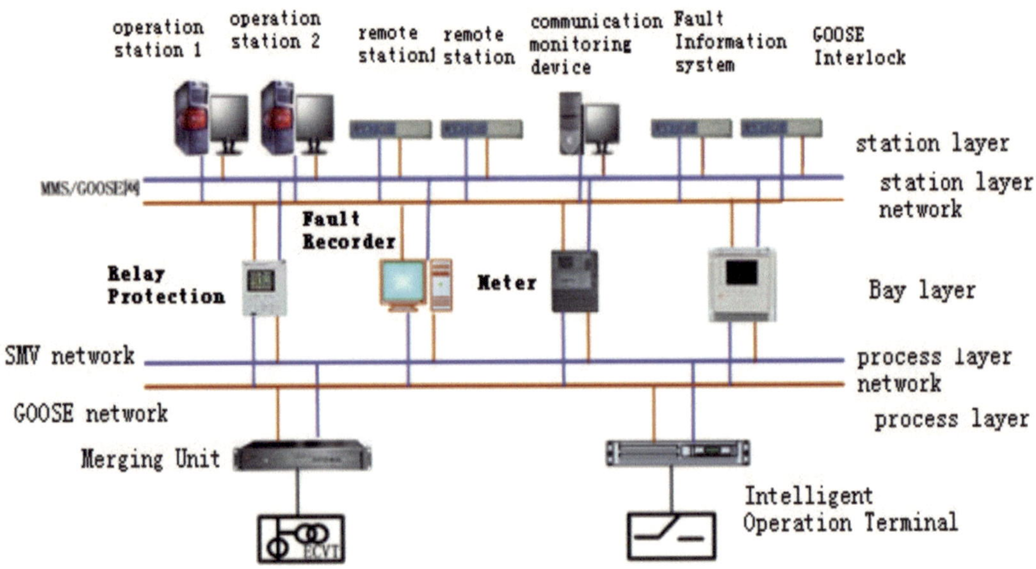

Figure 26. The structure of network

4.2. Ji-lin 500kV Chang-Chun substation

This substation is new constructed with many new technologies, the data acquisition is also through the network. This network is different with Shan-xi 750kV Yan-an substation. Although the merging unit and intelligent operation terminal is used but the sampling and GOOSE are in the same network and the network is redundant as A network and B network.

At the same time, the process layer network support the synchronization of IEEE1588. As the travel wave fault location need the requirements of high-speed sampling and the merging unit cannot meet it. So a separate high-speed sampling module is add in the CT/VT to realization the high-speed data acquisition.

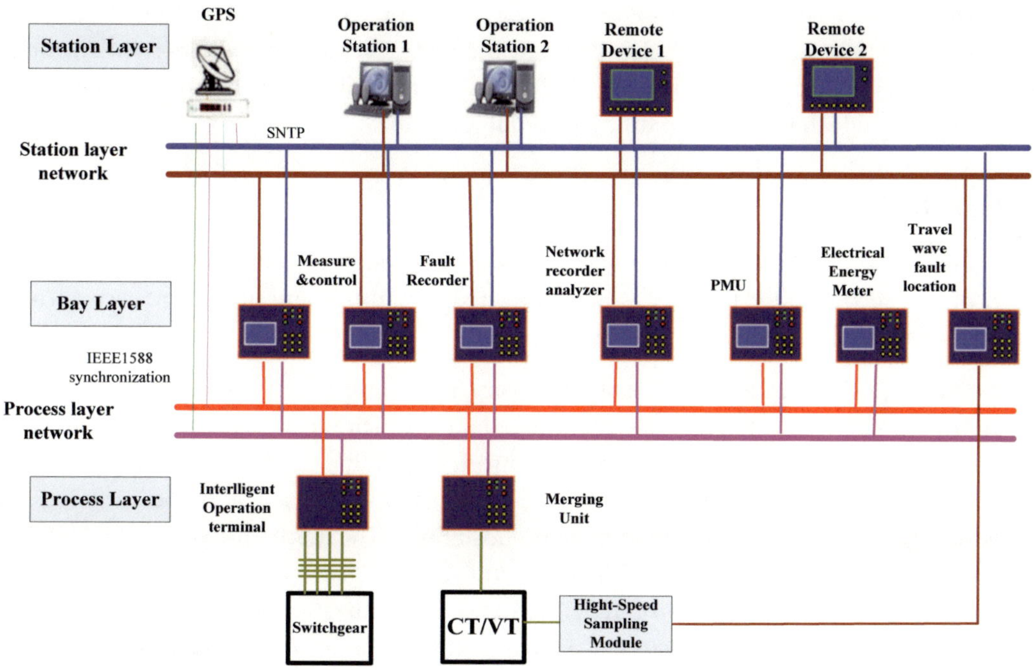

Figure 27. The structure of the network

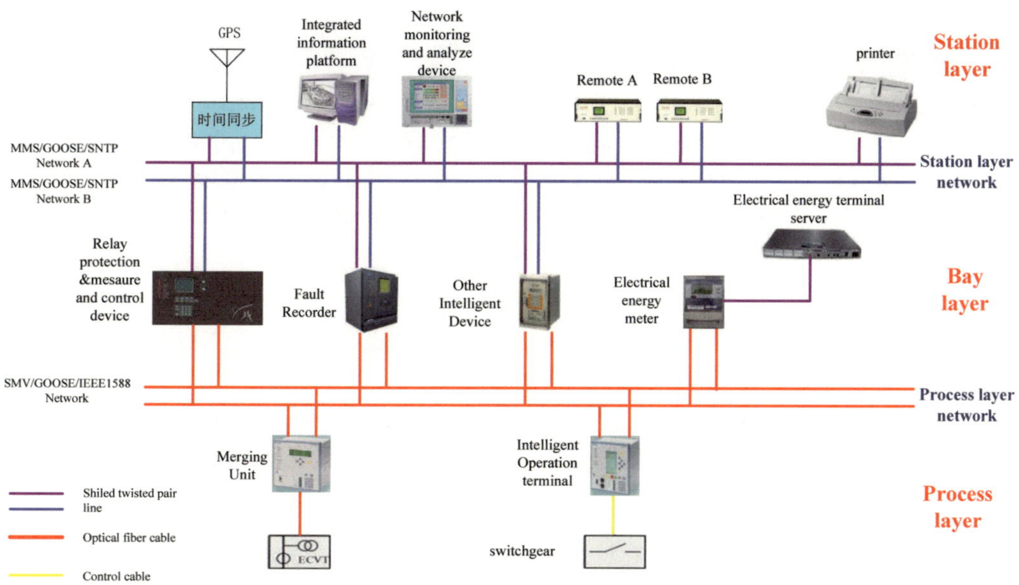

Figure 28. The structure of the network

4.3. Jiang-su 220kV Xi-jing substation

This substation is typical and many new devices and technologies are used. The data acquisition of this substation is also through the network but the SMV network which is based on 9-2, GOOSE network and IEEE1588 network are united which compose the process layer network which the data are full. The detail is as fig.28.

5. Conclusion

The construction of the first pilot projects of smart substation in China is developed and the plan of the second pilot projects is accomplished already. There are 41 new constructed substations have been operated until 2011.

The data acquisition in smart substation is very important to the security, reliability and economy of smart substation. The real-time data acquisition about the sampling value, status information and synchronization are introduced in this chapter. The sampling model and protocol based on IEC61850 and IEC60044-8 is widely used and the merging unit developed upon is now used in many smart substations. The mechanism of GOOSE and the configuration of the virtual terminal is the useful ways to make sure the status information transmit reliable. The principle of IEEE1588 and the realization of synchronization with IEEE1588 in merging unit is discussed which can make the error of synchronization below 1us and it has been used in pilot projects of smart substation.

The scheme of process layer network about the data acquisition which including the MSV, GOOSE and IEEE588 is significant to the security, reliability and economy of smart substation. The various solutions are compared and analyzed; it will be useful to the construction of the smart substation especially to the design of the process layer network.

According to the experience of the pilot project of smart substation of China, the smart substation will be constructed in large-scale in China and the plan that 6000 smart substations will be constructed in China until 2015 is publish by the Status Grid Corporation of China. The key technology of the data acquisition introduced in this chapter will play important role in the future.

Author details

Chen Fan

China Electric Power Research Institute, State Grid Electric Power Research Institute, China

6. References

[1] XU Yan, WU Yong-fei, XIAO Xia. Realization of the merging unit in electronic instrument transformer by using FPGA&DSP[J]. High Voltage Engineering. 2008, 34 (2): 275-279.

[2] DOU Xiao-bo,WU Zai-jun, HU Min-qiang. Information model and mapping implementation of merging unit based on IEC61850. Power System Technology, 2006, 30 (2): 80-86.

[3] LIANG Xiao-bing, ZHOU Jie, YANG Yong-biao. Development of a new type of merging unit based on IEC 61850[J]. Automation of Electric Power Systems, 2007, 31 (7): 85-89.

[4] Communication networks and systems in substation—Part 9-1: Specific communication service mapping(SCSM)—sampled values over serial unidirectional multidrop point to point link[S].

[5] Communication networks and systems in substation—Part 9-2: Specific Communication service mapping(SCSM)—sampled values over ISO/IEC 8802-3[S].

[6] Implementation guideline for digital interface to instrument transformers using IEC 61850-9-2[S].

[7] IEC61850-7-1, Communication networks and systems in substatons, part 7-1: Basic communication structure for substation and feeder equipment-principles and models[S].

[8] IEC61850-7-2, Communication networks and systems in substations, part 7-2: Basic communication structure for substation and feeder equipment-abstract communication service interface(ACSI)[S].

[9] Communication networks and systems in substations-Part 7-3: Basic communication structure for substation and feeder equipment-Common data classes[S].

[10] Communication networks and systems in substations-Part 7-4: Basic communication structure for substation and feeder equipment-Compatible logical node classes and data classes[S].

[11] Lars Andersson, Klaus-Perter Brand, Dieter Fuechsle. Optimized architectures for process bus with IEC61850-9-2[C].Proceedings of CIGRE, Paris, 2008.

[12] Joachim Schmid, Martin Schumacher. IEC61850 merging unit for the universal connection of conventional and non-conventional instrument transformers[C]. Proceedings of CIGRE, Paris, 2008.

[13] LIU Kun, ZHOU You-qing, ZHANG Wu-yang. Method for solving the synchronization of merging unit in electronic transducer[J].Telecommunication for Electric Power System, 2006, 27 (161): 71-75.

[14] ZHOU Jie, YANG Yong-biao, SHEN Jian. A kind of analog merging unit based on AC signal[J]. 2009, 37 (2): 65-68.

[15] Yin Zhi-liang, Liu Wanshun, Yang Qi-xun. New method for implementing the synchronization of merging unit according to the IEC61850 standard[J].Automation of Electric Power Systems. 2004, 28 (11): 57-61.

[16] Q/GDW441-2010.Technical specifications of protection for smart substation. State Grid Corporation of China.2010.

[17] FAN Chen,NI Yi-min, SHEN Jian. The Research of the application of IEEE 1588 in merging unit based on IEC61850-9-2[J]. Automation of Electric Power System, 2011, 35 (6): 55-58.

[18] IEEE 1588 Standard for a precision clock synchronization protocol for networked measurement and control systems[S],2008.

Chapter 7

Subsampling Receivers with Applications to Software Defined Radio Systems

José R. García Oya, Andrew Kwan, Fernando Muñoz Chavero, Fadhel M. Ghannouchi, Mohamed Helaoui, Fernando Márquez Lasso, Enrique López-Morillo and Antonio Torralba Silgado

Additional information is available at the end of the chapter

http://dx.doi.org/10.5772/49959

1. Introduction

There are currently a large number of different communication standards, due to the widespread acceptance of wireless technologies. As a consequence, there is a tendency to design transceivers for multiple standards [1-8]. A similar problem arises in the test industry, where providers of testing and certification services to the wireless communication industry need multi-standard receivers, in order to reduce the cost in testing equipment.

With the topology of a multi-standard receiver, the placement of the analog-to-digital converter (ADC) within the front-end chain is crucial, as shifting of the analog blocks (filter, mixer and amplifier) to the digital domain increases the flexibility of the receiver. The extreme case is known as the software defined radio (SDR) paradigm [9,10], where the ADC is placed right behind the antenna to directly digitize the radio frequency (RF) signal. For current communication standards, this approach imposes requirements on the ADC beyond the state of the art, where the ADC is limited to 7-8 bits for a sampling rate of 3 GS/s.

Different receiver architectures have been proposed to overcome this problem, such as direct conversion [11], low intermediate frequency (IF) [12], and subsampling [13,14]. In subsampling receivers, the RF signal is sampled using a frequency lower than twice the maximum input frequency, but larger than two times the signal bandwidth. One of the low-frequency replicas resulting from the sampling process, which contains the baseband signal, is then directly digitized.

Flexibility is the main advantage of a subsampling technique when using a sample and hold device (S&H) to produce low-frequency replicas of the RF signal, because most of the signal processing is done in the digital domain. In addition, it reduces the number of analog building blocks and relaxes the specifications of the ADC. On the other hand, the drawbacks of subsampling are the demanding specifications required for the S&H (wide input bandwidth and low aperture jitter) and high noise, due to folded thermal noise in the band of interest. In order to reduce the folded noise effect, a technique based on multiple clocking is proposed.

Due to the emergence of several coexisting wireless technologies, subsampling techniques can be useful in the implementation of a receiver for multi-band applications [15]. A multi-band receiver subsampling technique may be used in other applications, such as the feedback loop for linearization of dual-band power amplifiers in RF transmitters [16]. In both nonlinear and multi-band cases, the data acquisition involved in the subsampling receiver has additional limitations, because the harmonics (nonlinear case) and other carrier frequencies (multi-band case) are subsampled and may overlap with the signal of interest. Therefore, determination of the valid sampling frequencies in these scenarios is a major challenge. In this chapter, a particular case for dual-band applications in a nonlinear environment is studied, integrating both effects. Possible architectures to optimize the data acquisition resolution are described.

A data acquisition board based on subsampling for high-performance low-cost multi-standard test equipment is presented. With a signal bandwidth of 20 MHz, it achieves an 8.5 bit resolution for a programmable carrier frequency ranging from 0 up to 3.3 GHz and resolutions of more than 8 bits up to 4 GHz. With the proper selection of the center frequency and signal bandwidth, the proposed board can be used to digitize the signal in most of the current wireless standards. This design is intended to be part of a test system, i.e., the input signal of the subsampling receiver is assumed to be filtered and free of interferences.

Finally, an improvement based on multiple clocking techniques is employed to improve the resolution of the presented data acquisition system. By using two consecutive subsampling stages, this approach allows the sampling frequency of the first stage to be increased, resulting in a lower contribution of the first S&H to the folded thermal noise. Considering a signal bandwidth of 20 MHz, the improved data acquisition system achieves an effective number of bits (ENOB) of more than 9 for a programmable carrier frequency up to 2.9 GHz and of 8 up to 6.5 GHz, presenting an improvement of 0.5-1 bit in the resolution.

This chapter is organized as follows: Section 2 reviews the signal representation and definitions for wireless communication signals, while Section 3 reviews the sampling theory. Section 4 describes the theoretical concept of subsampling techniques, detailing their advantages and main drawback of jitter and folded noise. An approach based on multiple clocking is proposed, in order to reduce the effect of folded noise on the resolution. In this section, the typical problems of subsampling techniques are extended to multi-standard and nonlinear applications, and an optimization for receivers in these scenarios is also proposed. Finally, Section 5 describes the implementation of a data acquisition system and presents a comparison with other published multi-standard receivers. Conclusions are described in Section 6.

2. Signal representation and definitions

In current wireless communication links (Figure 1), a complex modulated baseband signal, *s(t)*, containing the useful information can be expressed as:

$$s(t) = A(t)e^{j\varphi(t)} = I(t) + jQ(t) = A(t)\cos\varphi(t) + jA(t)\sin\varphi(t) \tag{1}$$

where *A(t)* and $\phi(t)$ are the amplitude and phase of the complex baseband signal, and *I(t)* and *Q(t)* are the in-phase and quadrature-phase representation of the signal. This signal is usually up-converted to an RF bandpass signal around the carrier frequency, f_c, to be transmitted through a wireless channel and detected by a receiver and converted back to baseband. The bandpass transmitted signal can be written as follows:

$$\tilde{s}(t) = \Re[s(t)e^{jw_ct}] = \Re[A(t)e^{j\varphi(t)}e^{jw_ct}] = A(t)\cos(w_ct + \varphi(t)) \tag{2}$$

where $w_c=2\pi f_c$ and the transmitted signal, $\tilde{s}(t)$, is the real part ($\Re[.]$) of the complex envelope of the RF bandpass signal after up-conversion. In practical situations, the bandwidth of the baseband signal is much less that the carrier frequency, f_c.

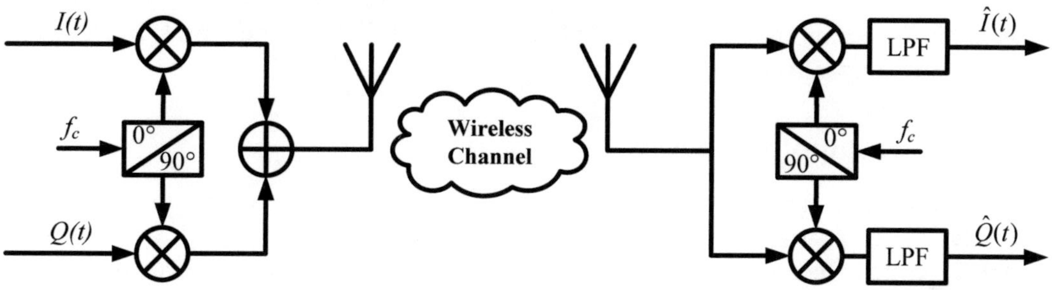

Figure 1. A typical wireless link

The radio channel is modeled as a linear time-invariant system; however, due to the different multipath waves that have propagation delays, which vary over different spatial locations of the receiver, the impulse response of the linear time-invariant channel should be a function of time, *t*, and the position of the receiver, *d*. The channel can, therefore, be described by *h(d,t)*.

The bandpass signal at the mobile receiver can be expressed as:

$$\tilde{s}_R(d,t) = \tilde{s}(t) \otimes h(d,t) \tag{3}$$

In the case of a stationary receiver, Equation (3) can be reduced to:

$$\tilde{s}_R(t) = \tilde{s}(t) \otimes h(t,\tau) = \int_{-\infty}^{t} \tilde{s}(t)h(t-\tau)d\tau \tag{4}$$

The received baseband signal can be obtained from a frequency down-conversion and channel equalization of the received bandpass signal as follows:

$$\hat{s}(t) = (\tilde{s}_R(t)e^{-jw_c t}) \otimes h^{-1}(t,\tau)$$
$$= \tfrac{1}{2}\hat{A}(t)\cos\hat{\varphi}(t) + \tfrac{1}{2}\hat{A}(t)\cos\hat{\varphi}(t)\cos 2w_c t - \tfrac{1}{2}\hat{A}(t)\sin\hat{\varphi}(t)\sin 2w_c t \tag{5}$$
$$+\tfrac{1}{2}j\hat{A}(t)\sin\hat{\varphi}(t) - \tfrac{1}{2}j\hat{A}(t)\sin\hat{\varphi}(t)\cos 2w_c t - \tfrac{1}{2}j\hat{A}(t)\cos\hat{\varphi}(t)\sin 2w_c t$$

The high-frequency components ($2\omega_c t$) are filtered out using low-pass filters (LPFs), as shown in Figure 1. The in-phase/quadrature-phase (I/Q) component of the received baseband signal can be expressed as:

$$\hat{I}(t) = \hat{A}(t)\cos\hat{\varphi}(t) \quad and \quad \hat{Q}(t) = \hat{A}(t)\sin\hat{\varphi}(t) \tag{6}$$

Knowing the transmitted signal, $s(t)$, and the received and equalized signal, $\hat{s}(t)$, one can calculate the normalized mean squared error (NMSE) as follows:

$$\text{NMSE}[\%] = \sqrt{\frac{\sum_{n=1}^{N} \left| s[n] - \hat{s}[n] \right|^2}{\sum_{n=1}^{N} \left| s[n] \right|^2}} \times 100\% \tag{7}$$

where N is the length of the data segment, and $s[n]$ and $\hat{s}[n]$ are the sampled versions of $s(t)$ and $\hat{s}(t)$, respectively.

3. Review of sampling theory

At the receiver end of the communication system, the RF signals are decomposed into their respective I and Q baseband components. A continuous time domain signal, x(t), should be sampled, so that the signal can be reconstructed without losing any information. Using ADCs, the continuous time domain signal is converted to a discrete time domain signal, x[n], through a uniform sampling process taken during the sampling period, T_s; and, their relation is $x[n]=x(nT_s)$.

Discrete time sampling affects the resolution of the final time domain signal being processed. If we consider a sine wave operating at 200 Hz and the continuous time domain signal representation as shown in Figure 2a, with a sampling frequency of 10 kHz, the sine wave is still visible in Figure 2b. However, the use of a sampling rate of 2 kHz, as in Figure 2c, results in a less accurate representation of the sine wave.

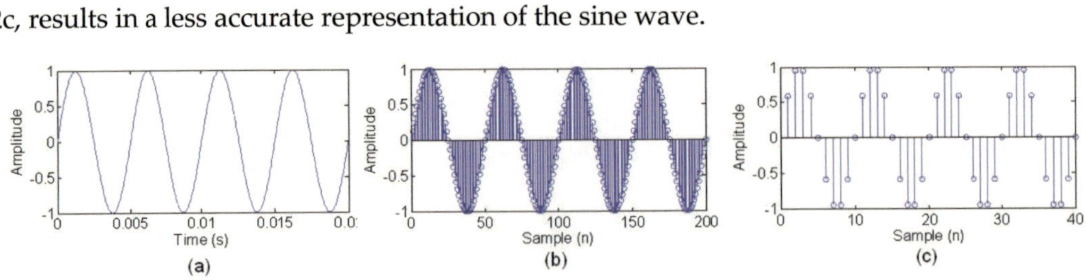

Figure 2. Time domain representation of (a) 200 Hz continuous sine wave (b) sampled at 10 kHz and (c) sampled at 2 kHz

The discrete time signal, *x[n]*, can be viewed as a multiplication of the continuous wave function, *x(t)*, with a train of impulse functions [17]. The sampled version of the signal can be expressed as:

$$x_S(t) = x(t)\delta_T(t) = \sum_{n=-\infty}^{\infty} x(nT_S)\delta(t - nT_S) \tag{8}$$

The impulse train can be further expressed as a Fourier series:

$$\delta_T(t) = \sum_{n=-\infty}^{\infty} \delta(t - nT_S) \xleftrightarrow{\Im} \omega_S \sum_{k=-\infty}^{\infty} \delta(\omega - k\omega_S) \tag{9}$$

where $\omega_s=2\pi/T_s$.

Since a multiplication in the time domain results in convolution in the frequency domain, the Fourier transform of the sampled signal, $X_s(\omega)$, in relation to the RF signal's Fourier transform, $X(\omega)$, is:

$$X_S(\omega) = \frac{1}{2\pi} X(\omega) * \left[\omega_S \sum_{k=-\infty}^{\infty} \delta(\omega - k\omega_S) \right] = \frac{1}{T_S} X(\omega) * \sum_{k=-\infty}^{\infty} \delta(\omega - k\omega_S) \tag{10}$$

Using the convolution property of the impulse function, the simplified version of the impulse-modulated signal becomes:

$$X_S(\omega) = \frac{1}{T_S} \sum_{k=-\infty}^{\infty} X(\omega - k\omega_S) \tag{11}$$

This shows that the spectrum is replicated every ω_s.

Choosing a sampling frequency for a band-limited signal affects the reconstruction process. A band-limited signal with total bandwidth (*BW*) is illustrated in Figure 3. For Figure 3a, the sampling frequency, $f_s=1/T_s=\omega_s/2\pi$, is much larger than the bandwidth; and, perfect reconstruction is possible. Similarly, for the case when $f_s=BW$ as in Figure 3b, the spectra do not overlap or alias over each other; and, the signal can still be decoded properly. However, in Figure 3c, f_s is less than *BW*, and aliasing occurs over the signal. This aliasing corrupts the information in the signal, making it unrecoverable. The minimum sampling rate (or the Nyquist sampling rate) should be $f_s >= BW$ in order to correctly decode the signal.

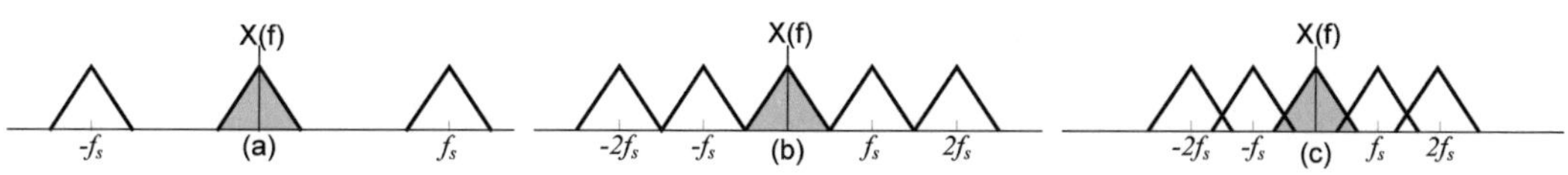

Figure 3. Sampling of a signal using (a) $f_s >> BW$ (b) $f_s = BW$ and (c) $f_s < BW$

4. Theory of operation

This section introduces the subsampling concept and details the method to select the optimal sampling frequency. Then, the two main limitations of the subsampling based systems, i.e., jitter and folded thermal noise, are described. Finally, the concept of subsampling is extended to nonlinear systems and multi-band applications, describing a method to optimize the performance in terms of noise.

4.1. Concept of subsampling

As mentioned before, moving the ADC closer to the antenna increases the flexibility of the receiver; however, this conversion just after the antenna prohibitively increases the ADC's bandwidth and sampling frequency requirements. Nevertheless, the bandwidth of a bandpass signal is usually a fraction of its center frequency, so that it is possible to subsample the signal (i.e., violating the Nyquist condition), thereby avoiding aliasing between replicas.

Subsampling is the process of sampling a signal with a frequency lower than twice the highest signal frequency, but higher than two times the signal bandwidth. An ideal S&H with a sampling frequency of f_s generates harmonics at f_s, $2f_s$...mf_s, where m is an integer. In the case for Figure 4a, a bandpass RF signal is centered at f_c, while the mth closest harmonic generated by the S&H and lower than f_c is k, where $k = floor(f_c/f_s)$. The replicas of the signal that are generated by the S&H exist at $-mf_s + f_c$, while the mirrored versions replicas exist at $(m + 1)f_s - f_c$. Figure 4b shows these replicas, and the signal replica within the 0 to $f_s/2$ range (centered at f_{if}=f_c-kf_s) can be used to extract the original RF signal.

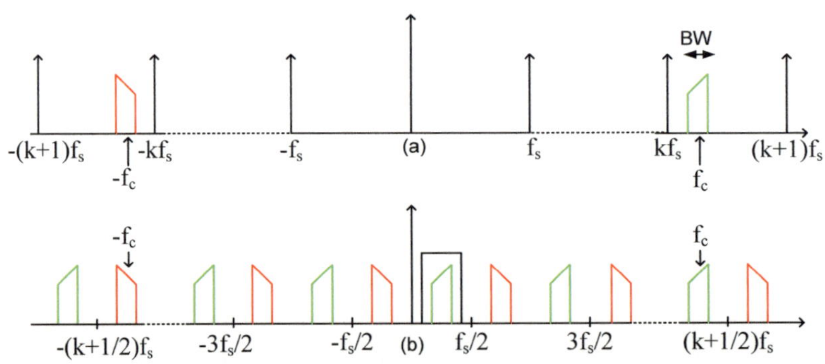

Figure 4. Illustration of the concept of subsampling: (a) frequency domain representation of the RF bandpass input signal along with the subsampling frequency and S&H harmonics and (b) signal replicas following subsampling process when selecting f_s=(f_c-f_{if})/k and f_s>BW

4.2. Selecting the sampling frequency

This section provides the method to select the optimal sampling frequency (f_s) for a given signal bandwidth (BW) and carrier frequency (f_c). Usually, the minimal sampling frequency is determined by the Nyquist theorem: f_s>2(f_c+BW/2). However, for a bandpass signal, a sampling frequency lower than the Nyquist frequency can be selected if Expression (12) still holds [14]:

$$2(f_c - BW/2)/(m-1) > f_s > 2(f_c + BW/2)/m \qquad (12)$$

where m is the number of replicas of the signal spectrum in the range $[0, f_c\text{-}BW/2]$ and lies between 1 and *floor* $((f_c\text{+}BW/2)/BW)$. An appropriate value is $f_s=4f_c/m_{odd}$, which produces a replica at $f_s/4$. Using an odd integer m_{odd} ensures that the signal is at $f_s/4$, while m_{even} generates the low-frequency alias of the signal at $3f_s/4$.

An example that illustrates the convenience of sampling at $4f_c/m_{odd}$ can be observed in Figure 5, which shows the output spectrum when an input signal at 1070 MHz is sampled at the f_s of 475.56 MHz (Figure 5a). Figure 5b shows the effect of selecting a non-optimal sampling frequency of 480 MHz; in such a case it can be seen how the second-order harmonic of the input signal is subsampled to 220 MHz, and falls closer to the subsampled fundamental at 110 MHz. Therefore, sampling at $4f_c/m_{odd}$ results in a larger subsampling frequency bandwidth and relaxes the filtering requirements after the S&H. As f_s, f_c and f_{if} are all directly related, there are bandwidth and frequency tradeoffs when selecting the subsampling frequency.

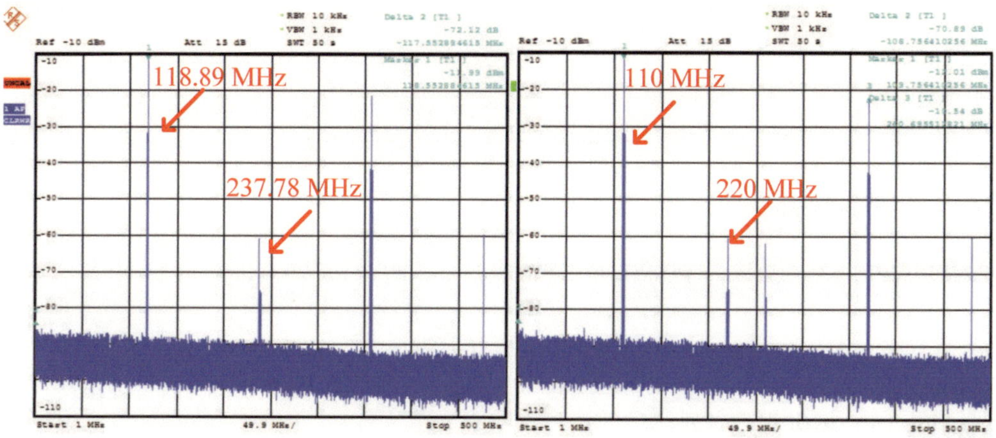

(a) (b)

Figure 5. Output spectrum of the subsampler when a 1070 MHz RF signal is subsampled at the f_s of (a) 475.56 MHz (m_{odd}=9 and f_{if}=118.89 MHz) and (b) 480 MHz (f_{if}=110 MHz)

4.3. Main non-idealities of a subsampling system

A general scheme for a subsampling receiver is shown in Figure 6. It should be mentioned that this receiver is very simple, especially if compared to conventional heterodyne architecture. However, as the S&H processes high-frequency signals, its requirements are much more restrictive than those expected from the signal bandwidth. The main non-idealities to be considered in the S&H are jitter and folded thermal noise, which are described in Subsections 4.3.1 and 4.3.2.

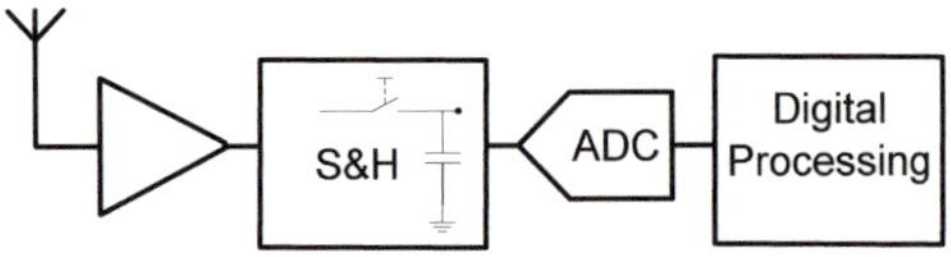

Figure 6. Subsampling receiver scheme

4.3.1. *Jitter*

Clock jitter is an important limitation in data acquisition systems at high signal frequencies, leading to sampling time uncertainly. Jitter is the deviation of the reference edges of the clock signal with respect to their ideal position in time. In this chapter, we consider this deviation as a random noise. As shown in Figure 7, a random error, τ_n, from the nominal sampling time instant, t_n, causes a random error, $\varepsilon_\tau(n)$, in the amplitude of the sampled signal [18]. This effect can be seen as an addition of noise to the output signal, resulting in a degradation of the output signal-to-noise ratio (SNR).

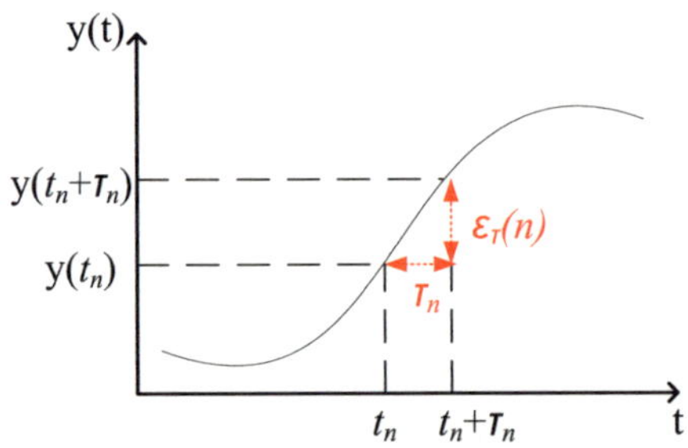

Figure 7. Concept of jitter

The amplitude error (v_{error}) is proportional to the derivative of the input signal [19]:

$$v_{error} = \Delta t \frac{dv_{in}}{dt} \tag{13}$$

With a jitter value of Δt.

For a sine wave of frequency f_{in} and amplitude A_{in}, the maximum error is [19]:

$$v_{error\_\max} = \Delta t A_{in} 2\pi f_{in} \tag{14}$$

There are two main sources of jitter noise: the phase noise associated with the clock reference, and the aperture jitter of the S&H. The aperture jitter of an S&H implemented with a MOS (metal oxide semiconductor) transistor is signal dependent, as the transistor threshold voltage depends on the input signal. There are two primary mechanisms that cause jitter in the system clock: the thermal noise, and the coupling noise. The latter can be caused by crosstalk and/or ground loops within, or adjacent to, the area of the circuit. Special care has to be taken in the design of the power lines in the data acquisition board, as described in Section 5.1.

In a first-order approach, these two sources of jitter noise can be considered as uncorrelated Gaussian stochastic processes: each one with a particular standard deviation. With Δt_{rms} as the standard deviation (or root mean square) of jitter, which usually defined as a percentage of the sampling period, the sampling error in Expression (13) can be rewritten as [19]:

$$\sigma(v_{error}) = \Delta t_{rms}\sigma(dv_{in} / dt) = \Delta t_{rms} 2\pi f_{in} \frac{A_{in}}{\sqrt{2}} \tag{15}$$

where $\sigma(.)$ is the standard deviation.

Therefore, the resulting SNR on the sampled signal is [19]:

$$SNR_{jitter} = 20\log\left(\frac{A_{in} / \sqrt{2}}{\Delta t_{rms} 2\pi f_{in} \frac{A_{in}}{\sqrt{2}}}\right) = -20\log(\Delta t_{rms} 2\pi f_{in}) \tag{16}$$

Note that the SNR is degraded when the input frequency increases.

This approximation is true if $2\pi f_{in}\Delta t_{rms} << 1$; otherwise, the general expression for the SNR, due to the uncorrelated random jitter noise for a sinusoidal input signal, can be expressed as follows [18,20]:

$$SNR = 20\log\left(\begin{cases} 1/4\pi^2 f_{in}^2 \Delta t_{rms}^2 : 2\pi f_{in}\Delta t_{rms} << 1 \\ 1/2(1-e^{-2\pi^2 f_{in}^2 \Delta t_{rms}^2}) : otherwise \end{cases}\right) \tag{17}$$

The expression of SNR for $2\pi f_{in}\Delta t_{rms} << 1$ is valid for all jitter distributions, while the other SNR expression only applies to a random jitter with a Gaussian distribution ($N(0, \Delta t_{rms})$) [18]. Moreover, small jitter noise can be regarded as approximately sampled additive white Gaussian noise (AWGN); whereas this assumption is not valid for large jitter.

In the particular case of subsampling, jitter noise is an important limitation, due to the high input frequencies that are processed. Thus, in order to validate this theoretical study, jitter noise is simulated using typical values for subsampling based receivers, i.e., input frequencies in the GHz range, sampling frequencies around 500 MHz (which is a typical limit for high-resolution commercial ADCs, as is described in Section 5.1) and a 20 MHz signal bandwidth, because it is a typical value for many communications standards and is used to experimentally characterize the data acquisition board proposed in Section 5.1.

Using these values, jitter noise has been simulated as a stochastic process (using MATLAB) with the average equal to zero and the standard deviation equal to Δt_{rms}. Figure 8a illustrates the maximum admitted jitter (X-axis) to obtain a concrete SNR (Y-axis) for three different input frequencies (1, 2 and 4 GHz) sampling at the optimal frequency (from equation $f_s = 4f_c/m_{odd}$) immediately lower than 500 MHz. In this example, the jitter noise is integrated in a signal bandwidth equal to 20 MHz; and, it can be observed that the SNR decreases around 6 dB each time the input frequency is doubled, as can be predicted by Expression (17).

This traditional method, based on Expression (17), to obtain the SNR as a function of clock jitter and signal frequency has some limitations, such as the assumption of a full-scale scenario. Although this situation may happen in some applications, the input signal energy is most commonly spread over some bandwidth. In these cases, it is more realistic to study the jitter effect from the spectrum domain. Since the spectrum of jitter is very difficult to measure directly [19], the most common method to study its effect is the measurement of the phase noise, which is the most widely employed parameter to compare between different clock sources and oscillators.

Phase noise is defined as the frequency domain representation of the phase modulation of the clock signal due to jitter. Since the clock signal is a sine wave of frequency f_s [19]:

$$v_{clock} = A\sin(2\pi f_s(t+\Delta t(t))) = A\sin(2\pi f_s t + \varphi(t)) \tag{18}$$

where $\phi(t)$ is the phase noise in the time domain. Assuming $\phi(t)$ has a small variation around zero, Equation (18) can be written as [19]:

$$v_{clock} \cong A\sin(2\pi f_s t) + A\cos(2\pi f_s t)\varphi(t) \tag{19}$$

The second term of Expression (19) is the additive noise due to phase modulation. Since the phase noise appears multiplied by a cosine in the above time domain expression, the spectrum of the phase noise in the frequency domain, $\Phi(f)$, is convolved with the noise-free clock and appears as sidebands around its center frequency. This noise is usually represented as $L(f)$ (single-sideband phase noise power spectrum) and is equal to the noise power spectral density per Hertz at the frequency of f_s+f, normalized by the clock or oscillator signal power, $A^2/2$. It is single-sideband, because only one side of the noise power is taken into account; hence, it includes only half the noise energy. Thus [19]:

$$\begin{aligned} L(f) &= 10\log\left(\frac{1}{2}\Phi^2(f)\right) \\ \varphi(f) &= \sqrt{2\cdot 10^{L(f)/10}} \end{aligned} \tag{20}$$

$L(f)$ is measured in dBc/Hz.

Figure 8b shows an example of phase noise for a clock frequency equal to 1.9 GHz, which is in the typical frequency range for the S&H clock source in the implemented systems, as is detailed in Section 5.1. These experimental measurements show a phase noise of around -95 dBc/Hz, -110 dBc/Hz and -125 dBc/Hz at 100 Hz, 1 KHz and 10 KHz, respectively. From Expression (18), the relationship between $\phi(t)$ and jitter is [19]:

$$\varphi(kT_s) = 2\pi f_s \Delta t(kT_s) \tag{21}$$

This is equivalent to referencing jitter to the clock period. In the frequency domain, where the clock phase noise is most commonly represented, it is then equal to the clock jitter scaled by $2\pi f_s$ [19]:

$$\Phi(f) = 2\pi f_s \Delta T(f) \tag{22}$$

Therefore, we have the following expression to obtain the total jitter from phase noise [19]:

$$\Delta t_{rms} = \frac{1}{2\pi f_s}\sqrt{\int_0^{\infty} \Phi^2(f)df} = \frac{1}{2\pi f_s}\sqrt{2\int_0^{\infty} 10^{L(f)/10}df} \tag{23}$$

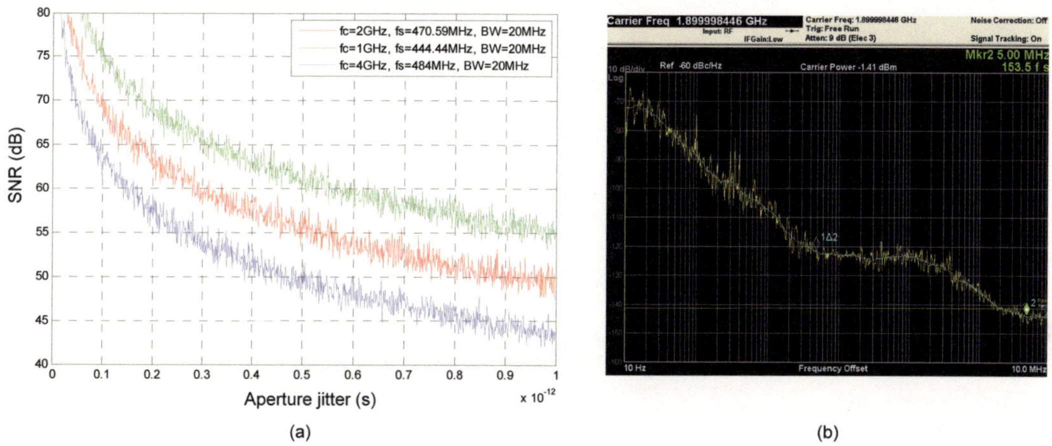

Figure 8.

4.3.2. *Folded thermal noise*

The other main non-ideality of the systems based on subsampling is the folded thermal noise. With the S&H modeled as shown in Figure 9a [18], this thermal noise is introduced by the switch and has a power spectral density (PSD) equal to $S_{in}(f)=4kTR_{on}$, where k is the Boltzmann constant, T is the absolute temperature and R_{on} is the on-resistance of the switch. This noise is AWGN and is folded in the band of interest by the subsampling process, as is described in this section (Figure 9b [7]).

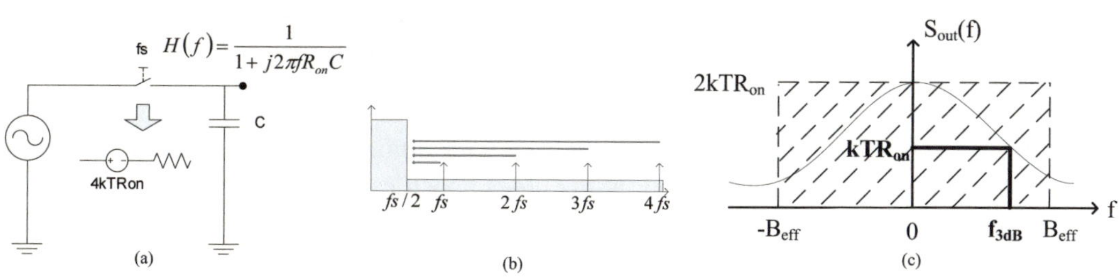

Figure 9. (a) Model of the S&H, (b) thermal noise folded in the band of interest and (c) effective noise bandwidth

R_{on} and C model a low-pass (LP) filter (Figure 9a) with a transfer function of $H(f)=1/(1+j2\pi f R_{on}C)$, whose 3-dB cutoff frequency is equal to $f_{3dB}=1/(2\pi R_{on}C)$. Considering the one-sided representation of $S_{in}(f)$, the output PSD is [18]:

$$S_{out}(f) = S_{in}(f)\left|H(f)\right|^2 = 2kTR_{on}\frac{1}{1+4\pi^2 f^2 R_{on}^2 C^2} \quad (24)$$

The total noise power (with a two-sided representation) is:

$$P_{out} = \int_{-\infty}^{\infty} S_{out}(f)df = \frac{kT}{C} \quad (25)$$

For modeling purposes, the output noise can be considered to be a Gaussian thermal noise filtered by a brick-wall filter with a bandwidth equal to B_{eff} (i.e., noise bandwidth, see Figure 9c) [18]:

$$B_{eff} = \frac{1}{4R_{on}C} = \frac{\pi}{2} f_{3dB} \quad (26)$$

Therefore, the power noise can be rewritten as follows [18]:

$$P_{out} = \frac{kT}{C} = 2kTR_{on} \cdot (2B_{eff}) \quad (27)$$

On the other hand, the SNR in $[-B_{eff}, B_{eff}]$ is defined as [14]:

$$SNR = \frac{P_s}{N_i + (m-1)N_o} \quad (28)$$

where P_s is the signal PSD, and N_i and N_o are the in-band and the out-of-band noise PSDs, respectively. As $2B_{eff}=mf_s$ if m=1, the Nyquist theorem is met, and the SNR is not affected by the folded noise. On the other hand, if m>1, and assuming N_i=N_o=N:

$$SNR = \frac{P_s}{mN} = \frac{P_s}{N(2B_{eff} / f_s)} \quad (29)$$

The out-of-band folded noise, therefore, reduces the SNR by a factor $2B_{eff}/f_s$, with the entire wideband noise being folded inside the band of interest. From Expression (29), we can observe how the noise decreases around 3 dB when the sampling frequency is doubled.

It is convenient to select the largest sampling frequency among the set of possible sampling frequencies set by the digital signal processing block specifications. This is considered as the optimal sampling frequency (from equation $4f_c/m_{odd}$).

This effect was corroborated experimentally, as shown in Figure 10. This figure illustrates how the folded noise increases when a lower optimal sampling frequency is employed for an input signal centered at 1473 MHz.

A limitation of the data acquisition systems based on subsampling is the maximum sampling frequency, which is determined by the ADC's specifications and is around 400-500 MHz for commercial ADCs with large enough resolution.

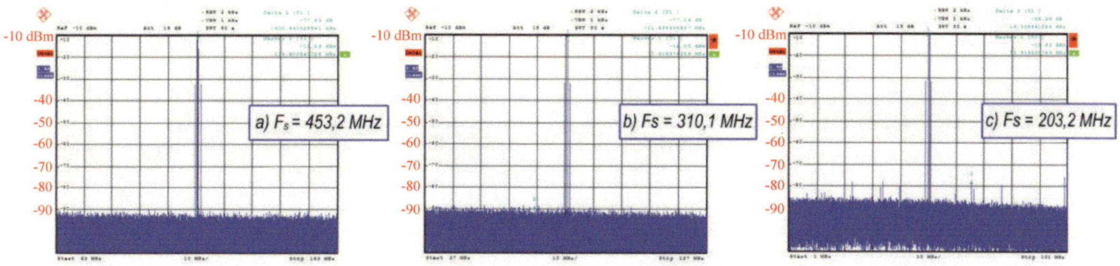

Figure 10. Thermal noise effect depending on the sampling frequency

In order to reduce the folded noise effect, a method to improve the resolution has been proposed [8], employing two consecutive subsampling stages. The use of two subsampling processes allows the sampling frequency of the first stage to be increased, resulting in a lower contribution of the first S&H to the folded thermal noise [8].

Figure 11 shows two different alternatives for the implementation of a subsampling based receiver. Figure 11a illustrates the scheme for a unique subsampling process that was implemented in [7], while Figure 11b illustrates the scheme with two different clocks, as proposed by [8].

Assuming the noise of both S&Hs in Figure 11 are uncorrelated, the output PSD due to the white noise of the S&Hs in Figures 11a and 11b are, respectively [8]:

$$P_{N(a)} = \frac{2B_{eff1}}{f_s} N_1 + \frac{2B_{eff2}}{f_s} N_2; \quad P_{N(b)} = \frac{2B_{eff1}}{f_{s1}} N_1 + \frac{2B_{eff2}}{f_{s2}} N_2 \tag{30}$$

where N_1 and N_2 are the noise power introduced by $S\&H_1$ and $S\&H_2$, respectively, with B_{eff1} and B_{eff2} as their respective noise bandwidths.

We can observe how the second term only depends on N_2 in Figure 11b, because of the signal is filtered at IF in both cases, using a bandpass filter. In fact, an additional advantage of using a higher sampling frequency is that the requirements of the bandpass anti-aliasing filter are relaxed. This is illustrated in Figure 12 [20], where we can observe how the nearest unwanted replica is placed further away from the desired signal when the sampling frequency is increased.

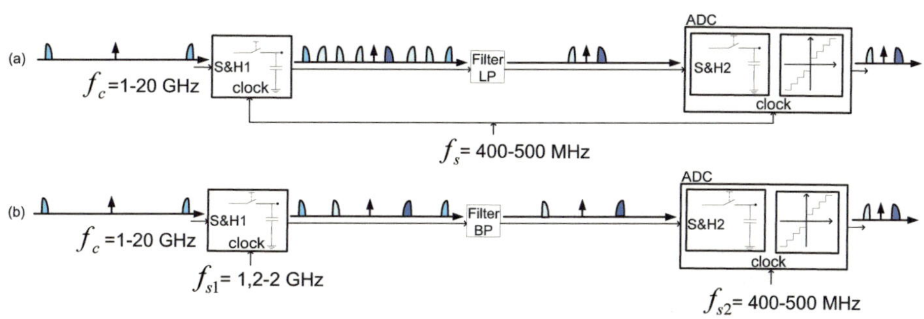

Figure 11. Clocking schemes for (a) a unique clock source and (b) two clock sources

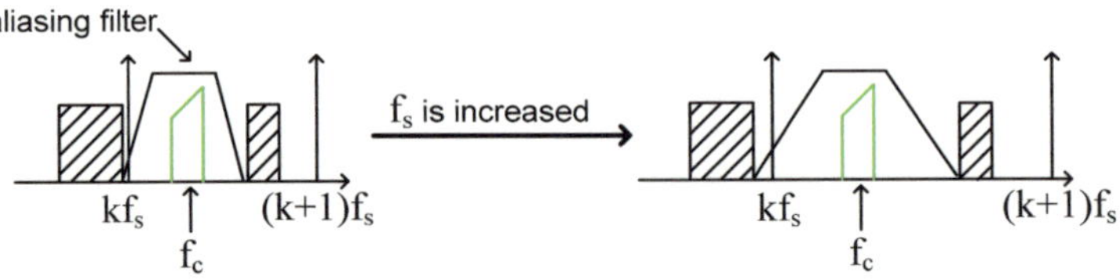

Figure 12. Bandpass anti-aliasing filtering requirements in subsampling

Thus, there is no folding of N_1 during the second sampling process. Therefore, the SNR improvement obtained with this sampling frequency plan is given by [8]:

$$\frac{SNR_{(b)}}{SNR_{(a)}} = \frac{P_s / N_{(b)}}{P_s / N_{(a)}} = \frac{B_{eff1}N_1 + B_{eff2}N_2}{\frac{f_s}{f_{s1}} B_{eff1}N_1 + \frac{f_s}{f_{s2}} B_{eff2}N_2} \quad (31)$$

The first S&H processes high-frequency signals, $B_{eff1} >> B_{eff2}$. In addition, the noise PSDs of both S&Hs can be assumed to be of the same order of magnitude. Expression (31) can then be approximated by [8]:

$$\frac{SNR_{(b)}}{SNR_{(a)}} \approx \frac{1}{\frac{f_s}{f_{s1}} + \frac{f_s}{f_{s2}} \frac{B_{eff2}}{B_{eff1}}} \quad (32)$$

where f_{s1}/f_s is the most influential term in this improvement; the higher the ratio, the better the SNR improvement.

Some drawbacks of the proposed system are higher complexity and higher power consumption than a one-stage subsampling receiver.

4.4. Subsampling in multi-band and nonlinear systems

As previously mentioned, the two main drawbacks of systems based on subsampling are the jitter and thermal folded noise, making system implementation even harder for multi-band or nonlinear applications.

There is a challenge in utilizing subsampling techniques in nonlinear systems, because the replicas of the generated harmonics are folded in the band of interest and may overlap with the desired signals. This issue has been addressed and studied in [21], where a universal formula for bandpass sampling in nonlinear systems was developed. The extension of this approach for dual-band nonlinear systems was employed in [22].

For dual-band applications, the main problem of subsampling is the possible overlapping between the two desired signals in the IF frequency band. Although this drawback has been studied in [23], [22] extended this approach in designing the subsampling based receiver and optimized the system with respect to the typical non-idealities of subsampling receivers, i.e., jitter and folded noise.

4.4.1. Subsampling for dual-band and nonlinear systems

The effect of subsampling a dual-band signal in a third-order nonlinear system is illustrated in Figure 13 [22], showing the spectrum due to in-band intermodulation and cross modulation.

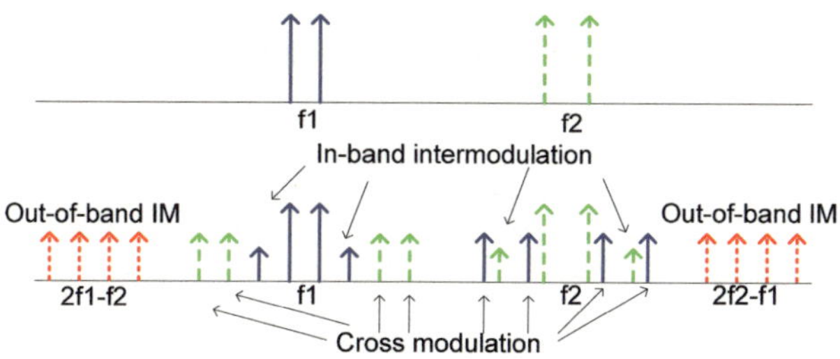

Figure 13. Power spectrum at the input (top) and the output (bottom) of a nonlinear system

On the other hand, when an input signal centered at f_1 (Figure 14a) [21] drives a nonlinear system, the output signal of this system may produce multiple spectra centered at integer multiples of f_1 (if_1 in Figure 14a). Moreover, each spectrum may have different bandwidths. Therefore, if we let two spectra, i and j (with bandwidths B_1 and B_2, respectively), be considered, where $j>i$ and $j-1=k$, and f_s is the sampling frequency, there must exist an integer such that [21]:

$$if_1 + n_k f_s \le jf_1 < if_1 + (n_k + 1) f_s \tag{33}$$

where $n_k = floor\ ((jf_1 - if_1)/f_s)$. On the other hand, an algorithm to find the range of valid subsampling frequencies for multi-band systems was presented in [23]. The subsampling frequency for a dual-band input spectrum, as shown in Figure 14b, must be chosen to ensure that the two signals do not overlap in the subsampled domain.

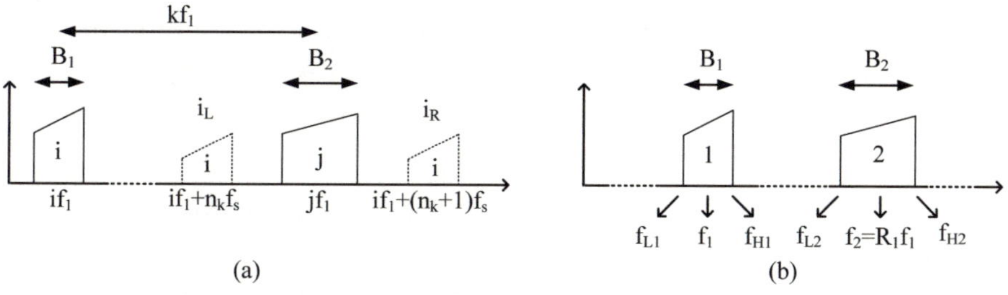

Figure 14. (a) Frequency locations in the sampled output spectrum and (b) spectrum of the dual-band RF signal at the input of the S&H with ratio $R_1=f_2/f_1$

From the general equations obtained in [23] and considering a dual-band case, the maximum replica order of the lower band (n_1) meets the following equation:

$$n_1 = \left\lfloor \frac{f_{L1}}{f_s} \right\rfloor \le \left\lfloor \frac{f_{L1}}{2((f_{U1} - f_{L1}) + (f_{U2} - f_{L2}))} \right\rfloor \tag{34}$$

where f_{L1} and f_{U1} are the low and high limits of the lower band, respectively, and f_{L2} and f_{U2} are the low and the high limits of the upper band, respectively. Knowing $f_2=R_1f_1$, replica orders of the upper band (n_2) meet the following constraint:

$$\lfloor R_1 n_1 \rfloor \le n_2 \le \lfloor R_1 n_1 + R_1 \rfloor \tag{35}$$

Therefore, the eight possible ranges for dual-band applications are listed in the Table 1 [23]:

Case	Range of valid f_s	Case	Range of valid f_s
1	$\frac{f_{U2}}{n_2+1/2} \le f_s \le \min\left(\frac{f_{L1}}{n_1}, \frac{f_{L2}-f_{U1}}{n_2-n_1}\right)$	5	$\max\left(\frac{f_{U1}}{n_1+1}, \frac{f_{U2}}{n_2+1/2}\right) \le f_s \le \frac{f_{L1}+f_{L2}}{n_1+n_2+1}$
2	$\frac{f_{U2}}{n_2+1} \le f_s \le \min\left(\frac{f_{L1}}{n_1+1/2}, \frac{f_{L2}-f_{U1}}{n_2-n_1}\right)$	6	$\max\left(\frac{f_{U1}}{n_1+1/2}, \frac{f_{U2}}{n_2+1}\right) \le f_s \le \frac{f_{L1}+f_{L2}}{n_1+n_2+1}$
3	$\frac{f_{U1}+f_{U2}}{n_1+n_2+1} \le f_s \le \min\left(\frac{f_{L1}}{n_1}, \frac{f_{L2}}{n_2+1/2}\right)$	7	$\max\left(\frac{f_{U1}}{n_1+1}, \frac{f_{U2}-f_{L1}}{n_2-n_1}\right) \le f_s \le \frac{f_{L2}}{n_2+1/2}$
4	$\frac{f_{U1}+f_{U2}}{n_1+n_2+1} \le f_s \le \min\left(\frac{f_{L1}}{n_1+1/2}, \frac{f_{L2}}{n_2}\right)$	8	$\max\left(\frac{f_{U1}}{n_1+1/2}, \frac{f_{U2}-f_{L1}}{n_2-n_1}\right) \le f_s \le \frac{f_{L2}}{n_2}$

Table 1. The boundary constraints for the dual band case

Thus, the final sampling ranges are given by the following expression:

$$F = F_{db} \cap F_{imd} \cap F_{cmd} \cap F_{hmd} \tag{36}$$

where F is the intersection of all the valid ranges calculated from Expressions (33) and (34), F_{db}, F_{imd}, F_{cmd} and F_{hmd} are the valid sampling frequency sets for the fundamental signals, intermodulation, cross modulation and harmonic distortion, respectively.

4.4.2. *Optimization of multi-standard receiver architecture*

In order to optimize the noise performance of a dual-band receiver in a nonlinear scenario, a particular case has been researched [22], where seven input frequencies were selected to study the selective combinations for different dual-band applications. These chosen standards were WCDMA (Wideband Code Division Multiple Access) (V) at 880 MHz, GSM-DCS (Global System for Mobile Communications – Digital Cellular System) at 1.82 GHz, WCDMA (I) at 2.12 GHz, Bluetooth at 2.4 GHz, WiMAX (Worldwide Interoperability for Microwave Access) at 3.5 and 5.8 GHz, and IEEE 802.11a at 5.2 GHz.

Since the main focus is the coverage of a maximum number of standards, it is mandatory that an S&H be placed before the ADC, in order to have enough analog bandwidth. The S&H from Inphi with part number 1821TH has been selected as the reference for this work, due to its high input analog bandwidth (up to 18 GHz), minimum aperture jitter (50 fs) and a maximum clock frequency equal to 2 GHz.

The first study scenario (Case 1) is based on a high-resolution ADC with a high sampling frequency, in order to reduce the folded noise effect. With this focus in mind, the selected ADC was a 12-bit ADS5400 from Texas Instruments with a maximum clock frequency of 1 GHz. Using a sampling frequency of almost 1 GHz, it is possible to cover all the dual-band applications, as illustrated in Figure 15a (Case 1) [22], where the meaning of X-axis is illustrated in Table 2 [22]. Using a typical SNR of the ADC of 58 dB as the reference, the theoretical SNR for each dual-band application is calculated from Expressions (16) and (29).

Another option is the use of a higher resolution ADC, such the 14-bit ADS5474 from Texas Instruments (Case 2 in Figure 15a). This device was selected because its maximum sampling frequency is 400 MHz; therefore, the folded noise is only around 4 dB higher than Case 1.

X-Axis	1	2	3	4	5	6
Input Frequency (GHz)	0.88-1.82	0.88-2.12	0.88-2.4	0.88-3.5	0.88-5.2	0.88-5.8
X-Axis	7	8	9	10	11	12
Input Frequency (GHz)	1.82 -2.12	1.82-2.4	0.88-3.5	1.82-5.2	1.82-5.8	2.12-2.4

Table 2. Correspondence between dual band applications and axis X

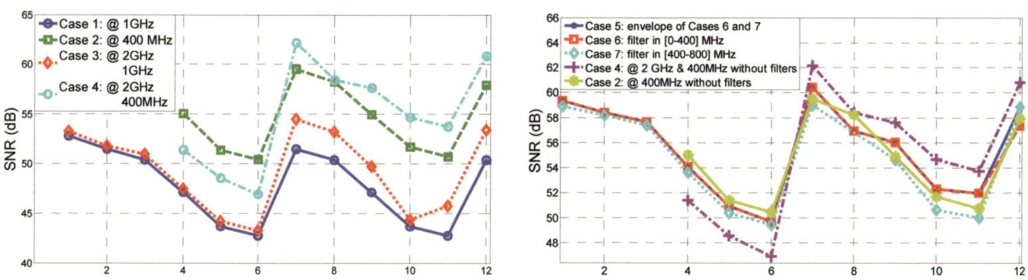

Figure 15. Expected SNR (a) for single and multiple clock architectures and (b) for different architectures based on bandpass filters

In order to improve the SNR without losing flexibility, a two-step subsampling approach is proposed, where the sampling frequency of the S&H is set at around 2 GHz and the sampling frequency of ADC at around 1 GHz (Case 3 in Figure 15a). Although this architecture improves the SNR by approximately 3 dB from Expression (29) in respect to Case 1, it is necessary to implement a second subsampling process; therefore, a new folded noise effect is added.

The last option is the use of a multiple ADC architecture employing the ADS5474 (Case 4 in Figure 15a) and a first sampling frequency of around 2 GHz. Theoretically, the SNR is improved by around 4 dB, in respect to Case 3. In this case, due to the second subsampling process, folded noise effects must also be added.

For the rest of combinations of frequencies, the curves present the same tendency, so that it is possible to cover all the scenarios (Cases 1-4). However, since Cases 2 and 4 provide the best results for the SNR, the next step is the coverage of all the dual-band applications for these cases. The proposed solution is the use of a bank of bandpass filters between the S&H and the ADC. This solution is applied to Case 4, because it has a more flexible architecture, with a higher number of available valid ranges. Using this solution, some harmonics are removed, and the flexibility of the receiver is increased. The solution is based on two bandpass filters with ranges of 0 – 400 MHz and 400 – 800 MHz. The maximum sampling frequency is selected, in order to have both fundamental replicas in each range. The selected filter corresponds to the higher of these two frequencies (Case 5 in Figure 15b [22]).

Another solution is a unique bandpass filter for all the applications (Cases 6 and 7 in Figure 15b). In these cases, it is possible to cover almost all the standards with only one of these filters, without considerably reducing the resolution. In order to maximize the flexibility and the SNR, the optimal architecture is like the one illustrated in Figure 16 [22]. For a more concrete application or more relaxed SNR specifications, a single bandpass filter can be used in order to reduce the complexity of the system.

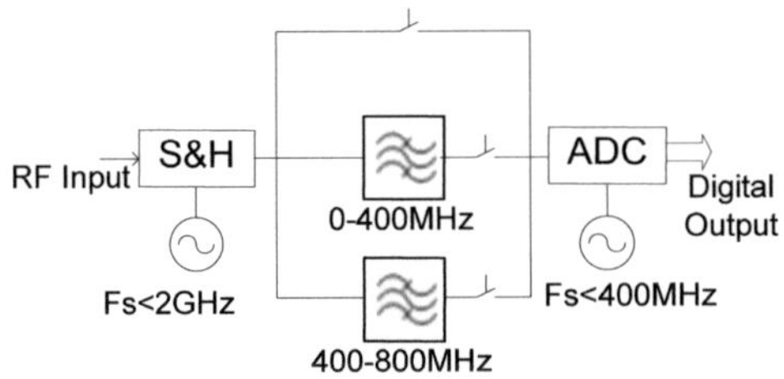

Figure 16. Optimized architecture based on multiple clocks and bandpass filters

4.4.3. Subsampling applications for multi-band and nonlinear systems

A subsampling receiver for multi-band applications is more advantageous than a wideband receiver, because it limits the minimum sampling rate to twice the information bandwidth, instead of twice the Nyquist frequency [24]. The reduced sampling frequency allows lower speed commercial ADCs to be used. Two applications are presented: spectrum sensing for cognitive radio applications, and selective multi-band down-conversion for amplifier linearization.

4.4.3.1. Spectrum sensing in cognitive radios

Wireless spectra are regulated by government bodies and are assigned a fixed frequency slot for transmission. Studies reveal that licensed spectra are highly underutilized and suggest a more efficient and flexible way for spectrum management [25]. Cognitive radio systems aim to reuse these underutilized spectra through dynamic spectrum allocation, which must integrate a wideband / multi-band receiver for scanning these spectra.

A subsampling receiver may allow the cognitive radio to sense different bands to check and see if they are in use. A bank of bandpass filters precedes the input of the receiver to control any interfering signals that may alias over the signal when subsampling. Figure 17a shows a block diagram of the subsampling receiver architecture proposed in [15], along with its corresponding validation setup (Figure 17b).

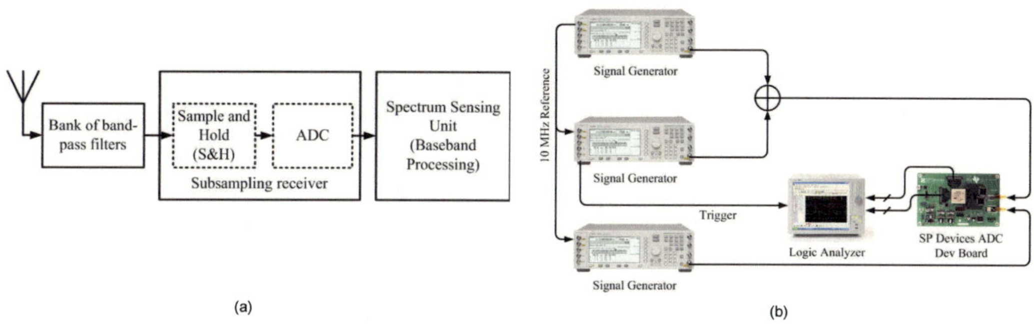

Figure 17. (a) Subsampling based receiver for spectrum sensing in cognitive radio systems and (b) measurement setup for validating spectrum sensing concept using subsampling receiver

As an example for spectrum sensing using a subsampling receiver, two RF bands are selected: the official digital video broadcasting (DVB) band at 698 – 752 MHz, and an unlicensed band at 902 – 928 MHz. With these two bands and using the formula described in the previous section, a subsampling frequency of 255 MHz is selected.

Figure 17b [15] shows the measurement setup used for spectrum sensing. Two signal generators are used to simulate the two RF bands, and the bands are then combined using a power combiner and passed into the receiver. A SP Devices development board and two Texas Instruments' ADS5474 ADCs operating in a time-interleaved manner are used as the subsampling device. A logic analyzer is used to capture the digital data streaming from the ADC board, while another signal generator provides a clock source for the ADC.

A three-channel signal is sent in the DVB band, while a 2-channel signal is sent in the unlicensed band. Different power levels are configured for each channel to simulate different received signals. Figure 18a shows the spectra of these two bands in the RF domain. Figure 18b [15] shows the two bands subsampled using a frequency of 255 MHz. Since the ADCs are operating in a time-interleaving fashion, the differences between each ADC may cause gain mismatches and timing skews [26]. These errors result in attenuated replicas of signals that are being subsampled, specifically at $f_s/2 - f_{in}$, where f_{in} is the subsampled signal frequency.

Figure 19 [15] shows the input signals overlaid with their subsampled output after digital demodulation. With the subsampling receiver, the captured signal has approximately a 50 dB signal-to-noise floor.

The technique may be extended to multiple bands, where changing the subsampling clock may allow different RF bands to be demodulated concurrently. In [15], the cognitive radio senses up to 14 bands, sensing two bands at any given time.

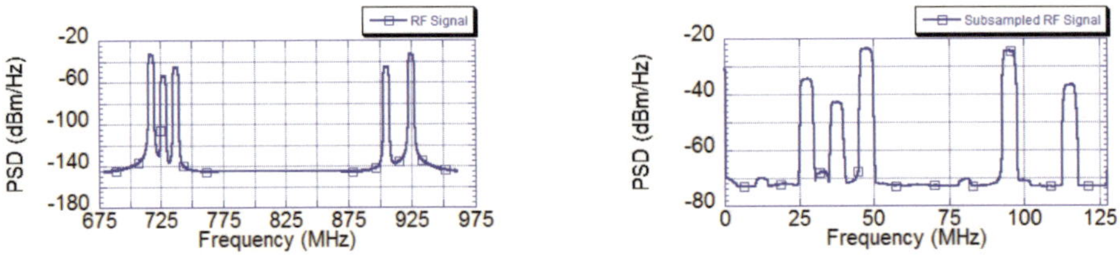

(a) (b)

Figure 18. Spectra of (a) the input RF signal to the receiver and (b) the subsampled RF signal for bands (698 – 752 MHz, 902 – 928 MHz) using a subsampling frequency of 255 MHz.

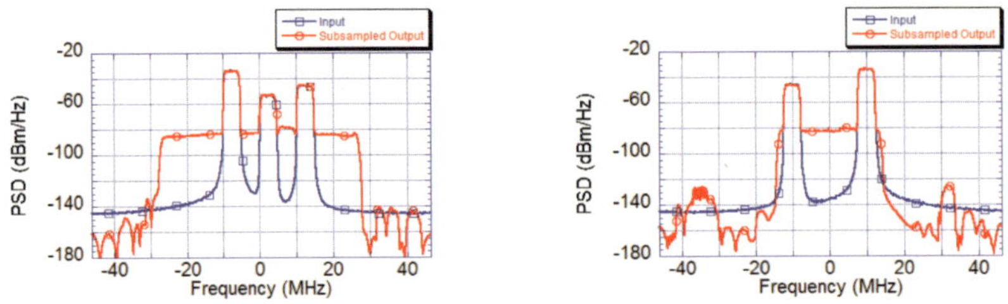

(a) (b)

Figure 19. Spectra of the input and filtered output baseband signals for (a) the 698 – 752 MHz band and (b) the 902 – 928 MHz band

4.4.3.2. Subsampling feedback loop for concurrent dual-band power amplifier linearization

The power amplification unit is typically the most inefficient component in wireless transmitters. This is caused by the inverse relationship that exists between efficiency and signal quality based on the signal power being transmitted [27]. At low input power, efficiency is low, and the power amplifier (PA) exhibits linear behavior, which results in good signal quality at the amplifier output. However, operating the amplifier at its highest efficiency state close to the maximum output power causes the gain characteristics to become compressed, and the input-output relationship becomes nonlinear. The nonlinear behavior reduces the in-band signal quality and causes out-of-band spectral regrowth. Nonlinearity is further complicated in a dual-band operation, where the device produces many intermodulation and cross-modulation signals. This inverse relationship causes difficulties for the wireless operator, and typically a linear operation mode is used, so that signal quality is good and that spectral regrowth is minimal and does not cause interference in other channels.

Digital predistortion allows for the operation of signal in the high-efficiency region, while reducing spectral regrowth and improving signal quality [28]. This is performed by analyzing the input and output signals of the PA and generating an inverse behavioral model (predistorter) of the amplifier. The cascade of both the digital predistorter and the PA results in a linear gain at the output for the full power range.

A dual-band PA operating at 880 MHz and 1978 MHz is used to test the subsampling feedback loop for concurrent dual-band linearization [16]. Two communication signals with

5 MHz bandwidths are sent at the center of these bands. The PA is predicted to have a 5th-order nonlinearity; and, all the harmonics, intermodulation and cross-modulation products up to 4 GHz are represented. In addition, a 25 MHz guard band is placed around each band frequency to account for the spectral regrowth that happens during the initial analysis stage.

Since the baseband communication signals are known, only the output signals at each band are needed. The harmonic, cross-modulation and intermodulation signals may be ignored; their only restriction is to not lie inside of the guard band of the signals. The subsampling algorithm outlined in the previous section calculated the minimal subsampling frequency of between 619.7 MHz and 620.1 MHz. Figure 20a shows a simulation of the RF spectra of all the components up to 4 GHz, while Figure 20b shows the subsampled components using a frequency of 619.8 MHz [16].

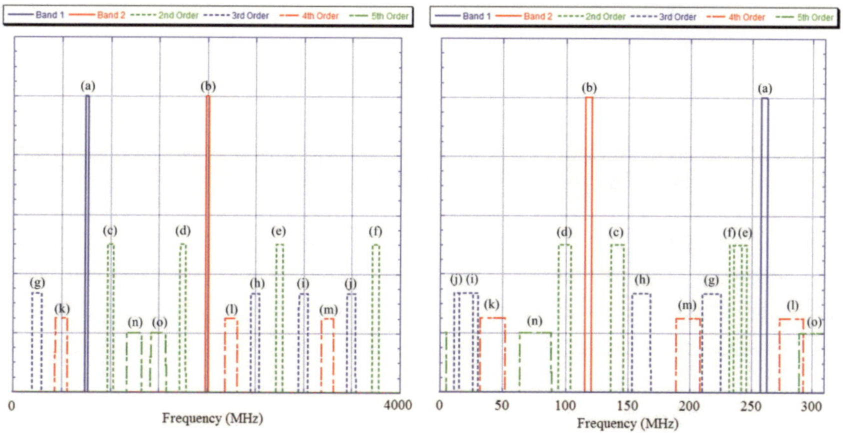

(a) (b)

Figure 20. (a) Predicted RF fundamental and harmonics up to 4 GHz and (b) subsampled result using a sampling frequency of 619.8 MHz

The same setup described in Figure 17b is used to generate the dual-band signal and capture the RF output. Figure 21a shows the RF spectra at the output of the PA [16]. Compared to Figure 20a, there is an extra term, p, which is a 7th-order intermodulation product at 436 MHz. The rejection of the i and j terms are due to the design of the PA output matching network. As explained previously, the time-interleaved ADC architecture causes attenuated signal replicas, a_i and b_i. Figure 21b [16] shows the normalized spectra of the subsampled RF PA output. There is attenuation from the upper band signal caused by the limitation of the ADC's bandwidth of 1.4 GHz. The captured time domain signal may be digitally demodulated, filtered and resampled to retrieve the amplifier output of the two bands; and, further post-processing can determine the digital predistortion model.

5. Implemented systems for multi-standard applications

If a multi-standard receiver is implemented by stacking different receivers for different standards into a single receiver, the area and power consumptions are extremely high.

Therefore, a properly designed multi-standard receiver must share hardware resources and use tunable and programmable devices, in order to reduce the area and power consumption, which is a very important approach for battery powered devices. Otherwise, the main constraint for multi-standard applications, such as instrumentation or validation, is the capability of covering the maximum possible number of standards.

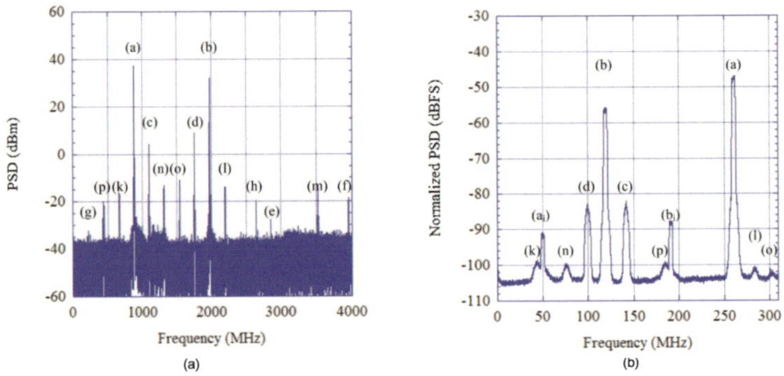

Figure 21. (a) RF spectra at the output of the PA and (b) normalized spectra of the captured subsampled signal using an ADC operating at 619.8 MHz

Multi-standard receivers can implement a narrowband or wideband strategy. A narrowband strategy is implemented by receivers that are designed for some specific standards, while a wideband strategy is implemented by receivers that cover a higher number of wireless standards. Therefore, narrowband receivers may provide a finer optimization for specific standards, and wideband receivers may be considered universal receivers and are used for more general applications.

Multi-standard receivers can be classified by their architectures, i.e., systems based on mixing or subsampling techniques. Although subsampling techniques have some problems, such as the folded thermal noise effect or aliasing in multi-band scenarios, they are very convenient for SDR applications, placing the ADC stage as close the antenna as possible.

5.1. Multi-standard receiver based on subsampling

A data acquisition module for high-performance low-cost multi-standard test equipment is presented in [7]. This work provides high resolution over a large bandwidth with only a low-jitter wideband S&H and an IF ADC by means of subsampling. Using commercial devices on a multilayer printed circuit board (PCB), experimental results show a resolution of more than 8 bits for a 20 MHz signal bandwidth with a center frequency up to 4 GHz, enough to cover the requirements of test systems for most of the current wireless communication standards.

From the theoretical analysis and a set of simulations, the specifications of the main building blocks of the module, i.e., the S&H and the ADC, can be derived. In order to obtain a total resolution larger than 8 bits for a maximum input frequency of 4 GHz and a signal bandwidth of 20 MHz, the main specification for the S&H is an aperture jitter lower than 100 fs. For the ADC, a sampling frequency larger than 400 MHz is selected, in order to reduce the folded noise effect.

After a study of the available commercial ADCs, an external S&H is selected, since the bandwidth of presently available internal S&Hs is limited to approximately 3 GHz for an equivalent number of bits (ENOB) of less than 8 bits. The selected ADC is the E2V AT84AS001. The Inphi 1821 TH is chosen as the S&H, because of its low aperture jitter (50 fs). For the target application, other relevant features of this S&H are its large bandwidth (18 GHz) and its large frequency range (0-6 GHz) for 10-bit linearity. In addition, it is able to sample at an IF of 500 MS/s, which is the maximum sampling frequency for the selected ADC that guarantees a spurious-free dynamic range (SFDR) larger than 60 dBc.

These devices are the main components of the proposed data acquisition system for which a multilayer PCB prototype was designed and fabricated (Figure 22a [7]). Other components, such as bias tees and low-pass passive filters (Minicircuits LFCN-160), are included between the S&H and the ADC. This design uses a Class 7 board with DE104i FR4 dielectric, six metal layers and microstrip lines adapted to 50 Ω. The rules and expressions employed to adapt the components (designing the dimensions of traces and layers) were obtained from [29].

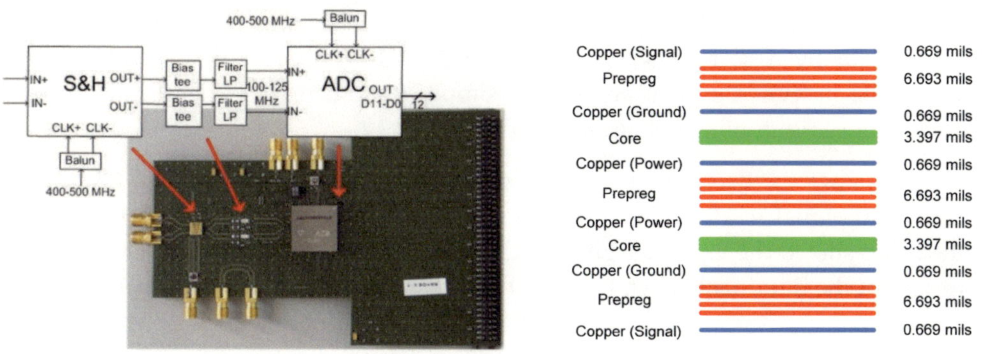

Figure 22. (a) Block diagram and designed PCB prototype and (b) the stack-up implemented in [6]

Employing the external metal layers (1 and 6) for signals, the adjacent metal layers for grounding (2 and 5) and the most internal layers (3 and 4) for power supplies, the resultant stack-up is as shown in Figure 22b.

The circuit is carefully laid out, in order to minimize the jitter effect. The distances between signal tracks, pads and metal layers are carefully chosen, in order to reduce crosstalk and inter-symbol interference, which cause jitter. Other rules followed to reduce jitter are a correct decoupling from the power lines and the so-called picket fences technique, which consists of placing closely spaced vertical interception accesses (vias) between different grounding planes. A distance between vias equal to 1/20 wavelength is selected.

Finally, this board achieves (for a 20 MHz signal bandwidth) an experimental ENOB of 8.5 bits for a programmable carrier frequency ranging from 0 up to 3.3 GHz. An example of the output spectrum is illustrated in Figure 23a.

In order to reduce the folded thermal noise effect, a new approach using two consecutives subsampling stages was implemented in [8]. The use of two subsampling processes allows the sampling frequency of the first stage to be increased, resulting in a lower contribution of the first S&H to the folded thermal noise.

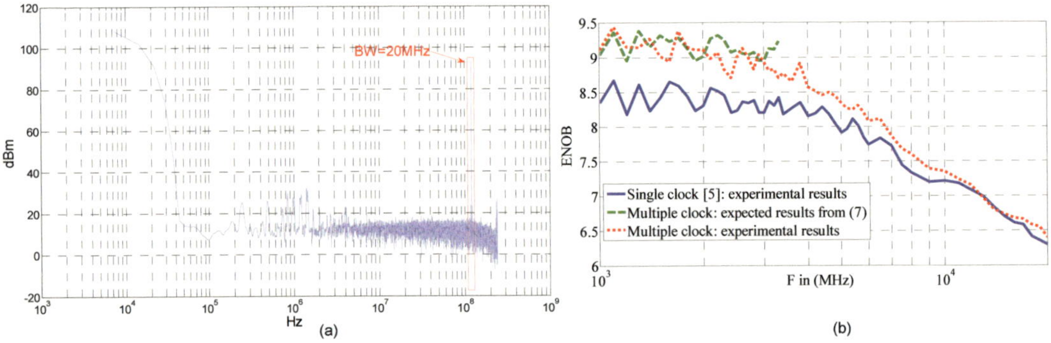

Figure 23. (a) Output spectrum for an input signal at 3 GHz sampled at 480.2 MHz and (b) ENOB versus carrier frequency (20 MHz signal band)

In this work, a sampling frequency of between 1.2 GHz and 2 GHz for the first S&H is selected, obtaining a band-limited signal at the output. After filtering, the resulting signal is subsampled again by a second S&H at 400 – 500 MHz (Figure 11b). However, some drawbacks of the proposed system are higher complexity and higher power consumption than the one-stage subsampling data acquisition system.

Figure 23b [8] shows the ENOB as a function of the carrier frequency up to 20 GHz, for a signal bandwidth equal to 20 MHz. The solid line shows previous results obtained in [7]. The dashed line shows the expected ENOB calculated with Expression (32), which is met, while jitter is not the dominant effect. Finally, the dotted line shows the experimental results obtained in [8].

These experimental results show how the proposed system reduces the effect of the folded noise, increasing the ENOB by 0.5-1 bits in the band of interest. Therefore, it provides an ENOB larger than 9 bits up to 2.9 GHz, 8 bits up to 6.5 GHz, 7 bits up to 12 GHz, and 6.4 bits up to 20 GHz. The results for linearity and power consumption are similar to those obtained in the previous work [7].

5.2. Comparison with other implemented multi-standards receivers

The receiver in [7,8], which is described in Section 5.1 may be an approach to a universal receiver for SDR applications. Other works have also studied multi-standard receivers. However, some of these works were based on mixing techniques, thereby losing part of the flexibility and simplicity provided by subsampling based systems. On the other hand, there were also multi-standard receivers that, although they were based on subsampling, were optimized for a given number of wireless standards, without covering all the applications.

Therefore, there are two main research fields for multi-standard receivers: digitalization techniques (i.e., mixing or subsampling based systems), and band strategies (i.e., wideband or narrowband strategy).

Examples in both research directions are present in the literature. There are examples of works that employ wideband strategies [1,5]. In [5], a receiver front-end is presented for multi-standard wireless applications, which is composed of a wideband amplifier, source followers, passive mixers and transimpedance amplifiers, with an analog bandwidth of up to 3.5 GHz. In [1], a wideband, multi-standard receiver, consisting of a wideband low-noise amplifier (LNA), a highly linear down-converter and a programmable digital baseband that performs decimation and filtering, is proposed. This work can be considered as a universal receiver, covering input frequencies between 0.8 and 6 GHz and based on mixing techniques. Although [1] is a more complex solution than [8], this work has a larger tuning range and other benefits, such as high linearity and low power consumption, because of its implementation in an integrated circuit (IC). Since the receivers of [1,5,7,8] offer wideband solutions, the RF front-end must meet the requirements for each standard; however, the solutions are not optimal for any standard.

Using a narrowband strategy, an alternative multi-standard receiver solution is proposed by [2], separating into two different RF channels, one for 2.4 and 5 GHz wireless local area networks (WLANs) and the other for Global System for Mobile Communications (GSMs). The different channels shared a common programmable baseband. This solution was highly efficient, because every path was optimized to a specific standard. On the other hand, in addition to the limitation of the number of standards, the main drawback of this work was area consumption, because the high selectivity was achieved by the utilization of many inductors.

An example of a solution based on narrowband strategies is shown in Figure 24a [3]. In this receiver, dedicated Bluetooth and Global Positioning System (GPS) links allow connectivity when making a phone call and/or sending or receiving data through a WLAN. The WLAN path connects to IEEE802.11a/b/g/n routers, while the cellular-dedicated channel can switch from one of the GSM bands to UMTS (Universal Mobile Telecommunications System) / WCDMA. Moreover, the selection is provided by off-chip surface acoustic wave (SAW) filters, which relax the linearity requirements.

Other works provided a high level of hardware sharing, where the different specific standards employed a common acquisition and digitalization stages. In [4], a solution for Bluetooth, GSM, UMTS and WLAN was presented, where the last three standards share the same circuitry after the filter bank (Figure 24b), allowing for reuse of some building blocks in the receiver architecture. This maximization of hardware sharing meant minimal area consumption, which was possible because all the considered standards (except Bluetooth) did not need to be covered at the same time, i.e., when an application was active, the others could be switched off, in order to save power.

Data acquisition systems for different communications standards use subsampling techniques, in order to process high-frequency signals with only a few components. In [6], a subsampling receiver was proposed for three different standards (GSM, UMTS and IEEE 802.11g), which validated these topologies at a simulation level, so that they could be applied to multi-standard radio design. An additional goal of this work was the design of RF and IF filters for the different standards, in order to avoid the aliasing caused by the subsampling process. Moreover, the constraints for the IF filter, the band of which is fixed, was relaxed due to the subsampling process in the first stage.

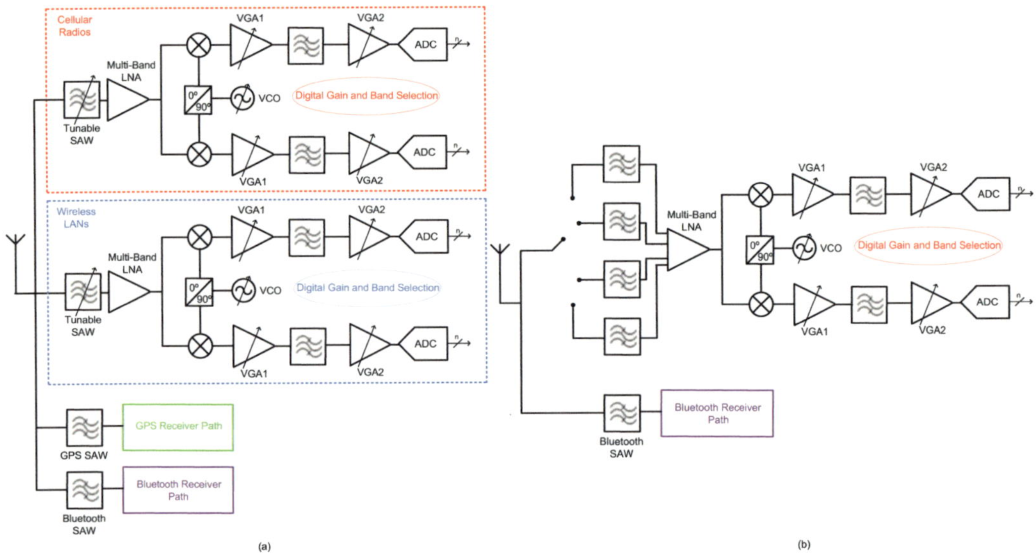

Figure 24. Multi-standard receiver architectures proposed in (a) [3] and (b) [4]

	Standard	GSM 1800	UMTS (I)	Blue-tooth	802.11b/g	802.11a
Standard requirements	Carrier Frequency (MHz)	1805.2-1879.8	2110-2170	2400	2400	5000
	Signal Bandwidth (MHz)	0.2	5	1	20	20
	ENOB (bits)	9	6	11	8	9
	NF (dB)	9.3	4.6	10.7	6.5	18.2
Experimental results of previously published acquisition systems	ENOB [7] (bits)	11.76	9.56	10.36	8.2	7.41
	NF [7] (dB)	6.1	6.5	8.3	8.3	13.1
	NF [2] (dB)	5.2	5.6		5.8	
	NF [5] (dB)	5.8	6	6.5	6.5	
	NF [6] (dB)		7.5		7.2	
	Noise PSD [31] (dBm/Hz)				-131	

	Standard	GSM 1800	UMTS (I)	Blue-tooth	802.11b/g	802.11a
Experimental results of [8]	ENOB (bits)	12.47	9.97	10.86	8.7	8.34
	NF (dB)	3.6	4.4	6.2	6.2	9.3
	Noise PSD (dBm/Hz)	-129.7	-128.8	-126.9	-126.9	-123.8

Table 3. Standard specifications and results

In other published works, the receivers based on subsampling were implemented experimentally for only fixed bands. Thus, low-noise subsampling implementations for the 2.1 GHz band [30] and for 2.4 GHz (IEEE 802.11a/g WLAN standards) [31] have been proposed. In [30], an IC receiver designed in 0.18 μm CMOS (complementary metal oxide semiconductor) was presented, the main goal of which was a tunable LC (inductor, capacitor) filter implementation. In [31], a 0.18 μm CMOS receiver represented the most complete subsampling receiver reference, due to the optimization performed for parameters, such as thermal noise level, jitter-induced noise and nonlinearity. Finally, there were also receivers based on subsampling for ultra wideband (UWB) applications, such the one in [32], which operates in the 3.1 – 10.6 GHz band with low power consumption.

Table 3 [8] shows the specifications for most of common wireless communication standards [2] and the results obtained in some of these previously published works on noise performance. These results are compared with those obtained in [8], in order to observe the benefits of implementation of a multiple clock technique for multi-standard receivers based on subsampling. It can be seen that, when employing the data acquisition system designed in [8], only the ENOB specifications for the IEEE 802.11a standard are not achieved, although they are very close. It should also be noted that some specifications, such the noise figure (NF) for UMTS (I) and IEEE 802.11b/g or the resolution for Bluetooth, are not achieved without the improvement proposed in [8], i.e., when a unique clock source is used [7]. Compared with the other published work, similar results for NF and noise PSD can be observed with respect to [8], showing a larger influence of the jitter (i.e., reducing the resolution with the input frequency) in the work presented in [8].

6. Conclusions

In this chapter, a brief review of sampling theory and the advantages of subsampling techniques in the context of wireless communication transceivers have been presented. In particular, the usefulness and potential of subsampling techniques in the design of a simple and flexible universal receiver are discussed. A data acquisition module for testing wireless receivers based on subsampling has been presented, which covers most present wireless communication standards requirements with only one single board. The main benefits have been presented, and a novel method based on multiple clocking techniques to reduce the folded noise effect has been proposed, obtaining an analytical expression for the improvement factor in the SNR with respect to a single clock solution. The presented board shows an experimental ENOB larger than 8 bits up to 4 GHz for a 20 MHz signal bandwidth; and, the selected frequency plan with two successive subsampling processes shows the ENOB improved by approximately 1 bit. Measurement results show that the design covers the most important wireless standards (i.e., GPS, GSM, GPRS, UMTS, Bluetooth, Wi-Fi, WiMAX), in terms of tuning frequency, linearity and noise. Another characteristic of the implemented module is its simplicity, with only a few components on a printed circuit board. These results show that, for testing purposes, the subsampling based receiver is a viable alternative to other typical frequency mixing based receiver architectures, with enhanced reconfigurability and programmability.

Moreover, the subsampling concept has been extended to multi-band and nonlinear systems, where there is an additional problem with the harmonics and different channels that may be folded in the band of interest. In this chapter, the challenges and issues on finding the valid subsampling frequencies in multi-band and nonlinear systems are discussed. For this scenario, the noise performance of a dual-band multi-standard receiver has been optimized, proposing different architectures based on multiple clocking techniques. Finally, two different applications (spectrum sensing in cognitive radios and a subsampling feedback loop for concurrent dual-band power amplifier linearization) are proposed and characterized experimentally, in order to demonstrate the functionality and capability of subsampling techniques for multi-band and nonlinear environments, reducing the cost and the complexity of the receiver architectures.

Author details

José Ramón García Oya*, Fernando Muñoz, Fernando J. Márquez,
Enrique López-Morillo and Antonio Torralba Silgado
Electronics Engineering Group (GIE), Electronics Department, University of Seville, Seville, Spain

Andrew Kwan, Fadhel M. Ghannouchi and Mohamed Helaoui
iRadio Lab, Department of Electrical and Computer Engineering, Schulich School of Engineering, University of Calgary, Calgary, AB, Canada

Acknowledgement

This work was supported in part by the Andalusian Regional Government (under the program entitled "Programa de Incentivos para el Fomento de la Innovación y el Desarrollo Empresarial de Andalucía") and the Andalusian Technological Corporation (CTA) and in part by the Andalusian Regional Government, under projects MUPHY and TIC-6323-2011, respectively. The authors also acknowledge Alberta Innovates - Technology Futures (AITF), the Natural Sciences and Engineering Research Council of Canada (NSERC), and the Canada Research Chairs (CRC) Program for their financial support.

* Corresponding Author

7. References

[1] Bagheri R, et al. (2006) An 800-MHz–6-GHz Software-Defined Wireless Receiver in 90-nm CMOS. IEEE Journal of Solid-State Circuits. j. 41, no.12: 2860-2876.

[2] Agnelli F et al. (2006) Wireless Multi-Standard Terminals: System Analysis and Design of a Reconfigurable RF Front-End. IEEE Circuits and Systems Magazine. j. 6: 38-59.

[3] Svelto F, Vahidfar M.B, Brandolini M (2008) Reconfigurable Si RF Receiver Front-Ends for Multistandard Radios. Proceedings of the 1st European Wireless Technology Conference, 2008: 33-36.

[4] Brandolini M, Rossi P, Manstretta D, Svelto F (2005) Toward Multistandard Mobile Terminals – Fully Integrated Receivers Requirements and Architectures. IEEE Transactions on Microwave Theory and Techniques. j. 53, no. 3: 1026-1038.

[5] Vidojkovic M, Sanduleanu M.A.T, Vidojkovic V, van der Tang J, Baltus P, van Roermund A.H.M (2008) A 1.2V Receiver Front-End for Multi-Standard Wireless applications in 65nm CMOS LP. 34th European Solid-State Circuit Conference. ESSCIRC 2008: 414-417.

[6] Barrak R, Ghazel A, Ghannouchi F.M (2009) Optimized Multistandard RF Subsampling Receiver Architecture. IEEE Transactions on Wireless Communications. j. 8: 2901 - 2909.

[7] Oya J.R.G, Muñoz F, Torralba A, Jurado A, Garrido A.J, Baños J. (2011) Data Acquisition System Based on Subsampling for Testing Wideband Multistandard Receivers. IEEE Transactions on Instrumentation and Measurements. j. 60: 3234-3237.

[8] Oya J.R.G, Muñoz F, Torralba A, Jurado A, Márquez F, López-Morillo E (2012) Data Acquisition System Based on Subsampling using Multiple Clocking Techniques. IEEE Instrumentation and Measurements. Accepted.

[9] Mitola J (1995), The software radio architecture. IEEE Communications Magazine. j. 33, no. 5: 26-38.

[10] Harris F, Lowdermilk R.W (2010) Software Defined Radio: Part 22 in a Series of Tutorials on Instrumentation and Measurement. IEEE Instrumentation & Measurement. j. 13: pp. 23-32.

[11] Abidi A.A (1995) Direct-conversion radio transceivers for digital communications. IEEE Journal of Solid-state Circuits. j. 30, no. 12: 1399-1410.

[12] Crols J, Steyaert M (1998) Low-IF topologies for high-performance analog front-ends for fully integrated receivers. IEEE Journal of Solid-state Circuits. j. 45, no. 3: 269-282.

[13] Grace D, Pitt S.P (1968) Quadrature sampling of high frequency waveforms. Journal of the Acoustical Society of America. j. 44: 1432-1436.

[14] Vaughan R.G, Scott N.L, White D.R (1991) The theorem of bandpass sampling. IEEE Transactions on Signal Processing. j. 39: 1973-1984.

[15] Kwan A, Bassam S.A, Ghannouchi F (2012) Sub-sampling Technique for Spectrum Sensing in Cognitive Radio Systems. IEEE Radio and Wireless Symposium, RWS 2012: 347-350.

[16] Bassam S.A, Kwan A, Chen W, Helaoui M, Ghannouchi F.M (2012) Subsampling Feedback Loop Applicable to Concurrent Dual-Band Linearization Architecture. IEEE Transactions on Microwave Theory and Techniques. Accepted.

[17] Phillips C.L, Parr J, Riskin E (2008) Signals, Systems and Transforms 4th Edition. Upper Saddle River, NJ: Prentice Hall.

[18] Sun Y.R (2006) Generalized Bandpass Sampling Receivers for Software Defined Radio. Doctoral Dissertation, School of Information and Communication Technology (ICT), Stockholm, Sweden.

[19] Azeredo-Leme C (2011) Clock Jitter Effects on Sampling: A Tutorial. IEEE Circuits and Systems Magazine. j. 11: 26-37.

[20] Karvonen S (2006) Charge Domain Sampling of High Frequency Signals with Embedded Filtering. Thesis, Faculty of Technology, Department of Electrical and Information Engineering, University of Oulu, Finland.

[21] Tseng C.H (2009) A Universal Formula for the Complete Bandpass Sampling Requirements of Non Linear Systems. IEEE Transactions on Signal Processing. j. 57, no. 10: 3869-3878.

[22] Oya J.R.G, Kwan A, Bassam S.A, Muñoz F, Ghannouchi F.M (2012) Optimization of Dual Band Receivers Design in Nonlinear Systems. IEEE International Microwave Symposium, IMS 2012.

[23] Tseng C.H, Chou S.C (2006) Direct Downconversion of Multiband RF Signals Using Bandpass Sampling. IEEE Transactions on Wireless Communications. j. 5, no. 1: 72-76.

[24] Kim J. H, Wang H, Kim H-J, Kim J-U (2009) Bandpass Sampling Digital Frontend Architecture for Multi-Band Access Cognitive Radio. IEEE Global Telecommunications Conference, GLOBECOM 2009: 1-6.

[25] Haykin, S (2005) Cognitive Radio: Brain Empowered Wireless Communications. IEEE Journal on Selected Areas in Communication. j. 48, no. 2: 201-220.

[26] Kurosawa N, Kobayashi H, Maruyama K, Sugawara H, Kobayashi K (2001) Explicit Analysis of Channel Mismatch Effects in Time-Interleaved ADC Systems. IEEE Transactions on Circuits and Systems I Fundamental Theory Applications. j. 48, no. 3:261-271.

[27] McCune E (2005) High-efficiency, Multi-mode, Multi-band Terminal Power Amplifiers. IEEE Microwave Magazine. j. 6, no. 1:44-55.

[28] Ghannouchi F.M, Hammi O (2009) Behavioral Modeling and Predistortion. IEEE Microwave Magazine. j. 10, no. 7:52-64.

[29] Mitzner K (2007) Complete PCB Design using OrCad Capture and Layout. Oxford: Elsevier.

[30] Pekau H, Haslett J.W (2007) A 0.18μm CMOS 2.1GHz Sub-sampling Receiver Front end with Fully Integrated Second- and Fourth-Order Q-Enhanced Filters. IEEE International Symposium on Circuits and Systems, 2007: 3103-3106.

[31] Jakonis D, Folkesson K, Dabrowski J, Eriksson P, Svensson C (2005) A 2.4-GHz RF Sampling Receiver Front-End in 0.18-μm CMOS. IEEE Journal of Solid-State Circuits. j. 40: 1265-1277.

[32] Vanderperren Y, Dehane W, Leus G (2006) A Flexible Low Power Subsampling UWB Receiver Based on Line Spectrum Estimation Methods. IEEE International Conference on Communications, ICC 2006. j. 10: 4694-4699.

Section 2

Medical Applications

Chapter 8

Data Acquisition in Pulmonary Ventilation

Bogdan Marius Ciurea

Additional information is available at the end of the chapter

http://dx.doi.org/10.5772/48363

1. Introduction

Breathing is the fundamental physiological process during which gas exchange between the organism and the environment is done. Respiration has three main components: external respiration, transport respiration and cellular respiration. The external respiration is significant for this chapter and it is defined as exchange of gases between the lungs and the external environment. Transport breathing facilitates the transport of gas through the blood inside the organism, and cellular respiration ensures the exchange of substances, including gas, at cellular level.

External respiration is carried out in two phases, called inspiratory breathing and expiratory breathing. During inspiratory breathing, a volume of air is inhaled through the airways (moth / nose, pharynx, larynx, trachea and bronchial tree) into the lungs. In the lungs air is mixed with carbon dioxide – rich gas coming from the blood. After that the mixed gas (air and carbon dioxide) is exhaled through the same airway to the atmosphere. Man can not live without oxygen, so, in case of reduced respiratory function, he could die.

There are natural cases, in which, due to illness (e.g. polio) or injury, the breathing process is affected. There are many people leading an apparent normal life, but they have respiratory disorders during sleep. The collapse of the respiratory system can appear also because of artificial causes (injections of anesthetic). During surgery, for pain relief and for muscle relaxation, artificial breathing is used. In those cases was observed that a lot of people have partly or completely affected the respiratory function, regardless that the phenomenon was predicted or not.

In case of respiratory function disturbance, to ensure the necessary quantity of oxygen in the lungs and at the cellular level, some equipment that supports breathing is used. These machines are called ventilators and their induced breathing is called ventilation. The ventilator must insert the gas mixture needed for a good oxygenation in safe conditions into the patient's lung. For this, it must be very precise.

Respiratory function depends on many parameters which makes the equipment for artificial respiration to be highly complex. Proper functioning of the ventilation equipment is required to ensure the success of the medical act.

To develop and test the ventilators it is important to know what the doctors need. There are three important ideas to know before understand ventilation: ventilation process (that means what the ventilator are doing during ventilation), ventilation parameters and ventilation modes. In this chapter some things about the ventilation parameters are presented.

Considering the speed with which the medical staff must intervene for saving the patients lives, ventilator should be easy to handle and ventilation parameters must be set and read quickly. Medical staff must easily monitor the ventilation process quality, and the ventilator must provide much information. These data should be viewed easily and in real time. Both set (wished) and realized parameters should be viewable at the same time.

There are used various sensors to determine directly or indirectly the values of the. Sensors must measure in some special places of the ventilation system and at certain time moments, different parameters. Signals from the sensors must be processed so that the values of the desired physical parameters appear on the display. Measured values are stored in order to observe their variation in time. This allows the efficiency of the medical care to be observed or, if it is necessary, to change and improve the medical process.

Because functioning of the ventilator must be safe, it must be tested from time to time. Testing consists of checking the parameters and the patient blocks. For testing are used specific sensors. Signals from these sensors are transmitted to a microprocessor and processed to obtain the real values of the measurements used in ventilation. To test the patient blocks special stands are constructed. Various valves and sealings must be tested. For this purpose gas is inserted or extracted into and from the system using solenoid valves. The sensors and the valves are connected to a computer or microprocessor through a device called Data Aqusition Board.

The program that processes data from the sensors and controls the actuators is a dedicated software for a DAQ board. The dedicated software (driver) is used to convert the DAQ board language into the computer's language. Inside the computer other softwares (application software) are used to process and display the DAQ board information. For this chapter the softwares are developed in LabView. For a good understanding of ventilation parameters determining process it is important to know the DAQ system, what DAQ means, what is needed for a DAQ system, how a DAQ works (some example that presents the DAQ system are given).

It is also important to know what is a sensor, an actuator and their working principle. The relationship betwen the electrical signal from the sensor and the physical parameter measured represent the sensor's calibration. To determine this relationship it is necessary to develop a calibration system. It is also important to know a lot about the sensors' and the actuators' power supplies, the actuators' electronic comands and others.

This paper presents the main parameters used in ventilation and how these can be determined with a DAQ board. For this purpose a DAQ system general presentation is made and some specific examples for the ventilation area are given. A system, which is meant to be a part of a ventilator tester, that can determine the leakage for a patient block is presented.

2. The main physical parameters used in ventilation

The ventilator introduces inside the patient gas with a certain flow rate and pressure to provide the oxygen needed for living. Blood oxygen concentration is monitored as a SpO_2 parameter and should be close to 100%. The doctor needs to adjust and monitor a set of parameters, named ventilation parameters, to ensure a proper ventilation. These are pressures, flow rates, volumes, gas concentrations.

2.1. Ventilatory pressures

Basically, inside the lung, during the process of external respiration the pressures varies as in Fig. 1. and during ventilation as in Fig. 2.

Pressures are very important in ventilation. Ventilatory pressures may not be too large, not to destroy the alveolar wall, but not too small either, to ensure that the lungs are filled with the necessary amount of gas.

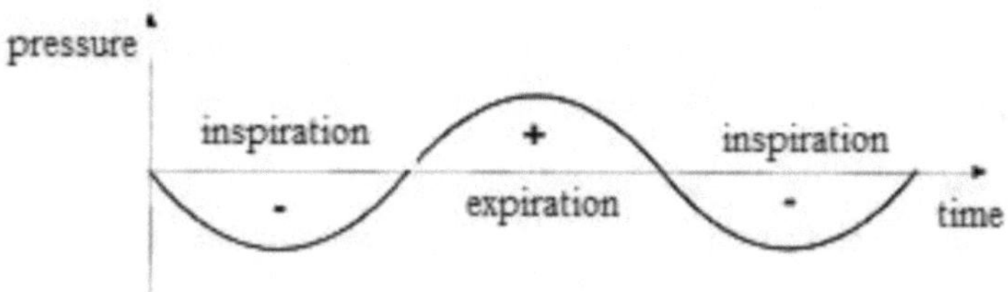

Figure 1. Pressure variation during respiration

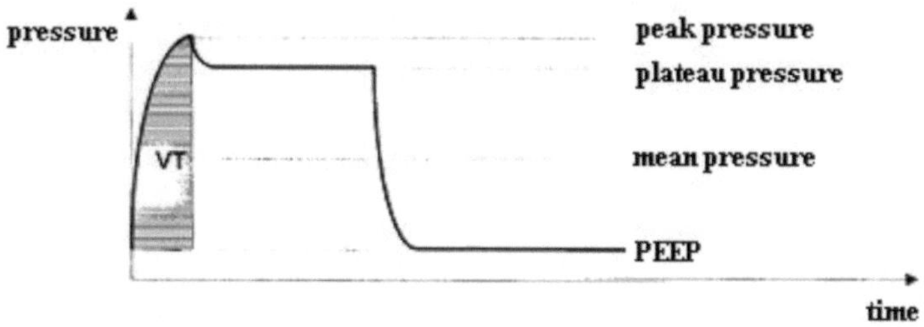

Figure 2. Pressure variation for lung ventilation (IPPV)

The pressure inside the airways is denoted by p_{aw}.

The mean pressure, denoted by p_{mean}, is the average pressure in the lung during ventilation cycle and is defined by the following relation:

$$p_{mean} = \frac{1}{T}\int_0^T p_{aw} dt \tag{1}$$

where: T – ventilation period,
p_{aw} – airway pressure,
t – time.

Inspiratory breathing's pressure in ventilation has two levels:

- $p_{\max}$ – the maximum pressure inside the lung; this pressure is set at maximum value by the physician; the ventilator must not introduce gas with a pressure above the preset maximum pressure inside the lung.
- $p_{plateau}$ – the plateau pressure, the pressure for which the lung is kept inflated to allow enought gas exchange, smaller than $p_{\max}$.

The pressure determined by the physician and created by the ventilator to produce expiration shall be called expiratory pressure, denoted by $p_{\exp}$. In general, the pressure at the end of the expiration breathing is called for short PEEP (Positive End-Expiratory Pressure).

2.2. Respiratory times

The time in which inspiratory breathing is done, is called inspiratory time, denoted by t_{insp}, and is composed of two other times:

- t_1 – lung filling time until $p_{\max}$,
- t_2 – plateau time, necessary to maintain the inflated lung for gas exchange.

$$t_{insp} = t_1 + t_2 \tag{2}$$

The time period necessary to empty the lung is called expiratory time, denoted by $t_{\exp}$.

The time period, denoted by T, in which the breath is fully done:

$$T = t_{insp} + t_{\exp} \tag{3}$$

Respiratory frequency, denoted by f, is defined by the following relation:

$$f = \frac{1}{T} \tag{4}$$

2.3. Volumes, flow rates

The gas flow introduced by the ventilator into the patient's lung is called inspiratory flow, $\dot{V}_i$, and the gas flow exhaled from the patient's lung is called expiratory flow, $\dot{V}_e$.

$$\dot{V}_e = -\frac{\Delta p}{R} \cdot e^{-\frac{t}{\tau}} \quad (5)$$

$$\dot{V}_i = \frac{\Delta p}{R} \cdot e^{-\frac{t}{\tau}} \quad (6)$$

where: t – the time,
τ – the time constant,
e – the base of the natural logarithm (≈2,72),
R – the resistance:

$$R = \frac{\Delta p}{\Delta V} \quad (7)$$

Δp – the maximum pressure variation:

$$\Delta p = p_{\max} - PEEP \quad (8)$$

where: $p_{\max}$ – the maximum pressure in airways,
PEEP – the PEEP pressure,
$\dot{V}$ – gas flow.

The volumes are determined as the product betwen the gas flow, $\dot{V}$, and the gas flow time, t.

$$V = t \cdot \dot{V} \quad (9)$$

The inhaled volume is called the inspiratory Tidal Volume, denoted by VT_i and the exhaled volume is called expiratory tidal Volume, denoted by VT_e or VT. Ideally, the two volumes are equal.

$$VT_i = \bar{\dot{V}}_{insp} \cdot t_{insp} \quad (10)$$

$$VT_e = \bar{\dot{V}}_{\exp} \cdot t_{\exp} \quad (11)$$

The Minute Volume is the amount of air volume inhaled or exhaled per minute and is defined as:

$$MV = f \cdot VT \quad (12)$$

2.4. Oxygen concentration

The gas mandatory for life is oxygen. For the human body's it is a necessary a certain amount of oxygen in the blood (SpO_2). To increase this parameter to 100% SpO_2, it is necessary to enrich the inspiratory gas with oxygen. When the lung is working normally and a large amount of oxygen in the mixture, O_2, is not needed, the concentration must be decrease to 21% O_2, only air. The oxygen concentration of inspiratory gas is denoted by FiO_2.

2.5. Temperature and humidification of ventilation gas

Because the gas is introduced directly into the lungs and in some cases it does not pass through the nose, it is necessary for gas to be heated to the patient's temperature and humidified. The nose's role is taken, during ventilation, by the humidifier.

3. Determination and comand of various physical paramters with a DAQ (Data AcQuisition) board

Data acquisition is the collection process of measured data from various sources, in a precise manner, organized and synchronized in time and is the monitoring part of a real physical system. Generally, data acquisition, involves a meshing process, which means sampling and quantifying, for analog signals to be converted into accessible digital computer, numerical representation. For short, data acquisition mean the process of sampling signals that measure physical conditions in real world and converting the resulting samples into digital numeric values that can be manipulated by a computer. Data acquisition systems (abbreviated with the acronym DAS or DAQ) typically convert analog waveforms into digital values for processing.

Data acquisition control system means generating data for process control as part of a real regulation system. In most cases control signals must be analog. Real-time operating systems are characterized by the ability to monitor and control in a predetermined time interval.

A functional diagram for an acquisition and control system is presented in Fig. 3. A process from a real system is characterized by a set of physical parameters, most often nonelectric. Sensors convert physical parameters into analog or digital electrical signals. Signals are handled, processed, analyzed and presented by the computing system. It also generates control signals through the control actuators in the real system. In the computer which has the driver and the application software data are saved, stored, then processed and analyzed. After processing the data are presented in an intuitive and intelligible manner. Some data are used to generate signals for the actuators to control the system.

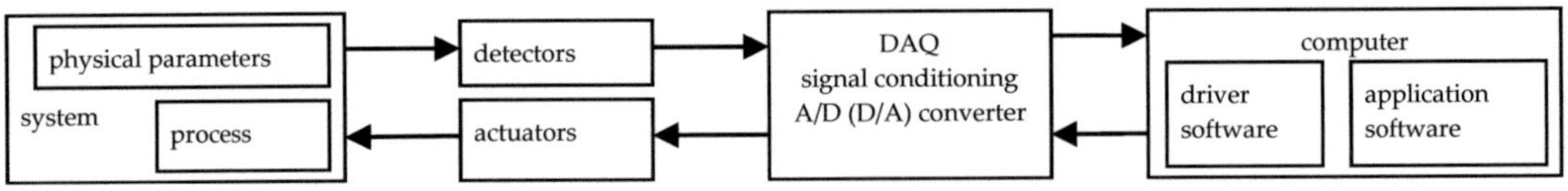

Figure 3. A real system

The acquisition and control system have two main parts, one is the hardware and the other is the software.

3.1. The hardware zone

A data acquisition hardware sytem is has sensors and / or actuators, a DAQ device, connection cables and a computer with dedicated software.

3.1.1. Sensors and actuators

A sensor is a converter that measures a physical parameter and converts it into a signal which can be read by an observer or by an instrument. In DAQ sistem a sensor, also called a transducer, converts a physical phenomenon into a measurable electrical signal.

An actuator is a type of motor for moving or controlling a mechanism or system. An actuator is the mechanism by which an agent acts upon an environment.

3.1.2. DAQ device

DAQ hardware acts as the interface between a computer and the signals from the outside world.

A DAQ system means any device which measures input electrical quantities and can be connected to a PC. A DAQ contains at least one converter, an interface that transforms analog signals into digital signals.

These hardware devices may only convert the input signals into digital signals without processing them. All calculations must be done by the PC software. The same device can measure a lot of parameters, simply by modifying the transducers used and the software that retrieves and analyzes the data. Universal DAQ have greater flexibility allowing their use in many applications with the disadvantage of user time lost for designing and developing application software for each system. These devices can be internal or external for a PC. The most common are the DAQ-boards. They are universal DAQ devices like extension boards that connect through an internal PC bus.

The overall structure of a data acquisition boards is shown in Fig. 4.

The analog signals, collected by the sensors, coupled to the **analog inputs** of the DAQ, are sampled and converted into digital format by **A / D converter**. Internal bus connects all blocks of DAQ. Digital data are available on the internal bus. **Bus interface and control block** connects the internal DAQ bus with PC bus extension and transfer data between them. **D/A converter** transform the digital signals from the computer into analog signals for the analog outputs.

I/O digital ports are programmable ports as inputs or outputs digital data. They provide acquisition and generate digital signals coupled to physical **I/O digital ports**.

Interrupts controller synchronizes events with the software.

Programmable Counter block assures functions: events counting, wave generation, time modulated signals and others. Interaction with the environment is achieved by **digital input / output count**.

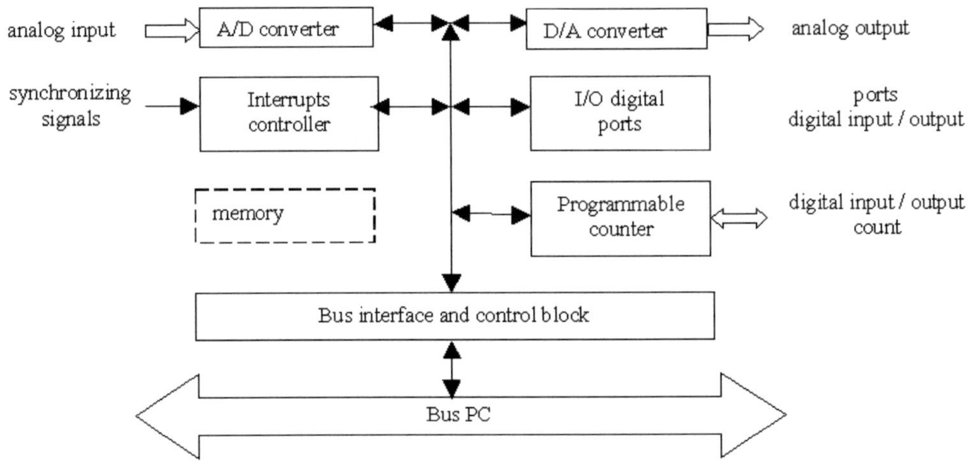

Figure 4. DAQ

Memory is a buffer for temporary storage of data in DAQ.

Actuators are usually complex devices that can not be directly controlled by control signals generated by the system. Interfaces that control these devices, according to orders received from the data generated, are called **controllers.** They actually translate simple commands from the computing system into complex signals that control the actuators.

Sometimes controllers are complex systems with microprocessors and control loops.

Few companies worldwide are dedicated to producing the DAQ, like: National Instrumets, ADLINK Technogy, LabJack Corporation, ACCES I/O and others.

3.2. The software zone

A computer with programmable software controls the operation of the DAQ device and is used for processing, visualizing and storing data. The software zone has two parts: the driver software and the application software.

The driver software is a very important software element for communication between the application software and the peripheral devices, like DAQ. It simplifies communication with the DAQ device by abstracting low-level hardware commands and register-level programming. A driver is a collection of functions (subprograms) that implements the necessary controls to interface the software with the hardware.

The driver receives high level commands from the software application and generates low-level commands to the DAQ. It receives, processes, analyzes and scales DAQ response. Typically, the DAQ driver software has an application programming interface that is used within a programming environment to build application software.

The application software implements, beside measuremet functions, control and data display, and firmware, program included by the manufacturer in a specialized system, providing processing and analysis data and calculate the final results.

The application software facilitates the interaction between the computer and the user for acquiring, analyzing, and presenting measurement data. It is either a prebuilt application with predefined functionality, or a programming environment for building applications with custom functionality. Custom applications are often used to automate multiple functions of a DAQ device, perform signal-processing algorithms, and display custom user interfaces.

Some commercial application softwares are: LabView, HP-VEE, DIA-dem, DASY Lab, Python, QtiPlot and others, or microcontrollers software based on C++.

To create application software it is important to know the main DAQ's features:

- Supported input voltage range from DAQ should be correlated with the voltage provided by the sensors. The sensor output range should be fully included into the DAQ's input range.
- **The accuracy and precision** defines quantitative how exactly are represented the analog input signals by the digital output signals. It is defining converter accuracy and analog components precision.
- **The conversion time** represents the time a converter needs to achieve a conversion for a sample of the analog signal in the equivalent digital representation.
- **The resolution** represents the precision of the digital representation of an analog input, resulting from the division of input domain by 2^n, where n is the number of bits for the analog / digital converter.
- **The sampling rate** is the maximum frequency that the DAQ can achieve, sample and convert the output signal.
- **The transmission rate** is given by the number of samples per second that DAQ can send to the computer.
- **The number of analog input and output channels** represents the number of physical connections on which analog signals can be read and generated.
- **The buffer capacity** represents the capacity of the used memory for temporary digital storage of the samples acquired until to their transmission to the PC. The buffer is very useful when the sampling rate exceeds the transmission rate or when multiple signals are acquired at different sampling rates.
- **The time synchronization** channels is very useful for collecting data on multiple channels.

4. Sensors and actuators used in pulmonary ventilation

In ventilation sensors for measuring pressure, flow rate, oxygen and anesthesic concentration, temperature and humidity are used.

4.1. Sensors

4.1.1. Diaphragm pressure sensors

The diaphragm pressure sensor uses a resistive element with variable resistance pressure-dependent. The resistors are applied on a ceramic membrane with thin film technology. The pressure acting on the membrane produces a change in the resistance depending on its bending.

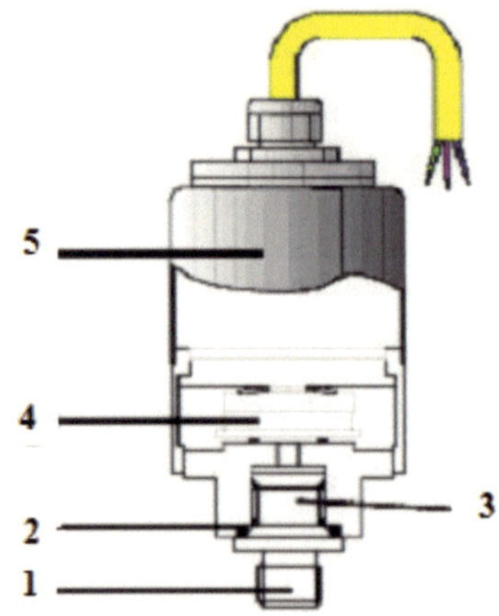

Figure 5. Pressure sensor: 1. connector, 2. o-ring, 3. coupling, 4. ceramic element with integrated metallic resistor, 5. housing

The main characteristics of pressure sensors are the maximum pressure that can be determined, accuracy, power supply voltage, temperature range in which the sensor has a linear characteristic.

For testing the ventilation and the patient blocks the maximum pressure is 110 mbar and the pressure sensor used can determine maximum pressure up to 120 mbar. For testing the gas supply pressure in the hospital is needed a pressure sensor that can measure values above 6 bar, and for the nebuliser testing at least 2 bar. The sensor used is for middle pressure, maximum 10 bar.

4.1.2. *Flow sensors*

Flow sensors used in ventilation can have a diaphram or a hot wire.

4.1.2.1. Diaphragm flow sensor

The measurement principle is simple, tthe diaphragm geometry is known, the pressure is measured downstream and upstream of the diaphragm simultaneous and using the fluid mechanics the flow rate can be determined with the following formula (13).

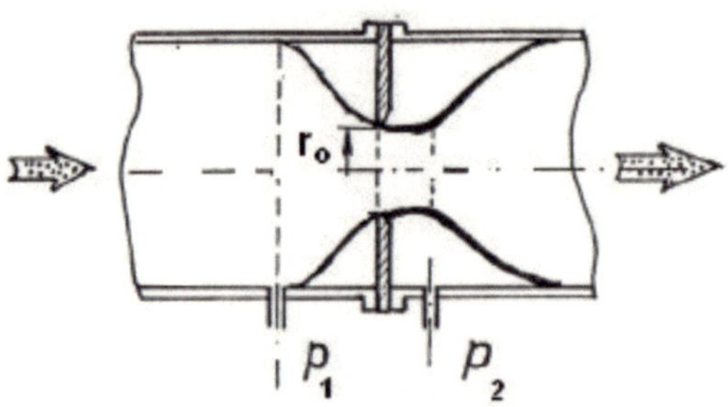

Figure 6. Diaphragm flow sensor

$$\dot{V} = \pi \cdot \frac{p_1 - p_2}{8 \cdot \eta \cdot l} \cdot r_0^4 \tag{13}$$

where: $\dot{V}$ – the flow rate,

p_1 – the gas pressure upstream the flow sensor,

p_2 – the gas pressure downstream the flow sensor,

r_0 – the flow sensor diaphragm's radius,

η – the dynamic viscosity.

4.1.2.2. Hot-wire flow sensor

Hot wire flow sensor operates according to the anaemometric principle of constant temperature hot wires flow meter. Gas flows along a very thin, electrically heated platinum wire in a measuring tube. The wire is heated to a temperature of 180°C. The gas flow that passes through sensor cools the platinum wire. To maintain a constant temperature additional electricity is required to pass through the resistor and the electrical current is proportional to the gas flow. The second platinum wire is used to compensate interferences of various gas mixtures. Various gases in the mixture have different thermal conductivity. The temperature lost in the second line is an indicator of the gas composition.

The main features of the flow rate sensor are the minimum and the maximum flow rate, pressure and temperature, gas type, input and output voltage.

When testing the ventilation flow rates of tens of liters/minute are used. For infants low flows and high accuracy are necessary. To determine leakage inside circuits and patient blocks a good sensor accuracy is necessary in the low flow rate area.

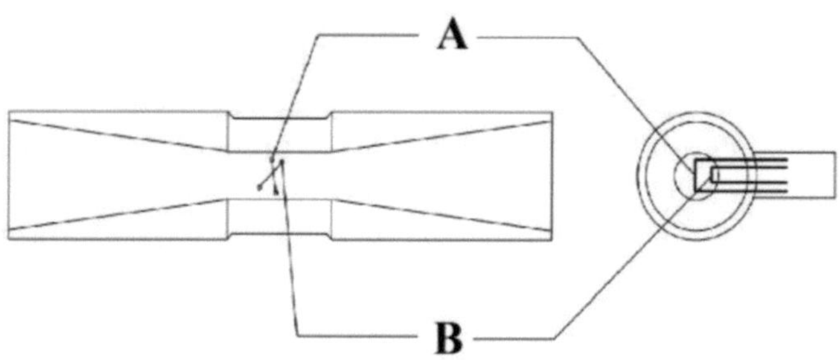

Figure 7. Hot-wire flow meter

4.1.3. Oxygen concentration sensors

Oxygen is the gas that ensures life. Depending on the amount of oxygen in the blood there are cases in which the inhaled gas should be enriched in oxygen. The oxygen introduced into the lungs must be strictly controlled and monitored, for this task sensors that determine the oxygen concentration are used. These sensors can be electrolytic or paramagnetic.

4.1.3.1. Electrolytic oxygen sensor

For this sensor the operating principle is electrochemical. The oxygen diffuses through a teflon membrane 1 into the electrolyte 5 and is reduced at the gold cathode 2. In the same time the lead anode 4 is oxidized. The reaction's results are lead and water. The oxidation process consumes anode 4 affecting the sensor's life. The teflon membrane makes the oxygen diffusion to be faster. For this reason the sensor response time is small. Chemical reaction produces a current proportional to the partial pressure of the oxygen inside the gas mixture. The chemical reaction is thermo-dependent. To eliminate the temperature dependence a thermistors 3 is introduced in parallel with the oxygen sensor.

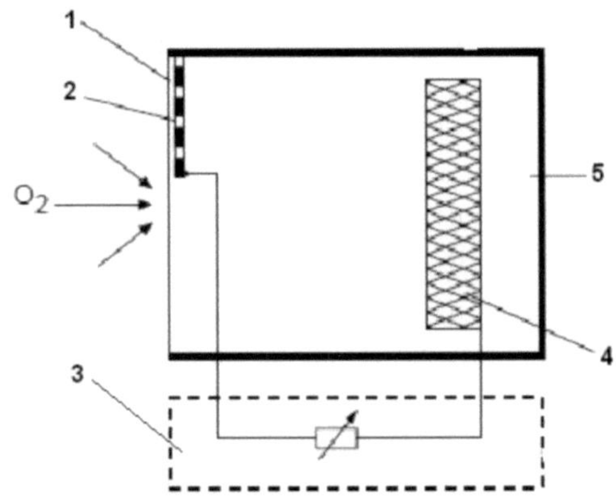

Figure 8. Electrolytic oxygen sensor. 1. teflon membrane, 2. gold cathode, 3. thermistor, 4. lead anode, 5. electrolyte.

For this sensor the operating principle is electrochemical. The oxygen diffuses through a teflon membrane 1 into the electrolyte 5 and is reduced at the gold cathode 2. In the same time the lead anode 4 is oxidized. The reaction's results are lead and water. The oxidation process consumes anode 4 affecting the sensor's life. The teflon membrane makes the oxygen diffusion to be faster. For this reason the sensor response time is small. Chemical reaction produces a current proportional to the partial pressure of the oxygen inside the gas mixture. The chemical reaction is thermo-dependent. To eliminate the temperature dependence a thermistors 3 is introduced in parallel with the oxygen sensor.

4.1.3.2. Paramagnetic O_2 sensor

The oxygen is a paramagnetic gas, which means that it is attracted by a magnetic field. This magnetic susceptibility is much greater than that of most other gas molecules and therefore this physical property is ideal for the oxygen level determination in a wide range of gases. The magnetic susceptibility of oxygen decreases inversely with its temperature. This principle has led to sensors like Dräger Pato and Michell XTP600.

The electromagnets generate an alternating field. The sampling gas flows through the cuvette and the gas path inside the sensor system. The heating element heats up the sampling gas to operating temperature and the thermoelement measures the temperature.

The outer alternating magnetic field influences the mobility of the oxygen contained in the sampling gas. The changing mobility alters the heat transfer in the sampling gas which results in the thermoelement measuring a changing temperature. The event of the heat transfer variation depends on the oxygen concentration in the sampling gas. An electronic module converts the temperature change in an oxygen concentration value which is then displayed on the connected patient monitor.

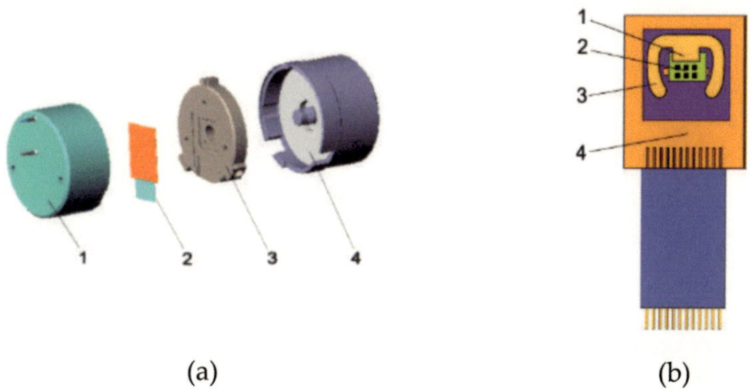

Figure 9. Sensor O2 – Pato. (a) 1. magnetic system, 2. sensor system, 3. cuvette, 4. magnetic system. (b) 1. measurement compartment, 2. heating element and thermoelement assembly, 3. gas path, 4. sensor element.

The main features of the oxygen sensor are the accuracy, the response time, the temperature and the voltage output.

Electrochemical sensors do not need power supply, but for the other types of oxygen sensors the inlet voltage is also important.

4.1.4. Anesthetic and capnography sensors

In anesthesia is very important The anesthetic's dosage to ensure that there is no pain and that there is muscle relaxation. An excessive dosage can lead to awakening problems and a small one can cause patient pain. Thus anesthesic must be accurately dosed and measured. For measuring an anestesic sensor is used.

The ILCA sensor measuring principle is the infrared absorption. Infrared radiation emitted by a source enters through a window and reaches the light beam where is divided into several parts. Each part goes through a fixed filter. The infrared optical filters (band-pass filters) are dimensioned in terms of their wavelength such that light is transmitted in three channels at the wavelength of the sampled gases. The remaining spectrum is blocked by these filters. When a gas is present the light is absorbed and the resultant change of intensity measured in the respective channel is a measure of the gas concentration. The fourth channel (reference channel) measures at a wavelength at which none of the sampled gases absorbs.

The CO_2 and anaesthetic sensor's characteristics are accuracy, measured gas type, temperature range, the supplying voltage and output voltage.

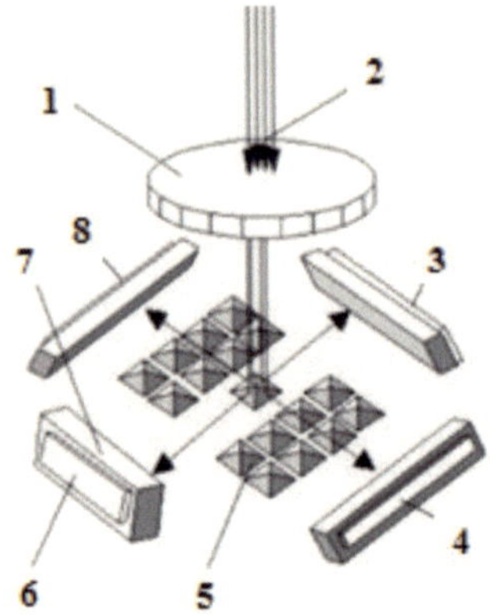

Figure 10. Senzor ILCA. 1. sensor window, 2. infrared light, 3. CO2 sensor chip, 4. reference, 5. beam splitter, 6. anesthetic gas sensor chip, 7. infrared filter, 8. NO_2 sensor chip.

4.1.5. Temperature sensors

Usually, the ventilation gas does not crosses through the nose to be heated. For this reason it is necessary to heat the gas which is done by a special divice named heater. Is it important to control and monitor the temperature and for this a temperature sensor is used. Temperature sensors used in ventilation are thermoresistive or thermocouple types.

The resistive sensor uses a resistive element, temperature dependent. Temperature variations produce proportional variations of resistance. The resistive element is composed of a platinum wire inserted into a capillary tube.

Pt100 - as is known this sensor, do not have a linear characteristic. The characteristics may be linearized with electronic assemblies.

The thermocouple sensor is made of two metal wires encapsulated into a metal tube joined at one end (welded junction elements). When a temperature variation appears, in the junction a voltage variation occurs and it can be read at the other ends of the two conductors, providig the temperature in the junction.

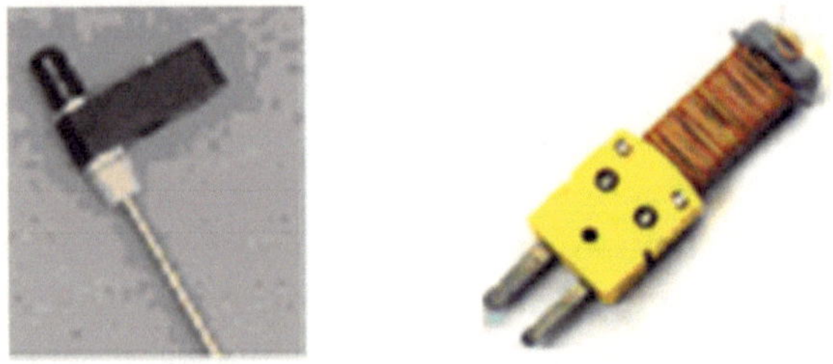

(a) (b)

Figure 11. Temperature sensors. (a) thermorezistive sensor. (b) thermocouple sensor.

For the temperature sensors the accuracy, the temperature range, the power supply and the internal resistances are important.

4.2. Actuators, solenoids

A valve is a device that regulates, directs or controls the flow of a fluid (gases, liquids) by opening, closing, or partially obstructing various passageways. A solenoid is an electrically controlled valve. In ventilation they are needed to control gas flow towards the patient or for the patient block test. Usually flow rate can be varied between 0.1 and 60 l/min.

4.2.1. Flow control valve

Flow control can be achieved by strangulation (throttle) or pulse.

Setting by strangulation is achieved by modifying the valve opening area.

Pulse adjustment is achieved by varying the open/close pulse times for a valve with a fixed diameter. To ensure there are no big variations of the instantaneous flow (fixed for the valve) from the average flow (regular) the open/closed sequence is done with high frequency.

Figure 12. Flow control valve

The main features of the flow control valves are the minimum and the maximum flow rate, the working pressure, the gas type, the maximum voltage supply, the response time, the internal resistance and the maximum current.

To test ventilators valves for pressure up to 6 bar with good flow control under 2 liters /minute are used.

4.2.2. Solenoid valve for pressure regulation

Is very important to control the pressure, for safety reasons, in the patient system.

Pressure control is achieved by means of pressure regulators with coils.

The pressure valve consists of a membrane which acts as a flow control regulator and is controlled by a plunger. A coil drives the plunger. The plunger moves the membrane and opens the valve. Proportional to the current through the coil is the displacement of the plunger and the valve's opening. (0 mA will correspond to –1 mbar, 500 mA to 120 mbar).

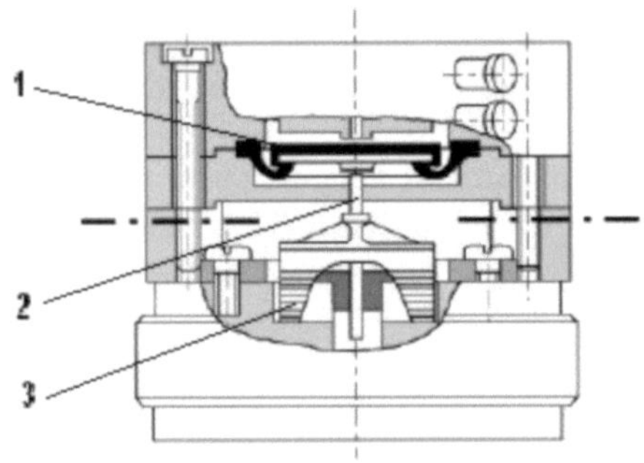

Figure 13. Solenoid valve for pressure regulation. 1. membrane, 2. plunger, 3. coil.

For the pressure regulators the maximum pressure, the power supply and the electric drive are important .

5. The power supply and command of various subassemblies

In order to use sensors they must be connected to a voltage source (power supply). Generally, in ventilation, sensors are supplied with voltages of 5, 10, 12 Vcc. Reading data from the sensor is done by reading an electrical outlet parameter from it. Usually it is read the electrical voltage, the current or the resistance. A specific electronic circuits is designed for the sensor's electrical supply, to acquire the correct value of the electrical signal.

5.1. The power supply for the spirolog flow sensor

For some sensors different montages are required to allow sensor supply and ensure a good data reading from it. Such an example is Fig. 14 in which a montage for the spirolog flow sensor is presented.

The basic wiring diagram for the spirolog sensor is represented by a voltage amplifier for a Wheastone bridge. With the adjustable resistor R_{var} (10kΩ) a current is established through the Wheastone bridge and the gas flow sensor is positioned inside the maximum sensitivity area. The Wheastone bridge imbalance generates a variable current at its terminals, which is then picked of by a differential amplifier, the operational amplifier AO2. At the outlet of the differential amplifier a voltage equal to the amplification coefficient multiplied with the difference resulted from the Wheastone bridge is generated. AO_3 is a simple DC amplifier, with a amplification coefficient egual to A, the level's stability being ensured by the capacitor C_1. At the AO3 amplifier's outlet a voltage variation between 10V and 19mV, corresponding to a change in flow from 0 to 60 liters/ minute, can be measured.

The flow sensor's filament sterilization is done with the K1 switch and with the resistor Rs = 120Ω. When closing the switch K1, the current inside the filament increases ensuring a temperature of 200°C.

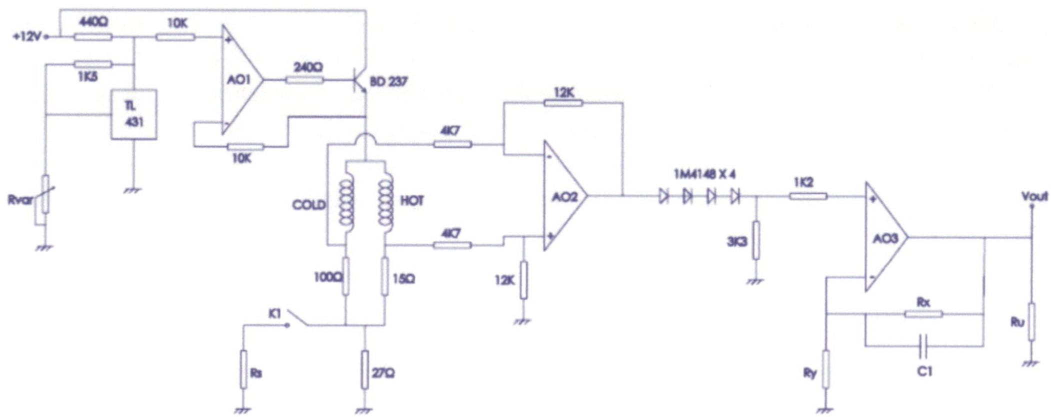

Figure 14. Electronic diagram for the spirolog flow sensor

5.2. The actuators' command

Actuators used in human ventilation can be commanded in voltage or current. Some data acquisition boards do not support the current command. For them an electronic device that switches the voltage command into a current command must be present.

5.2.1. The flow valve's command

The data acquisition board USB 6009 could assure a maximum voltage $U_{\max} = 5V$ and the maximum required for a flow control valve is $U_{\max} = 12V$. To command inside the full range of the flow valve the voltage command given by the data acquisition board is needed to be amplified.

The control of the flow control valve by the data acquisition board is done through a DC amplifier realized with an operational amplifier AO and a current amplifier realized with a transistor in Darlington configuration. The electronic scheme is shown in Fig. 15.

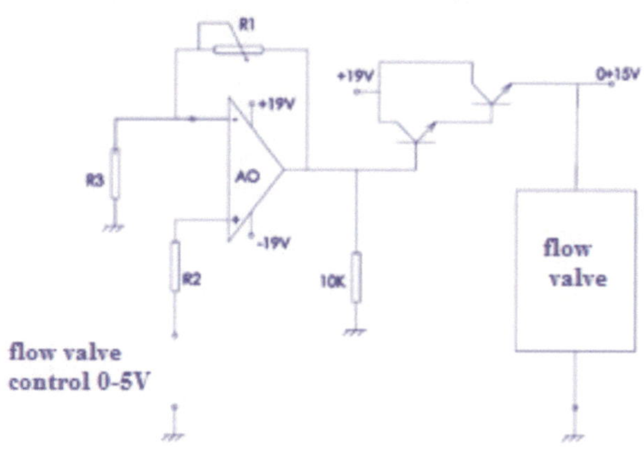

Figure 15. The electronic scheme for the flow control valve's power supply

The control voltage for the flow valve is set at the positive terminal of the AO amplifier. It is powered by a differential voltage +/- 19V. The Power amplifier is realized with transistors BD 139 and MJE 13009, medium power bipolar transistors. The amplifier input current is approximately 20 mA it is amplified with a value given by the product between the two transistors' β factors. The change in voltage on the noninverting input of the operational amplifier with 1V will generate to the output amplifier, respectively to the emitter of MJE 13009 transistor, a voltage of 3.2 V.

5.2.2. The pressure valve's command

An electronic system for the pressure valve's control is designed based on the control voltage's variation, variation between 0 to 5 V. The control system diagram is shown in Fig. 16.

The pressure control valve is controlled in current while the USB 6009 data acquisition board can control only in voltage.

For the pressure control valve a constant current generator is realized with an operational amplifier AO and a MOSFET transistor is used. Current through the pressure valve ($i_{pressure}$) is seted by the R_{set} resistance. A constant current generator controlled by a voltage is necessary to eliminate the impedance variations occured when the pressure valve is powerd, and it's core, consisting of a coil, is heated. $i_{pressure}$ is given by the following formula:

$$i_{pressure} = \frac{U_{pressure}}{R_{set}} \tag{14}$$

where: $i_{pressure}$ – the current through the pressure valve,

R_{set} – the resistance for the current regulation (1Ω),

$U_{pressure}$ – the electical DC voltage for the pressure valve.

The noninverting input of the operational amplifier is used to control the generator through the acquisition board.

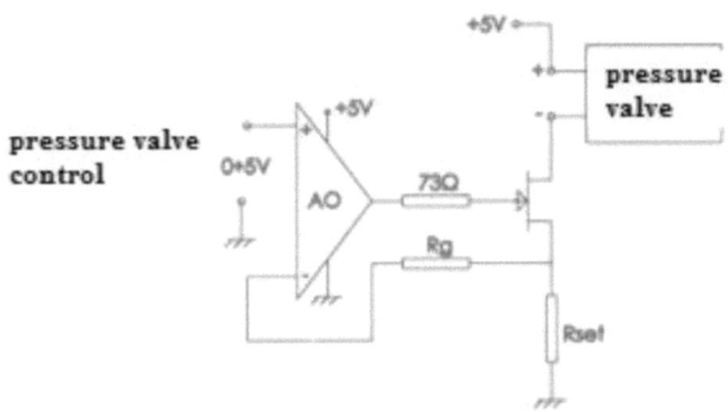

Figure 16. The electronic scheme for the pressure valve's power supply

The AO operational amplifier is powered from a single power surce with a constant voltage of 5V.

R_g (1kΩ) is the assembly's overall current response and it follows continuously the pressure valve's voltage changes.

6. Sensors and actuators calibration

The sensor calibration means finding an equivalent between the the sensor's measured electrical output and the physical parameter to be determined. To find the equivalent some calibration systems are created.

For calibration reasons it's necessary to be able to read on the computer's display the voltages provided by the calibrated sensor connected to it via the data acquisition board. A way to determine these voltages, for a pressure sensor, is shown in Fig. 17. This program was developed in LabVIEW 8.5, from National Instruments.

The software described in Fig. 17 is based on a "While" loop. This loop was chosen because it has the advantage that it can be easily stopped by the user when pressing the "stop" button connected in advance to the Conditional Terminal. The loop stops also in case of the acquisition board's erroneous functioning. In this case, the DAQ Assistant Express V.I. is connected via the output error ("error out") and the "OR" expression to the terminal conditioning of the "While" loop. The values from the sensor to be calibrated are introduced in the program through the data acquisition board and the DAQ Assistant Exprees V.I. Because to the acquisition board can be connected several sensors, using the function Select Signals the channel where the sensor is connected (to the DAQ board) is established. The signal from the sensor is filtered by the Express V.I. Filter. The filtered signal is displayed numerically using the indicator called, in this case, "pressure".

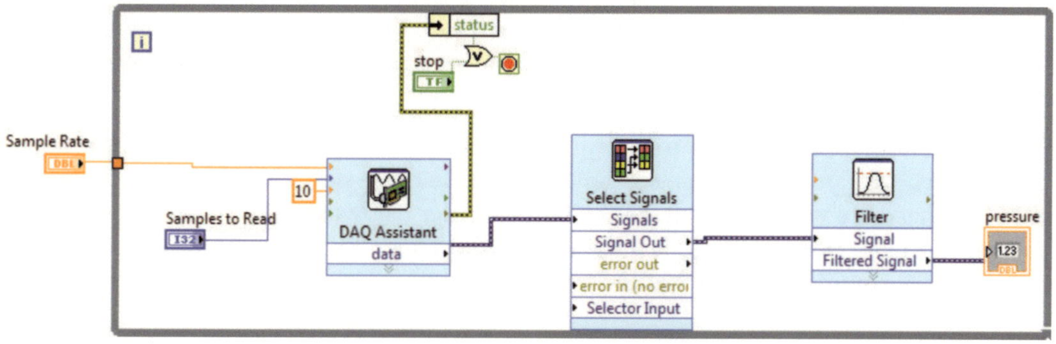

Figure 17. The software used to read the voltage from a pressure sensor

To determine the voltage from diferent sensors, like flow rate sensors, O_2 concentration sensors, anaestesic gas concentration sensors, the software, in LabView, is similar with the one shown in Fig. 17.

6.1. Pressure sensor calibration

6.1.1. Assembling for pressure sensor calibration

The pressure sensor to be calibrated is connected to the computer via the data acquisition board type NI USB 6009. On the computer's display, using the LabView 8.5 software, electrical signals provided by the the pressure sensor's output variation are viewed. To directly determine the pressure values it is necessary to find an equivalence between these voltages and the pressure values.

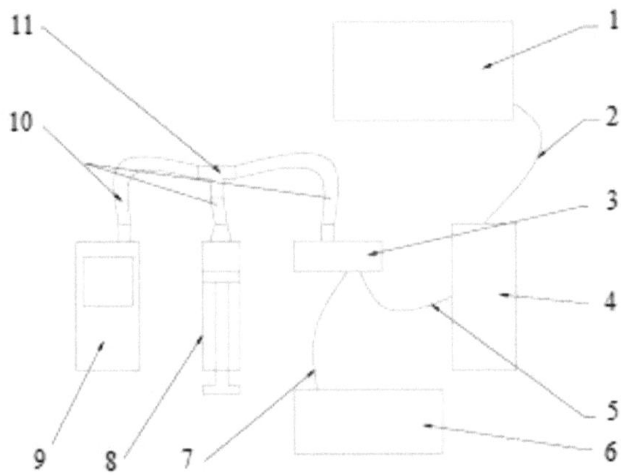

Figure 18. A diagram for a low pressure sensor calibration assembling. 1. computer, 2. connecting cable, 3. pressure sensor, 4. DAQ board, 5. connection cable, 6. power supply, 7. connection cable, 8. syringe, 9. pressure gauge, 10. hoses, 11. "T"-shaped connection piece

To calibrate the pressure sensor a montage shown in Fig. 18 is built. The system consists of a syringe for creating the pressure, connection hoses, calibrated sensor connected to a computer via the data acquisition board, the gauge (DPI 705 Druck Limited) metrological verified, connected in parallel with the sensor to be calibrated using a "T"-shaped connection piece. The sensor to be calibrated is powered from the power supply through a connection cable. The signals collected from the sensor are processed by the computer where they arrive through the data acquisition board and the connection cables.

Using a syringe various pressures which are monitored by the pressure sensor to be calibrated and the pressure gauge are generated inside the system. The data from the sensor to be calibrated are viewed as voltages by the computer using the software shown in Fig. 17, developed in LabView. The values measured by the sensor and pressure gauge, directly or indirectly, are summarized in Table 1.

P[mbar]	-20	-10	0	10	20	30	40	50	60	70	80	90	100	110	120
U[V]	-1,31	-1,17	-1,02	-0,88	-0,73	-0,58	-0,44	-0,29	-0,145	0,004	0,15	0,29	0,44	0,59	0,73

Table 1. Data for low pressure sensor calibration

Plot the curve that presents the pressure in relation with the voltage, according to the data from Table 1 and Fig. 19 is obtained.

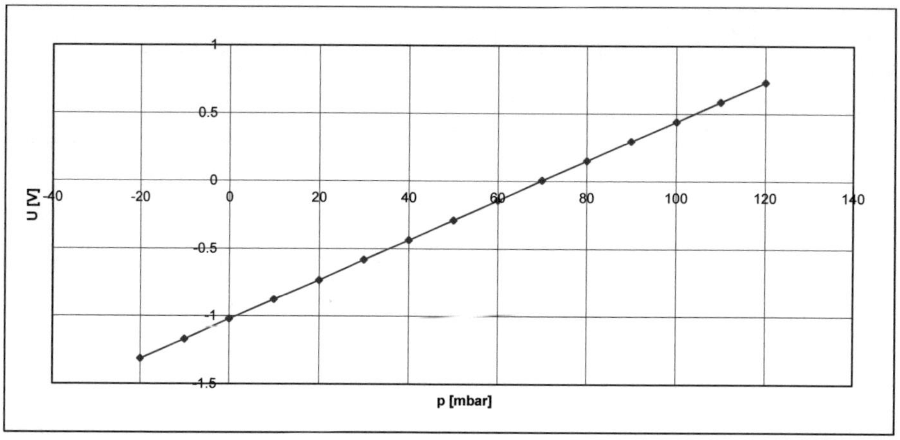

Figure 19. The pressure sensor's calibration curve

In the chart from Fig. 19 a linear pressure variation with the voltage can be observed. The equation governing the linear relationship is :

$$p = a \cdot U + b \qquad (15)$$

where: p – the pressure inside the calibration system,
U – the voltage at the data acquisition board,
a and b – constants.

For the equation (15) a and b are determined based on the data from Table 1 and the following values are obtained: $a = 68.4$ and $b = 71.82$.

More voltage measurements of the pressure sensor at different moments in time are done, creating pressures with values as random as possible. The data collected in this manner are summarized in Table 2 and in Fig. 20.

Be noticed that in Fig. 20 the curves U1-p, U2-p, U3-p, U4-p are parallel. Since the pressure sensor's calibration curves measured in different moments in time are parallel it means that in various moments in time the curve given by the relation (15) is translated with the factor k, defined by the following formula:

$$k = U_{n0} - U_{i0} \qquad (16)$$

where: U_{n0} – the calibration voltage for $p = 0mbar$, while operating the button "low pressure sensor calibration",

U_{i0} – the initial voltage calibration for $p = 0mbar$ (determined when the sensor was initially calibrated with the data acquisition board on which a and b from equation (15) have been determined, respectively $U_{i0} = -1.1V$).

For the pressure sensor's quick zero calibration to the atmospheric pressure, using relations (15) and (16), the following formula is considered:

p [mbar]	U1 [V]	U2 [V]	U3 [V]	U4 [V]
-20	-1,316	-1,311	-1,298	-1,295
-10	-1,172	-1,166	-1,15	-1,147
0	-1,022	-1,021	-1,004	-1
10	-0,878	-0,872	-0,858	-0,854
20	-0,734	-0,728	-0,712	-0,708
30	-0,583	-0,578	-0,566	-0,563
40	-0,438	-0,432	-0,421	-0,418
50	-0,291	-0,285	-0,277	-0,273
60	-0,145	-0,14	-0,13	-0,128
70	0,004	0,008	0,015	0,018
80	0,149	0,143	0,161	0,164
90	0,294	0,287	0,303	0,307
100	0,44	0,435	0,45	0,453
110	0,586	0,581	0,596	0,6
120	0,73	0,725	0,74	0,77

Table 2. Voltages of the pressure sensor for different pressure values measured in different moments in time

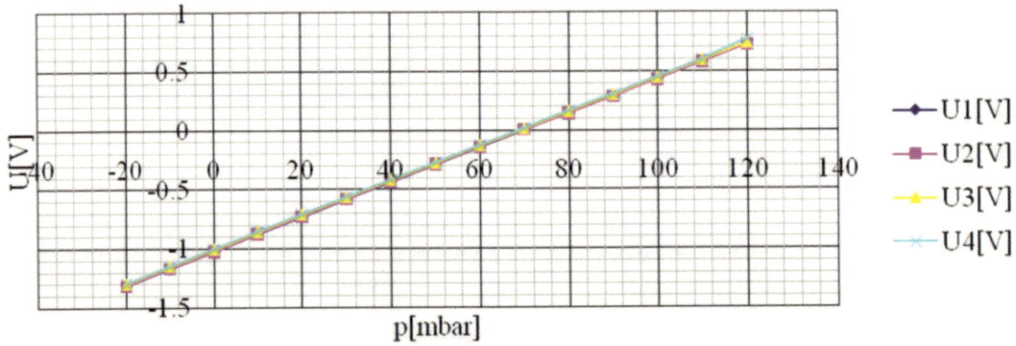

Figure 20. The pressure courves in different moments in time

$$p = a \cdot \left(U_n - U_{n0} + U_{i0} \right) + b \tag{17}$$

where: U_{n0}, U_{i0}, a and b – are the same as in formulas (15) and (16),

U_n – the voltage determined using the data acquisition board for pressure p.

U_n is determined with the pressure sensor. Its values are inserted into equation (17) (using a computer program developed in this paper) and the pressure values inside the system are determined. In this manner is obtained a digital manometer with zero calibration at atmospheric pressure.

6.1.2. An effective software for pressure determination

In Express V.I., "Select Signals" the channel through which the pressure sensor is coupled to the data acquisition board (in this case "0") is chosen for reading the collected data. After that the signal is filtered with the Express V.I. Filter. After filtering, the signal is introduced in the Express V.I. Formula 1. Formula 1 is the formula (17) representation in LabView. To calibrate the pressure sensor (a differential sensor) at zero value (atmosphere) a "Case Structure" is used. This diagram is controlled by the user via the OK button "connect the low pressure sensor to the atmosphere". When this button is activated U_{n0} is determined from equation (17). If the button is not activated, in Express V.I. Formula 1 the old value for U_{n0} is inserted. For this a Shift Register had been used. To view the pressure in relation with time curve the "pressure" Graph Indicator is used and for the numerical view the "pressure 2" numeric indicator.

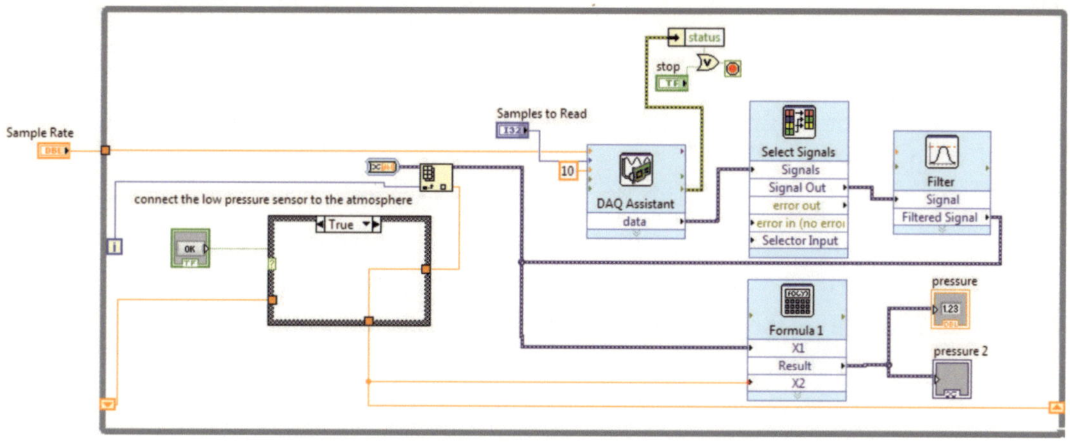

Figure 21. Low pressure sensor software

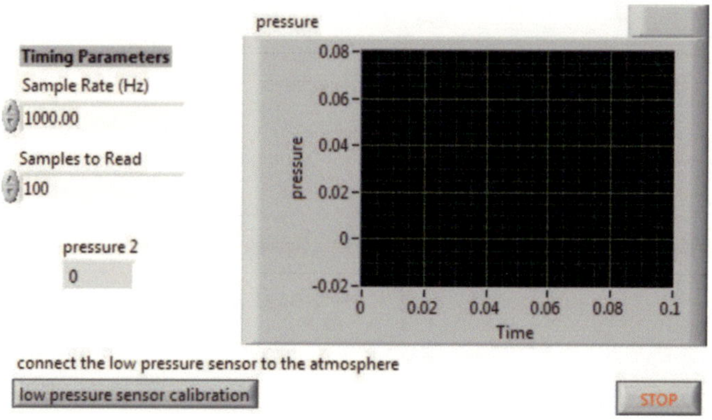

Figure 22. The user display of the low pressure sensor software

6.2. Flow sensor calibration

Honeywell AWM5000 flow sensor calibration is similar to the pressure sensor calibration except that the calibrated and metrological checked flow meter (Rota Yokogawa RAGL53) is connected in series with the flow sensor to be calibrated. The equations (15) and (17) become the equations (18) and (20):

$$\dot{V} = a \cdot U + b \tag{18}$$

where: U – the electrical voltage,

$\dot{V}$ – the gas flow,

a and b – constants:

$a = -18.23$ and $b = 32.63$ for $\dot{V} > 0$ ($U > 0.56$),

$a = -26.35$ and $b = 47.06$ for $\dot{V} < 0$ ($U \leq 0.56$).

k is defined with relation (19):

$$k = U_{n0} - U_{i0} \tag{19}$$

$$\dot{V} = a \cdot \left(U_n - k\right) + b \tag{20}$$

where: U_{n0} – the calibration voltage for $\dot{V} = 0l/\min$, when the button "flow sensor calibration" is pressed,

U_{i0} – the initial calibration voltage for $\dot{V} = 0l/\min$ (determined when the sensor was initially calibrated with the data acquisition board on which a and b from equation (18) have been determined, respectively $U_{i0} = 0.56V$)

a and b – are the same as in formula (18),

U_n – the voltage determined using the data acquisition board for flow $\dot{V}$.

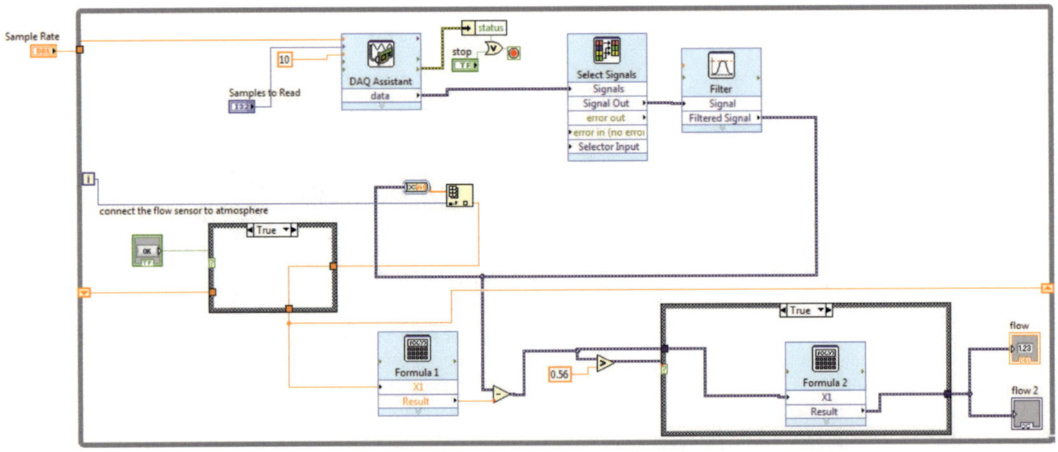

Figure 23. The flow sensor software

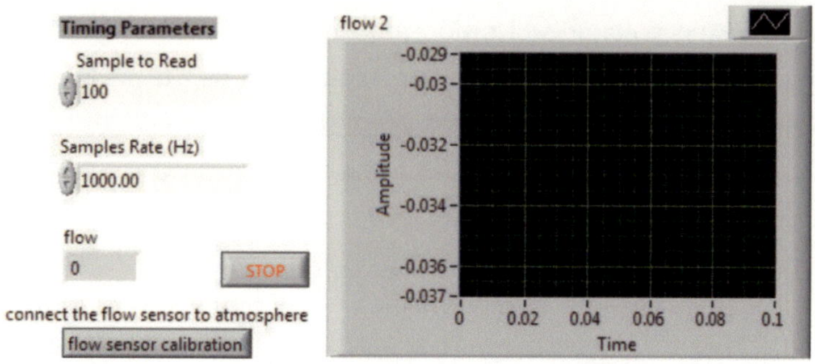

Figure 24. The user display of the flow sensor software

The software developed to read data from the flow sensor is similar to the pressure sensor calibration software. The voltage values obtained after filtration represent U_n from equation (20). The "Case Structure" connected to the OK button "connect the flow sensor to atmosphere" generates the U_{n0} voltage for equation (19). It is defined in LabVIEW with Express V.I. Formula 1. If the button is not activated, the old value for U_{n0} is inserted in Express V.I. Formula 1. For this a Shift Register had been used. The "Case Structure" connected after Express V.I. Formula 1 and containing Express V.I. Formula 2 or 3 represent equation (20) for those voltage / flow intervals. To view the curve flow in relation with time the Graph Indicator "flow 2" is used and for the numerical view the "flow" numeric indicator.

6.3. Oxygen sensor calibration

To calibrate the sensor for determining the oxygen concentration it's created a system where the sensor to be calibrated is connected in series with the already calibrated one. Determining the calibration relation is similar to determining the pressure sensor's calibration relation. Equations (21) and (21) are obtained.

$$FiO_2 = a \cdot U + b \tag{21}$$

where: FiO_2 – the oxygen concentration,
U – the voltage,
$a = 1316.67$ and $b = 1.25$.

The start calibration before each use is for 21% O2. Similar as for the pressure sensor is obtained the following relation:

$$FiO_2 = a \cdot \left(U_n + U_{i0} - U_{n0}\right) + b \tag{22}$$

where: a and b – are the same as in formula (21),
U_n – the voltage determined with the data acquisition board for the FiO_2,oxygen concentration,
U_{n0} – the voltage calibration for $FiO_2 = 21\%$, while operating the "FiO_2 sensor calibration" button,

U_{i0} – the initial voltage calibration for $FiO_2 = 21\%$ (determined when the sensor was initially calibrated with the data acquisition board on which a and b from equation (21) have been determined, respectively $U_{i0} = 0.015V$)

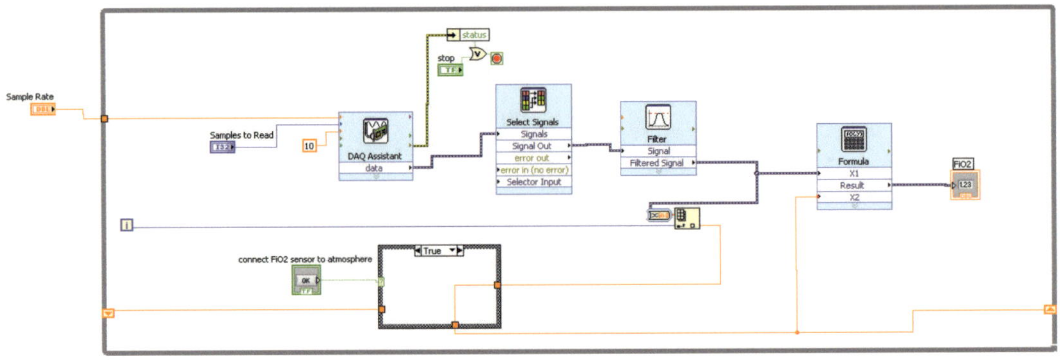

Figure 25. The FiO_2 sensor software

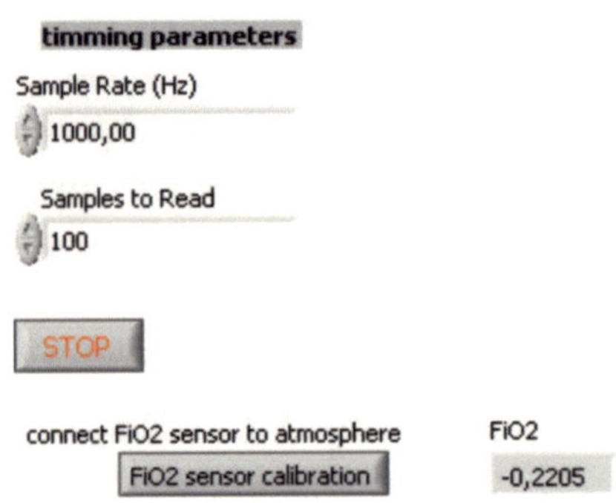

Figure 26. The user display of the FiO_2 sensor software

The software used to calibrate the oxygen concentration sensor is similar to the one used for calibrating the pressure sensor, noting that in Express V.I. "Formula" the data from formula (22) are introduced.

6.4. Flow valve calibration

An assembly diagram for the flow valve calibration is shown in Fig. 27.

The flow valve 12 is powered and controlled by the computer 1 through the data acquisition board 3 and the flow valve's 12 electronic control 5. It is powered by the power supply 7. The electrical connections are made using cables 2, 4, 6, 8. As for pneumatic, flow control valve 12 is connected to the main gas source 9 through the pressure regulator 11. The pneumatic connections are made with the hoses 10. The voltage command given by the computer for the valve 12, determines the valve's opening and through it is delivered a particular gas flow. Various supply voltages for the valve 12 are generated by the computer 1 through the data acquisition board 3. In this manner are generated various flow rates which are monitored by the calibrated and metrological checked flow meter 13 (Rota Yokogawa RAGL53). The voltages generated by the computer 1 and the flow values determined by the flow meter 13 are summarized in Table 3.

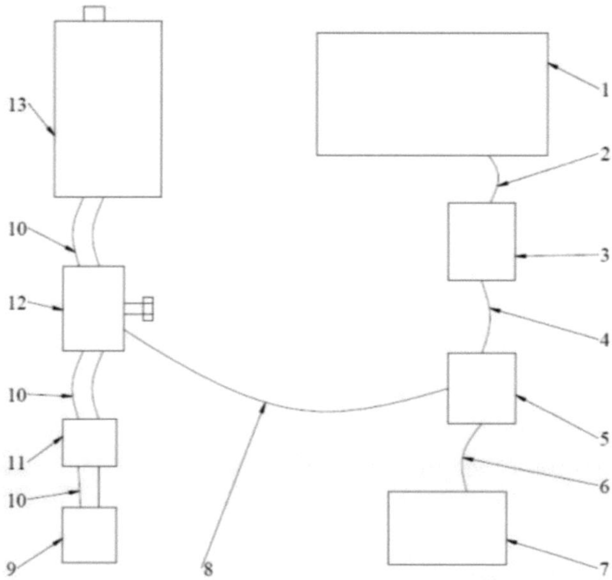

Figure 27. An assembling diagram for the flow control valve calibration

U [V]	0.7	0.8	0.9	1	1.1	1.11	1.12	1.13	1.14	1.15	1.2	1.3	1.4	1.5	2	2.5	3
$\dot{V}$ [l/min]	0.01	0.04	0.08	0.14	0.28	0.35	0.38	0.4	0.43	0.55	0.6	1.09	1.71	2.3	5.9	9.6	13.2

Table 3. Calibration data for the flow valve

The data from Table 3 are shown also in Fig. 28.

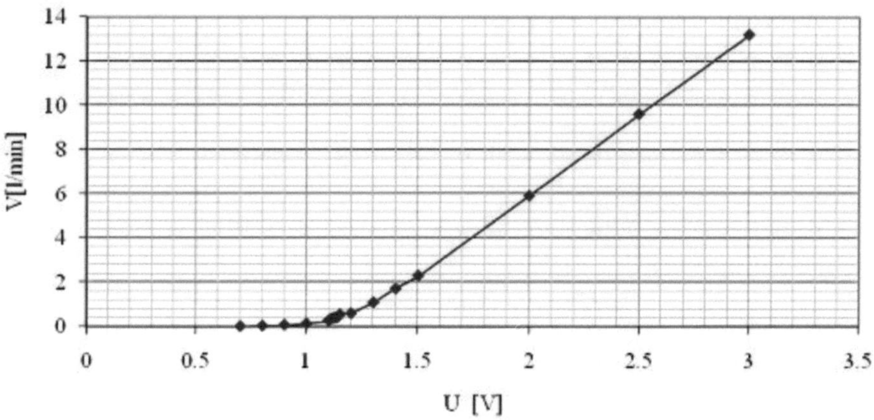

Figure 28. The flow valve's calibration curve

In Fig. 28, based on Table 3, the linearity variation on intervals of the gas flow depending on the voltage, can be observed. For a ventilator test system the voltage that controls the flow valve is interesting for obtain a certain gas flow.

The control voltage's variation depending on the flow equation is determined:

$$U_{\dot{V}} = a \cdot \dot{V} + b \tag{23}$$

where: $U_{\dot{V}}$ – the command voltage for the flow valve,

$\dot{V}$ – the flow rate,

a and b – constants.

Using Table 3 a and b are determined from the equation (23):

$$a = 0.695 \text{ and } b = 0.6916 \text{ for } \dot{V} < 0.55l / \min,$$

$$a = 0.137 \text{ and } b = 0.192 \text{ for } \dot{V} \geq 0.55l / \min.$$

A flow control system controlled by computer is create based on the relation (23) and with the components from the scheme shown in Fig. 27 (1-12).

6.5. Pressure valve calibration

The same way used to calibrate the flow valve is used to calibrate the pressure valve, resulting de relation:

$$U_p = a \cdot p + b \tag{24}$$

where: U_p – the command voltage for the pressure valve,

p – the pressure regulated with the pressure valve,

a and b – constants.

a and b are determined from equation (24):

$$a = 180, \ b = 10 \text{ for } U_p < 0.2V,$$

$$a = 120, \ b = 19 \text{ for } 0.2V \leq U_p < 0.5V,$$

$$a = 160, \ b = -1 \text{ for } 0.5V \leq U_p < 0.8V,$$

$$a = 380, \ b = -189 \text{ for } 0.8V \leq U_p$$

A pressure control system controlled by the computer is created using the relation (24).

To calibrate the flow and pressure valves the input data "flow" and "pressure" are connected directly with the DAQ Assistant Express V.I. The flow rate and the pressure are determined by the flow meter and pressure gauge and the equations (23) and (24) are obtain. For flow and pressure control these equations are introduced in Express V.I. Formula and Formula Node, thus achieving control for the valves. These Expres V.I are connected between the data input and the DAQ Assistant Express V.I.

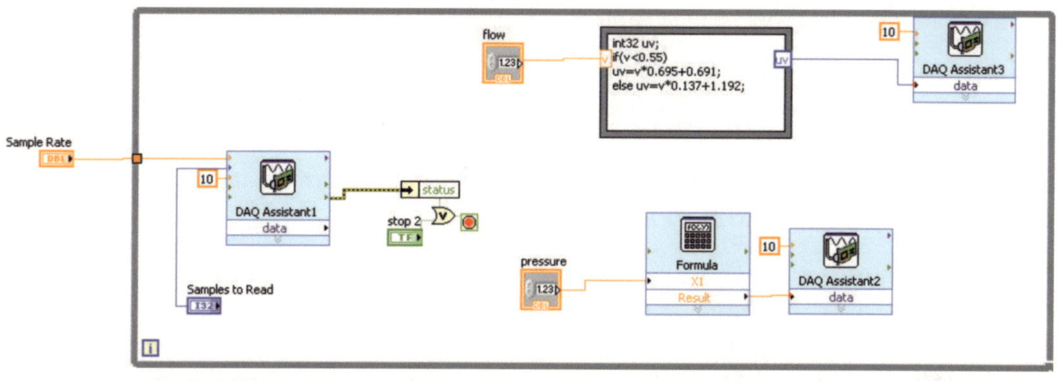

Figure 29. Sofware for pressure and flow valves

7. A system with sensors and actuators designed for the ventilation area

7.1. Lung's ventilation parameters determination

To detrmine the ventilation parameters the system shown in Fig. 30 is used.

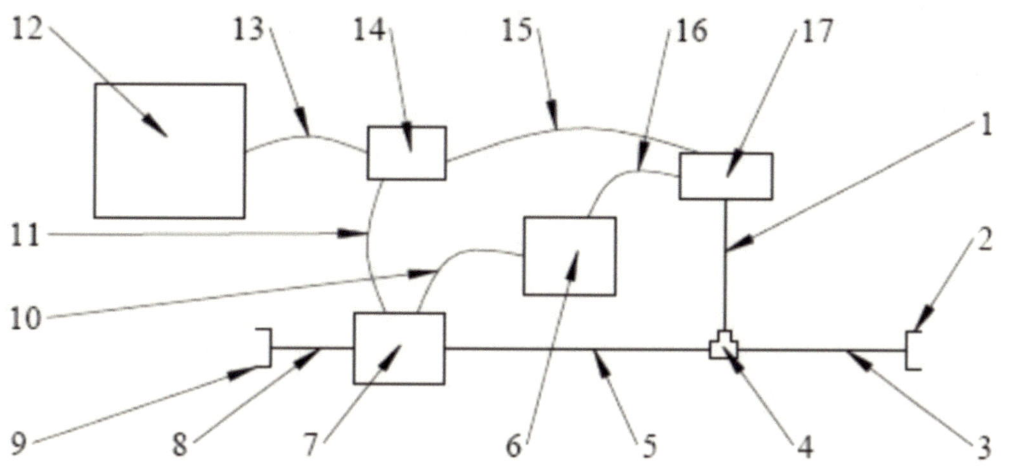

Figure 30. Test system diagram. 1. hose, 2. patient connector, 3. hose, 4. "T"-shaped piece, 5. hose, 6. power supply, 7. flow sensor, 8. hose, 9. ventilator connector (to a "Y"-shaped piece), 10. cable, 11. cable, 12. computer, 13. cable, 14. DAQ board, 15. cable, 16. cable, 17. pressure sensor

The pressure's and flow's versus the sensors supplied voltage variation diagrams were determined. The characteristic equations of these parameters are (15) and (18).

The data collected for the ventilators from the tester's sensors are retrieved with a certain sampling frequency (1000Hz in this case). This sampling frequency was chosen because the ventilators to be tested work with a respiratory frequency of one hundred breaths / minute, and a respiratory cycle consist of several different times (t_1, t_2, $t_{\exp}$).

To increase the time period in witch the ventilator parameters are analyzed (at least one respiratory cycle) the sensors measurements must be saved. To achieve this, data acquisition was introduced in a "while" loop. Because ventilator parameters can instantly change, the analysis is done on a complete respiratory cycle. It thus sets the samples number for a complete ventilation cycle to be included in a test.

With the pressure sensor and the LabView software the maximum pressure during the respiratory cycle is measured and it is considered as $p_{\max}$. The plateau pressure is calculated as the average pressure from it's beginning to its end (starts at the end of t_1 and lasts t_2). The PEEP pressure is calculated as the average pressure from the expiratory time when the flow rate is zero.

The positive flow rate appearance is considered the inspiratory phase start point and the negative flow rate appearance is considered expiratory phase start point. The positive and the negative flow rate means flow towards the patient and from the patient to the sensor. A complete cycle is considered to be the time period between two successive inspiratory phases. The inspiratory time's t_1 end is considered when the zero flow rate appears (no flow). At this point the plateau phase begins. In real human breathing between inhale and exhale (and vice versa) there are break times that allow the muscles to relax and the nervous system to change commands. In ventilation the resting phase is known as the plateau phase, t_2. The plateau phase ends with the appearance of the negative flow (reverse flow). At this point the expiratory time begins and ends at the appearance of the positive flow. The time period, the inspiratory time and the frequency are defined by formulas (3), (2) and (4).

Some uncommon cases when the end of the examined t_2 is previous of the end of t_1, so that the t_2 is negative, can be encountered. To eliminate these anomalies (negative time) some queries that check the time sequence are inserted. Calculation of t_1 is chosen so it depends on the beginning time of the inspiration before t_1. The t_2 value, where its end is before the end of t_1, is calculated according to a beginning inspiratory time before the end of the t_2 and the t_1 value.

$$t_2 = t_{end\_t_2} - t_1 - t_{begin\_inhale\_before\_t_2} \tag{25}$$

Based on relations (9-12), and considering the time interval between two measurements, that being the "*rate*", the volumes are calculated with the following formulas:

$$VT_i = \sum\left(rate \cdot \dot{V}_{pos}\right) \tag{26}$$

$$VT_e = \sum\left(rate \cdot \dot{V}_{neg}\right) \tag{27}$$

where: $rate$ – the sampling rate (10msec),
VT_i – the inspiratory tidal volume,
$\dot{V}_{pos}$ – the positive flow,
VT_e – the expiratory tidal volume,
$\dot{V}_{neg}$ – the negative flow.

The MV are defined and calculated with realtion (12).

The amount of negative volumes, VT, is determined. If the analyzed cycle is not a complete one, there is the risk that the VT's calculated value would be less than the real one. To eliminate this case the maximum VT is extracted from the analyzed period (more then one cycle), so a complete VT is determined, even if it is considered at a later time than the ventilation cycle's beginning. The same procedure is assumed for VT_i.

The software based on these explanation is presented in Fig. 31.

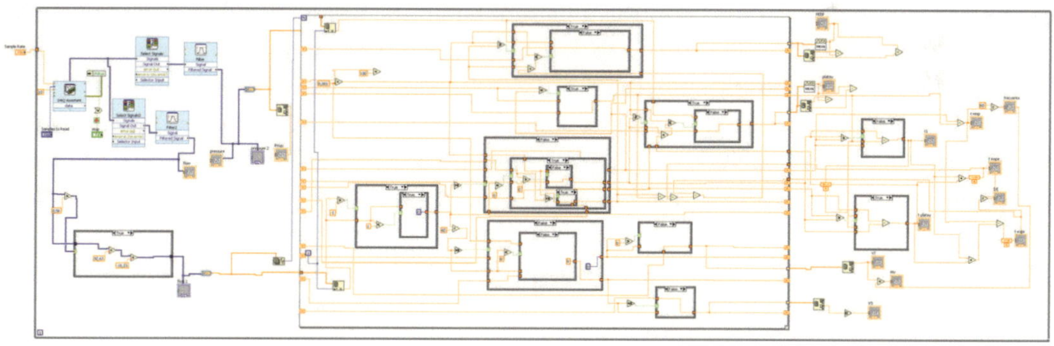

Figure 31. The ventilation parameters software

7.2. Determining the leakage flow in the patient unit

The gas leak flow from a system at a given pressure is represented by the flow needed to be permanently introduced into the system so that the pressure remains constant inside it.

For the patient unit leak testing, the ventilator (the anesthesia equipment) may be "off" or in "standby" mode and the gas control valves are closed. The "Y"-shaped piece of the ventilation circuit is connected to the coupling 1 (Fig. 32.).

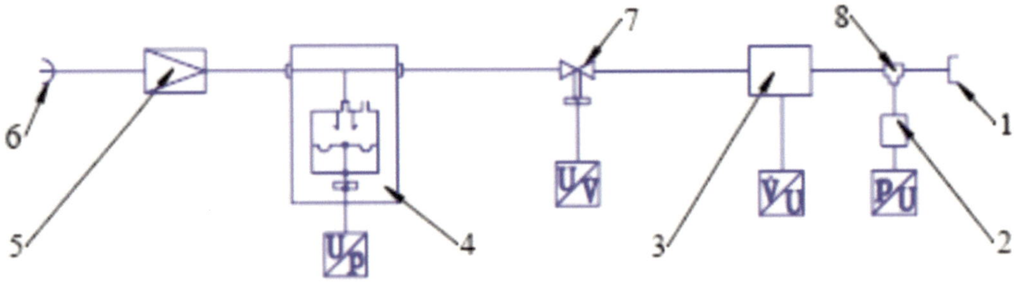

Figure 32. The test system scheme for the patient block leakage. 1. coupling to the patient system, 2. pressure sensor, 3. flow sensor, 4. pressure valve, 5. pressure regulator ($p = 1bar$), 6. coupling to the medium pressure gas supply, 7. flow valve, 8. "Y"-shaped piece

To determine the leaks from the patient unit gas is introduced until it reaches a certain preset pressure value. To maintain this pressure value the gas is introduced continuously. As illustrated in Fig. 32., the gas from the hospital's supply is entering into the system through coupling 6, passes through the pressure regulator 5, where the pressure is stabilized at the value of 1 bar, crosses the pressure control valve 4 and reaches the flow control valve 7. The pressure control valve is limiting the pressure at a safe value, usually with 10 mbar above the leaking test pressure. It establishes a certain gas flow to pass through valve 7, flow set by the computer. The gas reaches into the flow sensor 3 which is monitoring the flow, afterwards to the pressure sensor 2 connected to the "Y"-shaped piece 8. After monitoring the gas pressure the gas goes into the patient unit (not shown in the figure) through the coupling 1.

Pressure and flow valves are controlled by the computer using formulas (24) and (23).

The following parameters are considered:

- p_{test} – the pressure's value at which the leakage check is done, being specified in the technical documentation of the test equipment (e. g.: 30 mbar),
- Δp_{sig} – the safety pressure's value that is added to the test pressure value and results the value for the pressure valve, usually 10mbar,

- p_{dif} – the pressure test's accuracy level (e. g. 2 mbar),
- start flow ($\dot{V}_{start}$) – the test's start flow (a starting level for the system's filling flow is chosen, (e.g. 2 l/min)),
- max adm flow ($\dot{V}_{\max\_adm}$) – the maximum acceptable leakage flow specified in the manufacturer's documentation (e.g. 200ml/min).

The computer commands the flow control valve according to $\dot{V}_{start}$. The pressure p is monitored by the system using the pressure sensor 2 and the flow $\dot{V}$ (noted "leakage flow") with the flow sensor 3.

The system's maximum pressure seted by the pressure valve is determined as follows:

$$p_{\max} = p_{test} + \Delta p_{sig} \tag{28}$$

The $p_{\max}$ value is introduced in the pressure valve's control equation and it is controlled for $p = p_{\max}$.

The system's pressure is monitored cvasi constantly with the low pressure sensor 2 and it is compared with the test value. The following inequalities are considered:

$$p \geq p_{test} \tag{29}$$

$$p \leq p_{test} + p_{dif} \tag{30}$$

$$\dot{V} \leq \dot{V}_{\max\_adm} \tag{31}$$

Depending on the pressure p monitored by the sensor 2 the inequality (29) is checked:

- true, the inequality (30) is checked:
  - true, then $\dot{V}$ is the leaking flow,
  - false, the flow through the valve flow is halved by decreasing the control voltage and then inequality (29) is checked for the new value of the flow,
- false , the flow through the valve flow is increased by 50% by increasing the control voltage and then inequality (29) is checked for the new value of the flow,
  - flow control valve's control voltage is limited to a maximum of 4V.

After determining the leakage flow the inequality (31) is checked. If inequality (31) is true, the leak test is considered successful and the message "leakage level: ok" appears on the computer's screen, otherwise the test is failed and the displayed message is "leakage level: too high", while displaying the flow, $\dot{V}$.

The software developed in LabView 8.5 based on relations (23-24), (28-31), for determining the leakage flow in the patient block, is presented in Fig. 33.

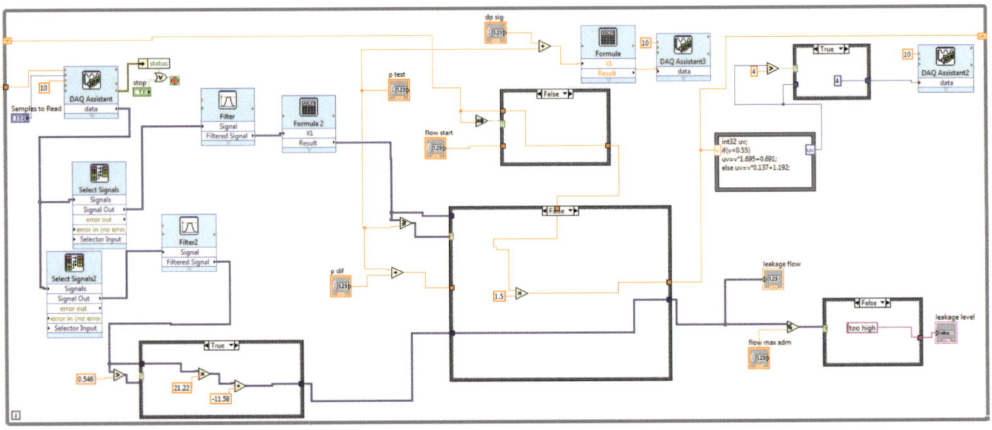

Figure 33. The Software for determining the leakage flow in the patient unit

8. Conclusions

The present chapter has discussed the most significant aspects needed to determine the ventilation parameters with a DAQ board.

A good knowledge of the ventilation phenomenon transforms the problems of determining the ventilation parameters and testing the ventilators into simple issues of data acquisition.

This paper offers some practical solutions that can be used to determine the ventilation parameters. Doctors need a lot of information to choose the best approach to treat the respiratory problems. A large part of this information is represented by the ventilation parameters. Using solutions like the ones presented in this chapter, DAQ system can offer this amount of information.

Time is very important for saving the patient's life, so the ventilation parameters must be set and read quickly. They can change fast and that means that the monitoring must be instantaneous. In this chapter a real time determination of some parameters, using a system based on DAQ, was presented. Inside the ventilator one can find some DAQ systems, so the problem of setting the ventilator becomes a simple DAQ problem, which can be solved with a simple interface and a good automation.

With DAQ systems the ventilation parameters can be set and view in real time and the medical staff can act in the best manner using the fastest way.

The problem of storing some parameters for a long period of time is solved by digitizing and saving their values inside a special memory. If all parameters are stored for long periods of time the doctors can view the quality of the healing progress and can perform the necessary changes.

The ventilator's functioning must be safe, so it must be tested. Note that testing the ventilation and the ventilators' blocks can be realized simply using a few specific sensors, a

DAQ board and a computer equipped with specialized software. It is essential to understand these parameters and their underlying relationships to be able to determine them.

Starting from these few examples complex ventilators test equipment can be built easily, ones that can automatically recognize the ventilation mode and the ventilation' accuracy.

It should be noticed that there are a lot of ventilation parameters obtained with just two sensors, a pressure sensor and a gas flow sensor. This can lead to the conclusion that the complex measurements may be done using simple systems.

Author details

Bogdan Marius Ciurea
Dräger Medical Romania

9. References

http://ro.wikipedia.org/wiki/Respira%C8%9Bie
R. L. Chatburn, Fundamentals of Mechanical Ventilation, Manu Press Ltd., Ohaio, S.U.A., 2003
R. Rathjen, Basisseminar, version 1.00, ENGLGRU.DOC, Dräger, Lubeck, Germany,1995
http://en.wikipedia.org/wiki/Data_acquisition
S. Pasca, Instrumentatie virtuala, lectii practice LabView, Cavallioti, Bucuresti, 2007
http://en.wikipedia.org/wiki/Sensor
http://www.ni.com/dataacquisition/whatis/
*** Technical documentation, Evita XL, Drager Medical, revision 59.0, Lübeck, Germany , 2005
http://www.michell.com/au/technology/thermo-paramagnetic-sensor.htm
*** Technical documentation, Primus Anaesthetic Workstation, Drager Medical, revision 6.0, Lübeck, Germany , 2008
*** Technical Documentation, Vamos Variable Anesthetic Gas Monitor, Drager Medical, revision 7.0, Lübeck, Germany , 2006
http://www.sincro.ro/produse.html?page=shop.browse&category_id=77
http://www.norgren.com/document_resources/en/EN_224_226.pdf
http://sine.ni.com/nips/cds/print/p/lang/en/nid/201987
http://www.ssec.honeywell.com/pressure/datasheets.html
http://sensing.honeywell.com/index.php?ci_id=50053
B. M. Ciurea, D. D. Palade, S. Kostrakievici, "Lung ventilators parameters determination", University "Politehnica" of Buchares Scientific Bulletin Series D: Mechanical Engineering, volume 73, issue 2, 2011, pp. 107-120, Ed. Politehnica Press (ISSN 1454-2358)
http://www.testequipmentdepot.com/druck/pdf/dpi705.pdf

http://aspzone.us.yokogawa.com/downloads/MI/General%20Specifications/General%20Specification/GS1R1B8-E-H(E3).pdf

Mobile Functional Optical Brain Spectroscopy over Wireless Mobile Networks Using Near-Infrared Light Sensors

Salah Sharieh, Franya Franek and Alexander Ferworn

Additional information is available at the end of the chapter

http://dx.doi.org/10.5772//46205

1. Introduction

The purpose of this research is to determine the feasibility of providing quality medical data with an acceptable time duration (event-to-action: in real time or near real time) using full mobility in everyday environments using a system that utilizes heterogenic nodes and a near-infrared light sensor designed to monitor brain function in humans. Multiple wireless networks employing different protocols are used for data transmission to provide new freedom to conduct tests in real environments outside a lab. Measurements of changes in the concentration of oxyhemoglobin (HbO_2) and deoxyhemoglobin (Hb) in the real-life environment may lead to better understanding of tissue pathologies.

A fully mobile functional brain Spectroscopy system was developed in this research to allow the possibility of testing subjects to be monitored in their real environments. The developed application introduces a model (four-node-model) to build fully mobile medical applications that support quality medical data and acceptable time duration (event-to-action time) for medical purposes.

The system introduces a newly created application level protocol to increase data quality and reduce event-to-action time duration. Moreover a new algorithm was created to minimize data loss. Finally a mathematical model was created to calculate the acceptable event-to-action time for particular physiological data based on the number of nodes and the type of nodes that data will go through.

To test this hypothesis, communication software was developed to allow for the collection of physiological data from a mobile near-infrared sensor via a mobile telephone. This system was then used to track changes in concentrations of HbO_2 and Hb during various activities and send data to a computer at a monitoring site using the protocol and algorithm created. The resulting data's accuracy was compared with other methods where the medical data collection was local to the test subject and observer.

Data was captured using a wireless near-infrared light sensor (Node 1: Client), transmitted to a mobile phone (Node 2: Mobile Server) using Bluetooth. The mobile phone sent the data to a central server (Node 3: Central Server). Finally the data was displayed on a monitoring station (Node 4: Monitoring Client).

Large amounts of data and small amounts of data can be captured from the biological tissues for different purposes in different situations. The amount of data, the type of data, the type of tissues, and the event-to-action requirements can effect the quality of captured data. Three data types were tested in this research: three biological events to ensure enough sample scenarios to test the hypothesis. The first data type was the effect of cigarette smoke on the human brain five minutes of smoking. The second data type was the effect of breathing on the human brain during a two–minute time period. The third data type was the response of a Canine when presented with its favourite toy one minute after detecting explosives. The responses from the activities can be inferred from the changes in concentration of HbO_2 and Hb. The data types used in this research have a direct relationship with the acceptable time duration of event-to-action and a direct relationship with the acceptable data quality that has been gathered. As a result, this has a direct effect on the packet size that is needed to be transmitted and on the acceptable time of transition.

2. Related work

2.1. Heterogenic networks

Networks – whether infrastructure based or non-infrastructure based – play an important role in our lives [1]. Wired networks, such as the Internet, provide us with global data access, while wireless networks, such as the Global Standard for Mobile Communications (GSM), give us mobility. Non-infrastructure-based networks (ad-hoc networks), such as Bluetooth networks, give us the freedom to communicate at no cost over short ranges [2].

Bluetooth devices utilize the unlicensed frequency of 2.4 GHz that offers a 10 to 100 meter range and a data transfer rate of up to 1 MBps [3]. Bluetooth technology offers point-to-point and point-to-multiple-points communication [4]. It performs communication through a protocol stack divided into hardware and software layers [5]. Bluetooth standards were created to provide guidelines to device manufacturers to facilitate interoperability between devices from different vendors. Moreover, Bluetooth standards specify profiles that determine the usage of the device and the services offered by it [6]. Standardization, low cost, minimum hardware, low power requirements, and the free use of unlicensed bandwidth all contribute to the wide spread use of Bluetooth devices [7].

GSM is widely used in more than 200 countries around the world, having an estimated subscriber base of over two billion users [8]. Roaming is one of the value-added features introduced by the GSM standard. This capability allows mobile users to travel the world and still be able to use their phones to connect with local operators. The introduction of data communication has also helped GSM standards to become more and more popular. GSM networks currently offer wide varieties of services, ranging from basic voice services to more advanced capabilities, such as allowing Internet access.

GSM's many features make it possible to use this type of network to assist in the monitoring of people's physiological parameters in everyday life regardless of their location [9]. GSM networks use different frequencies for upload and download links, which offer various data transfer rates between the network and the device. The data transfer rates can reach up to 9.6 KBps, which allows the networks to offer basic data services to their users [10]. The introduction of General Packet Radio Services (GPRS) – data services to GSM networks – has made it possible to run more varieties of applications than ever before at lower costs and faster speeds [11]. GPRS was added to the traditional GSM network to allow network operators to offer better data communications. GPRS is a packet-switched communication method where the communication channel can be employed by other users, unlike other data communication methods such as circuit switched data. With GPRS download rates reaching 236 KBps and upload transfers reaching up to 118 KBps, GPRS offers enhanced speed over the traditional GSM network [12].

2.2. Sensor networks

Several types of sensors have been created and used to monitor different object functions [13]. These sensors have been used in a variety of fields: health, medicine, manufacturing, telecommunications, security, and the natural environment [14, 15].

Often some sensors can communicate with each other directly or indirectly to form sensor networks [16]. Currently there are wide varieties of sensor networks used in different facilities to perform different monitoring tasks with different subjects: humans, machines, products, and workers [17]. Monitoring people, machines or products within a physical location does not necessarily require full mobility or full wireless connectivity since everything is in close proximity.

Some applications require variable degrees of wireless support or mobility support or a combination of both. For example, full wireless support is required when monitoring habitat without disturbing the surrounding environment for an extended period of time [18]. Monitoring people while they are on the move is an example where full wireless mobility support is required.

Each application has its own requirements and some technologies currently support these applications to some level. On the other hand, monitoring human brain using full mobility to collect medical data is a challenge and the current technology does not fully support it.

Sensor networks differ in their technical capabilities and implementation (hardware, software, communication protocols, algorithms, etc). Currently, available sensors and sensor networks support long-range and short-range communication (433 MHz-5.9 GHz) [19].

Some health care sensor networks combine short- and long-range communications to monitor patients [20]. They utilize mobile phone networks and Bluetooth networks together to achieve better coverage [21]. Wireless networks have wide variations of data transfer rates. Some have a low transfer rate (Spike, 35 KBps) and others have a high transfer rate (WLAN, IEE 802.11a, 54 000 KBps). Transfer rate requirements are highly dependent on the type of application. Some applications require a high transfer rate [22] because they generate large amounts of data that must be dealt with quickly. Sensor networks remain an active research area with focus on different components: networks, sensors, data acquisition, protocols, performance [23].

2.3. Protocols

Transmission Control Protocol (TCP) protocol is a reliable protocol used in communication when a reliable connection is required [24]. It allows two hosts to communicate and exchange data streams and guarantees the data delivery [25]. Data packets are delivered in the same order they were sent. In contrast, User Datagram Protocol (UDP) does not provide guaranteed delivery and does not guarantee packet ordering [26]. Selecting which protocol to choose for a particular application mainly depends on the application requirements. These protocols have proven their value and made their way into Bluetooth and GSM networks.

Bluetooth networks support both TCP and UDP communications [27]. Applications running on the Bluetooth networks can use any of these protocols to send and receive data. The most common way to send TCP and UDP packets over Bluetooth is using Bluetooth Radio Frequency Communications (RFCOMM) [28]. RFCOMM is a transport protocol that provides RS-232 serial port emulation. Bluetooth Serial Port Profile (SPP) is based on this protocol [29].

GSM networks are similar to Bluetooth networks and wired local area networks (LANs). They support TCP and UDP communication protocols [30]. Since wireless networks support the same communication protocol as wired LANs, applications running on wireless networks can communicate and exchange data with the applications running on wired LANs.

Application level protocols are created to support specific applications. These protocols can run on top of either TCP or UDP protocols. The protocol in this research is an example of such protocols. MDTP is a packet-oriented protocol created to support data exchange between heterogenic nodes. MDTP is a protocol created in this research to allow global communication between sensors, mobile data devices, and stationed servers over Bluetooth and GSM networks.

2.4. Functional Optical Brain Spectroscopy

Functional Optical Brain Spectroscopy using Near-infrared Light (fNIRS) has been used as a method to conduct functional brain analysis. fNIRS is a method that uses the reflection of infrared light to observe changes in the concentration of HbO_2 and Hb in the blood, and can provide a similar result to Functional magnetic resonance imaging (fMRI) [31]. fNIRS takes advantage of the absorption and scattering of near-infrared light to provide information about brain activities [32]. For a long time, it was thought that it was only possible to collect information from the superficial layers of tissue (e.g., microscopy) due to light scattering. However, about 25 years ago, it was discovered that functional information could be obtained from brain tissue using light shone at the scalp and detected from the scalp. This discovery motivated the development of diffuse optics as a method for brain monitoring. This method has different names: Near-infrared Spectroscopy (NIRS), Diffuse Optical Tomography, and/or Near-infrared Imaging (NIRI). Today, several types of NIRS devices have been built to image brain functions. These devices differ in their capabilities, designs, and costs [33, 34].

The NIRS devices can be classified into three main types: Continuous Wave Spectroscopy (CWS), Time-resolved Spectroscopy (TRS), and Frequency Domain Spectroscopy (FDS). The CWS device consists of a continuous light source, which transmits light waves with constant amplitude, and a detector that locates the attenuated incident light after it passes through the tissues. The TRS device transmits short incidents of light pulses into tissues and measures the light after it passes through the tissues. On the other hand, the FDS device transmits a sinusoidal modulated light wave into the tissue [33].

Each of these types of NIRS devices has limitations and strengths [35]. CWS has the advantage of low cost; however, with CWS it is difficult to distinguish contributions of absorption and scattering to the light attenuation. FDS, on the other hand, is known for its good spatial resolution, penetration depth, and accurate separation of absorption and scattering effects. Nevertheless, FDS is significantly more expensive than CWS. As for TRS, although theoretically it can provide a better spatial resolution than FDS, it has a lower signal-to-noise ratio. Since TRS requires short pulsed lasers and photon counting detection, it is the most expensive type of the NIRS instrumentation. Despite the advancements in NIRS technology, NIRS still has limitations, such as the short path length and the artefacts' movements during measurements.

NIRS relies on a simple principle: light in the range of near-infrared light emitted on the organ of interest passes through the different layers above the organ. When it passes through the tissues, light photons go through physical interactions, such as scattering and absorption that lead to a loss of energy in the emitted light. When the remaining light exits the organ, it is measured by a detector.

Near-infrared light, in the range of 700-900 nm, can travel relatively deep into body tissues. It is also worth mentioning that such light can easily travel through soft tissues and bones, such as those of neonates and infants. Therefore, it is suitable to use near-infrared devices to monitor brain activities or other oxygen-dependent organs in this category of humans [36].

Absorption and scattering are the main physical processes effecting the transmission of light photons in tissues. Light photon absorption and scattering causes the light intensity to decrease. Both absorption and scattering are wavelength dependent. The amount of absorbed light photons is also impacted by the concentration of blood HbO_2 and Hb in tissues that vary in time, reflecting physiological changes in tissues' optical properties [31].

When light photons travel through tissues, they are scattered several times before finally reaching the receiver. Scattering increases light's optical path length, causing photons to spend more time in tissues that in turn affects the tissues' absorption characteristics. NIRS measures the optical properties of HbO_2 and Hb concentrations in near-infrared light. The effects of the changes in concentration levels of HbO_2 and Hb in the blood stream on light absorption can be described by the Beer-Lambert's Law. A Modified Beer-Lambert Law can be used to predict the amount of blood chromophoers (HbO_2 and Hb) in tissues [34].

3. Hardware architecture

This system, developed for this research, consists of three main hardware components The first component is a Bluetooth wireless sensor (built by Arquatis GmbH, Rieden, Switzerland), which is the data acquisition device The second component is a PDA and is the main controller for the measurement process and the data communication bridge between the sensor and the central computer. The third component is a central computer (Server, or Host Computer, or PC) that stores the data for later analysis. Figure 1 displays the system's architecture.

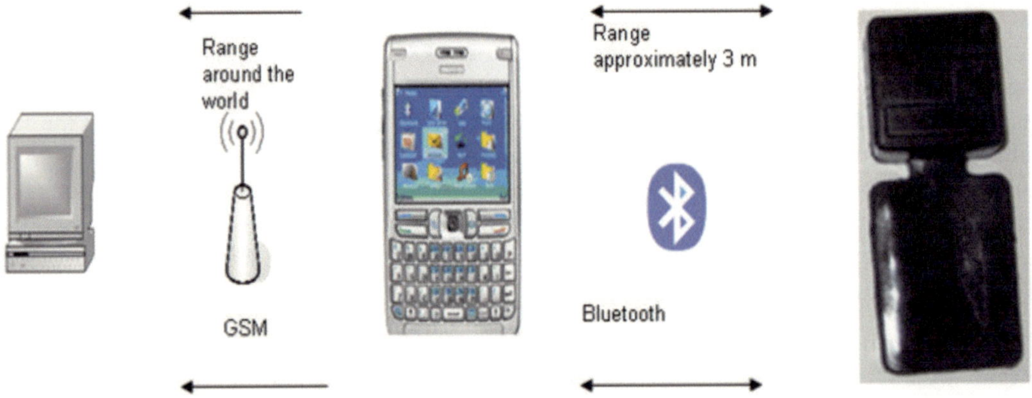

Figure 1. Hardware Architecture

3.1. The sensor

The sensor is a wireless near-infrared imaging sensor developed by Arquatis GmbH, Rieden Switzerland (Figures 2).The sensor quantifies changes in the concentration of HbO2 and Hb in tissues and sends information to a computer using wireless Bluetooth technology. The sensor has the following components: four light sources; each light source has two LEDs (Light Emitting Diodes) emitting at 730 and 830 nm. It has four light detectors (PIN silicon photodiodes) with a sampling rate of 100 HZ. An analog LED controller controls the emitted light. A microcontroller has an analog/digital (A/D) controller to manage the light intensity signal detection and the conversion of the signal into data. The accuracy of the A/D is 12 bits. The Bluetooth transceiver sends and receives data between the sensor and the Bluetooth networks within a range of 3 m. The sensor requires a power supply and uses a 3.7 volt rechargeable lithium-ion battery that can last up to 3 hours. The sensor's total weight is about (40 grams); its dimensions are (90 x 34 x 20 mm). To achieve better measurements, the sensor components are mounted on a rigid-flexible printed circuit board (PCB).

3.2. The Mobile Phone (PDA)

The personal digital assistance (PDA) device is a commercially available cell phone with data access capabilities, Bluetooth communication support, and Java support. The mobile phone used in this project is a Nokia E62 smart phone that runs Symbian operating system (Figure 3). It has extensive features and capabilities, however not all are necessary to run the developed system. It supports the following Bluetooth profiles SPP. The developed system uses only the SSP profile to carry out the communication between the sensor and the mobile phone. The developed system uses mobile information device profile (MIDP) v2.0, connected limited device configuration (CLDC) 1.1, and the optional Java package for Bluetooth (JSR 82).

The phone has single ARM 9 CPU with clock rate of 233 MHZ. The available memory allows the system to acquire and save data for at least 8 continuous hours; it has 80 MB by default. The battery can last up to 5.5 hours when the system is in full use.

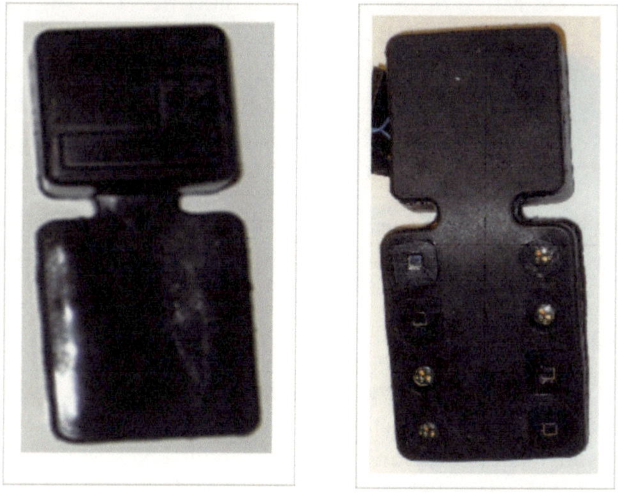

Figure 2. Wireless Sensor

Figure 3. Mobile Phone (PDA)

3.3. The host PC (Server)

The host PC is a regular desktop personal computer with 2 GB RAM and dual core Intel processor.

4. Software

4.1. Software components

Java portability allows it to run on a wide range of operating systems and devices. Sun Microsystems realized that one size does not fit all; it grouped Java into three main editions, each targeted at a specific range of devices. Java Enterprise Edition (J2EE) is targeted for enterprise servers to create large scalable applications. Java Standard Edition (J2SE) is targeted for desktop applications. Java Micro Edition (J2ME) is targeted for small devices with limited hardware capabilities. J2ME was used to build the mobile phone application and J2SE and J2EE was used to build the server application. The sensor application was built using C language.

Eclipse and Netbeans are among the most popular integrated development environments (IDE) used to build and debug Java applications. Both IDE's are used in this research.

4.2. Software architecture

The system software architecture (Figure 4) has three major layers: a data acquisition layer (DAL), a control layer (CL), and a data storage layer (DSL). The DAL software component in the sensor controls data acquisition and packet transmission. It is composed of a set of programs that implement the data communication protocol, the RFCOMM Bluetooth protocol, and the sensor's low-level controls. The second layer (CL) resides on the PDA and acts as the central control unit for the application. The majority of the system components reside in this layer. The third layer (DSL) is mainly used to accept connections from the PDA and store the received data packets in the server for later analysis. The PDA creates a persistent connection with the sensor and with the PC during the duration of the measurements. The system is designed to support a wide range of measurements and acquisition activities. Several types of tests can be performed using the system without the need to modify the programs. Most of the components are designed to be configuration-driven. The system architecture provides high interoperability between heterogeneous hardware and software.

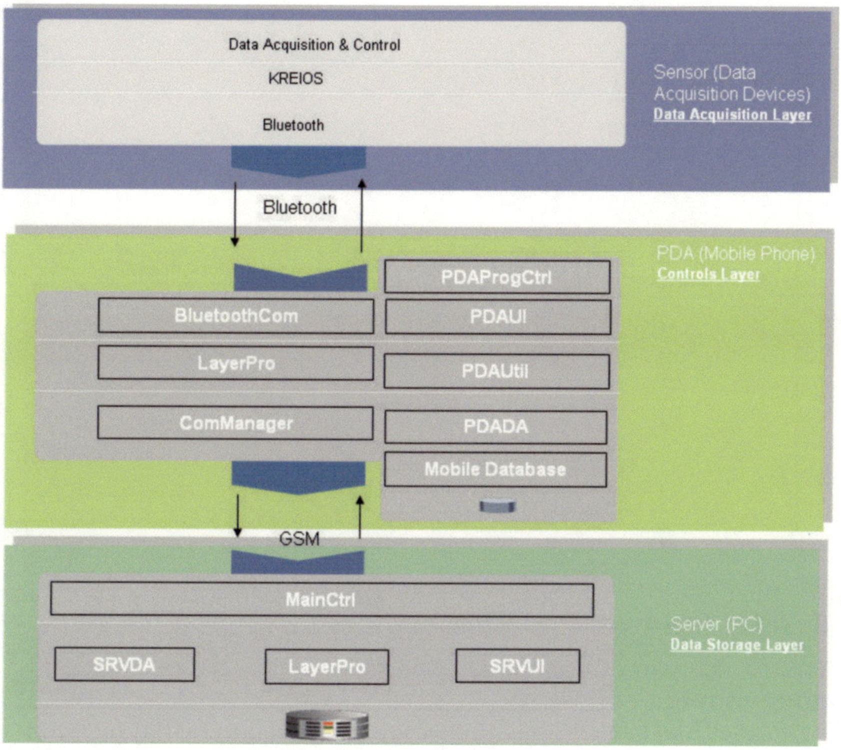

Figure 4. The System Software Architecture

4.3. Overall system component interaction

The overall system interaction is depicted in the sequence diagram in Figure 5. The sequence diagram shows the steps and the sequences of the steps in relation to time.

The system administrator starts the server. The sensor is carried by a test subject. The test subject fixes the sensor on a test area and starts the measurement process from the PDA software. The sensor emits light directly in the test area and starts the data collection. The sensor transmits the data back to the PDA. The PDA receives the data packet and forwards it to the server and at the same time the PDA will save a local copy to the file system. The server receives the data packet and displays the data on the screen at the same time it saves the packet in the server's local file system. Once the test is completed, the data is extracted and analyzed.

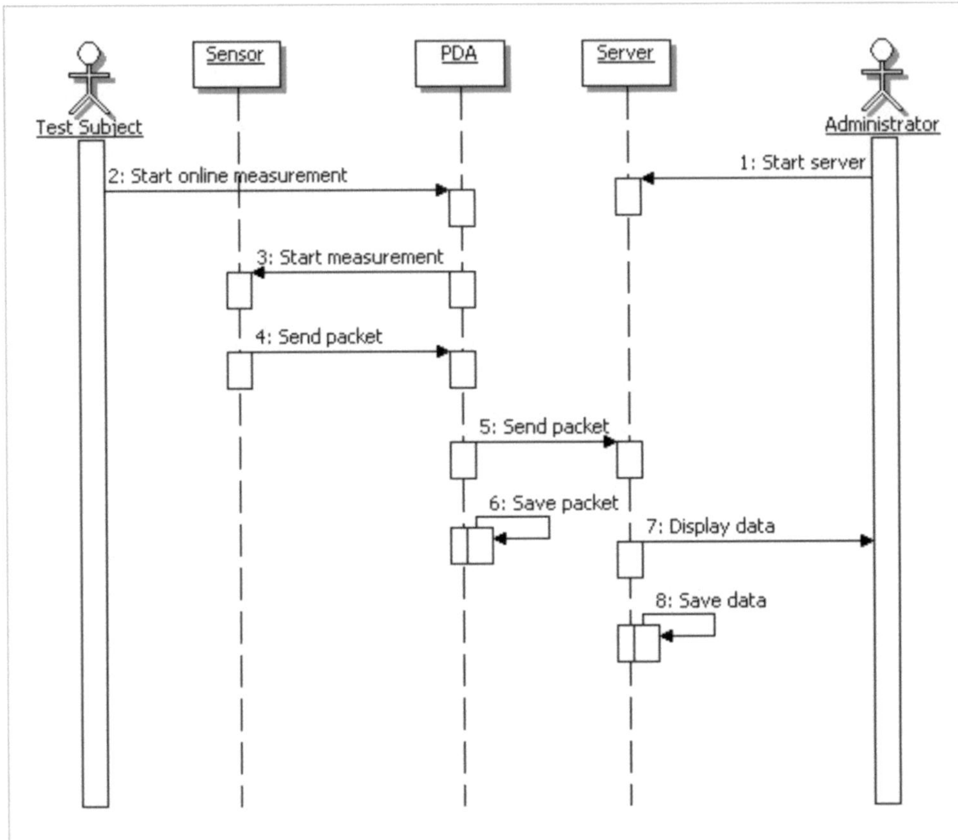

Figure 5. The Overall System Sequence Diagram

5. Four-node model

The four-node model (Figure 6) depicts the minimum necessary devices and networks required to support an affordable and practical solution to monitor biological tissues with an acceptable event-to-action time duration. In the proposed model, in order to support real near-time (event-to-action) mobility monitoring of biological tissues, a minimum four types of device and three types of networks are required.

The first node (Node 1) is a wireless sensor closely attached to the body that supports short-range communication. The sensor can be a device that implements any data collection approach (near-infrared, ECG, etc.). The purpose of this node (the sensor) is to closely monitor specific biological data in the body. Multiple sensors can be attached to the body to collect more specialized data from different type of tissues. The sensor can have different frequencies used to sample data from tissues. The system built to test this model used a sensor with 100 Hz sample rate and data accuracy of 12 bits.

The second node (Node 2) is a data buffer and a long-range data communication device (a Cell phone support data communication). The purpose of this node is to act as a data buffer for the data collected from the sensor. This node can also act as a network speed regulator between the sensor and the wide area network (WAN). The node implements a data integrity algorithm to minimize data losses due to data transmission over multiple networks. When integrating networks with different throughputs, data loss can occur due to capacity problems. The amount of captured data from the sensor sometimes cannot be sent fast enough to the central server; this node can prepare the data and store it to be forwarded to the central server. Finally this node adjusts its receiving speed based on the sensor transition speed.

Node 1 and Node 2 provide full mobility support in this model. These two nodes can be used in several scenarios. For example, in one scenario a doctor can monitor patients in their real environment (work, home, etc). Today most people carry cell phones that can be used as Node 2. The monitored subject can move freely while carrying a light weight sensor. Depending on the data type that needs to be monitored, the subject can carry a specific type of sensor that is capable of collecting the required data type. In this scenario the data can be transmitted to a central location or stay in local storage. The data is transmitted or downloaded at a later time when the event-to-action time duration is not critical.

In another scenario, doctors can carry their own communication device and their own sensors. While administrating to patients either in their clinic or in the hospital, they can collect data from their patients. The data ist stored and the doctor can analyze the collected data at a later time when the event-to-action time duration is not critical.

The third node (Node 3) is a central server that acts as a communication and long-term storage node. Node 2 communicates with Node 3 over any type of long-range network. In the implemented application in this research, a combination GSM network and the internet were used to test the four-node model.

During the communication between Node 2 and Node 3 a special consideration, based on the number of networks that are involved in the transmission process, is required. If a public infrastructure is used to transmit data, control over the priority of the transferred medical data over these networks is not guaranteed. The lack of control over the priority can cause delay or data accuracy issues.

This dependency can make the medical data less useful. The data might become less useful due to the two reasons discovered in this research: event-to-action time duration and data accuracy. These issues can be addressed by introducing a combination of a new protocol and a new algorithm that can make public networks appropriate to transfer medical data with acceptable event-to-action time durations and acceptable data accuracy. Later this article will explain briefly the proposed protocol and the proposed algorithm.

The fourth node (Node 4) is a monitoring device that is used to observe the monitored subject remotely. This node can be stationary or mobile. If the node is a stationary device then a wired network can be used to transmit data from the central server (Node 3). If the node is a mobile device, a combination of wireless and wired networks can be used to transmit the data.

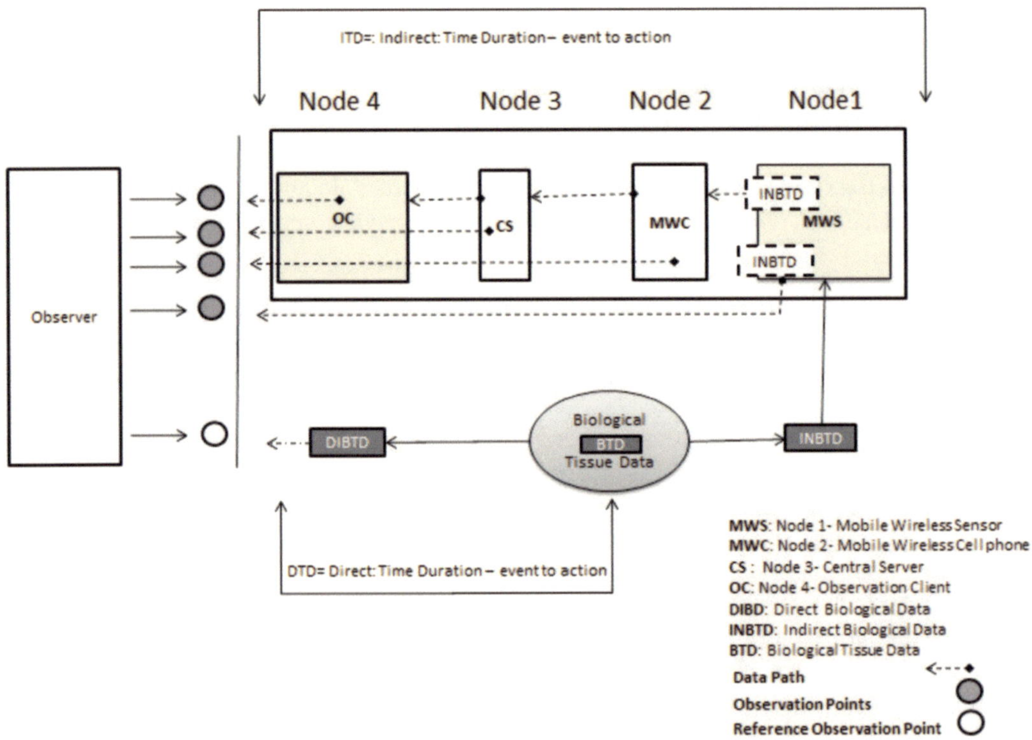

Figure 6. Four-Node Model

These four nodes are the minimum required nodes necessary to support full mobility to monitor biological tissues in near real time (acceptable event-to-action time durations with acceptable data accuracy) for most medical data types. To support this model, three network types are required: short-range wireless network; long-range wireless network; and wired network. Finally three types of protocols are required: protocol to transmit data over the short-range wireless network; protocol to transmit the data over the long-range wireless network; and finally a protocol to transmit the data over the wired network. One of the enhancements this research contributes is eliminating the need for three different protocols to transmit the data over these networks. This contribution enhances the event-to-action time duration and data accuracy. One more contribution of this research is, due to eliminating the need for multiple protocols, an algorithm can take into account the speed and data priority difference between the different networks.

6. Medical data

6.1. Data types

Large number of data types can be gathered from biological tissues for medical purposes. The data type that can be used for medical purposes varies based on the organ that is being monitored, the parameter being collected and the event-to-action time duration required. In this research the focus was on the brain as an organ, the amount of blood oxygenation as a parameter and the event-to-action time duration after a specific activity.

We monitored one data type – HbO_2 and Hb concentrations in the brain during three activities. Two activities dealt with the human brain and one activity dealt with the Canine brain. The HbO_2 and Hb concentrations were observed in human brain during breathing and during smoking. The HbO_2 and Hb concentrations were observed in the Canine brain after an explosion detection exercise.

The time duration required to observe the changes in the data was recorded during the above mentioned activities.

The first experiment was designed to generate observer data during human breathing over 120 seconds. The observed time duration during the experiment indicated that over the time duration of 20 seconds, we can see that each breath holding trial had a clear measured impact on the HbO_2 and Hb concentrations. From the experiment we can infer that an acceptable event-to-action time duration when monitoring breathing is 20 seconds. Based on this timing, the generated data were 2,000 (20 seconds x sensor sample rate is 100 Hz) state changes in HbO_2 and Hb concentrations during one breath. The experiment lasted for 120 seconds. The total amount of data during this experiment was (120 X 100) 12,000 state changes.

The second experiment was designed to gather data during 900 seconds when a human smoked a real cigarette (complete cigarette). The observed time duration during the experiment indicated that over the time duration of 100 seconds, we can see that each inhalation of cigarette substances (nicotine and other chemicals) had a clear measured impact on the HbO_2 and Hb concentrations. From the experiment we can infer that an acceptable event-to-action time duration when monitoring a human smoking is 100 seconds. Based on this time, the generated data were 10,000 (100 seconds x sensor sample rate is 100 Hz) state changes in HbO_2 and Hb concentrations during one inhalation of cigarette substances. The experiment lasted for 900 seconds. The total amount of data during this experiment was (900 x 100) 90,000 state changes.

The third experiment was designed to gather data after rewarding a Canine for detecting an explosive substance over a duration of 180 seconds. The observed time duration during the experiment indicated that over the time duration of 20 seconds, we can see that the effect of detecting an explosive substance had an impact on the HbO_2 and Hb concentrations but was not clear. From the experiment we can infer that an acceptable event-to-action time duration when monitoring explosives discovery is 20 seconds. Based on this timing the generated data were 2,000 (20 seconds x sensor sample rate is 100 Hz) state changes in HbO_2 and Hb concentrations during one detection of explosive substances. The experiment lasted for 120 seconds. The total amount of data during this experiment was (180 x 100) 18,000 state changes.

6.2. Data observation points

Medical personnel can observe biological changes through four observation points in the four-node model. The first observation point is the output data from the sensor (Node 1).

The second observation point is the output data from the cell phone (Node 2). The third observation point is the central server (Node 3). The last observation point is the observation client (Node 4). At each observation point data was examined to validate data accuracy and event-to-action time duration.

In order to validate the collected data accuracy and timing requirements using this model, a reference observation point was used. The reference observation point is data collected using an fMRI system.

6.3. Data transmission path

Speed and throughput of networks and nodes that are involved in transmitting data need to be able to transmit data with a speed that can meet the timing requirements. Otherwise, the data might be less useful to provide acceptable event-to-action time duration results. At the same time, networks and nodes need to ensure no data loss during transition. Data loss during transmission can compromise data quality, which in turn may make data less useful.

Data captured by Node 1 goes through a specific path to reach Node 4. The data is passed from Node 1 to Node 2 that ensures the integrity of the transmitted data over the heterogenic networks. When data arrives at Node 3, data is checked for integrity. Once the data integrity is complete, data is passed to Node 4. In case of data integrity issues, Node 3 requests a retransmission of data from Node 2. Node 2 resends the data and goes through the same process again.

In typical situations, the longer the path the more time is taken to transmit data and the more likely data integrity can be compromised. The proposed protocol and the proposed algorithm can reduce the effect of data path length effect.

7. Data integrity and event-to-action time duration

During data transmission over heterogenic networks and heterogenic nodes, data accuracy might be compromised due to network load or node processing speed. The time duration to transfer data from Node 1 to Node 4 might not be enough to meet the required event-to-action time duration of the monitored biological data. In order to overcome the above two challenges, the research proposed an algorithm and a protocol to enhance the data accuracy and the event-to-action time duration of.

7.1. The protocol: Medical Data Transfer Protocol (MDTP)

MDTP (Figure 7) is a binary application layer protocol for using heterogenic networks to transfer medical data. The protocol encapsulates biological data along with some data integrity identifiers that identify the medical data that is being transferred. The protocol consists of a small number of transactions and is stateless. It has three transactions: open, send, close. The protocol is bi-directional. Each participant node needs to establish a connection. The source node establishes a connection (Seed Connection). The target node establishes, in return, another connection back to the source node. The two connections make up a session with a full handshake. The two connections are required to complete the handshake and request data in cases of data loss. The target node can use this connection to ask Node 1 to resend the missed data using this connection. Once the session is established, the source node starts sending data with a sequence number identifying the sent packet. When data reaches an end, the source node sends a close transaction to terminate the session. The target node also sends a close transaction to the source node to complete the session termination.

The size of the data packet is small and has a variable length. The length of the packet depends on the medical data type that is to be sent and the sensor type. The packet consists of two parts: head and tail. The head is of fixed size; the tail is variable based on the data type. The variable length helps the protocol to transmit the data within acceptable event-to-action time durations for the specific data type.

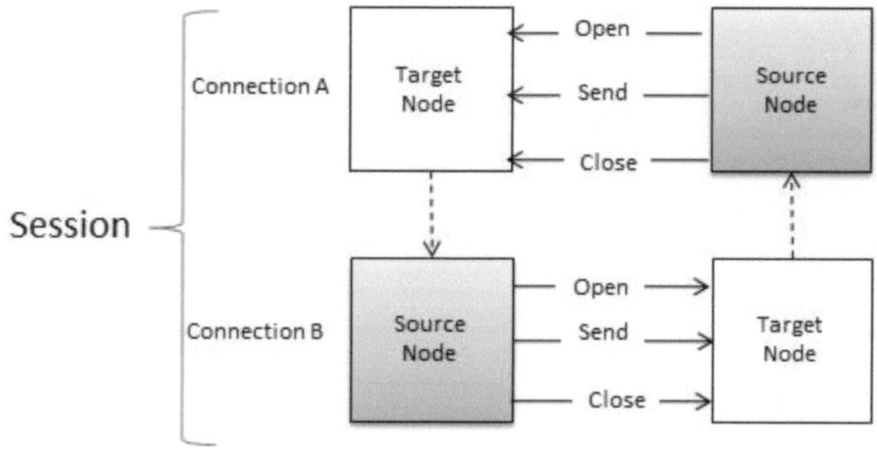

Figure 7. MDTP

7.2. Data Integrity Algorithm (DIA)

To ensure data integrity the data is validated at each node. The algorithm (Figure 8) validates the sequence number of each packet. If the data is valid, the protocol sends the data to the next node, otherwise the target node asks the source node to resend the data using the second connection. The algorithm on the target node tries to merge data after it ensures the correct sequence of packet has been received. Based on data type, the algorithm tries to reconcile the received packet or simply ignores any missed packets. Any packets losing medical data, such as changes in HbO_2 and Hb concentrations during detection of explosive substances, can make the data less useful. In this case the timing requirement for such state changes is not critical, but the data integrity is more important. On the other hand, a data packet loss during monitoring changes in HbO2 and Hb concentrations while smoking is not critical and neither is data accuracy. In this case, the changes occur over a longer time period and the algorithm can establish a pattern even if data loss occurs. In the case of monitoring changes in HbO_2 and Hb concentrations during breathing, the time requirements and the data accuracy is different. Even if a packet is lost, the observer still can infer the changes. Finally there might be a case where data integrity and event-to-action time duration is short and important. In this case the algorithm might be less useful.

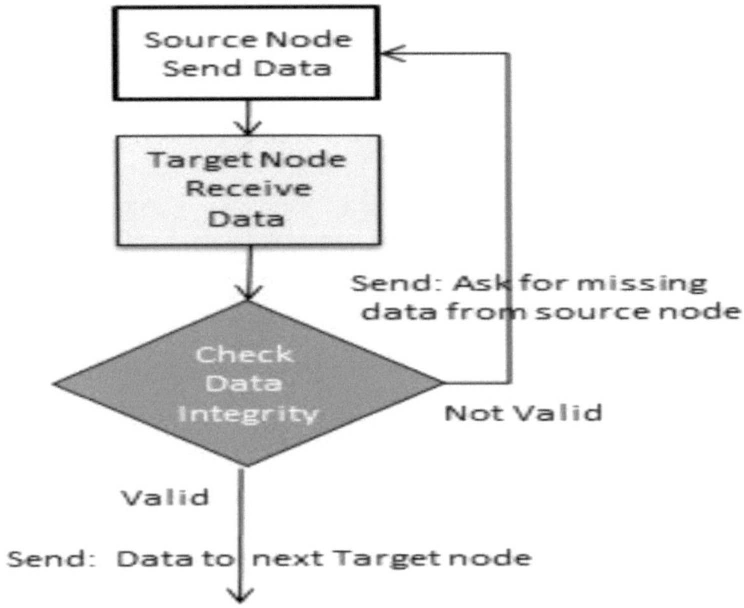

Figure 8. DIA

7.3. Event-to-action time duration

It is important to understand the event-to-action time duration and the data integrity requirements when monitoring HbO_2 and Hb concentrations during a specific activity. Based on the requirements, the proposed model, algorithm, and protocol can be useful or less useful.

In this research in order to validate the event-to-action time duration, we use the following formula to calculate time duration.

$$ITD \leq DTD$$

ITD: Indirect Time Duration – event to action
DTD: Direct Time Duration – event to action

$$ITD = \sum_{0}^{N} Tn$$

$$n \in N$$

N: Set of nodes data pass through
T_n: Processing and transfer time for node n

8. Experiment and results

The proposed model was designed to support a wide range of measurement and activities. We wanted to verify the model using an actual experiment. In order to achieve this goal, we conducted several tests inside and outside a lab environment. HbO_2 and Hb concentration changes in brain and tissue were collected under different circumstances. Figure 9 shows the event-to-action time duration during breathing. The result (Figure 4) was compared with a lab method [37] and was similar. At the start of the transmission we found there was a shift, but after the transmission stabilized the data went back to a synchronous state.

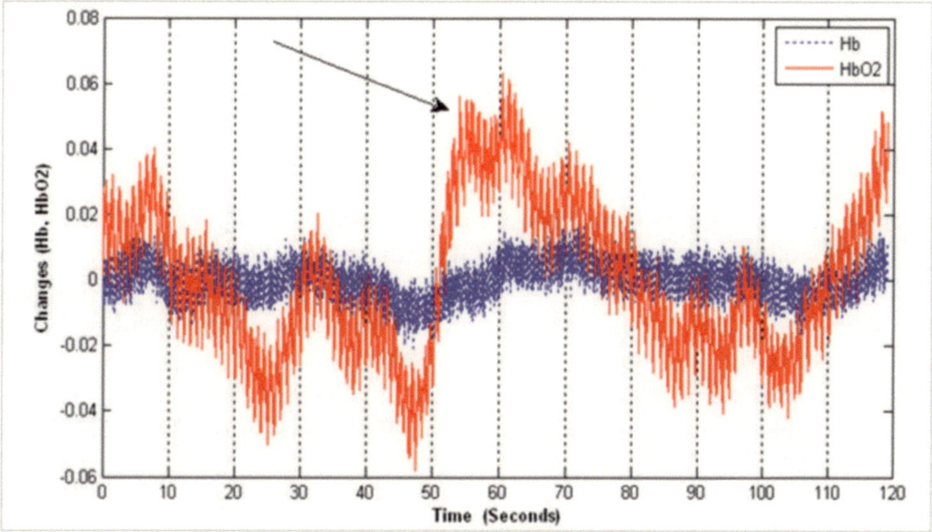

Figure 9. Time Duration and HB, HbO_2 Concentration Changes During Breathing

9. Conclusions and future work

The need to deal with different biological data that has variable timing requirements led to the introduction of a new algorithm that can be used to provide acceptable data quality. Sending and exchanging data over multiple nodes with acceptable quality and time durations (event-to-action) requires a protocol that can ensure these requirements met despite the lack of control over these heterogenic nodes. Medical Data Transfer Protocol (MDTP) was introduced to address this challenge.

The specific aims of this research were: create a model that can be used to represent the minimum node to build a fully mobile medical system that uses heterogenic nodes to monitor human physiological data in near-real time; provide quality medical data; transmit data within acceptable time durations (event-to-action). As a result this model might also allow health care providers to take effective action within acceptable time frames when possible. Moreover this may lead to a better understanding of tissue pathologies. The main aims of the project were achieved. The results have shown that it is possible to utilize heterogenic networks and near-infrared technologies to collect useful medical data. The proposed model was initially tested on a system to monitor HbO_2 and Hb concentrations in the human brain and tissues with acceptable event-to-action time durations. Further work will be required to ensure that the system provides better event-to-action time durations for changes that have shorter time duration requirements.

Author details

Salah Sharieh and Franya Franek
Department of Computing and Software, Faculty of Engineering, McMaster University, Canada

Alexander Ferworn
Department of Computer Science, Faculty of Engineering, Ryerson University, Canada

10. References

[1] Thomas Lagkas, Pantelis Angelidis, Loukas Georgiadis(2010),Wireless network traffic and quality of service support : trends and standards,Hershey, PA : Information Science Reference.

[2] Boukerche, Azzedine(2009).Algorithms and protocols for wireless and mobile ad hoc networks,Hoboken, N.J. : Wiley, c2009.0470383585.

[3] Bluetooth Core Specifications Version 2.1. 2007. available at http://www.bluetooth.com/NR/rdonlyres/F8E8276A-3898-4EC6-B7DAE5535258B056/6545/Core_V21__EDR.zip.

[4] Bray, J. (2002). Bluetooth: Connect without Cables, 2nd ed. Prentice Hall, Upper Saddle River, NJ.

[5] Ganguli, M. (2002). Getting Started with Bluetooth. Premier Press, Cincinnati, Ohio.

[6] Muller, N.J. (2001). Bluetooth Demystified. McGraw-Hill, New York.

[7] Barnes S.J. (2002). Under the Skin: Short-range Embedded Wireless Technology. International Journal of Information Management, 22, no. 3, (June), 165-79.

[8] Keshav, S. (2005). Why Cell Phones will Dominate the Future Internet. SIGCOMM Comput. Commun. Rev., 35, no. 2 (April), 83-86.

[9] Varshney, U. (2007). Pervasive Healthcare and Wireless Health Monitoring. Mob. Netw. Appl. 12, no. 2-3 (March), 113-27.

[10] Delord, X., Perret, S., and Duda, A. (1998). Efficient Mobile Access to the WWW over GSM. In Proceedings of the 8th ACM SIGOPS European Workshop on Support For Composing Distributed Applications, EW 8. (Sintra, Portugal, September). ACM, New York, NY, USA, 1-6.

[11] Eberspächer, J., Vögel, H.J, and Bettstetter, C. (2001). GSM: Switching, Services and Protocols, 2nd ed. John Wiley & Sons, Toronto.

[12] Chakravorty, R., Clark, A., and Pratt, I. (2003). GPRSWeb: Optimizing the Web for GPRS Links. In Proceedings of the 1st International Conference on Mobile Systems,

Applications and Services, (San Francisco, California, May). ACM, New York, NY, USA, 317-30

[13] Sasan Adibi,et al.(2010) Quality of service architectures for wireless networks : performance metrics and management,Hershey, PA : Information Science Reference

[14] Lorincz, K., Kuris, B., Ayer, S. M., Patel, S., Bonato, P., and Welsh, M. (2007). Wearable wireless sensor network to assess clinical status in patients with neurological disorders. In Proceedings of the 6th international Conference on information Processing in Sensor Networks (Cambridge, Massachusetts, USA, April 25 - 27, 2007). IPSN '07. ACM, New York, NY, 563-64.

[15] Soo-Hwan Choi, Byung-Kug Kim, Jinwoo Park, Chul-Hee Kang, and Doo-Seop Eom (2004). An implementation of wireless sensor network. Consumer Electronics, IEEE Transactions on Volume 50, Issue 1, Feb 2004, 236–44.

[16] Kumar, V. (2003). Sensor: the atomic computing particle. SIGMOD Rec. 32, 4 (Dec. 2003), 16-21.

[17] Kansal, A., Goraczko, M., and Zhao, F. (2007). Building a sensor network of mobile phones. In Proceedings of the 6th international Conference on information Processing in Sensor Networks (Cambridge, Massachusetts, USA, April 25 - 27, 2007). IPSN '07. ACM, New York, NY, 547-48.

[18] Mainwaring, A., Culler, D., Polastre, J., Szewczyk, R., and Anderson, J. (2002). Wireless sensor networks for habitat monitoring, Proceedings of the 1st ACM international workshop on Wireless sensor networks and applications, September 28-28, 2002, Atlanta, Georgia, USA.

[19] Junnila, S. and Niittylahti, J. (2003). Wireless technologies for data acquisition systems. In Proceedings of the 1st international Symposium on information and Communication Technologies (Dublin, Ireland, September 24 - 26, 2003). ACM International Conference Proceeding Series, vol. 49. Trinity College Dublin, 132-37.

[20] DeRenzi, B., Anokwa, Y., Parikh, T., and Borriello, G. (2007). Reliable data collection in highly disconnected environments using mobile phones. In Proceedings of the 2007 Workshop on Networked Systems For Developing Regions (Kyoto, Japan, August 27 - 27, 2007). NSDR '07. ACM, New York, NY, 1-5.

[21] Ni, Y., Kremer, U., Stere, A., and Iftode, L. (2005). Programming ad-hoc networks of mobile and resource-constrained devices. In Proceedings of the 2005 ACM SIGPLAN Conference on Programming Language Design and Implementation (Chicago, IL, USA, June 12 - 15, 2005). PLDI '05. ACM, New York, NY, 249-60.

[22] S. Zeadally and A. Kumar (2004). Protocol support for audio streaming between bluetooth devices. IEEE Radio and Wireless Conference, 303-306.

[23] Auletta, V., Blundo, C., De Cristofaro, E., and Raimato, G. (2006). Performance evaluation of web services invocation over Bluetooth. In Proceedings of the ACM international Workshop on Performance Monitoring, Measurement, and Evaluation of Heterogeneous Wireless and Wired Networks (Terromolinos, Spain, October 02 - 02, 2006). PM2HW2N '06. ACM, New York, NY, 1-8.

[24] Comer, D. (1997). In Stevens D. L. (Ed.), Internetworking with TCP (Windows sockets version. ed.). Prentice Hall, Upper Saddle River, N.J..

[25] Stevens, W. R. (1994-). Addison-Wesley Pub. Co., TCP. Reading, Mass.

[26] Comer, D. (2007). The internet book: Everything you need to know about computer networking and how the internet works, 4th ed. Pearson Prentice Hall, Upper Saddle River, NJ..

[27] Bray, J. (2002). Bluetooth: connect without cables, 2nd ed., Prentice Hall, Upper Saddle River, NJ.

[28] Ganguli, M. (2002), Getting started with Bluetooth. Premier Press, Cincinnati, Ohio.

[29] Huang, A. S. (2007). In Rudolph L. (Ed.), Bluetooth essentials for programmers. New York, NY: Cambridge University Press.Muller, N.J. (2001).

[30] Delord, X., Perret, S., and Duda, A. (1998). Efficient Mobile Access to the WWW over GSM. In Proceedings of the 8th ACM SIGOPS European Workshop on Support For Composing Distributed Applications, EW 8. (Sintra, Portugal, September). ACM, New York, NY, USA, 1-6.

[31] Villringer, A. and Chance, B. (1997). Non-invasive optical spectroscopy and imaging of human brain function. Trends in Neuroscience, 20(10), 435-42.

[32] Gratton, E., Fantini, S., Franceschini, M.A., Gratton, G., and Fabiani, M. (1997). Measurements of scattering and absorption changes in muscle and brain. Philosophical Transactions: Biological Sciences, 352(1354), 727-35.

[33] Strangman, G., Boas, D.A., and Sutton, J.P. (2002). Non-invasive neuroimaging using near-infrared light. Biological psychiatry, vol. 52, no. 7, pp. 679-93.

[34] Bozkurt, A., Rosen, A., Rosen, H., and Onaral, B. (2005). A portable near infrared spectroscopy system for bedside monitoring of newborn brain. Biomedical engineering online, vol. 4, no. 1, 29.

[35] Hong, L., Worden, K., Li, C., Murray, T., Ovetsky, Y., Pidikiti, D., and Thomas, R. (1998). A novel method for fast imaging of brain function, non-invasively, with light. Optics Express, vol. 2, 411.

[36] Germon, T.J., Evans, P.D., Manara, A.R., Barnett, N.J., Wall, P., and Nelson, R.J. (1998) Sensitivity of near infrared spectroscopy to cerebral and extra-cerebral oxygenation changes is determined by emitter-detector separation. Journal of clinical monitoring and computing, vol. 14, no. 5, 353-60.

[37] Zhang, X., Toronov, V., Webb, A. (2005). Methodology development for simultaneous diffuse optical tomography and magnetic resonance imaging in functional human brain mapping. In Proceedings of SPIE, Vol 5686, (April), 453-63.

Chapter 10

Calibration of EM Sensors for Spatial Tracking of 3D Ultrasound Probes

Andrew Lang, Vijay Parthasarathy and Ameet Jain

Additional information is available at the end of the chapter

http://dx.doi.org/10.5772/50695

1. Introduction

Ultrasound (US) imaging is one of the modalities commonly used for interventional guidance. It offers many advantages over other imaging systems such as MRI, CT, and fluoroscopy in that it is considerably cheaper, is portable, offers real-time imaging, and has no radiation exposure. Recent developments have led to the advancement of 3D US technology, making it a more feasible alternative to 2D US imaging, despite its higher cost. Among 3D US technology includes real-time 3D transesophageal echocardiography (TEE) enabling US imaging of the heart from within the body. Unfortunately, there are many disadvantages of US that must be addressed. Due to the presence of speckle, the image quality is very poor, especially away from the focal zone. The imaging field-of-view (FOV) is also quite limited, due to the size of the US transducer. These disadvantages significantly limit the usability of US for many interventional procedures.

To make US a more feasible interventional tool, it should be fused with information from another modality or a tracking system. The tracking system allows tools to be visualized in the US volume, especially helpful when imaging a needle or a catheter. Overlaying information from other modalities gives the clinician more information allowing them, for example, to see outside the limited FOV of the US. Often times, the fusion of multiple modalities is done using a tracking system as an intermediate link between them. Calibration of the tracking system to each individual modality is thus required. Calibration of a US probe is a well-studied problem with a variety of methods available to be used. Multiple types of systems can also be used for tracking, including optical and electromagnetic (EM) tracking. The methods of calibrating the US can generally be applied to any type of tracking system.

There are several papers that provide comprehensive reviews of the various methods for calibrating a tracking system to US imaging [8, 11]. These papers focus primarily on the calibration of 2D US systems, but some of these methods can be extended to 3D. Other reviews have been done specifically for the calibration of 3D US, which compare new methods made possible through the use of a 3D probe [5, 14].

Among methods for the calibration of a US probe, there are two commonly used categories of techniques: phantom-based and tracked stylus-based. There are numerous phantom-based calibration methods. Some of the more common types of phantom designs use "N-wire" fiducials [6, 13]. Other phantom designs consist of plane phantoms [15, 16], point phantoms [4], and cross-wire phantoms [15].

It is perhaps more beneficial to calibrate the US without using a phantom. First and foremost is the simplicity of the calibration using a readily available tracked stylus or needle. Also, manufacturing of a phantom may require additional cost and time to develop. Hsu et al. [9] provide an overview of stylus-based calibration methods. The simplest method of calibration using a tracked stylus or needle is to image the tip of the needle precisely in the scan plane of the US image. Given that the needle is tracked, the tip can be segmented from the US images and the collection of all positions can be registered using a point-based registration method [12, 19]. Zhang et al. [19] showed an accuracy of up to 3.5 mm using this method with only nine images for each calibration. In 2D, this method has a problem in that it is very difficult to precisely position the stylus tip in the US scan-plane. Even in 3D the image resolution and artifacts make it difficult to locate the needle tip position accurately. Poon and Rohling [14] performed a similar stylus calibration for a 3D US probe using five pairs of points. They showed an RMS accuracy of 2.36 mm. An optical tracking system was used which has a significantly better accuracy then EM tracking systems.

Another similar stylus-based method depends only on the intersection of the stylus with the imaging plane [10]. The intersection of the US scan-plane with the needle will show a point that is easily segmented. The calibration transformation can be estimated using these measurements. Unfortunately, the calibration accuracy was not quantifiably analyzed here and was only performed for 2D. The biggest problem with this method is that the stylus must be imaged at a wide range of angles and positions.

In this paper we examine the problem of EM-to-TEE calibration for a 3D TEE probe by looking at two separate but similar solutions based off of prior 2D methods [10, 19]. We examine how these methods perform when extended to 3D using EM tracking. In addition, we further analyze the calibration errors using a statistical framework and also examine the effect of the speed of sound errors on the calibration.

2. Methods

The relationship between the TEE image volume and the attached EM sensor is shown in Figure 1. Two similar calibration methods are employed to calibrate the TEE probe and determine this relationship to the EM tracking. In both methods, the calibration is a multi-step process. The data acquisition step is first. Images of the needle from the TEE probe are acquired concurrently with the EM position information of the probe and needle sensors. Segmentation is then carried out to find the tip of the needle in the first method. In the second method, segmenting any point along the needle is sufficient. The calibration is finally performed either using a point-to-point or a point-to-line registration method.

2.1 Data acquisition

Ultrasound imaging was performed using an X7-2t TEE probe with a Philips iE33 echocardiography system. An EM sensor has been permanently mounted on the end of the

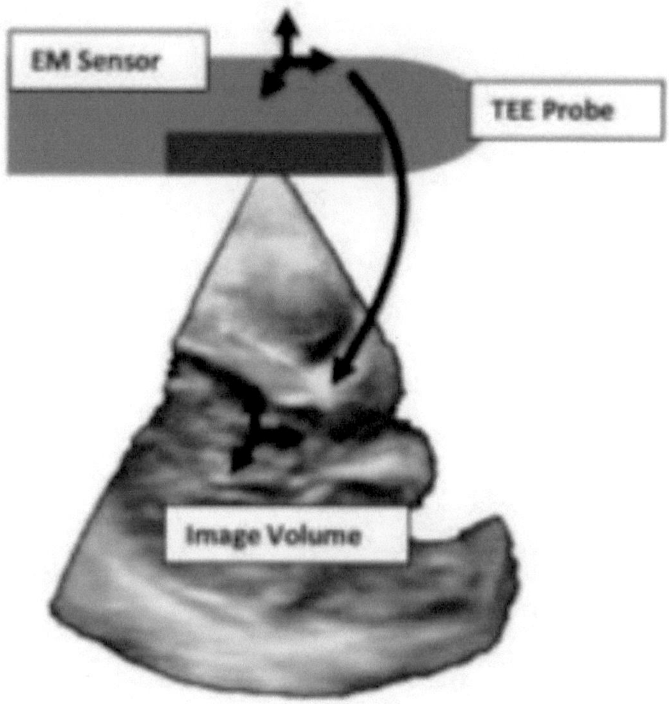

Figure 1. The relationship between the TEE image volume and the attached EM sensor.

probe (Figure 2). EM tracking was done using the Aurora Electromagnetic Measurement System (Northern Digital Inc, Waterloo, Canada). For each calibration experiment, a set of 30-50 volumes were captured, each containing the image of an EM tracked needle at a different orientation. It is important that these images are spread over a wide range of probe and needle positions to ensure the best accuracy of the calibration. Not doing so may introduce a bias to the calibration results. Additionally, all volumes are captured at a depth of 10 cm. TEE volumes are acquired in both the Live 3D (L3D) and Thick Slice (TS) imaging modes. L3D produces a volume size of 112 $\times$ 48 $\times$ 112 pixels or 91 $\times$ 47 $\times$ 100 mm in the width, height and depth directions. TS produces a volume size of 240 $\times$ 16 $\times$ 112 or 140 $\times$ 15 $\times$ 100 mm; almost twice the width as L3D with a very narrow thickness. Because of the narrow cross section, the TS volume can be thought of, in essence, as a 2D plane with some thickness. An overview of the acquisition system can be seen in Figure 3.

2.2 Needle segmentation

After the data is acquired, the needle must be segmented from the volumes in 3D. In both calibration methods the segmentation technique is the same. Needle segmentation is performed manually using three 2D maximum intensity projection images. Segmenting a needle point in two out of the three images is sufficient to identify the point in 3D. If the needle point is identified in all three views, the final 3D position will be the average position in all of the views.

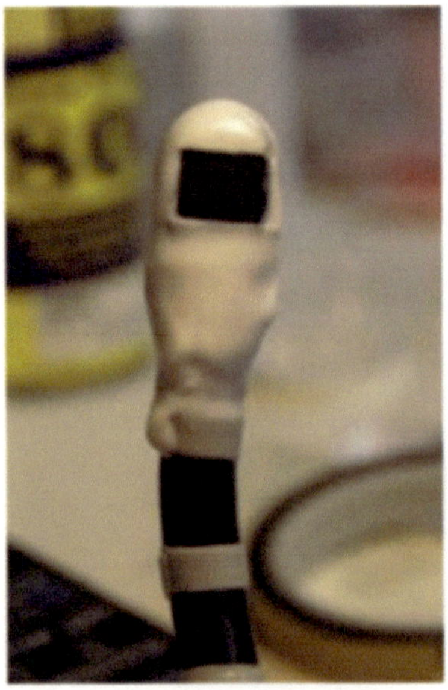

Figure 2. An image of a TEE probe with the EM sensor permanently mounted near the transducer face.

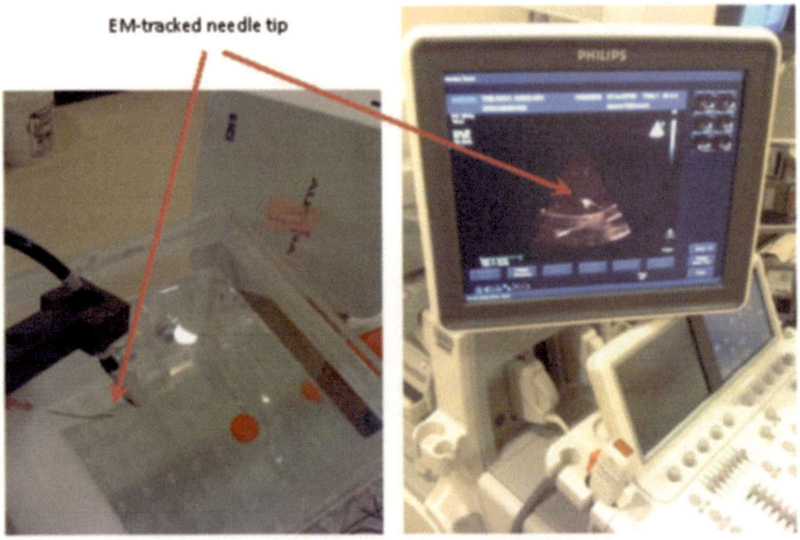

Figure 3. The TEE probe was calibrated by acquiring images of the needle at different orientations. The positions of the EM sensor attached to the TEE probe and the needle are concurrently saved with the image.

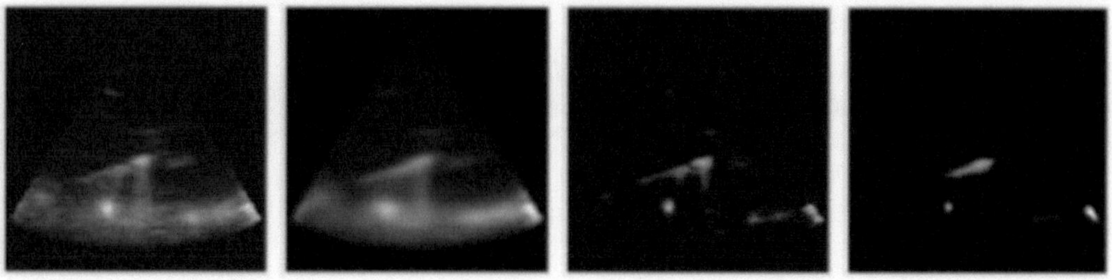

Figure 4. A look at the different modes of processing on the maximum intensity projections of the TEE volume. Left: original image. Left middle: anisotropic diffusion filtered image. Right middle: exponential filtered image. Right: exponential and anisotropic diffusion filtered image.

The images were processed to enhance the needle's appearance. Following the needle segmentation method described in Aboofazeli et al. [2], anisotropic diffusion [18] is first used for speckle reduction and smoothing with the subsequent application of an exponential contrast enhancement filter. The contrast adjustment filter has the form

$$I_c(x) = \exp\left(-\frac{1}{2}\left(\frac{I(x)-\mu}{\sigma}\right)^4\right) \tag{1}$$

where $I(x)$ is the intensity of the volume at voxel x, μ and σ are parameters specifying the range of voxel intensities representing the needle and $I_c(x)$ is the contrast adjusted intensity at voxel x. Values of $\mu = 190$ and $\sigma = 70$ were found to work well. The effect of these filters can be visualized in Figure 4.

2.3 Calibration

In order to calibrate the TEE probe to the EM tracking system, four different measurements are required as inputs. The first input is the set of segmented needle points, $\mathbf{p}_{TEE,i}$, where i is from 1 to the number of images acquired. Next we have two sets of measurements from the EM tracking. The first set of measurements are the positions of the TEE probe EM sensor, ${}^{EM}\mathbf{T}_{probe,i}$. Second are the measurements of the needle sensor, ${}^{EM}\mathbf{T}_{needle,i}$. The notation ${}^{b}\mathbf{T}_{a}$ represents the homogeneous transformation between coordinate systems a and b. The final input for the calibration is the position of the needle tip relative to the EM sensor, $\mathbf{p}_{needle}$. This position is a constant for all measurements determined prior to the experiments [19].

The purpose of calibration is to find the transformation between the TEE coordinate system and the TEE probe EM sensor coordinate system, ${}^{probe}\mathbf{T}_{TEE}$. After this transformation is estimated, a point measured in the TEE volume, $\mathbf{p}_{TEE}$, can be related back to the EM tracker coordinate system using the relation

$$\mathbf{p}_{EM} = {}^{EM}\mathbf{T}_{probe} \times {}^{probe}\mathbf{T}_{TEE} \times \mathbf{p}_{TEE} \tag{2}$$

where $\mathbf{p}_{EM}$ is that point in the EM coordinate system. Note that EM is simply the coordinate system of the stationary EM field generator, of which all EM sensor measurements are made relative to. It could alternatively represent the fixed location of a reference EM sensor.

2.3.1 Calibration using segmented needle tips

If the needle tip position has been segmented from each TEE volume, the needle tip position can be determined relative to the EM coordinate system using $\mathbf{p}_{EM} = {}^{EM}\mathbf{T}_{needle} \times \mathbf{p}_{needle}$, where $\mathbf{p}_{needle}$ is the calculated needle offset. Given a set of needle positions in EM and in the TEE volume, we can reformulate equation 2 to

$$^{probe}\mathbf{T}_{EM} \times \mathbf{p}_{EM} = {}^{probe}\mathbf{T}_{TEE} \times \mathbf{p}_{TEE}. \tag{3}$$

Since the points $\mathbf{p}_{TEE}$ are 3D, we can solve for $^{probe}\mathbf{T}_{TEE}$ using a closed-form least-squares solution proposed by Arun et al. [3] which uses the singular value decomposition. An alternative method must be used for 2D images [19].

2.3.2 Calibration using segmented needle points

The second calibration method is similar to that proposed by Khamene and Sauer [10] with an extension to 3D. In this method, any point on the needle may be segmented, not restricted to the needle tip as with the first method. However the calibration problem becomes more difficult to solve for. We must change our representation of the needle to that of a line, composed using two points. The first point, $\mathbf{p}_{l1}$ is taken to be the origin of the needle sensor measurements relative to the TEE probe sensor, or the translation vector of the transformation $^{probe}\mathbf{T}_{needle}$. The second point, $\mathbf{p}_{l2}$, is the position of the needle tip relative to the TEE probe sensor, or $^{probe}\mathbf{T}_{EM} \times \mathbf{p}_{EM}$.

We now have the problem of estimating the transformation that minimizes the distance between the TEE points and the line representing the needle. The general equation for the distance between a point, $\mathbf{p}_i$, and a line ($\vec{\mathbf{l}}_i = \{\mathbf{p}_{l1,i}, \mathbf{p}_{l2,i}\}$) is determined from the equation

$$d(\mathbf{p}_i, \vec{\mathbf{l}}_i) = \frac{\|(\mathbf{p}_{l2,i} - \mathbf{p}_{l1,i}) \times (\mathbf{p}_{l1,i} - \mathbf{p}_i)\|}{\|(\mathbf{p}_{l2,i} - \mathbf{p}_{l1,i})\|} \tag{4}$$

where $\times$ is the cross product. The calibration transformation is estimated using a nonlinear least-squares optimization framework. The equation to be minimized is

$$e = \sum_{i=1}^{N} d(\mathbf{T}_c \times \mathbf{p}_{TEE}, \vec{\mathbf{l}}_i)^2. \tag{5}$$

Here we are minimizing the distance of each individual needle point segmented in the TEE volume and the line representing the needle relative to the probe EM sensor. The TEE point is transformed by the transformation $\mathbf{T}_c$. The transformation $\mathbf{T}_c$ which minimizes 5 becomes the estimation of the calibration transformation $^{probe}\mathbf{T}_{TEE}$. Since no closed form solution exists to find this transformation, an iterative method must be used. The Levenberg-Marquardt algorithm is used here. The transformation $\mathbf{T}_c$ is represented by six parameters, the x, y, and z Euler angles as well as the x, y, and z translations. Also note that for increased efficiency, the denominator in equation 4 can be left out in the calculation of equation 5 since it is a constant equal to the needle tip offset, $\|\mathbf{p}_{needle}\|$.

Posing the calibration problem in this way, using the point-to-line distance, unfortunately is very susceptible to the optimization being caught in local minimum. It requires a close initial estimate of the solution. An approximation to the solution can be estimated by solving for 3 as seen in the previous section. This solution works well as an initial guess for $\mathbf{T}_c$ provided that the segmented points in the TEE volume are relatively close to the needle tip (within several mm). Also, as previously mentioned, the stylus must be imaged at a wide range of angles and positions. Note that in the extreme case of when all of the images are taken with the needle at the same orientation there would be uncertainty in the calibration translation along the direction of the needle.

2.4 Considerations for the speed of sound

For the best accuracy in calibration, careful consideration must be taken to account for the speed of sound (SOS) in water. The US machine assumes that the TEE probe is imaging human tissue, which has an approximate SOS of 1540 m/s. The SOS for water is different and depends on the water temperature. At room temperature (20° C), the SOS in pure water is approximately 1480 m/s [1]. There is therefore a mismatch in the speed of sound when the EM tracked needle is imaged in water by the US. Although the water temperature can be adjusted such that the SOS matches approximately 1540 m/s, maintaining the water at room temperature is more practical, especially for the lengthy calibration experiments carried out here.

When performing a calibration experiment in water, the voxel scaling can simply be changed to account for the SOS. Given water at room temperature, the voxel size must be multiplied by 1480/1540 in each direction. A key point to consider regarding the SOS of water is that the calibration transformation for experiments performed in water is not valid for experiments performed on real tissues. The physical size of the water and tissue volumes are now different for the same depth setting. At an imaging depth of 10 cm there would be a physical size difference between tissue and water volumes of about 4 mm along the depth direction. The error incurred by using the incorrect calibration matrix would depend on the location of the volume origin (Figure 5).

To illustrate the effect that the speed of sound has on the calibration, lets look at how the volumes compare for different speed of sound values. We will look at a 2D case where the speed of sound of water is *half* of that assumed by the US and the origin of the US image is in the top left corner of the image (SOS is exaggerated for visual purposes). Figure 5(a) shows the US image of several points at various locations in the image, with the imaged points denoted by red ×'s and their actual physical location denoted by blue ×'s. The arrow represents the calibration transformation between the US and EM sensor coordinate systems. Figure 5(b) displays the result of calibration using an incorrect SOS value. Figure 5(c) shows the result of calibration with the correct SOS value. Note that the acquired image is physically smaller and therefore the origin of the image has moved. With the origin of the image in a different location, the calibration transformation changes as well (Figure 5(d)).

In this figure, the calibration transformation in water that is calculated by scaling the voxels appropriately is seen in the interior square image of Figure 5(d). A volume acquired in real tissue will be larger requiring a different calibration transformation, as represented by the outer square image of Figure 5(d). Therefore, care must be taken to convert the calibration transformation when imaging in real tissues. This conversion can be done through a translation of the calibration transformation based on the origin of the volumes.

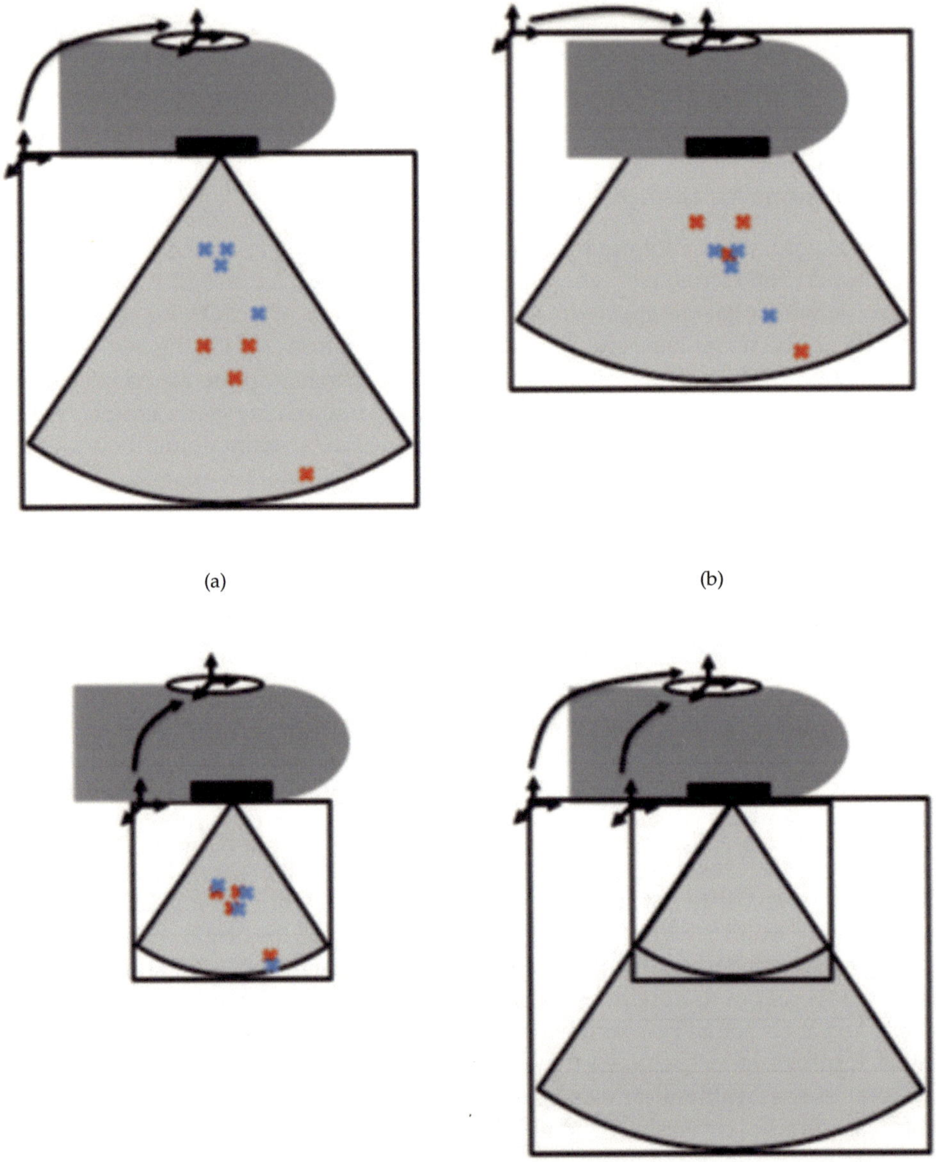

(a) (b)

(c) (d)

Figure 5. A illustration of the effect of the speed of sound on calibration. (a) US imaged points with an incorrect SOS (red $\times$'s) as compared to the correct physical location (blue $\times$'s) where the SOS value of the imaged points is half of the assumed SOS. (b) Calibration of points with an incorrect SOS. (c) Calibration of points with the correct SOS. (d) Calibration transformation changes for different SOS values depending on the image origin.

2.5 Statistical analysis

A statistical analysis can be performed on the data to remove outlying points and analyze the overall accuracy of the calibration. We wish to estimate the best points to include for a single calibration, as well as find the best calibration transformation with some indication of how well the calibration model fits. A single calibration using all available points can only provide a simple indication of the spread of the points. The analysis formed here includes outlier removal using RANSAC followed by a cross-validation analysis on the calibration using the remaining points. In this analysis, we will end up with a statistical view of the calibration accuracy using all available points.

A RANSAC framework is used for estimating outlying points [7]. The RANSAC algorithm examines random sets of "minimal" combinations of points. Minimal is taken to mean the minimum number of points required to perform the calibration. Three points are technically required, however, we choose to use 5 points since the calibration method of Section 2.3.2 is not robust to using only 3 points. A variation of RANSAC was used for our calibration called MLESAC, where each random sample set is ranked based on a likelihood function rather than the number of points that fit the model [17].

Having eliminated outlying points, we attempt to find the best calibration model from the remaining set of points. A random sample validation framework is used as an analysis tool to choose the best calibration transformation. Within this framework, we also look at the convergence of the calibration error as more points are used. By examining the convergence of the error, we are able to have confidence that enough points have been acquired for a successful calibration.

For the measure of error, when a simple calibration is carried out, the fiducial registration error (FRE) is calculated for how well the EM and TEE points fit together. This error consists of either the RMS point-to-point distance or RMS point-to-line distance for all points used in the calibration. Additionally, the target registration error (TRE) measures how well the validation points fit the calibration model. These points were not used to calculate the calibration transformation, and therefore provide a better indication of the accuracy of the calibration.

To examine the convergence of the calibration error, 5 points are used initially, incrementing by one up to $N - 3$ points, assuming that N points are available to be used for calibration. For each set of calibration points, three of the points that were not used in the calibration are used for validation (to calculate TRE). Because a single calibration at each interval will be biased towards the points included in the calibration, the calibration is repeated 1000 times at each interval. For each trial, the included points are randomized from the set including all points. The validation points are also randomized.

Given multiple FRE, TRE, and calibration values at each incremental number of calibration points, the mean and standard deviations can be calculated and plotted. Example plots of this information is given in Figure 6. The final calibration transformation is taken to be the average over all of the trials above the convergence point. The convergence point is the point at which the TRE mean and standard deviation values become "constant", when the differential values fall below a threshold (set to 0.01 mm for mean and 0.005 mm for standard deviation). A black vertical line represents the convergence point in Figure 6(a). If a convergence points

Probe	Calib Method	FRE	t_x	t_y	t_z	r_x	r_y	r_z
1	1 (L3D)	1.55	-2.2	54.6	22.6	-88.8	-2.5	-87.6
	2 (L3D)	1.22	-2.1	55.1	22.9	-86.8	-2.0	-88.5
	2 (TS)	1.66	-3.0	56.4	2.6	-90.8	-2.5	-91.5
2	1 (L3D)	1.89	-13.7	-59.4	33.4	96.4	-4.2	99.4
	2 (L3D)	1.76	-12.7	-59.1	33.6	94.5	-6.4	95.2
	2 (TS)	1.75	-10.0	-58.0	14.1	95.1	-7.1	101.4

Table 1. Calibration results for a single calibration using all of the points.

cannot be found, the calibration cannot be reliably used. Also, provided enough points are acquired, we can estimate the minimum number of experimental points required for a successful calibration.

3. Results and discussion

The calibration methods were analyzed for two separate TEE probes using each imaging mode (L3D and TS). Both probes were analyzed using each calibration method. TS volumes were only calibrated using calibration method 2 since the volume is too narrow to image the tip of the needle precisely. The speed of sound during calibration was assumed to be 1480 m/s based on the approximate water temperature, and the TEE volumes were scaled appropriately. We take method 1 to be the method described in 2.3.1 and method 2 to be as described in 2.3.2.

3.1 Single calibration

We first examine the results of a single calibration. The calibration result is calculated after discarding 10% of the points having the highest FRE. Looking at the results, method 2 gives a lower FRE value than method 1. The reason for this is that in method 1, the error is based on the point-to-point error of the needle tip position. There is more variation in segmenting the specific needle tip in the TEE volume. As a result, the distance will be larger. Also, the point-to-line distance is orthogonal to the needle direction. As the needle tip distance may not be orthogonal to the needle itself, this error is expected to be larger.

It should also be noted that the calibration parameters are different between the two calibration methods. We cannot tell based on this table which one is better, but can attempt to understand why they are different. Although the translational terms are relatively similar, all within 1.5 mm of each other, the rotational terms have larger differences, up to about 4 degrees. Again, one main reason for these differences is the difficulty in segmenting the needle tip. Also, there may be a bias in the needle tip segmentation, since the low resolution of the TEE volume makes it nearly impossible to determine which point is the tip. Looking back to Figure 4, there is generally a significant volume at the needle tip. The tip is located somewhere within this area. It was taken to be the center of this area for this work, but it could in fact be closer to the end.

Looking at the thick slice mode, we see similar parameters to the Live 3D mode. In fact, only one parameter, the z-translation, is dissimilar between modes. Since the other 5 parameters are similar, we can guess that the TS volume is located at a similar orientation as the L3D volume,

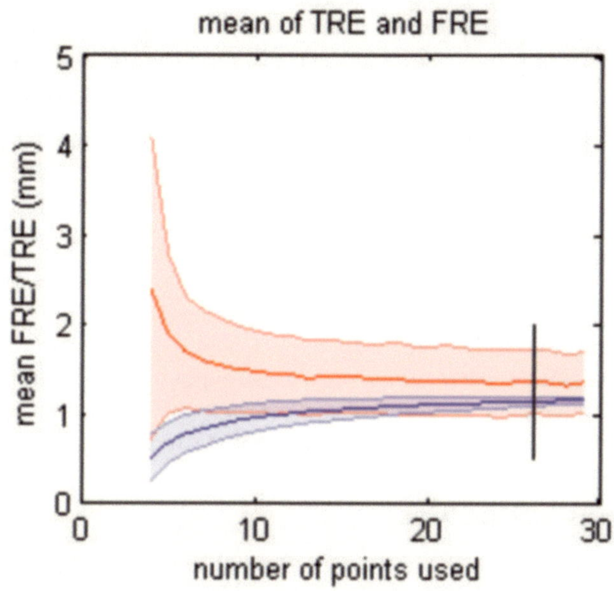

(a)

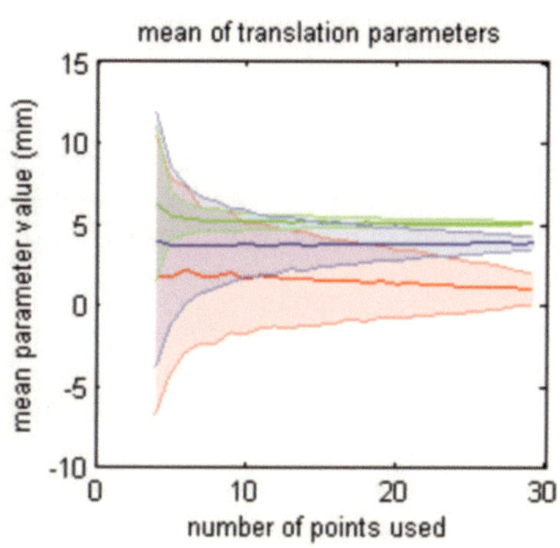

(b)

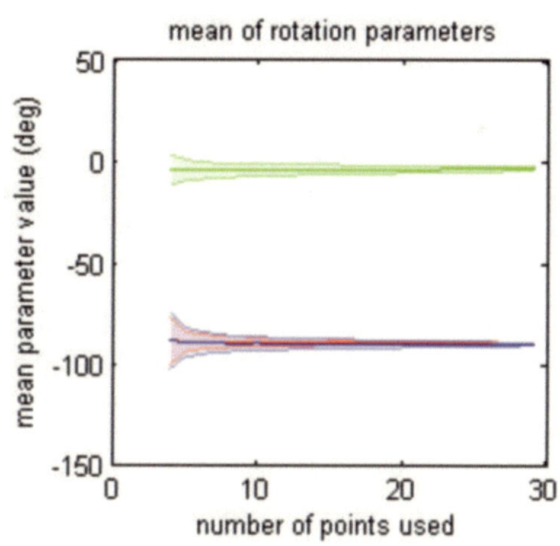

(c)

Figure 6. The resulting plots after the statistical analysis of the calibration. Note the scale of the Y-axis. (a) A plot of the convergence of the FRE (red) and TRE (blue) values as more points are used. For each number of points used, the average and standard deviation over 1000 trials is plotted. The black vertical line represents the approximate convergence point of these values. (b) The convergence of the x (red), y (blue), z (green) translation parameters of the resulting calibration matrices. (c) The convergence of the x (red), y (blue), z (green) Euler angle rotation parameters of the resulting calibration matrices.

Probe	Calib Method	FRE	TRE	t_x	t_y	t_z	r_x	r_y	r_z
1	1 (L3D)	1.37	1.48	-2.1	54.7	22.7	-88.9	-2.3	-86.3
	2 (L3D)	1.30	1.45	-2.0	55.1	22.8	-87.5	-2.8	-89.6
	2 (TS)	1.54	1.63	-2.8	56.5	2.7	-90.4	-2.0	-93.4
2	1 (L3D)	1.70	1.84	-13.6	-59.4	33.3	96.3	-4.2	99.9
	2 (L3D)	1.25	1.37	-12.1	-59.4	34.7	97.1	-7.7	96.1
	2 (TS)	1.59	1.69	-10.1	-58.2	13.9	95.1	-6.9	101.6

Table 2. Calibration results for a calibration statistical analysis.

only translated along one axis. In this case, the differences in the 5 similar parameters would be due error in calibration. Higher errors are expected in the TS mode because it is essentially a calibration in 2 dimensions. Also, many of the needle positions are along a similar direction, orthogonal to the slice axis. Since many of the needle positions were in along this direction, there will be a high error localizing the plane along this direction.

3.2 Calibration statistical analysis

Next, we examine the statistical analysis of the calibrations. The analysis described in Section 2.5 was performed on the data acquired from each probe in each imaging mode (L3D and TS). The resulting FRE, TRE and parameters are listed in Table 2. Figure 7 shows the convergence of the FRE and TRE as more points are included in the calibrations. Note the X and Y-axis scaling in these images for comparisons. In this figure, the results are displayed from both calibration methods.

In Table 2, we see a lot of similarities to Table 1. There is a lower FRE in method 2 as compared to method 1. The listed parameters are also quite similar between the two tables, with translational differences all within 1.5 mm and rotational differences all within 4 degrees. The differences may be attributed to the fact that a different number of outliers were rejected by the RANSAC than the single calibration.

Much of the information for the statistical analysis is in the plots that are generated, as displayed in Figures 7. In Figure 7, the TRE plots are the most important. They show how well the error for points not included in the calibration converges. In L3D mode, each method performs similarly. With only a few points used, the standard deviation is much higher for method two, however, both methods converge to similar values. Also, both methods seem to converge in about 20-25 points. The convergence of the thick slice was much slower however, converging in about 35 points.

3.3 Needle position error

Assessing the accuracy of the TEE calibration must be done using points not included in the calibration. Since the resulting calibration from the statistical analysis includes all of the points, a new set of points must be acquired. A new set of 10 TEE images of an EM tracked needle at different positions were acquired with their corresponding EM measurements. The needle tip was then manually segmented and the average distance error between the needle tip in the TEE volume and the tip in EM after applying the calibration transformation was

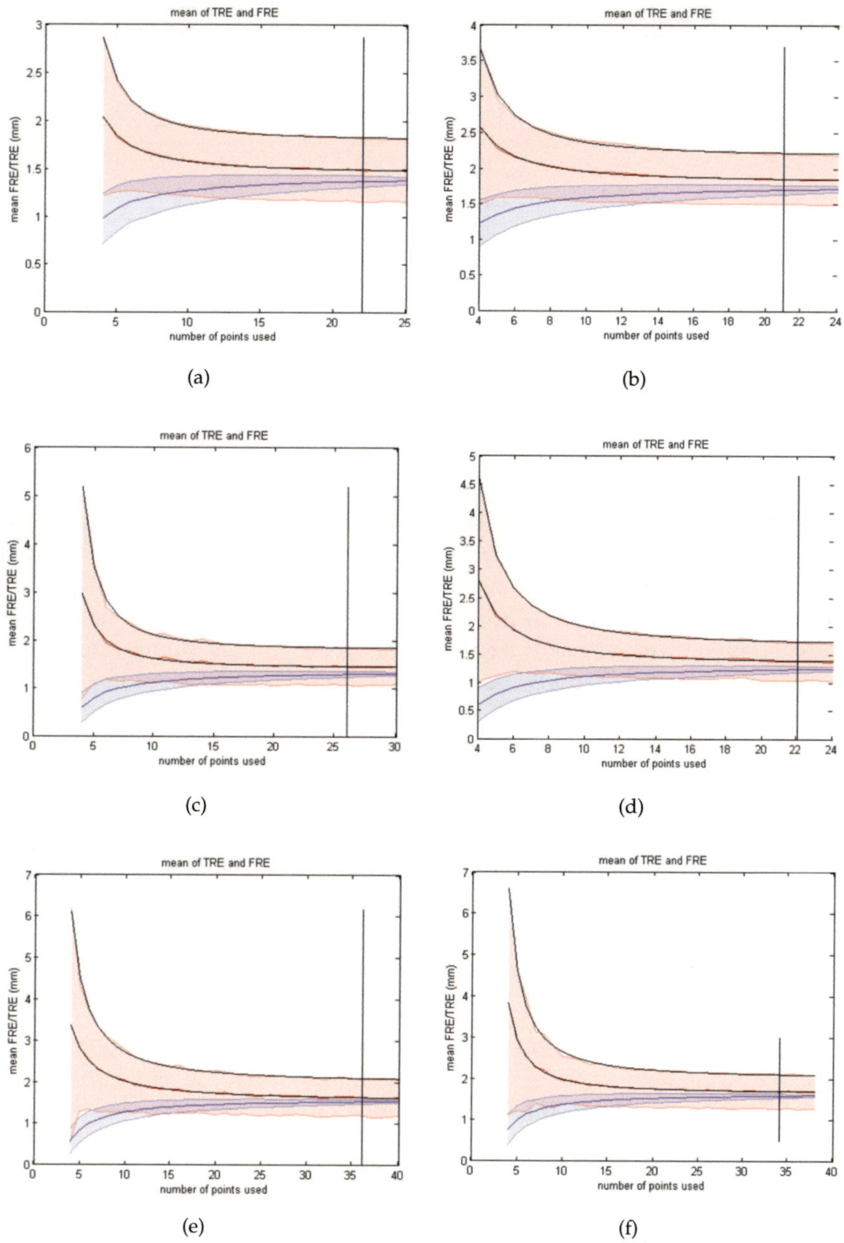

Figure 7. The convergence of the FRE (red) and TRE (blue) values after calibration for Probe 1 (left column) and Probe 2 (right column) calibration method 1 (top), method 2 - L3D (middle) and method 2 - TS (bottom)

Probe	Calib Method	FRE using default pixel scaling	FRE using SOS corrected pixel scaling	Percent Difference
1	1 (L3D)	1.66	1.55	6.6
	2 (L3D)	1.32	1.22	7.6
	2 (TS)	2.08	1.66	20.2
2	1 (L3D	1.92	1.89	1.6
	2 (L3D)	1.78	1.76	1.1
	2 (TS)	1.82	1.75	3.8

Table 3. Calibration results comparing the default pixel scale versus using a pixel scale adjusted for the speed of sound difference in water.

calculated. The average over all 10 points was 1.39±0.54 mm. This result was for Probe 2 using method 2. The error is reasonably close to the TRE seen in Table 2, as would be expected.

3.4 Effect of speed of sound

To look at the effect of the speed of sound on the calibration, we perform a single calibration on all points using pixel scaling having an assumed speed of 1540 and 1480 m/s. The FRE values are given in Table 3. A more significant increase in error is seen for Probe 1 than Probe 2. One possible reason is that Probe 2 was calibrated with much less variation in needle position. All of the segmented points are in a small area, whereas in Probe 1, the points are spread out much more. Having the points more spread out means that the calibration will be more effected by scaling errors.

4. Conclusions

A framework for the calibration of a 3D TEE probe to an EM tracking system was examined. The calibration framework consists of three basic steps: data acquisition, needle segmentation and calibration. We were able to analyze the results of the calibration of two separate TEE probes. Finally, two different calibration techniques for calibration using a needle were explored. The first method requiring the tip of the needle being segmented from the TEE volume, while the second method allows any point along the needle to be segmented.

It is very difficult to analyze which calibration method is better. Method 1 shows a faster convergence, requiring fewer images to be captured. However, it is more difficult to segment the needle tip from the TEE volume. A large imaging artifact at the needle tip prevents it from being precisely localized in the TEE volume. The likelihood of introducing a bias in method 1 due to segmentation error is much greater than in method 2. Therefore, method 2 is preferred. It does however require that more images are acquired. Greater than 30 images are recommended for good convergence properties. The speed of sound clearly also has an effect on the calibration accuracy. FRE values were improved after applying a scaling adjustment indicating that the segmented points had a better fit.

One potential for future work is to automate the calibration process. The presented calibration methods are not well suited for acquisition of more then a few dozen images since the acquisition is performed one image at a time with the needle being manually segmented.

Image acquisition can be made simpler by acquiring a continuous series of images while the user simply moves the needle around the needle field of view. A continuous data acquisition would lead to other problems however, such as a temporal delay between the US acquisition and the EM tracking data. The needle segmentation can be improved through the use of more sophisticated, automatic needle identification methods. There are several published needle segmentation algorithms [2]. One way of segmenting the entire needle is to use a form of 3D Hough transform. If the needle can be automatically segmented, the calibration method described in 2.3.2 can be extended to a line-to-line registration method. More information extracted from these volumes can only improve the calibration consistency and accuracy.

Acknowledgements

The authors are sincerely grateful to Philips Research North America to provide the much needed support to conduct the research that has been presented here.

Author details

Andrew Lang
Department of Electrical and Computer Engineering, Johns Hopkins University, Baltimore, MD, USA

Vijay Parthasarathy and Ameet Jain
Philips Research North America, Briarcliff Manor, NY, USA

5. References

[1] Ablitt, J. [2000]. Speed of sound in pure water, http://resource.npl.co.uk/acoustics/techguides/soundpurewater/. National Physical Laboratory.
URL: *http://resource.npl.co.uk/acoustics/techguides/soundpurewater/*

[2] Aboofazeli, M., Abolmaesumi, P., Mousavi, P. & Fichtinger, G. [2009]. A new scheme for curved needle segmentation in three-dimensional ultrasound images, pp. 1067–1070.

[3] Arun, K. S., Huang, T. S. & Blostein, S. D. [1987]. Least-squares fitting of two 3-D point sets, *IEEE Transactions on Pattern Analysis and Machine Intelligence* 9(5): 698–700.

[4] Barratt, D., Penney, G., Chan, C., Slomczykowski, M., Carter, T., Edwards, P. & Hawkes, D. [2006]. Self-calibrating 3D-ultrasound-based bone registration for minimally invasive orthopedic surgery, *IEEE Transactions on Medical Imaging* 25(3): 312–323.

[5] Bergmeir, C., Seitel, M., Frank, C., Simone, R. D., Meinzer, H.-P. & Wolf, I. [2009]. Comparing calibration approaches for 3D ultrasound probes, *International Journal of Computer Assisted Radiology and Surgery* 4(2): 203–213.
URL: *http://www.springerlink.com/content/011g2nlu31q42035/*

[6] Chen, T. K., Thurston, A. D., Ellis, R. E. & Abolmaesumi, P. [2009]. A real-time freehand ultrasound calibration system with automatic accuracy feedback and control, *Ultrasound in Medicine & Biology* 35(1): 79–93.
URL: *http://www.sciencedirect.com/science/article/B6TD2-4TK2PMY-1/2/0229366696d3a893ecd930204c77aed1*

[7] Fischler, M. A. & Bolles, R. C. [1981]. Random sample consensus: A paradigm for model fitting with applications to image analysis and automated cartography, *Communications of the ACM* 24: 381–395.

[8] Hsu, P.-W., Prager, R. W., Gee, A. H. & Treece, G. M. [2009]. Freehand 3D ultrasound calibration: A review, *in* B. H. Ch.W. Sensen (ed.), *Advanced Imaging in Biology and Medicine*, Springer Berlin Heidelberg, chapter 3, pp. 47–84.
URL: *http://www.springerlink.com/content/x271137049707865/*

[9] Hsu, P.-W., Treece, G. M., Prager, R. W., Houghton, N. E. & Gee, A. H. [2008]. Comparison of freehand 3-D ultrasound calibration techniques using a stylus, *Ultrasound in Medicine & Biology* 34(10): 1610–1621.
URL: *http://www.sciencedirect.com/science/article/B6TD2-4S97JGM-4/2/29347751b4b2b32d578f211a5d9eab11*

[10] Khamene, A. & Sauer, F. [2005]. A novel phantom-less spatial and temporal ultrasound calibration method, *Medical Image Computing and Computer-Assisted Intervention MICCAI 2005*, Vol. 3750 of *Lecture Notes in Computer Science*, Springer Berlin / Heidelberg, pp. 65–72. URL: *http://www.springerlink.com/content/4t0lr4pp0kqye7nx/*

[11] Mercier, L., Langø, T., Lindseth, F. & Collins, L. D. [2005]. A review of calibration techniques for freehand 3-D ultrasound systems, *Ultrasound in Medicine & Biology* 31(2): 143–165.
URL: *http://www.sciencedirect.com/science/article/B6TD2-4FFMNSK-3/2/c40fe8177f79a9cfddb543694f849b17*

[12] Muratore, D. M. & Galloway, R. L. [2001]. Beam calibration without a phantom for creating a 3-D freehand ultrasound system, *Ultrasound in Medicine & Biology* 27(11): 1557–1566.
URL: *http://www.sciencedirect.com/science/article/B6TD2-44N9J9C-G/2/b4c61cdbf56df1bf72c554537de449cb*

[13] Pagoulatos, N., Haynor, D. R. & Kim, Y. [2001]. A fast calibration method for 3-D tracking of ultrasound images using a spatial localizer, *Ultrasound in Medicine & Biology* 27(9): 1219–1229.
URL: *http://www.sciencedirect.com/science/article/B6TD2-444DTNW-9/2/fee010a12a55a764289158215f4d9b49*

[14] Poon, T. C. & Rohling, R. N. [2005]. Comparison of calibration methods for spatial tracking of a 3-D ultrasound probe, *Ultrasound in Medicine & Biology* 31(8): 1095–1108.
URL: *http://www.sciencedirect.com/science/article/B6TD2-4GT7XPW-F/2/b57f38b74e41675342283dee4aa55349*

[15] Prager, R. W., Rohling, R. N., Gee, A. H. & Berman, L. [1998]. Rapid calibration for 3-D freehand ultrasound, *Ultrasound in Medicine & Biology* 24(6): 855–869.
URL: *http://www.sciencedirect.com/science/article/B6TD2-3W01HPN-17/2/4e6d61757137c9fc45d5692665accb7b*

[16] Rousseau, F., Hellier, P. & Barillot, C. [2005]. Confhusius: A robust and fully automatic calibration method for 3D freehand ultrasound, *Medical Image Analysis* 9(1): 25–38.
URL: *http://linkinghub.elsevier.com/retrieve/pii/S1361841504000404?showall=true*

[17] Torr, P. & Zisserman, A. [2000]. MLESAC: A new robust estimator with application to estimating image geometry, *Journal of Computer Vision and Image Understanding* 78(1): 138–156.

[18] Weickert, J. [1998]. *Anisotropic Diffusion in Image Processing*, Teubner, Stuttgart.

[19] Zhang, H., Banovac, F., White, A. & Cleary, K. [2006]. Freehand 3D ultrasound calibration using an electromagnetically tracked needle, *Proc. SPIE*, Vol. 6141, SPIE, San Diego, CA, USA, pp. 61412M–9. URL: *http://link.aip.org/link/?PSI/6141/61412M/1*

Section 3

Scientific Experiments

Chapter 11

Data Acquisition in Particle Physics Experiments

V. González, D. Barrientos, J. M. Blasco, F. Carrió, X. Egea and E. Sanchis

Additional information is available at the end of the chapter

http://dx.doi.org/10.5772/48463

1. Introduction

This chapter presents an overview of technological aspects related to data acquisition (DAQ) systems for particle physics experiments. Being a general topic as data acquisition can be, particle physics experiments pose some challenges which deserve a special description and for which special solutions may be adopted.

Generally speaking, most of the particle physics experiments incur in the use of different types of sensors which information has to be gathered and processed to extract the biggest semantic contents about the process being analyzed. This fact implies the need for, not only a hardware coordination (timing, data width, speeds, etc.) between different sub-acquisition systems for the different types of sensors, but also an information processing strategy to gain more significance from the analysis of the data from the whole system that the one got from a single type of sensor. Also, from the point of view of hardware resources, each type of sensor is replicated several times (even millions) to achieve some spatial coverage. This fact directly drives to the extensive use of integrated devices when needed to improve cost and space utilization.

This chapter, thus, will cover the specific technologies used in the different stages in which a general DAQ system in particle physics experiments can be divided.

The rest of the chapter is organized following the natural flow of data from the sensor to the final processing. First, we will describe the most general abstraction of DAQ systems pointing out the general architecture used in particle physics experiment. Second, different common types of transducers used will be described with their main characteristics. A review of the different hardware architectures for the front-end system will follow. Then, we will get into several common data transmission paradigms including modern standard buses and optical fibers. Finally, a review of present hardware processing solutions will be done.

2. Data acquisition architectures

Data acquisition pursues the reading of the information from one or many sensors for its real-time use or storage and further off-line analysis. Strictly speaking we may establish four different activities in a sensor processing system: acquisition, processing, integration and analysis. However, most of the time we refer to DAQ system as the whole of these activities.

It is worth to say that not every DAQ system includes these four activities, depending on their complexity and application. For example, in single sensor systems neither integration nor processing could be necessary. On the other hand, in systems with replicated sensors, processing could be minimal, but the integration is crucial. If the system is based on different types of sensors, processing is necessary to make the readings of the various sensors compatible and the integration is needed to obtain comprehensive information of the environment. However, the majority of the DAQ systems will include the four activities: the physical variable is sensed in the acquisition activity; the data collected is processed properly (for example, performing scaling or formatting) before being transported to the integration activity; the output of the integration is a more meaningful information on which the analysis activity can base its tasks (storage, action on a mechanism, etc.).

2.1. Architectures of sensor systems

As we mentioned before, the DAQ system consists of four activities: acquisition, processing, integration and analysis. Depending on the characteristics of the process under study we will have to choose how to organize them, as we shall see now, to adapt it to our needs [1].

- Collection of sensors

A collection of sensors is a set of sensors arranged in a certain way. They can be in series, parallel or a mixed combination of these two basic arrangements.

The choice of the particular configuration will depend on the application. The integration of information is carried out progressively through the different sensors to get a final result.

- Hierarchical system

In a centralized system, data from the sensors are transmitted to a central processor to be combined. If the volume of data is large, this organization may require considerable bandwidth. For these cases, the DAQ system can be arranged as a hierarchy of subsystems.

Consider the example of the figure 1a. Data D_1 and D_2 are combined in the stage of integration in the feature F_{12}. Similarly, D_3 and D_4, D_5 and D_6 and D_7 and D_8 constitute characteristics F_{34}, F_{56} and F_{78} respectively. Features F_{12} and F_{34} are then combined in the stage of feature integration in a local decision *Dec 1-4*, and F_{56} and F_{78} generate *Dec 5-8*. Finally, local decisions are combined in the stage of decision integration in a global decision *Dec 1-8* .

The interesting aspect of this organization is that an increase in the "size" of the problem does not translate in a similar increase in the organization of the DAQ, i.e., the system does not grow linearly with the problem. This is true provided that the data and feature fusion stages reduce the volume of information.

- Multisensor integration

Figure 1b shows the integration of various sensors s_1, s_2, s_3 and s_4 (not all of the same type). We assume that s_1 and s_2 are of the same type, s_3 of a second type and s_4 of a third type. In this case, the integration of the information has to be done to ensure that data from the sensors are compatible.

The processing of the four readings must be carried out sequentially in three phases: $t_1 = F_1 (s_1, s_2)$, $t_2 = F_2 (t_1, s_3)$ and $t_3 = F_3 (t_2, s_4)$. The final output is $t_3 = F_3 (F_2 (F_1 (s_1, s_2), s_3), s_4)$. We must clarify that the function F_1 uses data from the two sensors competitively while F_2 and F_3 use complementary data.

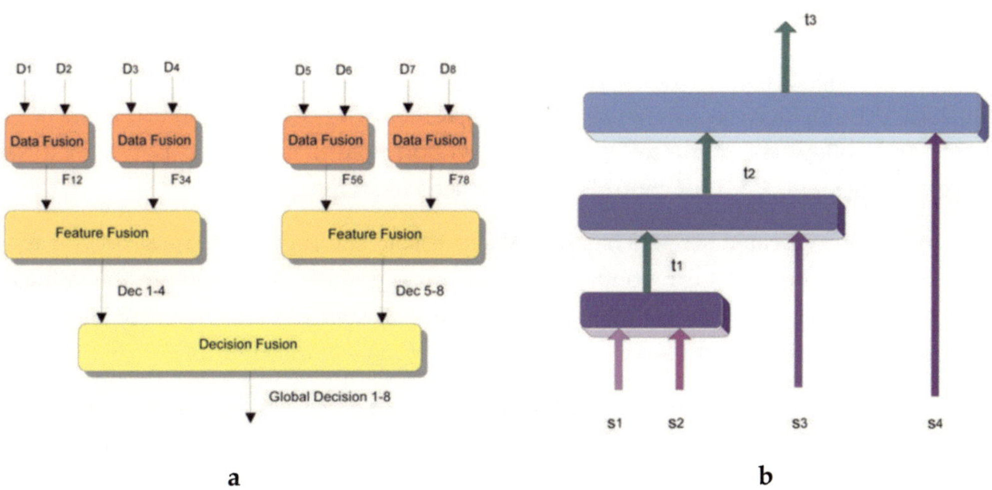

Figure 1. a) Hierarchical sensor integration. b) Multisensor integration

2.2. Distributed processing of sensors

In the following we will focus on DAQ systems where the four activities described before take place in a distributed way, known as distributed processing systems [2]. This case is of special interest as many of the present DAQ systems for particle physics follow it.

To better understand the different aspects of the processing of sensors let us consider a distributed processing system of sensors with the main objective of detecting targets present in the surveyed space. This example may apply to particle physics experiments but also to other fields like distributed control systems, sensory systems for robots, etc.

Let us assume that there is a finite number of resources (sensors and processors) in the distributed system. Consider a system in which there are N sensors (S_1 to S_N) and P processors (EP_1 EP_P). N sensors, for example, can track objects in observation space and we assume that they are all of the same type, that is, they conform a system based on physically replicated sensors. Let us suppose they have been organized in P sensors groups or *clusters*, for example 3, of N/P sensors each. In our example, there are three groups, each with three sensors and a processor to control them.

The main task, *T*, is to detect and possibly follow targets across the surveyed space. Consider two possibilities:

1. The space of observation is too broad and therefore cannot be efficiently covered by any of the clusters of sensors.
2. The space of observation can be covered by all the groups of sensors, but the system requires a response in real time for the follow-up of the target.

In the first case, part of the space can be assigned to each group of sensors. Collectively, they will cover all the surveyed space. In the second case, we can assign to each cluster the task of following some specific number of targets; ideally, each group should be following a single target.

In our example, the distributed processing system breaks down the main task *T* in *P* subtasks; this operation is known as *task decomposition*. The objective of each subtask T_i is to detect and follow the ith-target in the observation space. Each task is assigned with a processing element, EP_i, that controls the three sensors of the group.

Each group of replicated sensors has a local processor. The processor is responsible for local processing and control; it can control the sensors assigned to it and obtain the values from them. Ideally, the sensors of the clusters should always obtain the same value, but in practice they give different values following some statistical distribution.

Suppose that each group can see only part of the space, but the targets can move anywhere within this space. In this case, the system would require a communication between the local processors to share the information about the object and to know when it moves from one area to another.

Finally, the integrator is responsible for combining data from sensors and/or their abstractions. It should be noted that we started with nine sensors. There are three groups of three sensors each. The three sensors on each group provide redundant information. The processing of each group combines the redundant information to obtain a solution of a sub-problem - what object is the one the group is observing?

In this way, the integrator gets three sets of data, each coming from a group of sensors. With these data, the observer determines that there are three objects in the space of observation. The distance from the integrator to the sensor is not, in general, negligible, so the results of the local processing must be transmitted in some way.

In our example, the result obtained by the integrator is a map of the objects present in the whole surveyed space.

The DAQ system is assumed to have a knowledge base that can analyze and interpret the data and take the appropriate action depending on the result obtained. In our case, the system interprets that there are three objects that occupy the space of observation; the reaction of the system will depend on the knowledge base.

2.3. Distributed sensor networks

The use of different, intelligent and distributed sensors space and geographically has grown constantly in applications such as robotics, particle physics experiments, medical images, tracking radar, air navigation and control systems of activities on production lines, to name a few. These systems, and other similar, are called *distributed sensors networks* or *DSN* [1]. Otherwise, we could define a network of distributed sensors as a set of intelligent sensors distributed spatially and designed to obtain data of the environment that surrounds them, abstracting the relevant information and infer from it the observed object, deriving from all this, an action appropriate according to the scenario.

2.4. Data acquisition systems in particle physics experiments

The distributed sensor network (DSN) paradigm fits what we generally implement as DAQ systems in particle physics experiments. Because of the need of a spatial coverage or an identification scheme based on the detection of different types of particles, the DAQ system will include several sensors of the same type or different types of multiple replicated sensors. Hardware architectures to read out all them are implemented in a distributed and possibly hierarchical way due to high data volume, high data rate or geographical sensor distribution. Comparison of hierarchical DSN versus other type of solution may be found in [3, 4].

3. Radiation detection. Transducers

Radiation detection involves the conversion of the impinging energy in form of radiation into an electrical parameter which can be processed. In order to achieve this, transducers are the responsible for transforming the radiation energy into an electrical signal. The type of detector has to be specific for each radiation and its energy interval. In general, several factors must be taken into consideration as the sensitivity, the response of the detector in energy resolution, response time and efficiency of the detector.

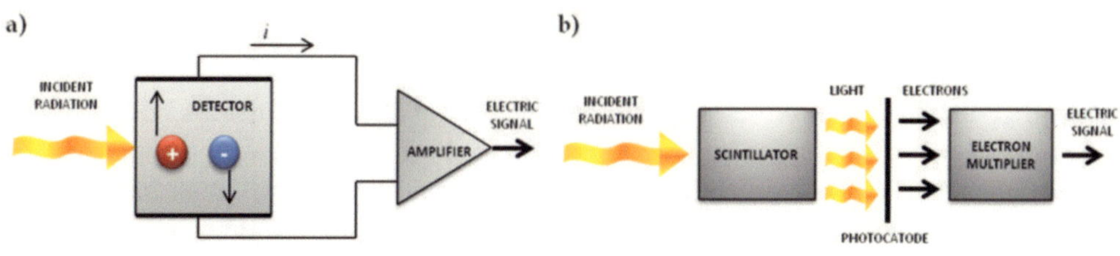

Figure 2. Radiation detection. (a) direct mode, (b) indirect mode

Energy conversion can be carried out whether in a *direct* mode, if the signal is directly detected through the ionization of a material (figure 2a), or in an *indirect* mode, when it performs different energy conversions before obtaining the electrical signal (light production plus electrical conversion, figure 2b). The following sub-sections describe the most commonly used devices for both medical as nuclear physics applications.

3.1. Direct detection

Direct detection with ionization chambers is a common practice. They are built with two electrodes to which a certain electrical potential is applied. The space between electrodes is occupied by a gas and it responds to the ionization produced by radiation as it passes through the gas. Ionizing radiation dissipates part or all of its energy by generating electron-ion pairs which are put in motion by the influence of an electrical field and consequently, by producing an electrical current.

Other possibility that provides good results in radiation detection is a semiconductor detector. They are solid-state devices which operate essentially like ionization chambers but in this case, the charge carriers are electron-hole pairs. Nowadays, most efficient detectors are made of Silicon (Si) or Germanium (Ge). The main advantage is their high energy resolution; besides, they provide linear responses in a wide energy range, fast pulse rise time, several geometric shapes (although the size is limited) and insensitivity to magnetic fields [5].

3.2. Indirect detection

3.2.1. Scintillators

Scintillators are materials which exhibit luminescence when ionizing radiation passes through them. Material absorbs part of the incident energy and reemits it as light, typically in the visible spectrum. Sir William Crooks discovered this property presented by some materials in 1903 when bombarding ZnS with alpha particles.

Organic scintillators belong to the class of the aromatic compounds like benzene or anthracene. They are made by combining a substance in higher concentration, solvent, and one or more compounds at lower concentrations, solutes, which are generally responsible for the scintillation. They are mainly used for the detection of beta particles (fast electrons with linear response from ~125 keV), alpha particles and protons (not linear response and lower efficiency for the same energies) and also for the detection of fast neutrons. They can be found in different states such crystals, liquid solutions, scintillating plastics with almost every shape and size and in gaseous state.

On the other hand, inorganic scintillators are crystals of the alkali metals such as NaI(Tl), Cs(Tl), LiI(Eu) and CaF_2(Eu). The element in brackets is the activator responsible of the scintillation with a small concentration in the crystal. Inorganic scintillators have in general high Z and for this reason they are mainly used for gamma particle detection, presenting a linear response up to 400 keV. Regarding to its behavior towards charged particle detection, they exhibit linear responses with the energy of the protons from 1 MeV and for alpha particles from 15 MeV. However, they are not commonly used to detect charged particles [5,6,7].

As it is shown in figure 2b, the scintillator produces a light signal when it is crossed by the radiation to be detected. It is coupled to a photodetector that will be responsible of transforming the light signal into an electrical signal.

3.2.2. *Optoelectronic technology for radiation detection*

Light detection is achieved with the generation of electron-hole pairs in the photosensor in response to an incident light. When the incident photons have energy enough to produce photoelectric effect, the electrons of the valence band jump to the conduction band where the free charges can move along the material under the influence of an external electric field. Thus, the holes left in the valence band due to prior removal and displacement of electrons, contribute to the electrical conduction and in this way, photocurrent is generated from the light signal.

3.2.2.1. *Photodetectors. Features*

One of the main characteristics of a photodetector is its spectral response. The level of electric current produced by the incidence of light varies according to the wavelength. The relationship between them is given by the spectral response, expressed in form of photosensitivity S (A/W) or quantum efficiency QE (%). Another important feature is the Signal to Noise (SNR) Ratio. It is a measure that compares the level of a desired signal to the level of the background noise.

The sensibility of the photodetector depends on certain factors such as the active area of the detector and its noise. The active area usually depends on the construction material of the detector; about the noise level, it is expected that the level of the signal exceeds the noise associated to the detector and its electronics, taking into account the desired SNR. One important component of the noise in the photodetector is the dark current [8, 9]; this current is due to the current flow existing in the photodetector even when they are in a dark environment, both in the photoconductive mode as in the photovoltaic mode. This current is known as dark current with intensities from nA to pA depending on the quality of the sensor.

The light coming from the scintillator is generally of low intensity and because of that, some photodetectors make avalanche processes to multiply the electrons for obtaining a detectable electric signal. Other parameters that determine the quality of the photodetector are the reverse voltage, the time response and its response against temperature fluctuations.

3.2.2.2. *Commercial photodetectors*

Photomultiplier Tubes (PMT) have been the photodetectors longer employed for a wide number of applications, mainly due to their good features and benefit results. They are used in applications that require measuring low-level light signals, for example the light from a scintillator, converting few hundred photons into an electrical signal without adding a large quantity of noise. A photomultiplier is a vacuum tube that converts photons in electrons by photoelectric effect. It consists of a cathode made of photosensitive material, an electron collecting system, some dynodes for multiplying the electrons and finally an anode which outputs the electrical signal, all encapsulated in a crystal tube. The research carried out in this type of detectors and the evolutionary trend is mainly focused on the improvement of the QE, achieved with the development of the photomultipliers with bialkali photocathode or GaAsP, but it has also been focused on obtaining better time response. In relation to the building material, four of them are commonly used depending on the detection requirements and the wavelength of the light, (Si, Ge, InGaAs and PbS, figure 3).

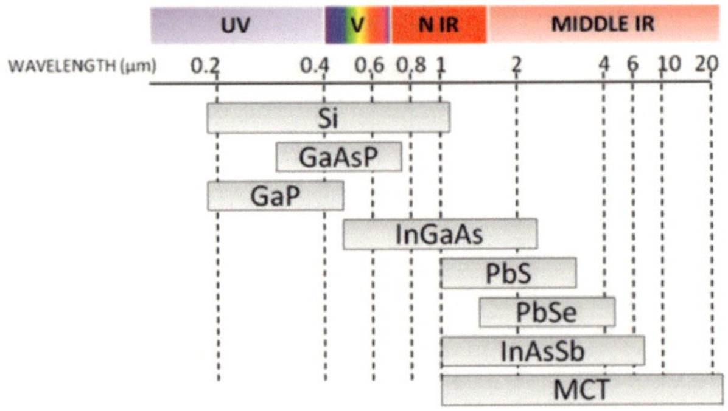

Figure 3. Sensitive material according to wavelength

In such applications where the level of light is high enough, photodiodes use to be the detectors employed due to their lower price but also to their remarkable properties and response. It is a semiconductor with a PN junction sensitive to the infrared and visible light. If the light energy is greater than the band gap energy, the electrons are pulled up into the conduction band, leaving holes in their place in the valence band. If a reverse bias is applied, then there is an electrical current. Thus, P layer in the surface with the N layer both act as a photoelectric converter.

Other important photodetectors such as Avalanche Photodiodes (APDs) have been developed in the last few years [10]. Compared to photodiodes, APDs can detect lower levels of light and they are employed in applications where high sensitivity is required. Although the principle of operation, materials and construction are similar to the photodiodes, there are considerable differences. It has an absorption area *A* and a multiplication area *M* which implies an internal gain mechanism that works by applying a reverse voltage. When a photon strikes the APD, electron-hole pairs are created and in the gain area, the acceleration of the electrons is produced; thus, the avalanche process starts with a chain reaction due to successive ionizations. Finally, the reaction is controlled in a depletion area. The output result is, after the incidence of a photon, not only the generation of one or few electrons but a large number of them. In this way, a high level of electric current is obtained from a low level of incident light with gain values around 10^8.

Silicon Photomultipliers (Si PMT) are promising detectors due to their characteristic features and probably its utilization in many applications will increase during the following years. It is a photon counting device consisting on multiple APD pixels forming an array and that operates in Geiger mode. The addition of the output of each APD results on the output signal of the device, allowing the counting of individual events (photons). One advantage is the low reverse voltage needed for its operation, lower than the one used with PMTs and APDs. When the reverse voltage applied exceeds the breaking reverse voltage, the internal electric field is high enough to produce high gains of the order of 10^6 [11, 12].

Finally, a CCD camera (charged-coupled device) is an integrated circuit for digital imaging where the pixels are formed with p-doped MOS capacitors. Its principle of operation is based on the photoelectric effect and its sensitivity depends on the QE of the detector. At the end of the exposition, the capacitors transmit their charge which is proportional to the amount of light and the detector is read line by line (although there are different configurations). They offer higher performances regarding QE and noise levels; however their disadvantages are the big size and high price. Figure 4 shows the general features of the different photodetectors.

Photo detector	λ (nm)	Gain	Rise Time (ns)	Active Area (mm^2)	V (V)	QE (%)
PD	200-2000	-	2-20	0.5-2 ·10^3	5-15	70-95
PMT	115-1100	10^3-10^7	0.7-15		300-3000	1-80
APD	300-1700	10-10^8	1-4	0.2-5	150-1500	50-85
Si PMT	400-550	10^5-10^6	~1	0.5-3	50-100	25-65
MCP	100-650	10^3-10^7	0.15-0.8	5-15 ·10^{-3} /channel	500-3500	~1
HPD	115-850	10^3-10^5	0.4-10	2-10	~10^4	25-45
CCD	200-1200	-	-	5-15 ·10^{-3} /pixel	5-15	70

Figure 4. General features of different photodetectors

4. Front-end electronics

When talking about front-end electronics in nuclear or particle physics applications, we usually refer to the closest electronics to the detector, involving processes from amplification, pulse-shape conformation to the analog-to-digital conversion. The back-end electronics are left apart further away from the detector for processing tasks.

In this section, we will introduce the common circuits used in the front-end electronics, such as preamplifiers, shapers, discriminators, ADCs, coincidence units and TDCs.

4.1. Unipolar and bipolar signals

In nuclear and particle physics, usually the signals obtained are pulse signals. Depending on the detector used, different parameters such as the rise or fall time, as well as the amplitude are different. Figure 5 (left) shows a typical pulse signal with all its important parameters. Mostly related to the rise time, it is important to remark the bandwidth of pulse signals, related to the fastest component of the pulse, usually the rise time. A typical criteria to choose the signal bandwidth based on the temporal parameters is to choose a bandwidth such that $BW=0.35/t_r$, where t_r is the signal rise time [13].

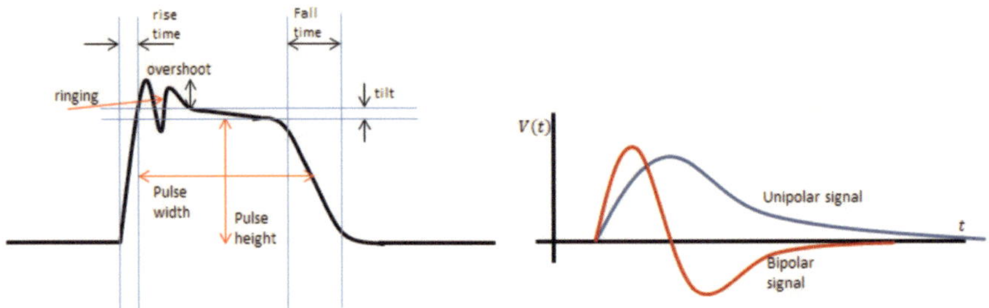

Figure 5. Left. Example of a typical pulse signal. Right. Example of a bipolar and unipolar signal

Unipolar or bipolar signals show better or worse performance depending on our needs, each of them with different advantages and drawbacks. By definition, a unipolar signal is an only positive or only negative signal while a bipolar signal involves both signs, more interesting for high-counting rate systems, while the unipolar is left for systems with lower counting rates, with a better SNR. On figure 5 (right), an example of a unipolar and bipolar signal can be seen. For more information about this, consult the references [6, 7].

4.2. Circuits

4.2.1. Preamplifiers

Often in particle physics nuclear and particle physics experiments, the signal obtained at the output of the amplifier is an electrical pulse whose amplitude is proportional to the charge produced by the incident radiation energy. It is quite impractical to provide directly the signal without a proper amplification, and for this reason, preamplifiers are the first stage seen by the pulse signal, usually placed the closest to the detector for noise minimization since noise at this stage is very critical. Two different types of preamplifiers are commonly used depending on the sensing magnitude: Voltage-sensitive amplifiers and charge-sensitive amplifiers.

4.2.1.1. Voltage-sensitive amplifiers

They are the most conventional type of amplifiers, and they provide an output pulse proportional to the input pulse, which is proportional to the collected charge as well. If the equivalent capacitance of the detector and electronics is constant, this configuration can be used. On the other hand, in some applications, as for example semiconductor detectors, the detector capacitance changes with temperature, so this configuration is not anymore useful. Hence, it is preferred to use the configuration called charge-sensitive preamplifiers. The basic schematic of the voltage-sensitive amplifier is shown on the figure 6 (left).

4.2.1.2. Charge-sensitive amplifiers

Semiconductors, such as germanium or silicon detectors are capacitive detectors itself with very high impedance. The capacitance, C_i, for these detectors fluctuates making the voltage-sensitive amplifier inoperable. The idea of this circuit is to integrate the charge using the feedback capacitor C_f. The advantage of this configuration is the independence of the amplitude with the input capacitance if the condition $A \gg (C_i + C_f)/C_f$ is satisfied. A picture of the charge-sensitive amplifier is shown on the figure 6 (right) [14].

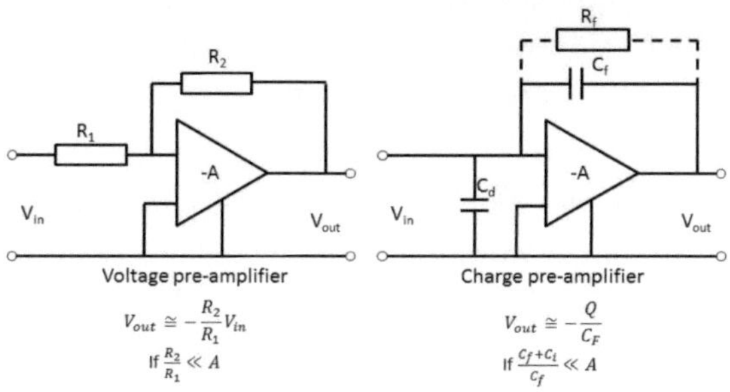

Figure 6. Voltage and charge preamplifiers schematic

The feedback resistor R_f is used to discharge the capacitor leading the signal to the baseline level with an exponential tail around 40-50 μs. This discharge is usually done with a high R in order to provide a slow pulse tail, minimizing the noise introduced, but a tail too slow can lead to pile-up effects. Another approach to get rid of the pile-up effect is the optical feedback charge amplifier [6, 7].

4.2.2. *Amplifiers and shapers*

After the pre-amplification process is carried out, it might be useful to provide a certain shape in order to simplify the measurements of certain magnitudes, preserving the interest magnitude intact. Pulse stretching and spreading techniques can be used for pile-up cancellation, timing measurements, pulse-height measurements and preparation for sampling. Other reasons to use pulse shaper is its SNR optimization, where a certain shape provides the optimal SNR ratio. Most of the shaper circuits are based on differentiator (CR) and integrator (RC) circuits. The circuit schematic and time response are shown in the figure 7 (left). For further information about these circuits, consult the references [7, 15].

4.2.2.1. *Shaper networks*

Three different pulse shapers will be introduced into this sub-section, although there exist many more. CR-RC network, CR-RC network with pole-zero cancellation and the double differentiating CR-RC-CR circuit are introduced here. CR-RC circuits are implemented as a differentiator followed by an integrator (figure 7a). The differentiated pulse allows the signal to return to the baseline level but it does show neither an attractive pulse nor allows easy sampling of the maximum point when extracting the energy with pulse height analysis (PSA). The integrator stage improves the SNR ratio and smoothens the waveform.

The choice of the time constant τ often is a compromise between pile-up reduction and the ballistic deficit, which occurs when the shaper produces an amplitude drop. This can be solved by choosing a high value of τ compared to the rise time, or the charge collecting time from the detector.

When considering a real pulse instead of a step ideal response, CR-RC circuits produce undershoot (figure 7b), which leads to a wrong amplitude level. This can be solved by adding a resistor to cancel the pole of the exponential tail, cancelling the undershoot. If the system counting rate is low, this strategy is useful, but when this counting rate increases, the pulses start to pile-up onto each other creating baseline fluctuations and amplitude distortion.

A solution for this problem is the double differentiating network CR-RC-CR (figure 7c), in which a bipolar pulse is obtained from the input pulse. The main difference resides on the fact that the bipolar pulse does not leave any residual charge, making it very suitable for systems with high-counting rates, but still for systems with low-counting rates, it is preferred to use the unipolar pulses, since its SNR ratio is fairly better.

Further shaping methods such as semi-gaussian shapers, active pulse shapers, triangular and trapezoidal shaping, as well as shapers using delay lines can be consulted on the references [6, 7, 15].

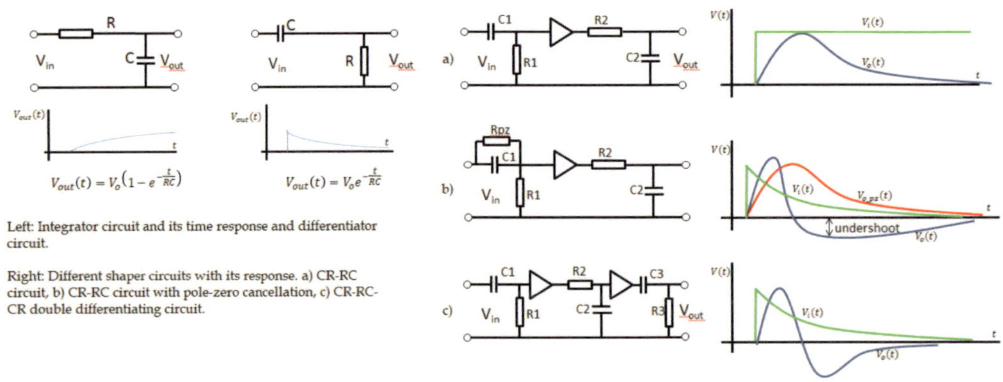

Figure 7. Left. Integrator and differentiator circuits. Right. a) CR-RC circuit, b) CR-RC circuit with pole compensation, c) CR-RC-CR double differentiating circuit.

4.2.3. Discrimination techniques

Discriminator circuits are systems that are activated only if the amplitude of the input signal crosses a certain threshold. Discriminators are used to find the events and to use them as trigger signals, commonly for time measurement. Besides, it blocks the noise coming from previous devices, such as the detector and other electronics stages.

The simplest method for pulse discrimination is the leading edge triggering. It provides a logic signal if the pulse amplitude is higher than a threshold. The logic signal is originated at the moment when the signal crosses the threshold but with the problem called the time-walk effect, which describes the dependence of the pulse discrimination with the signal rise time. This effect can be seen, on the figure 8 left.

Another undesirable effect for pulse discrimination is the time jitter effect (figure 8 right). This effect is caused by statistical fluctuations at the detector and electronics level, and as a difference from the time walks effect. The time jitter is shown as a timing uncertainty when the signal amplitude is constant. This effect comes from the noise introduced in the components, and also the detector sources, as for example the transit time from the electrons in a photomultiplier or the fluctuation of photons produced in a scintillator.

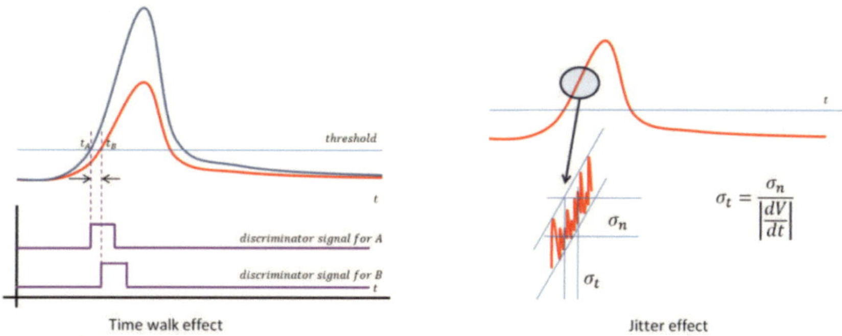

Figure 8. Time walk and jitter effects

Other methods to avoid or reduce these effects in discrimination systems are zero-crossover timing or constant fraction discrimination methods. Zero-crossover timing method is based on the double-differentiation of the pulse shape. This method, although improves the time resolution and makes independent the crossing point from the amplitude, the shape and rise time still influence the time resolution, making it unsuitable for applications where these fluctuations are very large. The constant fraction discriminators establish the threshold as a fraction of its maximum level. The most common way to implement it is based on the comparison between a fraction of the signal with a slightly delayed version, where the zero-crossing point of its difference makes the pulse independent of the amplitude with lower jitter [7].

4.2.4. A/D conversion (analog to digital conversion)

More sophisticated algorithms may be implemented digitally inside the logic devices (FPGA or GPUs). Nevertheless, before performing those algorithms, an analog to digital conversion is required, introducing inevitably a source of error due to the sampling and quantization processes. Two of the most common techniques used in nuclear or particle physics research proposals are the Wilkinson method and the FADC (Flash ADC) if a very high sampling rate is required, although other conversion methods such as successive approximation and sub-ranging ADC are used as well.

The main difference between the Wilkinson method and FADC sampling is that Wilkinson method takes one sample per event based on the time measured when a capacitor is discharged, where the time counted is proportional to the pulse charge. On the other hand, FADC takes several samples per event, where the digitized value is taken when comparing the input voltage with a set of resistors forming a voltage divider across all the possible digitized values. Although FADC technique leads to the fastest architecture, as far as the number of bits required is higher, the amount of comparators increases exponentially [6, 16, 17].

The analog-to-digital conversion performance can be tested by measuring certain parameters, such as the differential and integral nonlinearities (DNL and INL), which cause missing codes, noise and distortion, as well as the effective number of bits (ENOB), which quantifies the resolution loss when the distortion and nonlinearities come in. Further information about ADC parameters con be found in [17] and its measuring method in [17, 18].

4.2.5. Coincidence and anti-coincidence units

These circuits are used to know whether an event has been detected in several detectors at the same time or to detect events only occurring at only one detector. This is especially useful in detector arrays in order to discard fake events. The way to implement it, is based on simple logical operations between the signals from the discriminators [6, 7].

4.2.6. TDC (Time-to-digital converter)

In most of the applications in nuclear and particle physics, the measurement of time intervals will be a primary task. Basically the way to measure time intervals, is based on a start and stop signals, usually given by discriminator circuits. Then, a value proportional to the time interval between the start and stop signals is digitized. Different architectures lead to different performance, but the most notorious for TDC is the time resolution, defined as the minimum time τ the TDC is capable to measure. Among different architectures, we can mention the TAC (Time-to-amplitude converter), the direct time-to-digital converter, and for higher resolutions, the differential TDC and the Vernier counter [15].

5. Data Bus systems for back-end electronics

In this section we present the most popular standards used today to build DAQ systems in particle physics experiments. All the systems presented are modular systems with each module carrying out a specific function. This technique allows the reuse of the modules in other systems and makes the DAQ system scalable.

Most of the features of these modular systems as mechanics, data buses characteristics or data protocols are defined in standards. Many DAQ system manufacturers develop their own products according to these standards. The use of standards implies many benefits as the use of third party products and support [19].

5.1. NIM Standard

NIM stands for Nuclear Instrumentation Module and was established in 1964. NIM standard does not include any kind of bus for data transfer communications since NIM crates only provide power to the NIM modules.

The advantage of the NIM standard is that modules are interchangeable and work as a standalone system allowing the set up of DAQ systems in a simple way, where a module can be replaced without affecting the integrity of the rest of the system [20]. These advantages make the NIM standard very popular in nuclear and particle experiments, and it is still used for small experiments. However, NIM has disadvantages since lacks of a digital bus, not allowing a computer based control or data communication between modules.

5.1.1. Crate and modules

Standard NIM crates have 12 slots for modules and include a power supply that provides AC and DC power to the modules. The power supply is distributed via the backplane to the NIM modules that comprise many different functions like discriminators, counters, coincidences, amplifiers or level converters, for example.

Figures 9a and 9b show a standard NIM crate where we can see the NIM connector in the bottom, and a standard NIM module.

a

b

Figure 9. a) Standard NIM crate, b) Standard NIM module

5.2. VME standard

The Versa Module Europa (VME) is a standard introduced by Mostek, Motorola, Philips and Thompson in 1981. It offers a backplane that provides fast data transfer allowing an increase of the amount of transferred data and, therefore, an increase of the channel count coming from the front-end electronics. This fact makes VME standard the widest standard used in physics experiments.

5.2.1. Crate and modules

VME crates contain a maximum of 21 slots where the first position is reserved for a controller module; the other 20 slots are available for modules that can perform other functions.

There are different types of VME modules, each having a different size and a different number of 96-pin connectors that define the number of bits designed for address and data buses.

5.2.2. VMEBus

VME systems use a parallel and asynchronous bus (VMEBus) with a unique arbiter and multiple masters. VMEBus also implements a handshaking protocol with multiprocessing and interrupt capabilities. VMEbus is composed by four different sub-buses: Data Transfer Bus, Arbitration Bus, Priority Interrupt Bus and Utility Bus [20].

While VMEBus achieves a maximum data transfer of 40 MBps, some extensions of the VME standard as VME64, VME64x and VME320 standards have enhanced its capabilities increasing the number of bits for address and data and implementing specific protocols for data communication [21]. In this way, VME64 systems achieve data transfers up to 80 MBps, while VME64x support data transfers up to 160 MBps and VME320 between 320 MBps and 500 MBps.

Also, VXS standard is an ANSI/VITA standard approved in 2006. VXS standard maintains backward compatibility with VME systems combining the parallel VMEbus with switched serial fabrics. VXS systems achieve a maximum data transfer between modules of 3050 MBps [22].

5.3. PCI standard

PCI stands for Peripheral Component Interface and was introduced by Intel Corporation in 1991. The PCI bus is the most popular method used today for connecting peripheral boards to a PC providing a high performance bus using 32 bit or 64 bit bus with multiplexed address and data lines. PC-based DAQ systems can be easily built using PCI systems as PCI cards are directly connected to a PC.

5.3.1. PCI cards

The last PCI standard specifies three basic form factors for PCI cards: long, short and low profile [23]. PCI cards are keyed to distinguish between 5V or 3.3V signaling cards and they use different pin count connectors according to the data and address bus widths.

5.3.2. PCI Local Bus

PCI devices are connected to the PC via a parallel bus called PCI Local Bus. Typical PCI Local Bus implementations support up to four PCI boards that share the address bus, data bus and most of the protocol lines, but also having dedicated lines for arbitration. PCI local bus width and clock speed determines the maximum data transfer speed. Table 1 shows a summary of the achievable data transfer speeds in PCI and the extension version of the PCI, called PCI-X [24].

A disadvantage of the PCI standard is the use of a parallel bus for data and address lines. The skew between lines and the fact that only one master/slave pair can communicate at any time and the handshaking protocol limits the maximum achievable data transfer in PCI [19].

Further, in 1995, PICMG introduced the compact PCI (cPCI) standard as a very high performance bus based on the PCI bus using Eurocard format boards. But cPCI is not widely used in particle physics experiments due to some additional disadvantages, such as, small size cards, limited power consumption and limited number of slots [25].

Standard version	Bus width	Clock speed (MHz)	Data rate (Mbps)
PCI 1.0	32	33	133
PCI 2.1	32	66	266
	64	66	532
PCI-X 1.0	64	133	1064
PCI-X 2.0	64	266	2128
	64	533	4256

Table 1. Data transfer speeds for PCI and PCI-X standards

5.4. PCI Express

PCIe stands for Peripherial Compatible Interface Express. PCIe standard was introduced in 2002 to overcome the space and speed limitations of the conventional PCI bus by increasing the bandwidth while decreasing the pin count. This standard not only defines the electrical characteristics of a point to point serial link communication, but also a protocol for the physical layer, data link layer and transaction layer. Moreover PCIe standard includes advanced features such as active power management, quality of service, hot plug and hot swap support, data integrity, error handling and true isochronous capabilities [26, 27]. As PCI systems, PCIe systems allow the implementation of DAQ systems based on PC.

5.4.1. PCIe cards

PCIe uses four different connector versions: x1, x4, x8 and x16, where the number refers to the number of available bi-directional data path and correspond to 32, 64, 98 and 164 pin connectors respectively. There are two possible form factors for PCIe cards: Long and Short.

5.4.2. PCIe Bus

The PCIe serial bus transmits with a data rate of 2.5 Gbps using LVDS logic standard. But really, the effective data rate is reduced to 80% of the original data rate due to the use of the 8b10b codification [27]. A summary of the achieved data rates per direction using PCIe is shown in table 2:

Bus	Data rate (MBps)
PCI-Express x1	250
PCI-Express x4	1000
PCI-Express x8	2000
PCI-Express x16	4000

Table 2. Data transfer speeds for the PCIe standard

5.5. ATCA standard

ATCA stands for Advanced Telecommunications Computing Architecture and was introduced by PICMG in 2002 in the PICMG 3.0 specification. PICMG 3.0 and 3.x specifications define a modular open architecture including mechanical features, components, power distribution, backplane and communications protocols. This specification was created for telecommunication purposes where high speed, high availability and reliability are extremely needed. ATCA systems can deploy a service availability of 99.999% in time [28].

5.5.1. ATCA shelf

The shelf can allocate a different number of ATCA boards (blades) and it also allocates the shelf manager that is responsible for the power and thermal control issues. Figure 10a shows a 14 slots ATCA shelf with a height of 13U, and figure 10b shows a processor ATCA module.

a b

Figure 10. a) ATCA shelf of 14 slot 13U, b) Processor ATCA module

5.5.2. ATCA modules

Regarding the ATCA modules we can highlight three main types of ATCA blades for the data transport purposes: Front boards, Rear Transition Modules (RTM) and Advance Mezzanine Cards (AMC). All of these modules are hot swappable and have different form factors.

- Front boards are connected to the shelf backplane through the Zone 1 and Zone 2 connectors. Zone 1 connector is use to feed the module and Zone 2 connector is use for data transport signals. Moreover Front boards have a third connector, Zone 3, which provides a direct connection with the RTM.
- Rear Transition Modules are placed in the rear side of the shelf and it is used to expand the ATCA system functionalities.

- AMCs are mezzanine modules pluggable onto ATCA carriers enlarging system functionalities. Examples of AMCs include CPUs, DSP systems or storage.

Moreover, ATCA Fabric interface reaches data rates between modules of 40 Gbps using protocols such as Gigabit Ethernet, Infiniband, Serial Rapid IO or PCIe and network topologies such as dual star, dual-dual star or full mesh. These features provide a clear advantage of ATCA systems over other platforms.

5.6. MicroTCA

MicroTCA is a complementary specification to the PICMG 3.0 introduced by PICMG in 2006. It was defined to develop systems that require lower performance, availability and reliability than ATCA systems, and also lower space and cost, but maintaining many features from PICMG 3.0 such as shelf management or fabric interconnects [29].

5.6.1. MicroTCA shelf and modules

The shelf can allocate and manage up to 12 single or double size AMCs. AMCs are directly plugged into the backplane in a similar way than ATCA carriers. The function of the backplane is to provide power to the AMC boards and also connection with the data, control, system management, synchronization clock and JTAG test lines. The MicroTCA backplane can implement network topologies like star, dual star, mesh or point-to-point between AMCs. The protocols used for data communications in the MicroTCA backplane are: Ethernet 1000BASE-BX, SATA/SAS, PCIe, Serial Rapid IO or 10GBase-BX4. Data transfers between AMCs within the MicroTCA backplane can achieve speeds of 40 Gbps.

5.7. Transmission media

In the past, copper wires, as coaxial or twisted cables, were widely used to communicate front-end electronics and back-end electronics, or even modules in back-end systems. For example, many NIM and VME modules use coaxial cables with BNC, LEMO or SMA connectors for control or data communications.

But, nowadays, data transmission media for DAQ has moved to fiber optics due to the advantages of fiber optics over copper cables that make them the best option to transmit data in present particle physics experiments. Some of these features are: EMI immunity, lower attenuation, no electrical discharges, short circuits, ground loops or crosstalk, resistance to nuclear radiation and high temperatures, lower weight and higher bandwidth [30].

Due to the widespread use of fiber optics, optic modules play an essential role in present particle physics experiments. Optic modules are needed to convert electrical signals into optical ones for transmission via optic fibers. Some examples of optic modules that are used for data transmission in particle physics experiments and their data bandwidths are shown in the table 3 [31].

Type	Channels count/fiber ribbon	Bandwidth (max)
X2	1	10Gbps
XENPAK	1	10Gbps
SFP+	1	10Gbps
XFP	1	10Gbps
QSFP+	4	40Gbps
CFP	10	100Gbps
CXP	12	120Gbps
SNAP12	12	120Gbps
POD	12	120Gbps
MiniPOD	12	120Gbps

Table 3. Examples of parallel optic modules used in particle physics experiments

6. Back-end data processing

In the last decades, the improvements in the analog-to-digital converters, in terms of sampling rate and resolution, opened a wide range of possibilities for the digital data processing. The migration from the analog to the digital processing has proven a number of scenarios where the digital approach has potential advantages, such as system complexity, parameter setup changes or scalability. On the other hand, system designers have to deal with bigger amounts of data processed at higher sampling rates, which affects the complexity of the processing algorithms working in real time and the transport of those data at high rates.

For instance, digital processing has demonstrated significant advantages processing pulses from large-volume germanium detectors, where a good choice in the pulse shaping parameters is crucial for achieving good energy resolution and minimum pulse pile-up for high counting rates.

6.1. Common used algorithms

Following the inheritance of the analog data processing, some of the digital data processing algorithms perform similar tasks to the analog blocks; taking advantage of the digital information compiled in the ADCs. These algorithms can be divided in five groups:

- Shaping or filtering: When only part of the information from the detector pulses is relevant, such as, for instance, the height of the pulse, shaping techniques can be applied. They filter the digital data according to certain shaping parameters, which could be changed easier in the digital setup. Thus, the only difference in order to apply the same filters in the analog and digital approaches would remain in the continuous or discrete characteristics that differentiate them. In addition, apart from the time-invariant filters similar to the analog ones, in the digital world also adaptive filtering could be applied, changing the filter characteristics for a certain period of time.
- Pulse shape analysis: Exploiting the amount of digital information available in the fast digitalization process, different techniques for the analysis of the shape of the pulses

can be applied. According to the detector response, these algorithms could be used for obtaining better detector performance or distinguishing between different input particles, as show in Figure 11.

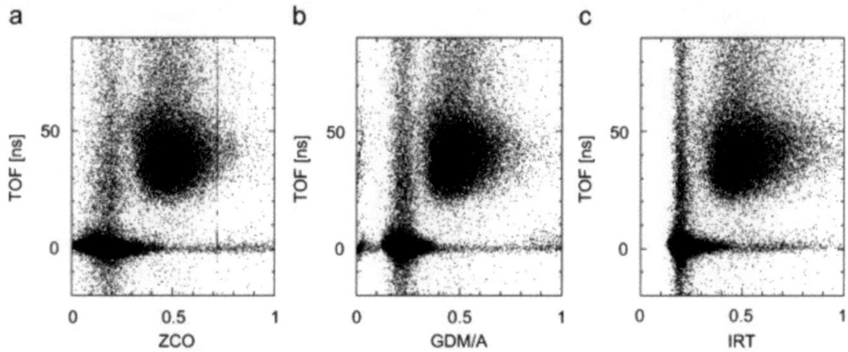

Figure 11. Comparison between an analog (left) and two digital algorithms in a neutron-gamma separation using Pulse shape analysis algorithms [32].

- Baseline restoration: During the time gap between two consecutive pulses, the baseline value can also be digitized and easily subtracted from the digital values of the waveform. Also sometimes more elaborated algorithms can be applied in order to calculate the baseline of the pulses. Thus, better system performance is achieved, avoiding changes due to temperature drifts or other external agents.
- Pile-up deconvolution: The pile-up effect consists on the accumulation of pulses from different events in a short time, which, in principle, avoids the study of those events. In the analog electronics, this effect usually causes an increment in the dead time of the system, as those events should be rejected. However, taking advantage of the digital characteristics, a further analysis of these pulses can be performed and, consequently, in some cases the information of the compound pulses can be disentangled.
- Timing measurements: Timing information is mainly managed in two ways:
    - Trigger generation: In a fully digital system, pulse information can be used for generating logical signals for validating certain events of interest. Furthermore, in complex systems with different trigger levels the generation of logic signals for the validation or rejection of events becomes very important. For this purpose, two methods are commonly used: leading edge triggering and constant fraction timing. The first is the simplest, and generates the logic pulse performing a comparison between the input pulse and a constant trigger level. In the second, a small algorithm generates the logic pulse from a constant percentage of the pulse height. There are other algorithms like the crossover timing, ARC timing, ELET, etc. but its usage is lower.
    - Measurement of timing properties: With the trigger information generated either analog or digitally, several logic setups can be performed. Thus, depending on the complexity of the experiment and its own characteristics, trigger pulses can be used for measuring absolute timing between detectors, perform new trigger levels

according to certain conditions or filter events according to a specific coincidence trigger.

Although the needs of the experiments and the complexity of the setups changes enormously, the processing algorithms usually can fit into one of the categories described previously. However, it is also common to combine several algorithms in the process, so the system architecture can be quite elaborated. The split of the system into several firmware and software blocks allows designers and programmers to manage the difficulty of the experiment.

6.2. Hardware choices

The complexity and performance of the algorithms previously presented varies depending on the input data, the sampling rate or the implementation architecture. For the last one, several options are presented according to the experiment needs:

- Digital Signal Processing (DSP): The DSPs are Integrated Circuits (ICs) that perform programmable filtering algorithms by applying the Multiply-Accumulate (MAC) operation. These devices have been used since more than 30 years, especially in other fields, such as audio, image or biomedical signal processing. The wide knowledge acquired with these devices has contributed to its use within the particle experiments network, taking advantage of its compactness or stability with temperature changes.
- Field-Programmable Gate Array (FPGA): These programmable ICs are composed by a large number of gates that can be individually programmed and linked, as it is depicted in figure 12. They are usually programmed using Hardware Description Languages (HDLs), like the Application-Specific Integrated Circuits (ASICs), so, in theory, they could implement any of the algorithms presented previously. Furthermore, these devices use to embed other DSPs or microprocessors, which allow performing different processing tasks, even concurrently.

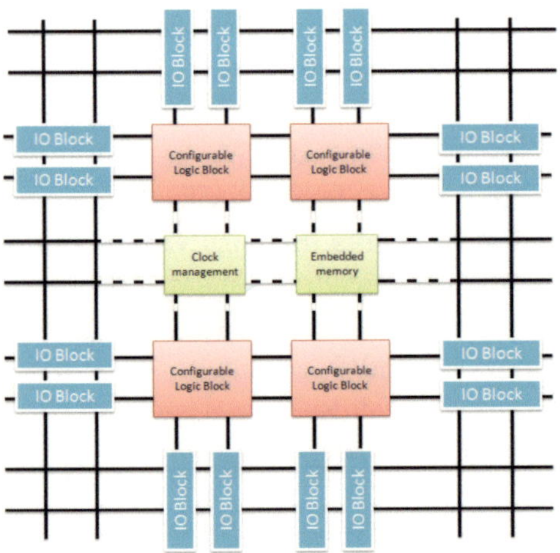

Figure 12. Block structure of a FPGA. It contains the main Input Output Blocks, the Configurable Logic Blocks and other embedded hardware blocks such as Clock management blocks or Embedded memory (SRAM or BRAM based) blocks

- Central Processing Unit (CPU): In some cases, a Personal Computer (PC) with specific memory or CPU characteristics is used. In this case, the data are treated with software programs together with the operating system. They are often included as an interface to long-term memories, i.e. to handle the storing process. However, sometimes additional data processing is required, and they are particularly efficient when there is a high amount of data, which are not needed to be processed at a high frequency. Moreover, data processing at this point sometimes requires a lot of computing resources, so these processes use to run in computer farms, which are handled by distributed applications or operating systems.
- Graphics Processing Unit (GPU): When parallel processing and the amount of data to manage increase, CPUs may not be the best hardware architecture to support it. Thus, the underlying idea of the GPUs is to use a Graphical card as a processing unit. They have been shown as very efficient hardware setups that can be more efficient than CPUs in some configurations.
- Grid computing: This technique, which is used in large experiments where the amount of data is not even manageable by computing processing farms, consists of taking advantage of the internet network to communicate computing farms or PCs in order to perform a large data processing with an enormous number of heterogeneous processing units. Obviously this technique is implemented with data without timing constraints, as the processing time for each unit may be different.

Among this short description of data processing hardware blocks, an overview of all possible units has been presented. However, it is important to remark that the final system requirements may advise to select a certain setup. For this purpose, the reader is encouraged to review the bibliography for further details.

7. Application examples

This section reviews at a glance some implementations of DAQ in particle physics experiments and medical applications in order to clarify the concepts on detectors, algorithms and hardware units previously described.

The first example regards to the data processing in the Advanced GAmma Tracking Array (AGATA) [33]. As it is a "triggerless" system, the detector signals (HPGe crystals) are continuously digitized and sent to the pre-processing electronics, which implement shaping, baseline restoration, pile-up deconvolution and trigger generation algorithms in FPGAs in a fully digital way. After that, crossing different bus domains, the data arrive to a PC that performs Pulse Shape Analysis algorithms to calculate the position of the interaction and add it to the energy information calculated in the preprocessing. Then, data coming from all detectors arrive to a PC (Event Builder), using a distributed Digital Acquisition program. When the event is generated, its information is added to the data from other detectors (ancillaries) in a PC called "Merger", that sends them to the tracking processor. This is another PC that performs tracking algorithms for reconstructing the path of the gamma-rays in the detectors. Finally, the data is stored in external servers.

In this example, most of the presented algorithms and hardware configurations are used. In addition, GPUs have been tested for the Pulse Shape Analysis and they have shown excellent performance characteristics. Also Grid computing techniques are used for data analysis and storage, so the hardware components previously presented are almost covered in this example.

The second example is the data processing in the ATLAS detector, at CERN [34]. In this case, the system is composed of several different types of sensors and the DAQ system is controlled by a three level trigger system. In the first level of trigger, the events of interest recorded in the detectors, mostly selected by comparators, are directly sent to the second level of trigger. In this level, the information from several sub-detectors is correlated and merged according to the experimental conditions. Finally, a third event filtering is carried out with the data from the whole system. Along these trigger levels, different processing algorithms are used, combined in different hardware setups. However, all of them can be included in one of the categories previously detailed. An example of the hardware systems developed for this particle physics experiment may be found in [35, 36].

The last example is from radiation therapy where ionizing radiation is used with medical purposes. Nowadays, radiologists make use of radioactive beams i.e. gamma particles, neutrons, carbon ions, electrons, etc. to treat cancer, but they also take advantage of the properties of the ionizing radiation and its application in the diagnosis of internal diseases through medical imaging. This field has involved the development of devices capable of, on one hand, producing the radioactive particle needed for a specific treatment and, on the other hand, to detect the radioactive beam (in some cases, the part of the radiation that has not been absorbed by the patient) to reconstruct the internal image. This is the case of the Computed Tomography (CT) scan, a medical imaging technique consistent on an X-Ray source (X-Ray tube) that rotates 360º around the patient providing at each rotation a 2D cross-sectional image or even a 3D image by putting all the scans together through computing techniques. The detection of the X-Rays is carried out whether in a direct or in an indirect way depending on the device; actually, the detection area consists from one up to 2600 detectors of two categories, scintillators (coupled to PMTs) or gas detectors. Another well-known imaging technique is the Positron Emission Tomography (PET). It provides a picture of the metabolic activity of the body thanks to the detection of the two gamma rays that are emitted after the positron annihilation produced by a radionuclide previously inserted into the patient. Gamma detection is achieved by placing scintillators generally coupled to PMTs but also to Si APDs.

8. Conclusion

In this chapter we have presented a review of the technologies currently used in particle physics experiments following the natural path of the signals from the detector to the data processing. Even these kinds of applications are well established there is not a comprehensive review, as this chapter tries in a very light version, of the overall technologies commonly in use. Being a wide field, we have tried to be concise and provide the interested reader with a list of references to consult.

Author details

V. González, D. Barrientos, J. M. Blasco, F. Carrió, X. Egea and E. Sanchis
University of Valencia, Dep. of Electronic Engineering, Spain

D. Barrientos and F. Carrió
Instituto de Física Corpuscular (IFIC), Valencia, Spain

Acknowledgement

This work is funded by Spanish Commission of Science and Technology under project reference FPA2009-13234-C04-02.

9. References

[1] Iyengar, S. S. et al. (1995) Advances in distributed sensor integration. Application and theory. Prentice Hall, 1995.
[2] Wesson, R. et al. (1981) Network structures for distributed situation assessment. IEEE Trans. on System, Man, Cybernetics. 11: 5 - 23
[3] González, V., Sanchis E., Torralba G. & Martos, J. (2002) Comparison of parallel versus hierarchical systems for data processing in distributed sensor networks. IEEE Transactions on Nuclear Science, 49: 394 – 400.
[4] González, V., Sanchis E. (2004) Comparison of data processing techniques in sensor networks, In: Ilyas Mahgoub , editor. Handbook of Sensor Networks: compact wireless and wired sensing systems. CRC Press. pp. 21.1 - 21.19.
[5] Tsoulfanidis, N. (1995) Measurement and detection of radiation (2nd Edition). Taylor & Francis.
[6] Leo, W.R. (1994) Techniques for Nuclear and particle Physics Experiments (2nd Edition). Springer-Verlag.
[7] Knoll, G.F. (2000) Radiation Detection and Measurement (4th Edition). John Wiley & Sons.
[8] Kaufmann K.J. (2000) Light levels and noise. Guide detectors choice. Photonics Spectra, 7.
[9] Kaufmann K.J. (2005) Choosing your detector. OE Magazine.
[10] Renker, D. (2006) Geiger Mode avalanche photodiodes, history, properties and problems. Nuclear Instruments and Methods in Physics Research A, 567: 48-56.
[11] Hamamatsu P. (2008) Characteristics and use of Si APD (Avalanche Photodiode) Technical information, SD-28.
[12] Hamamatsu P. (2009) Photodiode Technical Information. Application note, SD-03.
[13] Sobering, T.J. (1999) Bandwidth and rise time. Technote 2, SDE Consulting. May 1999.
[14] Hamamatsu P. (2001) Characteristics and use of the Charge Preamplifier, Application note SD-37, 2001.
[15] Rivetti, A. et al. (2011) Integrated circuits for time and amplitude measurement of nuclear radiation pulses. Short course on IEEE 2011 Nuclear Science Symposium and Medical Imaging Conference, Valencia, October 2011.
[16] Analog Devices. (2006) High Speed System Applications.

[17] Kester, W. (2004) The data conversion handbook, Analog Devices.
[18] Hofner T.C. (2002) Measuring and evaluating dynamic ADC Parameters. Microwaves & RF, pp. 78-94.
[19] Joos, M. (2012) Standards for Modular Electronics – the past, the present and the future. International School of Trigger and Data Acquisition 2012, Cracow, Poland.
[20] Ahmed, S. N. (2007) Physics and Engineering of Radiation Detection. Academic Press, Elsevier.
[21] VITA Technologies (2011) VME Technology FAQ. Available: http://www.vita.com/home/Learn/vmefaq/vmefaq.html. Accessed 2012 May 10.
[22] VITA Technologies. Frequently asked questions on VXS. Available: http://www.vita.com/home/MarketingAlliances/vxs/vxs_faq.pdf. Accessed 2012 May 10.
[23] PCI-SIG. (2002) PCI Local Bus Specification Revision 2.3, PCI-SIG.
[24] Digi International (2003) PCI Technology Overview. Available: http://www.digi.com/pdf/prd_msc_pcitech.pdf. Accessed 2012 May 10.
[25] Matveev, M. (2008) Databus Systems in High Energy Physics (HEP): Past, Present and Future, Rice University, Houston, Texas, USA.
[26] PCI-SIG. (2003) PCI Express Base Specification Revision 1.0a.
[27] Wilen,A. H.; Schade, J. P. & Thornburg, R. (2003) Introduction to PCI Express. A Hardware and Software Developer's Guide, Intel Press.
[28] PICMG. (2003) PICMG 3.0 - Advanced TCA Short Form Specification, Available: http://www.picmg.org/pdf/picmg_3_0_shortform.pdf. Accessed 2012 May 10.
[29] Jamieson, S. (2006) PICMG MTCA.0 R1.0 - Micro Telecommunications Computing Architecture Short Form Specification. Available: http://www.picmg.org/pdf/microtca_short_form_sept_2006.pdf. Accessed 2012 May 10.
[30] Gokhale, A. A. (2004) Introduction to Telecommunications, Cengage Learning.
[31] Chramowicz J., Kwan S., Prosser A. & M. Winchell (2011) Application of emerging parallel optical link technology to high energy physics experiments, Proceeding of 2nd International Conference on Technology and Instrumentation in Particle Physics 2011, Chicago.
[32] Söderström, P. A.; Nyberg, J. & Wolters, R. (2008) Digital pulse-shape discrimination of fast neutrons and γ rays. Nuclear Instruments and Methods in Physics Research Section A: Accelerators, Spectrometers, Detector and Associated Equipment, 594: 79-89.
[33] Akkoyun, S. et al. (2012) AGATA – Advanced Gamma Tracking Array. Nuclear Instruments and Methods in Physics Research Section A: Accelerators, Spectrometers, Detector and Associated Equipment, 668: 26 – 58.
[34] ATLAS Collaboration. (1994) ATLAS Technical Proposal for a General-Purpose pp Experiment at the Large Hadron Collider at CERN, CERN, Switzerland.
[35] González, V., Sanchis E. et al. (2006). Development of the Optical Multiplexer Board Prototype for Data Acquisition in the TileCal System. IEEE Transactions on Nuclear Science, 53: 2131 - 2138.
[36] Carrió F., Castillo V., Ferrer V., González V., Higón E., Marín C., Moreno P., Sanchis E., Solans C., Valero A. & Valls J. (2011) Optical link card design for the upgrade phase II of TileCal experiment. IEEE Transactions on Nuclear Science, 58: 1657 - 1663.

Chapter 12

Digital Signal Processing for Acoustic Emission

Paulo R. Aguiar, Cesar H.R. Martins, Marcelo Marchi and Eduardo C. Bianchi

Additional information is available at the end of the chapter

http://dx.doi.org/10.5772/48557

1. Introduction

Fast advances in several signal processing techniques, along with cost-effective digital technologies for their implementation, are ready to address important manufacturing and machine monitoring issues for which no solution currently exists. Among new technologies are advances in wavelet and time-frequency signal analysis. By virtue of their ability to characterize both transient phenomena and persistent harmonic structure, they appear well-matched to the signals associated with rotating machinery. Other recent developments, such as higher-order spectral theory, could also possibly contribute in these applications.

Because of the complexity into detection and categorization of faults are normally difficult to solve analytically or through mathematical modelling, and usually require human intelligence, thus, higher-level techniques such as neural networks and statistical pattern recognition and classification have demonstrated improvements over traditional approaches. These methods, with appropriately directed research, may offer solutions for the critical technology needs in manufacturing and machine monitoring. The growing interest in the use of artificial intelligence for the solution of engineering problems is visible from the considerable number of articles published in the last decade [1].

Thus, the present chapter aims to present results of statistical tools to detect faults in machining processes, by digitally processing the acoustic emission signals generated during the process.

2. Monitoring and process control of machining processes

The implementation of intelligent processes in industries utilizing computer numerically controlled machining is increasing rapidly. However, these systems are not enough reliable to operate without human interference so far. It is common to observe operators of CNC machines correct the process parameters or identify the end of the tool life [2].

In the grinding process, the workpiece quality depends to a great extent on the experience of the operator. This occurs because grinding is a very complex process affected by so many factors that a reproducible result is rarely obtained. The most important one is that the cutting ability of the grinding wheel changes considerably during the grinding time. In practice the grinding process is carried out with cutting parameters that are safe but not optimal. Another and no less important parameter to be controlled in grinding is dressing, which is the process of conditioning the grinding wheel surface in order to reshape the wheel when it has lost its original shape through wear [3-4].

Thus, there are three main goals related to grinding process monitoring: detection of problems during machining; provision of information necessary to optimize the process; and the contribution to the development of a database needed to determine the control parameters [5].

The use of acoustic emission (AE) to monitor and control the grinding process is a relatively recent technology [6], besides being more sensitive to the grinding condition variations, when compared with the force and power measurements [7], standing as a promising technique to the process monitoring.

Acoustic emission is the phenomenon in which elastic or stress waves are emitted from a rapid, localized change of strain energy in a material. Typically frequencies are in the range of 100 kHz to 2 MHz, well above the vibration frequencies of most machines and surroundings. At grinding process the AE signals are directly generated in the deformation zone. Thus, an important assumption is made: AE generated during the grinding process is assumed to contain information related to the micro mechanical phenomena of the grinding process and thus conditions of its components [8].

With the objective to determine features of the machining processes from the AE signal, techniques of signal processing are applied, and may include: root mean square (RMS), constant false alarm rate (CFAR), mean value dispersion statistic (MVD) etc. Features of the machining processes may be extracted as part of the particular monitoring system [9-10].

2.1. Root mean square (RMS)

The root mean square of the raw AE signal can be expressed by Equation (1):

$$AE_{RMS} = \sqrt{\frac{1}{\Delta T}\int_{0}^{\Delta t} AE^2(t)dt} = \sqrt{\frac{1}{N}\sum_{i=1}^{N} AE^2(i)} \tag{1}$$

Where ΔT is the integration time constant and N is the number of discrete AE data within ΔT. AE_{RMS} can be obtained by using an analog RMS filter or digitally by calculating with a chosen ΔT according to the right part of the equation. There is no general rule in selecting suitable ΔT to obtain AE_{RMS}, however ΔT=1 ms provides a good resolution for grinding process, and have been used for many researchers.

2.2. Constant false alarm rate (CFAR)

Constant false alarm rate (CFAR) is a statistic tool employed in detection of events, which is described by [11]:

$$T_{pl}(X) = \sum_{k=0}^{M-1} X_k^{\upsilon} \tag{2}$$

Where the X_k is the kth magnitude-squared FFT bin, υ is a changeable exponent and 2M is the total FFT bins. Respectively υ=1 and υ=∞ correspond to the energy detector and max{X_k}. Although υ between 2 and 3 provides a good performance for a wide frequency band of the studied signal, this statistic needs pre-normalized data. Due to the fluctuation of the AE signal during the grinding process, a constant false alarm rate (CFAR) power-law [12] is used. The CFAR power-law is based on an assumption that the spectrum of AE signal is flat. An alternative version of this tool was employed due to system distortions, which is expressed by the following equation [13].

$$T_{bcpl}(X) = \frac{\sum_{k=n1}^{n2} X_k^{\upsilon}}{\left(\sum_{n1}^{n2} X_k\right)^{\upsilon}} \tag{3}$$

Where T_{bcpl} is clearly not affected by signal amplitude. This version of the CFAR power-law statistics is band-limited by $n1$ and $n2$.

2.3. Mean value dispersion statistic (MVD)

The mean-value deviance (MVD) statistic quantifies in a certain way the average deviation of observations from its mean value. Unusually large value of $T_{mvd}(X)$ implies such deviation is too great to be explained using a simple exponential distribution model. This statistic is sensitive to small outliers, that is, observations with extremely small values [14].

The MVD statistic was used successfully in burn detection [15], and is defined by Equation (4).

$$T_{mvd}(X) = \frac{1}{M} \sum_{k=0}^{M-1} \log\left[\frac{\overline{X}}{X_k}\right] \tag{4}$$

Where $\overline{X}$ is the mean value of $\{X_k\}$; $2M$ is the total number of FFT bins, and is the kth magnitude-squared FFT bin.

2.4. Kurtosis and skewness statistics

The measurement if the distribution tail is longer than other is made by skew. In case of kurtosis, the tail size is expressed. Both statistics are utilized as an indicator to the acoustic emission variations. Thus, abrupt changes in the AE signal may result in spikes in these statistics. The Equation (5) shows the way of calculating kurtosis of an x signal.

$$K = \sum \frac{(x-\mu)^4}{N\sigma^4} - 3 \tag{5}$$

Where μ is the mean of x, N the number of samples in the range considered and σ the standard deviation.

Similarly, the expression given in Equation (6) is used to calculate skewness.

$$S = \sum \frac{(x-\mu)^3}{N\sigma^3} \tag{6}$$

2.5. Ratio of power (ROP)

It is instinctive to think about the different behaviours expected for a good part or bad one by observing the frequency spectrum of the AE signal. Hence, for each block of AE data ROP is given by Equation (7).

$$ROP = \sum_{k=n_1}^{n_2} \frac{|X_k|^2}{\sum_{k=0}^{N-1} |X_k|^2} \tag{7}$$

The denumerator eliminates the local effect of power in equation, where N is the size of a block of AE data; n_1 and n_2 define a frequency range to analyse.

2.6. Autocorrelation

The time correlation of a function Φ_{xy} is defined by Oppenheim [16] in Equation (8).

$$\phi_{xy}(t) = \int_{-\infty}^{+\infty} x(t+\tau)\,y(\tau)\,d\tau \tag{8}$$

Where Φ_{xx} is commonly referred to autocorrelation of x signal.

2.7. DPO

The combination of the RMS AE signal and the cutting power signal provided a parameter to indicate burning of the workpiece in surface grinding, which has been dubbed DPO, and consists of the relation between the standard deviation of the RMS AE signal and the maximum cutting force per grinding wheel pass [17]. Equation (5) represents the DPO parameter.

$$DPO = std(AE)\max(pw) \tag{9}$$

Where *std(AE)* is the standard deviation of the RMS AE and *max(pw)* is the maximum value of cutting power in the pass.

2.8. DPKS

The DPKS statistic was developed by Dotto [18] in order to increase the sensitivity of the DPO parameter. This parameter allows to identify the exact moment when grinding burn begins, and in the case of dressing, the exact moment to stop the process. The DPKS is calculated by multiplying the standard deviation of AE by the sum of the cutting power subtracted from its standard deviation elevated to the fourth power. Equation (6) represents the calculated DPKS statistic:

$$DPKS = \left(\sum_{i=1}^{m} \left(pw(i) - std(pw) \right)^4 \right) std(AE) \tag{10}$$

Where i is the power index which varies from 1 up to m points in each pass, *pw(i)* and *std(pw)* are, respectively, the instant value of the cutting power and standard deviation of the cutting power in the pass, and *std(AE)* is the standard deviation of the RMS AE in the pass.

2.9. Artificial neural network (ANN)

According to Kwak & Song [19], neural networks are composed of many non-linear computational elements operating in parallel. Because of their massive nature and their adaptive nature in using the learning process, neural networks can perform computations at a higher rate and adapt to changes in data learning the characteristics of input signals. The usefulness of an artificial neural network comes from the ability to respond to an input pattern in a desirable fashion, after the learning phase.

The artificial neural network efficiency has proved in previous investigations in the prediction of faults at machining processes. Thus, this technique is very promising and can also be applied successfully to industrial automation in a flexible and integrated fashion.

2.9.1. Multi layer perceptron (MLP)

Nathan et al. [20] state that there are three structural layers in a network, namely the input layer (which receives input from the outside world), the hidden layer (between the input and the output layers) and the output layer (the response given to the outside world). The neurons of different layers are interconnected through weights. Thus, processing elements at different layers, interconnections between them, and the learning rules that define the way in which inputs are mapped on to the outputs constitutes a neural network. The usefulness of an ANN comes from its ability to respond to an input pattern in a desirable fashion, after the learning phase. As such, the processing units receive inputs and perform a weighted sum of its input values using the connection weights given initially by user. This weighted sum is termed the activation value of the neuron, given by:

$$u = \sum w_i x_i + \theta \tag{11}$$

where w_{ij} is the weight interconnecting two nodes i and j; x_i is the input variable; and u is the threshold value. During the forward pass through the network, each neuron evaluates an equation that expresses the output as a function of the inputs. Using the right kind of transfer function is therefore essential. A sigmoidal function can be used for this purpose, and is given by:

$$f(x) = \frac{1}{\left(1 + e^{-u}\right)} \tag{12}$$

Depending on the mismatch of the predicted output with the desired output, the weights are adjusted by back-propagation of error, so that the current mean square error (MSE) given by the following equation is reduced:

$$MSE = \frac{1}{2NK} \sum_{n=1}^{N} \sum_{k=1}^{K} \left(b_{nk} - S_{nk}\right)^2 \tag{13}$$

where N is the number of patterns in the training data, K is the number of nodes in the network, b_{nk} is the target output for the nth pattern and s_{nk} is the actual output for the nth pattern.

Still, according to Hykin apud Nathan et al. [20], it should be noted that the MSE itself is a function of the weights, as the computation of the output uses them. During this learnig phase of the network the weights and the threshold values are adapted in order to develop the knowledge stored in the network. The weights are adjusted so as to obtain the desired output. The problem of finding the best set of weights in order to minimize the discrepancy between the desired and the actual response of the network is considered as a non-linear optimization problem. The most popularly used learning algorithm, namely the back-propagation algorithm, uses an interactive gradient-descent heuristic approach to solve this problem. Once the learning process is completed, the final set of weight values is stored, this constituting the long term memory of the network, which is used later during the prediction process.

2.9.2. The radial basis neural network

According to Musavi et al. [21] Radial Basis Function (RBF) technique provides an alternative tool to learning in neural networks. The main idea is to design a network with good generalization ability and a minimum number of nodes to avoid unnecessarily lengthy calculations as opposed to multilayer perceptron networks. The RBF classifiers which belong to the group of kernel classifiers utilize overlapping localized regions formed by simple kernel functions to create complex decision regions.

The structure of the radial basis ANN is like a MLP with three layers, an input layer, the radial basis function layer, and one linear layer output neuron [22]. This structure is shown in Figure (1).

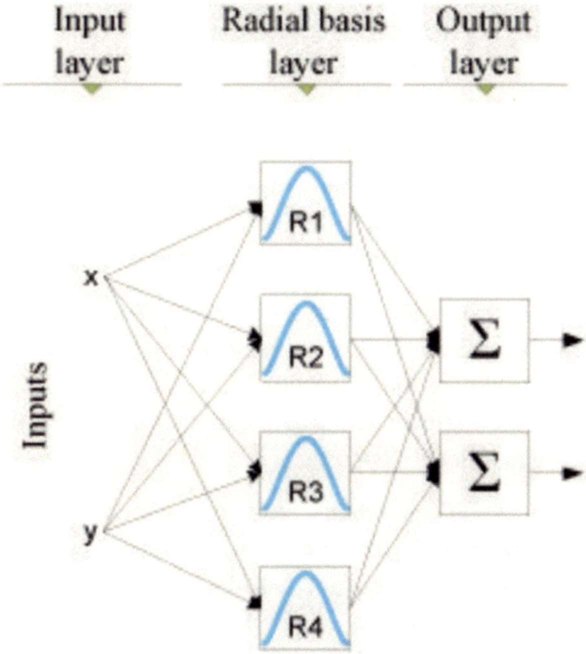

Figure 1. A generic radial basis network. Adapted from Jang [23].

The radial basis function (RBFs), which have been widely advocated [21], are approximations of the form

$$yr = \alpha + \sum_j \beta_j G\left(\left\|x - x_j\right\| / \sigma_j\right) \tag{14}$$

for centers x_j, where $G(r) = exp(-r2/2)$, σ is the covariance matrix. Using RBFs as the basis functions, one output can be represented by

$$y = b2 + \sum_{j=1}^{n_j} w2_j \exp\left(-b1_j^2 \sum_{i=1}^{n_i} \left(w1_{ji} - x_i\right)^2\right) \tag{15}$$

where x is the input vector with size n_i, n_i and n_j are separately the numbers of neurons used in input and the radial basis layer, $w1$ and $b1$ are the weight matrix and the bias vector with dimension n_j for the radial basis layer, $w2$ and $b2$ are the corresponding weight matrix and bias scale for the linear layer.

Just as any statistical analysis, an implied requirement for developing robust neural network models is that the training sets cover as many of the possible variations in the input and output vector as possible.

2.9.3. *Adaptive neuro-fuzzy inference system (ANFIS)*

The ANFIS system is based on the functional equivalence, under certain constraints, of RBF networks and Takagi-Sugeno-Kang (TSK) fuzzy systems [24-25]. A single existing output is calculated directly by weighting the inputs according to fuzzy rules, which are the knowledge base determined by a computational algorithm based on neural networks.

To produce an ANFIS model that performs well requires taking into account the initial number of parameters and the number of inputs and rules of the system [26]. These parameters are determined empirically and an initial model with equally spaced membership functions is usually created. However, this method is not always efficient because it does not show how many relevant input groups there are.

The subtractive clustering algorithm [27-28] is used to identify data distribution centers, which contain the membership curves with membership values equal to 1. The algorithm uses the cluster number or the size of the neighborhood radius and the number of iteration times. In each pass through the algorithm, the latter looks for a point that minimizes the sum of the potential with the neighboring points.

According to Lee et al. [29], ANFIS is a fuzzy inference system introduced in the work structure of an adaptive neuro-fuzzy network. Using a hybrid learning procedure, the ANFIS system is able to build an input-output map based on human knowledge and on input/output data pairs. The ANFIS method is superior to other modeling methods such as the autoregressive model, cascade correlation neural networks, back-propagation neural networks, sixth-order polynomials, and linear prediction methods [23].

3. Case study

3.1. In-process grinding monitoring by acoustic emission

This case aims to investigate the efficiency of digital signal processing tools of acoustic emission signals in order to detect thermal damages in grinding process. To accomplish such goal, an experimental work was carried out for 15 runs in a surface grinding machine operating with an aluminum oxide grinding wheel and ABNT 1045. A high sampling rate data acquisition system at 2.5 MHz was used to collect the raw acoustic emission. Many statistics have shown effective to detect burn, such as the RMS, correlation of the AE, CFAR, ROP and MVD. However, the CFAR, ROP, Kurtosis and correlation of the AE have been presented more sensitive than the RMS.

3.1.1. *Experimental setup*

The experimental tests were carried out upon a surface grinding machine where raw acoustic emission signals were collected for fifteen different runs at 2.5 million of samples per second rate. Data was collected from a fixed acoustic emission sensor of the Sensis manufacturer; model PAC U80D-87, which was mounted on the part holder. The major grinding parameters were kept constant during the runs, and can be seen in Table (1). However, the depth of cut was varied from light and aggressive cutting. All the parts were essayed post-mortem and the burn marks were identified.

Items	Specifications and conditions
Grinding wheel	Type: 38A80-PVS-Norton, size: 296.50 x 40.21 mm
Wheel speed	27.94 m/s (1800 rpm)
Coolant	Type: water-based fluid 4%
Workpiece	Material: ABNT 1045 steel, size: 98.58 x 8.74 mm
Workpiece speed	0.044 m/s

Table 1. Experimental specifications and conditions.

The Table (2) shows details of tests carried out for the ABNT 1045 steel. Besides the visual analysis, roughness and microhardness test were performed on the parts.

Test	Depth of cut (μm)		Cutting Profile	Comments
1	10			No burn
2	30			Slight burn
3	20			Severe burn
4	90	10		Severe burn
5	20	2.5		Severe burn
6	40	5		Severe burn
7	15			Burn at middle

Table 2. Tests with ABNT 1045 steel.

3.1.2. Results

Digital processing of the acoustic emission signals was accomplished for many statistical correlations such as kurtosis, skewness, autocorrelation, RMS, CFAR, ROP and MVD. These statistics were obtained by digitally processing the raw acoustic emission in blocks of 2048 samples. As a result, each statistics were computed along the 6 second-related test, which was composed of the grinding pass itself and some noise period before and after the grinding pass. The graphs for each workpiece obtained for these statistics are presented in Figure (2) for tests 1, 5 and 7 respectively.

From the results it can be observed that the RMS statistic had a stable level for the non-burning workpiece during all over the grinding pass while significant variations can be observed when severe burn occurred, as can be seen in Figure (2a) for non-burning and Figure (2b) for severe burning. Skewness and kurtosis presented variation when burn took place but positive amplitudes dos some tests and negative ones for others were observed, which are not useful for an indicator parameter to burn. The ROP turned out to be a good indicative to burn, since its behavior has shown quite sensitive to the studied phenomenon. Besides, its level is low to those non-burning parts and high to the burning ones.

Additionally, it has well characterized the contact between the wheel and piece. The MVD tool presented a behavior similar to the RMS statistic. The autocorrelation statistic was very sensitive to burn for the most tests performed but for a few it has shown useless by virtue of the decreasing observed when burn occurred. Similarly to the autocorrelation, the CFAR tool has behaved quite well to burn detection for most of the tests carried out but with no decreasing of signal at all, except for test 7 where a decreasing was observed during the grinding pass. This behavior, however, did not compromise the utility of CFAR tool, for the level of test 7 has kept higher than to the non-burning test.

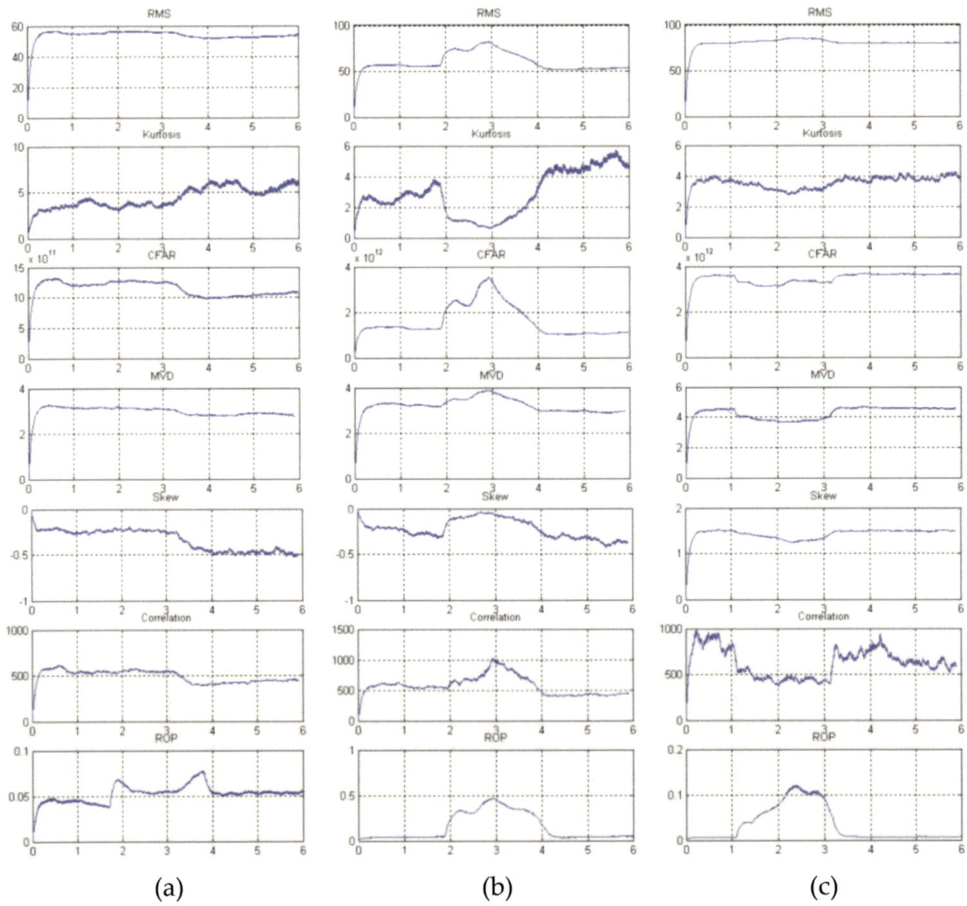

Figure 2. Results for Test 1, Test 5 and Test 7; Horizontal axis corresponds time in seconds and Vertical axis Volts multiplied by a constant; (a) Test 1 with no burn; (b) Test 5 with severe burn from close to the beginning to the end; (c) Test 7 with burn in the midst.

3.1.3. Case study conclusion

For this case study, the results show that several statistics have worked quite well to burn detection, as is the case of RMS, CFAR, ROP and MVD. Nevertheless, skewness and kurtosis statistics have presented an interesting behavior regarding the waveform of the signal and their variation along the grinding pass, though they are not effective to detect burn.

3.2. Classification of burn degrees in grinding by neural nets

The aim of this case study is to attain the classification of burn degrees of the parts ground with the utilization of neural networks. The acoustic emission and power signal as well as the statistics derived from the digital signal processing of these signals are utilized as inputs of the neural networks. The results have shown the success of classification for most of the structures studied.

3.2.1. Experimental setup

A surface grinding machine was used in the grinding tests equipped with an aluminum oxide grinding wheel, model ART-FE-38A80PVH. An acoustic emission sensor was placed near the workpiece and an electrical power transducer for measuring the electrical power consumed by three-phase induction motor that drives the wheel were employed. The acoustic emission (AE) and cutting power (Pot) signals were measured at 2.0 millions of samples per second. Table (3) list the parameters adjusted to the system.

Items	Specifications and conditions
Wheel speed	30 m/s (1800 rpm)
Coolant	Type: water-based fluid 4%
Workpiece	Material: SAE 1020 steel, size: 150 x 10 x 60 mm
Workpiece speed	0.033 m/s

Table 3. Experimental specifications and conditions.

The power transducer consists of a Hall sensor to measure the electric current and a Hall voltage sensor to measure the voltage at the electric motor terminals. Both signals are processed internally in the power transducer module by an integrated circuit, which delivers a voltage signal proportional to the electrical power consumed by the electric motor.

The tests were carried out for 12 different grinding conditions, and subsequently the burn degrees (no-burn, slight burn, medium burn, and severe burn) could be visually assessed for each workpiece surface. Dressing parameters, lubrication and peripheral wheel speed were adequately controlled in order to ensure the same grinding condition for each test. Each run consisted of a single grinding pass along the workpiece length at a given grinding condition to be analyzed.

3.2.2. Results

The digital signal processing phase started after all the 12 tests were carried out. The process generated seven new statistics, that is, the parameters DPO and DPKS, and the statistics CFAR and MVD. Seven structures were used for the neural network implementation as shown in Table (4). It can be noted in this table that besides the signals and statistics aforementioned the depth of cut a was also used as input.

In this case, the back-propagation algorithm of neural networks, which is one of the learning models, was used. The following parameters ware also found more suitable: downward gradient training algorithm; all data in the neural networks were normalized; training for 1000 epochs; square mean error value of 10-5. Cross-validation was used to estimate the generalization error of the model. The outputs of the neural network was configured in a binary way according to the degree of burn obtained, that is, 0001 for no no-burn, 0010 for slight burn, 0100 for medium burn, and 1000 for severe burn.

Structure	Inputs
I	Pot, AE, a
II	DPO, a
III	DPKS, a
IV	MVD, a
V	CFAR, a
VI	AE, a
VII	Pot, a

Table 4. Neural Network Structures.

Each statistic was represented by a vector of 3000 samples for each test subsequently the digital processing of the AE and power signals. The quantification of the grinding burn on every part surface was done by specific software for that purpose, which assessed the surface of a given part regarding the burn level through its digitalized picture. From the results of this characterization, input vectors ware separated and assigned to the corresponding type of burn. The input vectors were again divided into training, validation and test vectors.

Then, the process of optimization for the neural network was carried out. For each structure were tested some parameters like the number of neurons of the hidden layer, learning rate and momentum. The best results for all structures were obtained and presented in Table (5).

Structure	Neurons	Learning rate	Momentum
I	3 – 35 – 4	0.7	0.6
II	2 – 50 – 4	0.7	0.3
III	2 – 45 – 4	0.5	0.7
IV	2 – 30 – 4	0.3	0.7
V	2 – 50 – 4	0.7	0.3
VI	2 – 40 – 4	0.7	0.7
VII	2 – 20 – 4	0.5	0.3

Table 5. Final configuration for the 7 neural network structures.

The results for each structure were generated by inputting the corresponding data along with the depth of cut information, and the network output was interpreted in a bar graph fitting the form of the ground workpiece according to each burn level obtained. The digital picture of the workpiece with the corresponding bar graph for each structure was put all together for comparisons.

Figure (3) shows the results obtained when the signal vectors of Test 2, not used in the training, were inputted to the neural network. Thus, the data given to neural network are different from those it was used in training, testing this way its ability of classifying the burn levels. It can be observed that the structures were able to detecting well the changes in the burn levels occurred in this test. Some minor errors of classification were also observed as is the case of the Structure IV, Figure (3e), which has failed in classifying severe burn in the end of the workpiece.

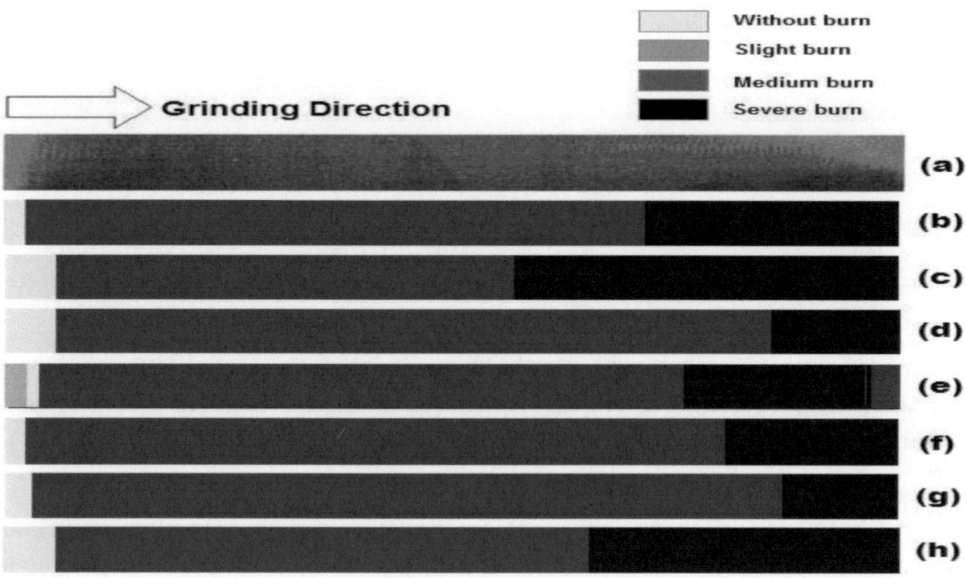

Figure 3. Results obtained for Test 2; (a) Workpiece picture; (b) Structure I; (c) Structure II; (d) Structure III; (e) Structure IV; (f) Structure V; (g) Structure VI; (h) Structure VII.

It can be observed in Figure (4) that all structures have presented a success rate quite good, with the exception of Structure IV that has presented a success rate of only 52.9%. The structure having acoustic emission, power and depth of cut was supposed to own a better position in the grading since these signals are widely employed in the grinding process monitoring. On the other hand, Structure II composed by DPO parameter and depth of cut has present the best result, this can also be explained due to the parameter DPO combines the variations of the RMS acoustic emission and the maximum amplitude of the electric power during the grinding pass, resulting in an excellent tool for detection of burn degrees. It can be emphasized that all structures detected slight burn quite well, and the grading showed was based on the success rate for all degrees of burn studied.

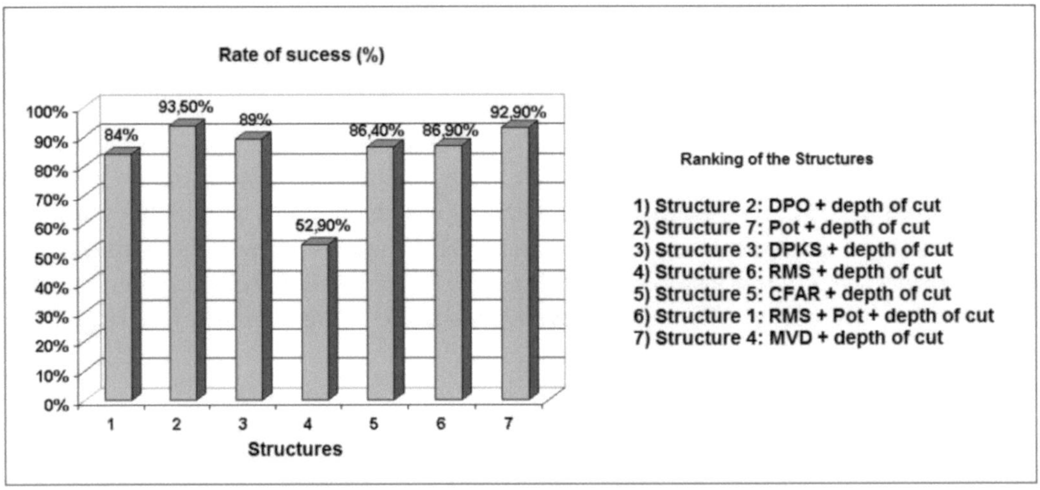

Figure 4. Rate of success for each structure and the ranking obtained.

3.2.3. *Case study conclusion*

The utilization of neural network of type multi-layer perceptron using back-propagation algorithm guaranteed very good results.

As all structures have detected correctly the degree of slight burn that is the first stage of change on thermal damage, it can be concluded that all structures worked well for classification of burn or non-burn occurrence.

The differences of errors found among the Structures II, VI and VII are quite small, that is, less than 1% for the set of input #7, and 6.6% for the set of input #6 with respect to Structure II. Therefore, the acoustic emission and electric power signals can also be employed successfully as inputs to the artificial neural networks for classification of burn degrees in grinding.

3.3. ANFIS applied to the prediction of surface roughness in grinding of advanced ceramics

In this case is introduced a methodology for predicting the surface roughness of advanced ceramics using Adaptive Neuro-Fuzzy Inference System (ANFIS). For this work, alumina workpieces were pressed and sintered into rectangular bars. The statistical data processed from the AE signal and the cutting power, were used as input data for ANFIS. The output values of surface roughness were implemented for training and validation of the model. The results indicated that an ANFIS network could predict the surface roughness of ceramic workpieces in the grinding process.

3.3.1. *Experimental setup*

To evaluate the behavior and collect the signals in surface grinding process of advanced ceramics, a test bench was created. A surface grinding machine was used, equipped with a synthetic diamond grinding wheel (type: SD 126 MN 50 B2). Dressing was carried out with a cluster type diamond dresser. The test pieces, consisted of rectangular bars of commercial alumina comprising 96% of aluminum oxide and 4% of flux oxides, were produced by pressing and sintering. Table (6) lists the parameters adjusted to the system.

A piezoelectric type sensor attached to the holder that fixes the workpiece collected the AE signal. The system's cutting power was recorded through an electrical power module connected to the power supply of the frequency converter. Surface roughness was measured with a Taylor Hobson Surtronic 3+ surface roughness tester. Tests were performed at three different cutting depths: 20μm, 70μm and 120μm to record the signals and surface roughness data.

The following statistics was obtained from the cutting power and AE signals: mean of AE, standard deviation of AE (std of AE), mean of cutting power (mean of PW), standard deviation of cutting power (std of PW), DPO and DPKS. These values were evaluated as inputs to the ANFIS system. Based on the surface roughness values, regressions were made to obtain more data for training the networks. Figure (5) illustrates this process.

Items	Specifications and conditions
Wheel speed	35 m/s (1800 rpm)
Workpiece speed	0.038 m/s
Coolant	Type: Conventional water and oil emulsion (Rocol Ultracut 370); Concentration: 5%
Fluid velocity	3 m/s
Fluid outflow	27.5 l/min (0.458 l/s)
Pressure of the fluid in the system	Lower than 0.2 kgf/cm2

Table 6. Experimental specifications and conditions.

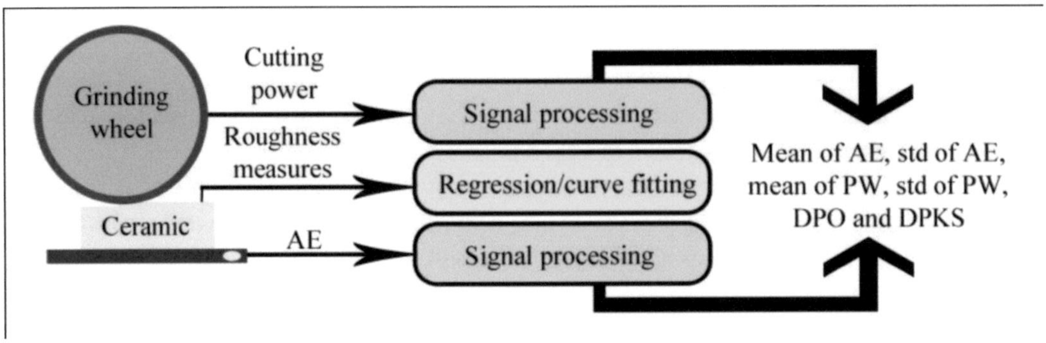

Figure 5. Data acquisition and signal processing scheme.

3.3.2. Results

For this case, the ANFIS model with three inputs composed by: acoustic emission, standard deviation of power and the DPO statistic. This model presented the lowest error and best represent the behavior of the system.

For the best model was conduced several test to find the ideal training parameters. The number of membership functions per input was varied, and the general error of the test set and the general error related to the real measurements were analyzed.

Table (7) lists the final parameters of the definitive ANFIS model for the prediction of surface roughness of a ceramic body. The five rules are in the form: Rule(k) – IF (mEA is In1cluster(k)) and (sPot is In2cluster(k)) and (DPO is In3cluster(k)) THEN (Roughness Outcluster(k)), where k is the rule number and varies from 1 to 5.

Parameter	Value
Number de Membership Functions per Input	5
Type of Membership Function	Gbellmf, Gaussian function
Target Error	0.001
Maximum Number of Iterations	100
Maximum Learning Coefficient	1.1
Training Method	Hybrid

Table 7. Definitive parameters of the ANFIS model.

The newly created model was validated using values generated by the surface roughness curve. The result is depicted in Figure (6), which shows a good prediction with a total error of approximately 4%.

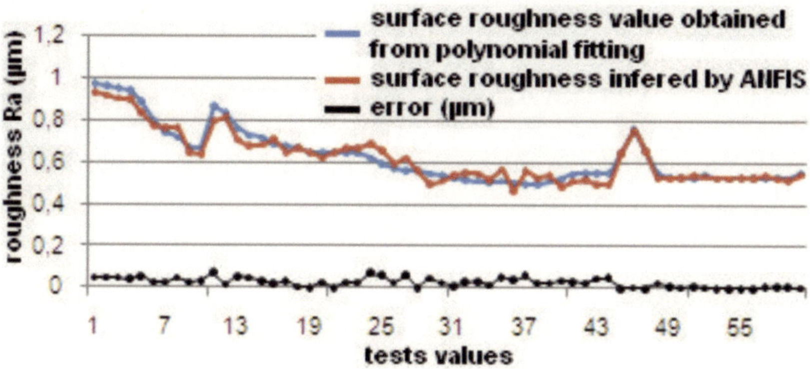

Figure 6. Inference of surface roughness by ANFIS for the test set generated by the fitted roughness curve.

3.3.3. Case study conclusion

The accuracy of the ANFIS network for predicting surface roughness demonstrates that this type of network is a good data prediction system, since its hybrid nature (neural and fuzzy) enables the correct prediction of the values of the system, which are not easily related.

The ANFIS network tested with three inputs showed a lower RMS error than the networks with one and two inputs, and the best set was the one whose parameters were the mean acoustic emission, the standard deviation of cutting power and the DPO.

The predicted surface roughness values showed a percent error of 7.54% for the measurements taken in the tests at 20µm of depth, 6.54% for the test at 120µm, and the lowest error of 4.73% for the test at 70µm. After building the ANFIS model and training it, it was possible to obtain the membership functions, with their allocated centers, the rule sets for predicting surface roughness, and the set of output equations of the model, enabling the system's application in a control environment.

4. Conclusions

The characterization and detection of anomalies during the grinding process were successfully performed by digitally processing the raw acoustic emission signal for several statistics studied and presented in this chapter. The first case study has shown good results for burn detection with the statistics RMS, CFAR, ROP and MVD.

Artificial neural networks (ANNs) proved to be very useful tool for pattern recognition of grinding burn degrees as well as estimating the wear of the grinding wheel indirectly. In addition, ANNs have presented good results in estimating surface roughness of advanced ceramics. This turns out to be a benefit towards the optimization of the grinding process, avoiding high reject rates, scrap, rework, and machine downtime.

Based on the studies presented, a contribution is given to the development of a database needed to determine the control parameters of the grinding process. It is therefore possible to determine safe regions to operate the grinding machine from mild to critical conditions, providing a system to the end user to start out with the optimal parameters, eliminating the need for trial and error, with increased productivity, reduced expenditures on consumables, scrap and rework reduction, and improved quality. The digital signal processing of the raw acoustic emission as well as the artificial neural network models applied to the grinding process provide valuable information necessary to optimize the process.

Author details

Paulo R. Aguiar, Cesar H.R. Martins, Marcelo Marchi and Eduardo C. Bianchi
Universidade Estadual Paulista "Júlio de Mesquita Filho" (UNESP), Bauru campus, Brazil

5. References

[1] Pham, D. T. & Pham, P. T. N. (1999). Artificial intelligence in engineering. *International Journal of Machine Tools & Manufacture,* Vol.39, No.6, pp. 937-949, ISSN 0890-6955

[2] Aguiar, P. R.; Willet, P. & Webster, J. (1999). Acoustic emission applied to detect workpiece burn during grinding, In: *Acoustic emission: Standards and Technology Update, ASTM STP 1353,* S. J. Vahaviolos, (Ed.), 107-124, American Society for Testing and Materials, ISBN: 0-8031-2498-8, West Conshohocken, Pennsylvania, USA.

[3] Aguiar, P. R.; Cruz, C. E. D.; Paula, W. C. F.; Bianchi, E. C.; Thomazella, R.; Dotto, F. R. L. (2007). Neural network approach for surface roughness prediction in surface grinding, *Proceedings of the 25th IASTED International Multi-Conference: Artificial Intelligence and Applications,* Innsbruck, 2007, pp. 96-106.

[4] Aguiar, P. R.; Souza, A. G. O.; Bianchi, E. C.; Leite, R. R.; Dotto, F. R. L. (2009). Monitoring the Dressing Operation in the Grinding Process, *International Journal of Machining and Machinability of Materials,* 5 (1), pp. 3-22.

[5] Inasaki, I. (1999). Sensor fusion for monitoring and controlling grinding processes, *The International Journal of Advanced Manufacturing Technology,* Vol.15, No.10, pp. 730-736, ISSN 0268-3768.

[6] Bennett, R. T (1994). *Acoustic emission in grinding,* Master Thesis, University of Connecticut.

[7] Webster, J.; Marinescu, I.; Bennett, R. & Lindsay, R. (1994). Acoustic emission for process control and monitoring of surface integrity during grinding, *CIRP Annals – Manufacturing Technology,* Vol.43, No.1, pp. 299-304, ISSN 0007-8506.

[8] Sachse, W.; Roget J.; Yamaguchi, K. (1991). Acoustic Emission: Current Practice and Future Directions, ASTM.

[9] Dornfeld, D. A. (1990). Neural network sensor fusion for tool condition monitoring, *Annals of the CIRP,* Vol.39, No.1, pp. 101-105.

[10] Fang, X. D. (1995). Expert system-supported fuzzy diagnosis of finish-turning process states, *International Journal of Machine Tools Manufacturing,* Vol.35, No.6, pp. 913-924, Elsevier Science.

[11] Nuttal, A (1997). Performance of power-law processors with normalization for random signals of unknown structure, Naval Undersea Warfare Center, *NPT Technical Report 10,760.*

[12] Nuttal, A. (1996). Detection performance of power-law processors for random signals of unknown location, structure, extent, and strength, *AIP Conference Proceedings*, Vol.375, No.1, pp. 302-324, ISBN 1-56396-443-0.

[13] Wang, Z. (1999). Surface grinding monitoring by signal processing of acoustic emission signals, Master Thesis, University of Connecticut.

[14] Chen, B.; Willett, P.; Streit, R. (1999) Transient detection using a homogeneity test, in: Proceedings of 1999 ICASSP, Phoenix, AZ, no. 1715, IEEE, Piscataway, New Jersey.

[15] Wang, Z.; Willet, P.; Aguiar, P. R. & Webster, J. (2001). Neural network detection of grinding burn from acoustic emission, *International Journal of Machine Tools & Manufacture*, Vol.41, No.2, pp.283-309, ISSN 0890-6955.

[16] Oppenheim, A. V. et al. (1997). Signals & Systems, 2sd. Edition, Prentice Hall Signal Processing Series.

[17] Aguiar, P. R.; Bianchi, E. C.; Oliveira, J. F. G. A. (2002). Method for Burning Detection in Grinding Process Using Acoustic Emission and Effective Electrical Power Signals. In: CIRP Journal of Manufacturing Systems. Paris, v.31, n.3, 253 – 257.

[18] Dotto, F. R. L.; Aguiar, P. R.; Bianchi, E. C.; Serni, P. J. A. & Thomazella, R. (2006). Automatic system for thermal damage detection in manufacturing process with internet monitoring. *Journal of Brazilian Society of Mechanical Science & Engineering*, Vol.28, No.2, pp. 153-160, ISSN 1678-5878.

[19] Kwak, J. S. & Song, J. B. (2001). Trouble diagnosis of the grinding process by using acoustic emission signals, *International Journal of Machine Tools & Manufacture 41*, pp. 899-913.

[20] Nathan, R. D.; Vijayaraghavan L.; Krishnamurthy R. (1999). In-process monitoring of grinding burn in the cylindrical grinding of steel, Journal of Materials Processing Technology, 91, 37–42.

[21] Musavi, M.; Ahmed, W.; Chan, K.; Faris, K. (1992). On the Training of Radial Basis Function Classifiers, Neural Networks, 5, pp. 595-603.

[22] Hopgood, A. A. (2000). Intelligent Systems for Engineers and Scientists, 2nd. Edition, Boca Raton: CRC Press.

[23] Jang, J. S. R. (1993). ANFIS: Adaptive-network-based fuzzy inference system, IEEE Transactions on Systems, Man and Cybernetics, 23 (3), 665-685.

[24] Sugeno, M. & Kang, G. T. (1988). Structure identification of fuzzy model, Fuzzy Sets and Systems, 28, 15-33.

[25] Takagi, T. & Sugeno M. (1985). Fuzzy identification of systems and its aplications to modeling and control, IEEE Trans. Syst Man Cyber, 15, 116-131.

[26] Lezanski, P. (2001). An intelligent system for grinding wheel condition monitoring, Journal of Materials Processing Technology, 109, 258-263.

[27] Chiu, S. L. (1994). Fuzzy model identification based on cluster estimation, Journal of Intelligent and Fuzzy Systems, 2, 267-278.

[28] Chiu, S. L. (1996). Selecting input variables for fuzzy models, Journal of Intelligent and Fuzzy Systems, 2, 267-278.

[29] Lee, K. C.; Ho, S. J.; Ho, S. Y. (2005). Accurate estimation of surface roughness from texture features of the surface image using an adaptive neuro-fuzzy inference system, Precision Engineering, 29, 95-100.

Chapter 13

Making Use of the Landsat 7 SLC-off ETM+ Image Through Different Recovering Approaches

Feng Chen, Xiaofeng Zhao and Hong Ye

Additional information is available at the end of the chapter

http://dx.doi.org/10.5772/48535

1. Introduction

Landsat program represents the world's longest continuously acquired collection of space-based moderate-resolution land remote sensing data. So far, the sensors include the Landsat1-5 Multispectral Scanners (MSS), the Landsat 5 Thematic Mapper (TM) and the Landsat 7 Enhanced Thematic Mapper Plus (ETM+). The Landsat imagery with nearly four decades (from 1972 to present, see Fig.1) provides a unique resource for researchers and common users who work in agriculture, geology, forestry, regional planning, education, mapping, and global change research. Currently, both Landsat 5 and Landsat 7 are still being operated in orbit for data collection, although they have exceeded the expected service time and always readily experienced malfunction.

The scan-line corrector (SLC) for the ETM+ sensor, on board the Landsat 7 satellite, failed permanently on May 31, 2003. Normally , the SLC compensates for the forward motion of the satellite. Under the abnormal situation, without an operating SLC, images have wedge-shaped gaps that range from a single pixel in width near the nadir point, to about 12 pixels towards the edges of the scene. The SLC anomaly results in about 22% pixels in these images are un-scanned. The consequence of the SLC failure (called SLC-off problem) hampers the use of the Landsat 7 ETM+ data. At the same time, Landsat 5 has suffered problems with its solar array drive which have affected data availability. It suggests that Landsat 5 would be at the end of its operational life and not be reliable on as a source of future imagery (Pringle et al., 2009). Additionally, TM sensor onboard the Landsat 5 has been suspended from 2011 November resulted from the failure of its electronic component vital to the data transmission, according to the news provided by the U.S. Geological Survey (USGS). The Landsat Data Continuity Mission (LDCM), to be called Landsat 8, which is regarded as a successor of the preliminary series (e.g. the Landsat 1-4, Landsat 5, and

Landsat 7), will be launched in December 2012 or January 2013 according to the passed schedule. Under the condition that no replacement of Landsat or Landsat-like sensor from the LDCM has been launched presently, along with the sensors failures mentioned above, there would be a period of data gap, probably ranging from 2003 to 2013. Fortunately, SLC-off has not affected the radiometric and geometric quality of the sensor, with approximately 80% of the pixels in each image being scanned (The USGS & National Aeronautics Space Administration [NASA], 2003). Although the SLC anomalies produce obviously negative impacts on the post-event Landsat 7 ETM+ data usability, for some applications the SLC-off ETM+ retains significant and important utility for scientific applications and some users still prefer these data over more costly alternatives (USGS & NASA, 2003). In order to resolve the SLC-off problem and enable the continuous usage of ETM+, we must find suitable way to estimate the values at un-scanned pixels.

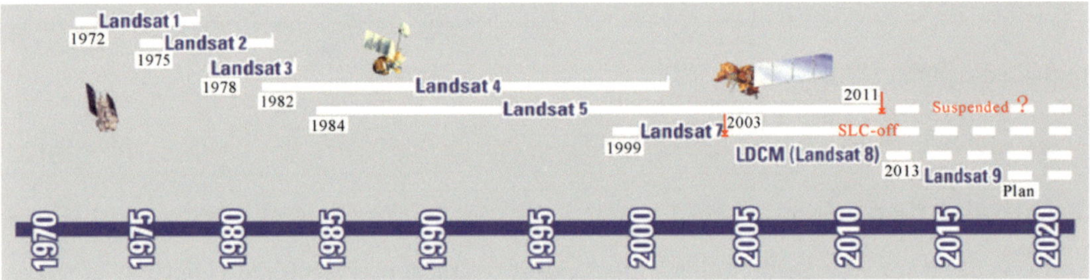

Figure 1. Landsat missions' timeline and their current status (modified for illustration, originally obtained from USGS (*http://landsat.usgs.gov/about_mission_history.php*))

Soon after SLC-off occurred, a report was compiled by the USGS (USGS & NASA, 2003). It suggested that, at the un-canned location, the reflectance of a particular ETM+ band could be estimated by compositing the target image, the SLC-off one need to be recovered, with the corresponding band of laterally overlapping ETM+ images, SLC-off or SLC-on ETM+ images (called fill image) of the same area from other dates (USGS & NASA, 2003). The means and the variances of the bands in the additional images can be adjusted, either globally or locally, to the means and variances of the bands in a target image (USGS & NASA, 2003). Based on this assumption, an expert group organized by the USGS proposed several recovering methodologies to tackle this issue, including global linear histogram match (GLHM), localized linear histogram match (LLHM), and adaptive window linear histogram match (AWLHM) (Scaramuzza et al.,2003; USGS & NASA, 2004). These methods are simple and easily to be put into application. Therefore, the un-scanned pixels in the SLC-off ETM+ images are able to be recovered with acceptable accuracy, given that the input scenes (the target and fill ones) are provided with high quality and represent comparable seasonal conditions (USGS & NASA, 2004).

However, in practice, there are shortcomings associated with these original methods, of which, the most obvious one is the restrict requirement on selecting the fill image (F. Chen et al., 2010). Thus, as an alternative to those methods, it is possible to use the information from a sensor other than ETM+, which is observed at the close time as a SLC-off ETM+ image, to estimate the un-scanned pixels. This assumption has been verified by several previous researches. For example, Reza and Ali (2008) used IRS products to recover the SLC-off ETM+ image, while Boloorani et al (2008a) and F. Chen et al (2010) demonstrated the possibility of estimating un-scanned pixels in SLC-off image by using EO-1/ALI and CBERS data as auxiliary information, respectively. Furthermore, Roy et al (2008) used the information observed by MODIS to calculate reflectance of the missing pixels, although the spatial resolution of MODIS sensor is much coarser than that of Landsat 7 ETM+.

Recovering procedures based on other concepts or methodologies were also discussed separately. Multi-scale segmentation approach was developed by Maxwell et al (2007) to fill gaps in the Landsat 7 SLC-off ETM+ images. By means of the geostatistical techniques, in which kriging or co-kriging was used, not only the value of the un-scanned pixels can be estimated, but also the uncertainty of the prediction can be quantified (Zhang et al.,2007; Pringle et al.,2009). Boloorani et al (2008b) developed a methodology called 'projection transformation'. A simple but effective method was proposed by J. Chen et al (2011) to fill the gaps, in which information about the neighbourhood similar pixels were incorporated for estimating the target un-scanned pixel. The recovered accuracy was improved consequently, especially in heterogeneous landscape areas (J. Chen et al., 2011).

As mentioned above, researches have been conducted widely for issues associated with recovering the Landsat 7 SLC-off ETM+ image, by interested individuals, institutions or organizations. However, while much attention has been paid to the reconstruction of its multispectral bands (e.g. visible and near infrared ones), few researches have been done to recover its thermal infrared band, although this band has been used widely, such as for urban heat island (X. L. Chen et al., 2006; Rajasekar & Weng, 2009), water environment (Wloczyk et al., 2006), volcanic activity (Flynn et al., 2001). Thus, the thermal infrared band of SLC-off ETM+ image should be useful for scientific applications, provided that a suitable recovering procedure is implemented(F. Chen et al., 2011). The modified AWLHM method was preliminarily proposed for recovering the thermal infrared band of Landsat 7 SLC-off ETM+ image, while the multispectral bands of CBERS were used as auxiliary data (F. Chen et al., 2011). Results illustrated this methodology's availability for getting brightness temperature directly from the SLC-off thermal infrared band. However, overestimation and underestimation were presented in cooler and warmer areas, respectively.

Moreover, in 2008, the USGS made a decision to make the Landsat standard data products freely available through the internet, which was served as a watershed event in the history of the Landsat program. This policy has triggered more and more studies by using Landsat series data, which had been limited previously by data costs and processing requirements. As stated by Wulder & Masek (2012), a special emphasis is placed on the burgeoning scientific and applications opportunities enabled by free access to the US archive, such as use of dense time-series data to characterize inter- and intra-annual land cover changes, new capabilities for continental-scale mapping, and applications focused on particular information needs. Meanwhile, the LDCM program, including the approaching launch of Landsat 8, and the proposed Landsat 9 and Landsat 10, will make sure the future continuity of the Landsat series, which is critical for understanding the Earth system and for providing a scientific basis for land management in the future. Nevertheless, the data gap for valid

Landsat 7 ETM+ data caused by the SLC-off problem, between 2003 and 2013, may prevent the full usage of the Landsat legacy to some extent.

In conclusion, further researches concerned on recovering the Landsat 7 SLC-off ETM+ image is necessary, mainly due to valuable legacy of the Landsat series and the freely distributed policy. In this chapter, we intend to review and show several solutions for making full use of the Landsat 7 SLC-off ETM+ image based on actual conditions, followed by methods comparison and discussion on the usage of the recovered ETM+ images.

2. The recovering approaches

As mentioned in the introduction (Section 1), different recovering approaches have been proposed based on different assumptions. Fig.2 shows an example of recovering SLC-off ETM+ image by using information from a precedent SLC-on ETM+ image. Under each ideal condition, recovered results were properly obtained, as illustrated in simulation studies. For practical application, these recovering approaches should be compared in depth, and thus the most suitable one should be selected at last.

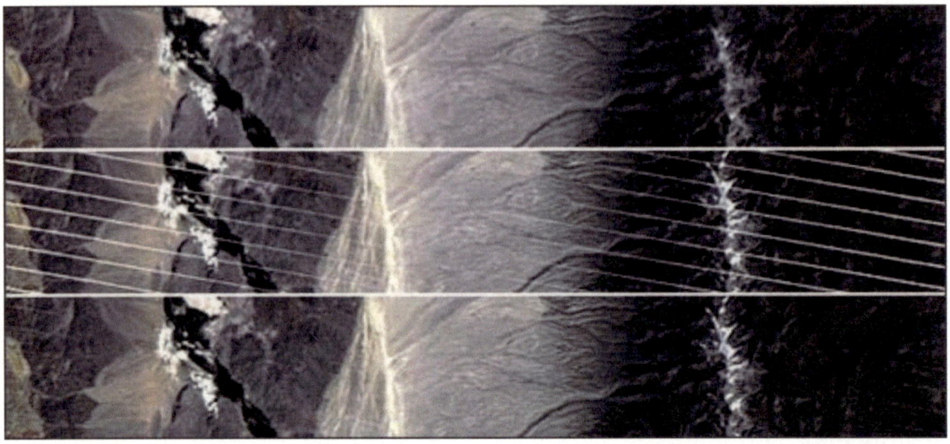

Figure 2. An example of recovering SLC-off ETM+ image: top image: Pre-SLC anomaly scene (SLC-on), middle image: Scene after SLC anomaly (SLC-off), bottom image: Scene after SLC anomaly, with interpolation. (Obtained from *http://landsathandbook.gsfc.nasa.gov/sysper/*)

2.1. GLHM and LLHM method

Soon after the SLC failed, experts from USGS initially provided two recovering methods, called GLHM and LLHM respectively, and they were served as the 'Phase One Methodology' (Scaramuzza et al., 2003).The basis for these methods is that linear relationship exists between one image and another, in view of band-by-band comparison, as shown in Fig.3. Generally, linear least squares estimate can be used to estimate the transformation parameters (e.g. gain and bias). For convenience, in the' Phase One Methodology', a simple procedure was adopted for calculating gain and bias (see equation (1)).

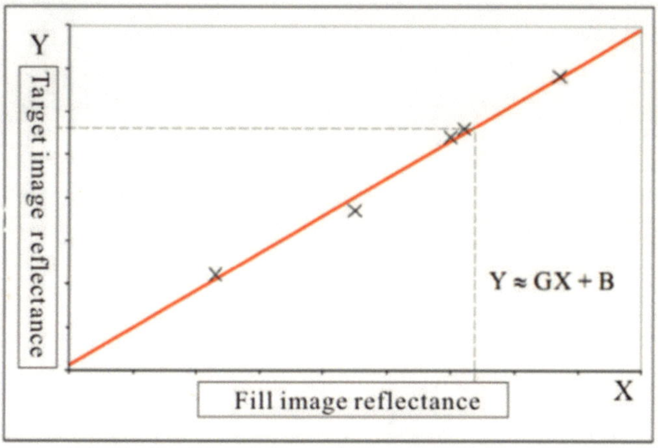

Figure 3. Linear model for GLHM method (modified from document (Scaramuzza et al., 2003) for illustration)

$$Y \approx gainX + bias \quad \text{with} \quad gain = \frac{\sigma_Y}{\sigma_X} \;;\; bias = \overline{Y} - gain\overline{X} \tag{1}$$

Where, X (also denoted $L(x_j, y_j, t_2, b)$ in following sections) is the pixel value in the fill image, and Y (also denoted $L(x_j, y_j, t_1, b)$ in the following sections) is the pixel value in the target image; σ_X is the standard deviation of the fill image, and σ_Y is the standard deviation of the target image; $\overline{X}$ is the mean of the fill image and $\overline{Y}$ is the mean of the target image.

When this transformation is applied to the entire image, it is called GLHM. GLHM is a very simple method, and all un-scanned pixels are estimated using the same gain and bias. It may perform well over scenes with invariant terrain such as deserts and rocky areas, but obviously visible errors are possible in scenes with transient. It is desirable to consider the inter-regional heterogeneity caused by factors such as atmosphere, topography, and land cover. For greater precision, gain and bias for estimating the un-scanned pixels can be calculated in a moving window around each un-scanned pixel, which is the original basis of the LLHM.

2.2. AWLHM method

'Phase Two Methodology' is an enhancement of the 'Phase One Methodology', which allows users to choose multiple images and to combine SLC-off images (USGS & NASA, 2004). AWLHM is an improved version of the LLHM. The AWLHM is based on the same assumption as LLHM, except that the moving window size is changeable. To obtain the correlation (or gain and bias) statistically, the number of effective pixels used for estimating each un-scanned pixel should be considered. The moving window around each un-scanned pixel should be adaptive according to the distribution of commonly scanned pixels (Fig.4). Based on the AWLHM method, the recovered image can be obtained through iteration process over all un-scanned pixels in the target image. Iteration for one un-scanned pixel is described as follows:

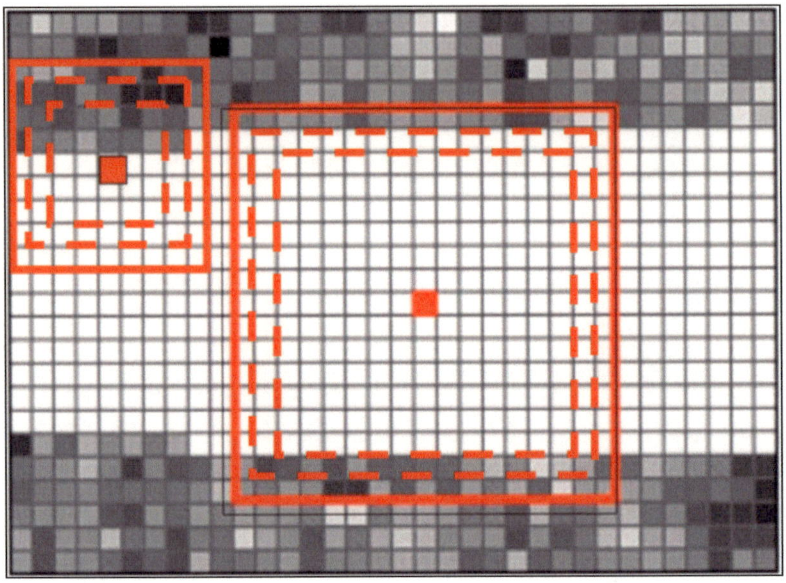

Figure 4. Illustration of the adaptive moving window process, the red pixels is the un-scanned ones needed to be recovered, and the rectangles with red dash lines represent the window searching process, while the red rectangles are the lastly determined windows (modified from document (USGS & NASA, 2004), just for methodology but not exact)

a. Extract an nxn window around the un-scanned pixel which is need to be recovered, in both target and fill images. Larger windows were found to yield essentially identical results but impose a significant performance penalty.
b. Find smallest square of pixels between the two blocks (windows in the fill image and the target one) which contains at least a minimum number of commonly scanned pixels (the valid data in both the target and fill images). Beginning with the smallest window size with 1x1 pixel, the number of valid common pixels between the target and the fill images is counted. If the minimum number of commonly scanned pixels is not met, the moving window size is expanded by one pixel on each side of the window. Then the commonly scanned pixels are counted again. The moving window is expanded gradually, with increasing size series, such as 3x3, 5x5, 7x7 ,…(Fig.4). Iteration continues until the minimum number of common pixels is met. If the minimum number of common pixels is not met before reaching the maximum extent of the window, all commonly scanned pixels in the moving window are used for obtaining the transformation parameters, regardless of the total number. In the 'Phase Two Methodology', the minimum number is defined as 144.
c. Using the common pixels in the lastly determined moving window around the un-scanned pixel, to estimate the bias and gain by means of the least squares solution for the linear equations, established based on the values of all selected common pixels in the moving window. It is necessary to check the estimated gain to see whether it is reasonable, and to prevent outliers from having a strong effect on the transform. If it is greater than the maximum allowable gain (Mgain) or less than the inverse (1/Mgain) of

the maximum allowable gain, then calculate gain and bias using the mean and standard deviation, just like the method mentioned in the 'Phase One Methodology'(Scaramuzza et al., 2003).

d. Estimate the value for the un-scanned pixel in the target SLC-off ETM+ image, using the linear relationship (see equation. (1)).

Complete this procedure for each un-scanned pixel in the target SLC-off ETM+ image, thus the recovered ETM+ image may be obtained. However, in some cases, there are still some un-scanned pixels remaining in the recovered image, resulted from many factors. Under this condition, the recovering procedure is need to be conducted again, and even several times, by assigning the lastly recovered image as target image and taking the other fill image or images to repeat the recovering process mentioned above.

Note that this method will encounter the problem for the proper window around the edges of the image, and expanding the extent of the image is needed thereby. In this study, a symmetrical extending procedure was implemented around the edges of the image with the length of 17 pixels, in order to make AWLHM available to estimate each un-scanned pixel including the marginal ones in the tested ETM+ SLC-off images.

Compared with GLHM and LLHM, the AWLHM is more rational; however, poor results are potentially suffered if the images being combined exhibit radical differences in target radiance. At the same time, the AWLHM can perform well when adjust the temporal changes happened in homogeneous areas such as agricultural field, airport (F. Chen et al., 2010), but it has difficulty when the size of the areas exhibiting change is too small. Generally, features smaller than the local window size (normally 19x19 pixels) are difficult to model if significant change occurred. That is why fill data are typically better matched in the large agricultural fields typical of the American Midwest and West than in the smaller fields of the Northeast and, presumably, much of Europe and Asia (USGS & NASA, 2004).Taking into account the shortcomings for AWLHM, especially for heterogeneous landscape, J. Chen et al (2011) proposed an improved method, referred to as the Neighbourhood Similar Pixel Interpolator (NSPI). More details on the NSPI method will be given in next section (Section2.3).

For obtaining recovered ETM+ image with good quality, selecting proper fill images is critical. According to the report written by USGS & NASA (2004), the most important criteria for selecting fill images are those related to the similarity of image content between the target and fill images. Any new data the similar fill image provide is likely to be of high quality, which will provide valuable additional information for transforming subsequent fill images. As suggested by USGS & NASA (2004), following guidelines for fill image selection are listed in order of priority:

a. Select fill images that are as free of clouds as possible and that contain as few obvious changes in image as possible.
b. Select SLC-off images that are as close time to target image as possible to minimize changes in vegetation conditions. Failing this, select fill images that are as close to an anniversary data as possible to take advantage of the similarities in seasonal vegetation cycles.

c. Select fill images that provide good predicted un-scanned coverage based on the un-scanned phase statistics.
d. Select SLC-off fill images that are within +/-4 WRS cycles of the target image, if possible.
e. For recovering image with multiple SLC-off images, including an anniversary date SLC-on image as the final fill image is recommended as a way of ensuring good image registration performance and providing complete un-scanned coverage.

2.3. NSPI method

The NSPI method is a simple but effective one, for estimating the values of un-scanned pixels in SLC-off ETM+ image. It is based on the assumption that the same-class neighbouring pixels around the un-scanned pixel have similar spectral characteristics, and that these neighbouring pixels and un-scanned ones exhibit similar temporal change patterns. Thus , as found in the initial research based on simulated and actual experiments, the NSPI method can restore the value of un-scanned pixels very accurately, and even performs well in heterogeneous areas(J. Chen et al., 2011). Another advantage of the NSPI method is that it can work well even if there is a relatively long time interval or obvious spectral changes between the fill and target images. Compared with the original AWLHM method, the NSPI method incorporates several other sub- procedures, including selection of neighbouring similar pixels, calculation of the weights for similar pixels, calculation of the target pixel value in view of temporal differences.

2.3.1. Selection of neighboring similar pixels

As same as AWLHM method, all commonly scanned pixels in the determined adaptive moving window around the un-scanned pixel (target pixel) are selected. Then, similar pixels are selected from these common pixels based on spectral similarity, which is defined as root mean square deviation (RMSD) between each common pixel and the target one.

$$RMSD_i = \sqrt{\frac{\sum_{b=1}^{n}(L(x_i,y_i,t_1,b) - L(x,y,t_1,b))^2}{n}} \tag{2}$$

Where, $L(x_i,y_i,t_1,b)$ are the value of common pixel i, which locates in (x_i,y_i), in band b for the fill image acquired at time t_1, while $L(x,y,t_1,b)$ is for the target pixel locating in (x,y); and n is the number of spectral bands. Larger RMSD value denotes larger spectral difference.

According to previous research conducted by Gao et al (2006), common pixels with lower RMSD values than the predefined threshold are identified as the similar ones:

$$RMSD_i \le \left[\sum_{b=1}^{n}\sigma(b) \times 2 / m\right] / n \tag{3}$$

Where, $\sigma(b)$ is the standard deviation of the entire fill image for band b, and m is the number of classes, which is a predefined value according to the complexity of the landscape.

Requirement for the minimum number (M) of similar pixels in the moving window is also need predefinition. Then, the initial moving window size can be estimated, and the number of selected similar pixels in this initial window is counted. Expanding the window iteratively, as described in Section 2.2, until either the requirement for minimum number of similar pixels (M) is met, or the window reaches the maximum size.

2.3.2. *Calculation of the weights for similar pixels*

The contribution of the selected similar pixels to the prediction of target pixel might vary according to their spectral similarity, temporal change difference and geographic distance related to the target pixel. Generally, similar pixels with higher spectral similarity and smaller distance to the target pixel are more important than other ones. The geographic distance between the j th similar pixel (x_j, y_j) and the target pixel (x, y) is calculated in Euclid space:

$$D_j = \sqrt{(x_j - x)^2 + (y_j - y)^2} \tag{4}$$

Then, the weight indicating the contribution of similar pixel j to the prediction of the target pixel is calculated by following equation:

$$W_j = (1/(RMSD_j \times D_j)) / \sum_{j=1}^{N} 1/(RMSD_j \times D_j) \tag{5}$$

The weight indicator W_j is a normalized one, with the range from 0 to 1. For the special situation, when some similar pixels have the same or distinct spectral characteristics as the target pixel, that is to say, their spectral similarities RMSD are 0, then the weight for the special pixels is set to an equal value, and all the information is given by these special similar pixels.

2.3.3. *Calculation of the target pixel value*

According to the statements by J. Chen et al (2011), two procedures can be used to estimate the target pixel value using the information provided by the similar pixels separately. However, the integrated value based on the two predictions is possibly more reliable (J. Chen et al., 2011).

The first method is based on the fact that the similar pixels have the same or at least approximate spectral value with the target pixel when they are observed at the same time, and the weighted average of all the similar pixels in the target image (SLC-off one) is calculated.

$$L_1(x,y,t_2,b)=\sum_{j=1}^{N} W_j \times L(x_j,y_j,t_2,b) \tag{6}$$

At the same time, it is rational that the value (e.g. radiance, reflectance) of the target pixel at t_2 (the acquisition time of the target SLC-off image) is the sum of its value at t_1 (the acquisition time of the fill image) and the temporal spectra difference between t_1 and t_2. It is also acceptable in most cases that the similar pixels undergo the similar temporal change as the target one. Then, the second method for estimating the target pixel value at t_2 is developed, by using the change information provided by the similar pixels:

$$L_2(x,y,t_2,b)=L(x,y,t_1,b)+\sum_{j=1}^{N} W_j \times (L(x_j,y_j,t_2,b)-L(x_j,y_j,t_1,b)) \tag{7}$$

Predicted values with more accuracy may be obtained by integrating these two estimated results, with a suitable weight framework, in which both the landscape heterogeneity and the temporal change are incorporated. In the work of J. Chen et al (2011), the averaged RMSD between the similar pixels and the target pixel ($RMSD_1$, see equation (8)) was used to indicate the heterogeneity, while the averaged RMSD of similar pixels between observations at t_1 and t_2 ($RMSD_2$, see equation(9)) is used to denote the temporal change between two images:

$$RMSD_1=\frac{1}{N}\sum_{j=1}^{N}\sqrt{\left[\sum_{b=1}^{n}(L(x_j,y_j,t_1,b)-L(x,y,t_1,b))^2\right]/n} \tag{8}$$

$$RMSD_2=\frac{1}{N}\sum_{j=1}^{N}\sqrt{\left[\sum_{b=1}^{n}(L(x_j,y_j,t_1,b)-L(x_j,y_j,t_2,b))^2\right]/n} \tag{9}$$

The combined weights are calculated through a normalized process，shown as follows：

$$T_1=(1/RMSD_1)/(1/RMSD_1+1/RMSD_2) \tag{10}$$

$$T_2=(1/RMSD_2)/(1/RMSD_1+1/RMSD_2) \tag{11}$$

Finally, the estimated value for the target pixel is an integrated result combined two initial results and two combined weights:

$$L(x,y,t_2,b)=T_1 \times L_1(x,y,t_2,b)+T_2 \times L_2(x,y,t_2,b) \tag{12}$$

However, it is worth to note that when there is no similar pixel selected, the AWLHM method（see Section 2.2）can be applied to estimate the value of the un-scanned pixel.

2.4. Projection transformation method

A recovering method based on projection transformation was evaluated through a simulated experiment, which called the PCT-gap-fill method (Boloorani et al., 2008b). The principal component transformation (PCT), which can make new representative data sets of the original ones, is mathematically lossless and vigorous invertible transformation. Over the obtained new components, if transformation be carried out, the original data sets can be recovered with no loss. The PCT-gap-fill method is to recover the un-scanned areas in the target image based on the scanned pixels from the fill image. Generally, this recovering procedure is mainly based on forward and backward principle component transformations. When the target and the fill images both have been normalized, such as transformed to reflectance, the PCT-gap-fill method can be applied as follows (Boloorani et al., 2008b):

a. Extract the scanned pixels in the target SLC-off image, and calculate the needed statistics for inverted PCT based on these pixels.
b. Extract the scanned pixels in the fill image, which were un-scanned in the target image, and apply the PCT to these selected pixels to get the transformed ones (denoted TFs).
c. Inversely transform the TFs using the statistics obtained from the scanned pixels in the target image (in step a.),to make new values for those pixels (NITFs) in the fill image selected in step b, then the un-scanned pixels in the target image can be recovered by means of setting the geospatially corresponding NITFs to them.

The step a. is important, where the scanned pixels in the target image need to be selected carefully due to the crucial role they play in the recovering procedure. In fact, the pixels selected for transformation statistics can be gotten either from the whole scanned area in the fill image or some samples of it. As suggested by Boloorani et al (2008b), the selected samples must be the real representative of the physical phenomena from the land surface. The previously simulated experiment shows that the PCT-gap-fill method recovered the SLC-off image with higher accuracy than the LLHM method, and preserved the radiometric characteristics better even in the areas with sharp radiometric changes. However, the simulated result also demonstrated that the gap lines were still visible in areas with sharp radiometric differences. The findings from this analysis based on simulated SLC-off image, provide a new concept for recovering the Landsat 7 SLC-off ETM+ image by means of data transformation, such as PCT, which is able to estimate the un-scanned pixels fully using the multispectral bands (e.g. Band 1-5, 7). Therefore, it is possible that the values of one specific un-scanned pixel in all bands can be estimated simultaneously by inverted PCT. Nevertheless, some other methods just are able to recover the Landsat 7 SLC-off ETM+ image band-by-band. In view of convenience for application, this methodology based on transformation is a good choice, given that several related problems is tackled properly, such as for heterogeneous area with sharp radiometric difference, the incorporation of the moving window tech.

2.5. Geostatistical method

Initially, the GLHM, LLHM and AWLHM methods were developed based on the basic assumption that there is a linear relationship between the target image and the fill one or ones. Thus, several images (SLC-on or SLC-off) need to be selected properly as the fill images for recovering the target SLC-off ETM+ image. The most important criteria for selecting suitable fill images are cloud free and associated with time interval. However , in fact, these criteria are difficult to meet, especially for regions with moist environment. Under this condition, the GLHM , LLHM and AWLHM methods are limited to use consequently. On the basis that the autocorrelation is one of the predominant phenomena in physical geography, pixels in a specific extent may correlate with each other to a certain degree. So, it is possible to estimate un-scanned pixels based on the pixel relationship rules within the image itself, and this methodology is served as interpolation. General interpolation methods, such as inverse distance weighted methods and triangulation methods may be not suitable for recovering un-scanned pixels in the SLC-off image, because information about spatial structure is not used fully by these interpolation methods. Understanding the magnitude and pattern in spatial variability is necessary for accurately interpolating the un-scanned pixels. Zhang et al (2007) and Pringle et al (2009) discussed the possibility that using geostatistical techniques (e.g. kriging methods) to resolve the un-scanned pixels issue, which provides unbiased estimation with minimum and known error.

As mentioned above, the fundamental idea of geostatistics is the first law of geography, that spatial data from locations close to each other are more similar than data from locations far apart. Variogram used to indicate the spatial structure can be applied to estimate values at un-sampled locations (here, are un-scanned pixels in SLC-off ETM+ image).

Variogram model the spatial dependence in a regionalized variable Z (here is reflectance, radiance or digital number (DN) in SLC-off ETM+ image) under the 'intrinsic' hypothesis that the increments ($Z(x_i, y_i, h) - Z(x_i, y_i)$) associated with a small distance h are weakly stationary (Zhang et al., 2007). For multispectral image, in practice, a semivariogram is computed using the values in each band, shown as follows:

$$\gamma(h) = \frac{1}{2N(h)} \sum_{i=1}^{N(h)} [Z(x_i, y_i) - Z(x_i, y_i, h)]^2 \tag{13}$$

Where, $N(h)$ is the number of pairs of pixel locating with h apart, and distance h is defined in Euclidean space. The larger value of $\gamma(h)$ indicate the pixel pairs distributing apart with h distance are less similar.

Similarly, in view of the two co-dependent variables, the joint spatial dependence is common, and is often modelled using a cross-semivariogram, shown as follows:

$$\gamma(h) = \frac{1}{2N(h)} \sum_{i=1}^{N(h)} [Z_1(x_i, y_i) - Z_1(x_i, y_i, h)] \bullet [Z_2(x_i, y_i) - Z_2(x_i, y_i, h)] \tag{14}$$

Where, Z_1 and Z_2 represents values in image 1 and image 2 (here referred to the target image and the fill image), respectively. Unlike semivariogram models, the cross-semivariogram may have negative values because of a negative cross-correlation between the two images.

The calculated semivariogram (cross-semivariogram) values based on the sampled pixels according to equations mentioned above, need to be fit for its further application in kriging.

Mathematical models frequently used for fitting semivariogram include nugget effect model, spherical model, exponent model, Gaussian model and power model. At the same time, for fitting cross-semivariogram, the basic models usually used are linear, spherical and exponential models.

Kriging is a family of generalized least-square regression algorithms that take advantage of the spatial dependence information given by the variogram. Ordinary kriging is the most common and robust one, which is able to rescale locally the random function model to a different mean value in different locations (Zhang et al., 2007). For estimating an un-scanned pixel (x_i, y_i) in the SLC-off ETM+ image, pixels locating in the local neighbourhood are only used, and the extent of the neighbourhood is determined by semivariogram. Therefore, the value of pixel (x_i, y_i) (denoted $Z_{OK}(x_i, y_i)$) is estimated through a linear model:

$$Z_{OK}(x_i, y_i) = \sum_{j=1}^{n} \lambda_j^{(OK)}(x_i, y_i) Z(x_j, y_j) \quad \text{with} \quad \sum_{j=1}^{n} \lambda_j^{(OK)}(x_i, y_i) = 1 \tag{15}$$

Where, $\lambda_j^{(OK)}(x_i, y_i)$ is the ordinary kriging weight for the pixel j locating in the neighbourhood of pixel (x_i, y_i), of which the value needs to be estimated, and n is the number of pixels locating in the neighbourhood of pixel (x_i, y_i).The ordinary kriging estimator is unbiased by forcing the kriging weights to sum to 1(see equation (15)).

Cokriging is an extended version of kriging, which incorporates more than one variable in the estimating procedure. Thus, generally, it can improve the accuracy, particularly when the primary variable is sparse and poorly correlated in space compared to the secondary one. Both the autocorrelation in each variable and the cross-correlation between the variables are taken into consideration in cokriging method. The value of pixel (x_i, y_i) (denoted $Z_{COK}(x_i, y_i)$) estimated by means of cokriging method is expressed as follows:

$$Z_{COK}(x_i, y_i) = \sum_{j=1}^{n1} \lambda_j^{(COK)}(x_i, y_i) Z(x_j, y_j) + \sum_{jj=1}^{n2} \lambda_{jj}^{(COK)}(x_i, y_i) Z_S(x_{jj}, y_{jj})$$

$$\text{With} \quad \sum_{j=1}^{n1} \lambda_j^{COK}(x_i, y_i) = 1 \quad \text{and} \quad \sum_{jj=1}^{n2} \lambda_{jj}^{COK}(x_i, y_i) = 0 \tag{16}$$

Where, $\lambda_j^{(COK)}(x_i, y_i)$ is the ordinary cokriging weight for the pixel j locating in the neighbourhood of pixel (x_i, y_i) for the primary variable, and n1 is the number of pixels locating in the neighbourhood of pixel (x_i, y_i) for the primary variable. Similarly, $\lambda_{jj}^{(COK)}(x_i, y_i)$ is the ordinary cokriging weight for the pixel jj locating in the neighbourhood of pixel (x_i, y_i) for the secondary variable, and n2 is the number of pixels locating in the neighbourhood of pixel (x_i, y_i) for the secondary variable.

As illustrated above (see equations (15) and (16)), two procedures are needed for estimating the value of the un-scanned pixel in advance, including determining the extent of local neighbourhood and thereby the valid sampling pixels, and calculating the kriging weights for each neighbourhood valid sampling pixel. Ordinarily, these procedures especially the last one need much time. The simplified versions for both ordinary kriging and cokriging were proposed for tackling the SLC-off issue by Zhang et al (2007), which are faster.

Extent of the local neighbourhood is mainly defined based on the variogram, which are well-structured and can be fitted well due to the abundant data available in the SLC-off ETM+ image (about 80%).The specific pattern of the un-scanned pixels makes it possible to recover the SLC-off ETM+ image accurately, which was verified by Zhang et al (2007). Mean while, the case study showed that the cokriging method provided little improvement in estimating the un-scanned pixels in the SLC-off ETM+ image compared with the ordinary kriging method(Zhang et al., 2007). That is to say, similar results were obtained by these two approaches separately. The ordinary kriging allows users to extract the maximum information from the individual scene of the SLC-off ETM+ image by considering spatial variability and dependence, and it also overcomes the inherent problems caused by radiometric differences and small georeferencing errors possibly suffered in the GLHM, LLHM and AWLHM methods.

However, according to the statement of Pringle et al (2009), ordinary kriging and cokriging can be used complementarily to interpolate the value of un-scanned pixels in the SLC-off images. In detail, cokriging can be implemented by default and kriging is used in some sub-regions where the secondary variable is under-sampled. The recovered experiment based on the geostatistical method and two fill images (both are cloud-free), of which one was collected a few weeks earlier than the target image and the other one was collected a few weeks later, demonstrated the superiority of the geostatistics to several compositing methods and the improved prediction of cokriging method in the sub-regions where the secondary variable was more numerous than the target one (Pringle et al., 2009).

These previous researches suggest that the geostatistical method, especially the ordinary kriging is a good alternative to these traditional methods (e.g. the GLHM, LLHM and AWLHM) for predicting the values of un-scanned pixels in the SLC-off ETM+ image, especially for regions where suitable fill images are difficult to obtain, mainly resulted from weather conditions, cloud and temporal interval between images acquisition. Also, as shown in the previous results, main reasons for the advantages of geostatistics are including, (1) all un-scanned pixels in the SLC-off image are able to be recovered; (2) recovered results agree more strongly with the observations, even when there is an abrupt temporal changes; (3) for each recovered pixel, geostatistical method provides an estimation variance associated with uncertainty. However, the disadvantages of the geostatistical method in recovering the SLC-off ETM+ image are associated with its relatively slow speed and the selection of neighbourhood pixels for kriging weights. To solve its disadvantage in time consuming, Pringle et al (2009) proposed a hybrid technique. Additionally, further research is needed to find how many valid pixels in local neighbour is most suitable for estimating the un-scanned pixel, considering the specific spatial distribution characteristics of the un-scanned pixels in the SLC-off ETM+ image (Zhang et al., 2007).

2.6. Using images from other sensors

As mentioned before, selecting the fill image is crucial for recovering the SLC-off ETM+ image, and that cloud free images (SLC-on or SLC-off) acquired temporally close to the target image are desirable. But, for regions with moist environment the valid fill images are few. Consequently, due to the limitation of data acquisition, e.g. temporal resolution and atmospheric condition, there are always a large number of overlapping areas filled with un-scanned pixels in two cloud-free SLC-off ETM+ images which are close in time. Ordinary kriging has been illustrated as a good tool for tackling this issue (Zhang et al., 2007). However, as an alternative to ordinary kriging, the image from a sensor other than Landsat 7 ETM+, which is observed at the close time as the target SLC-off ETM+ image, may be able to be used to estimate the un-scanned pixels. This assumption has been verified by several previous researches. For example, Reza and Ali (2008) used IRS products, Boloorani et al (2008a) and F. Chen et al (2010) adopted EO-1/ALI and CBERS data as auxiliary information, respectively, while Roy et al (2008) used the information observed by MODIS.

Our experiments conducted on exploiting CBERS data as the fill image are shown here. All provided bands (totally four) of CBERS-02B CCD sensor have a spatial resolution of approximately 20m. There is similarity more or less between CBERS-02B CCD and Landsat7 ETM+ VNIR bands (Fig.5.) as well as the medium spatial resolution of each band, which makes it possible to estimate the un-scanned pixels in the ETM+ SLC-off image considering the CBERS-02B as the fill image. After the main procedures, including image resampling, geometrical registration, radiometric correction, several methods (e.g. Simple Filling, GLHM, LLHM, and AWLHM) were applied. Findings show the availability that using CBERS image as the fill data, and the superiority of AWLHM compared to the rest methods. However, further researches should be conducted, such as recovering all multispectral bands of SLC-off ETM+, and improving the estimated accuracy in urban or sub-urban areas with obvious heterogeneity.

Generally, AWLHM along with CBERS-02B estimated un-scanned pixels well around which the neighborhood was relatively homogeneous, however, was less accurate for pixels in the context of heterogeneous land use/cover. It is clear that the procedure performed well near the International Airport (Fig.6 (B2), (B4)) but less properly near the mixture places (Fig.6 (U2), (U4)) with incompatible appearance, no matter which date is considered. Setting recovered results of ETM+ 021 as an example, Fig.7 demonstrates that the linear relationship is less proper between pixels around P1 in SLC-off ETM+ and corresponding ones in CBERS-02B, compared with the good linear relationship for the relatively homogeneous neighborhood around P2, shown in Fig.8. The imprecise relationship might impact the accuracy of estimation at P1.These findings suggest the necessity to resolve the issues associated with heterogeneity to recover the SLC-off images in urban and sub-urban regions. According to the previous researches, ideas incorporated into the NSPI method (J. Chen et al., 2011) may be worth learning.

Another problem is that the number of multispectral bands validly provided by CBERS (here is CBERS-02B) is less than that of Landsat 7 ETM+. It may limit the full usage of the recovered results; because recovering procedures are always operated band-by-band, except the recovering method based on projection transformation (see Section 2.4). The simple method by using the intra-bands relationship is possible, in addition to the methodology based on projection transformation. Reza and Ali (2008) adopted the simple method to fully recover the multispectral bands of the SLC-off ETM+ image using IRS/1D LISS-III as the fill image through two stages.

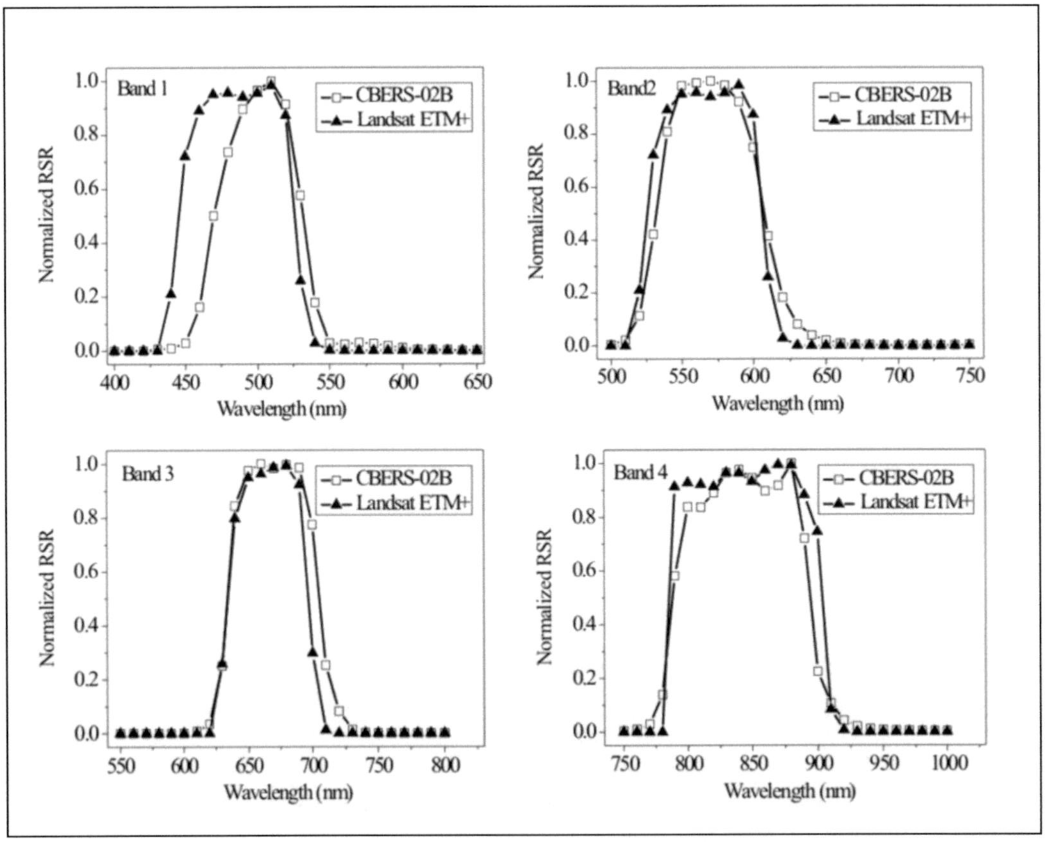

Figure 5. Comparison of relative spectral response (RSR) between CBERS-02B and ETM+ (Original data were provided by CRESDA (*www.cresda.com*) and NASA respectively, and each ETM+ RSR exhibited above was resampled to a spectral resolution of 10nm so as to compare)

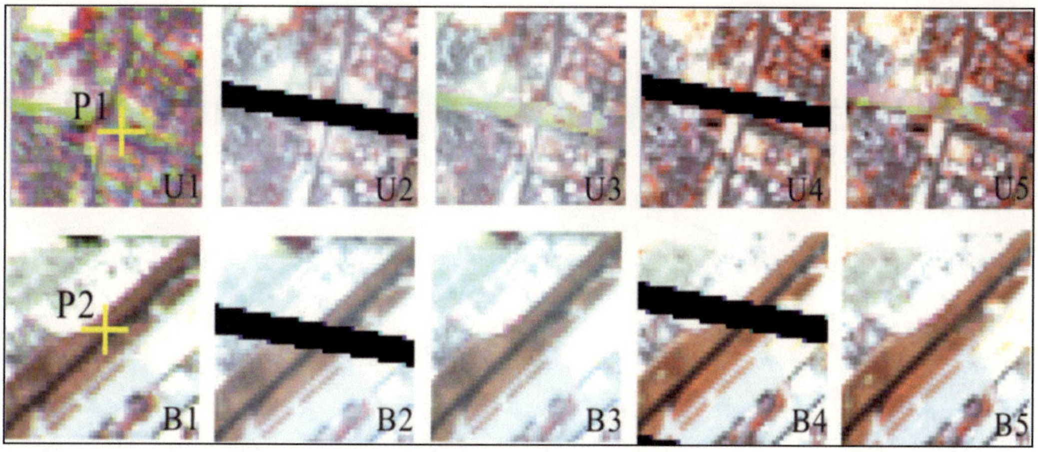

Figure 6. Detailed exhibition of small extracts (R:band4,G:band3,B:band2) (U1:from CBERS-02B，U2:from original ETM+ 021,U3:from recovered ETM+021,U4:from original ETM+ 309,U5: from recovered ETM+ 309; B1:from CBERS-02B,B2:from original ETM+021,B3:from recovered ETM+ 021,B4:from original ETM+ 309,B5:from recovered ETM+ 309) (in F. Chen, et al., 2010)

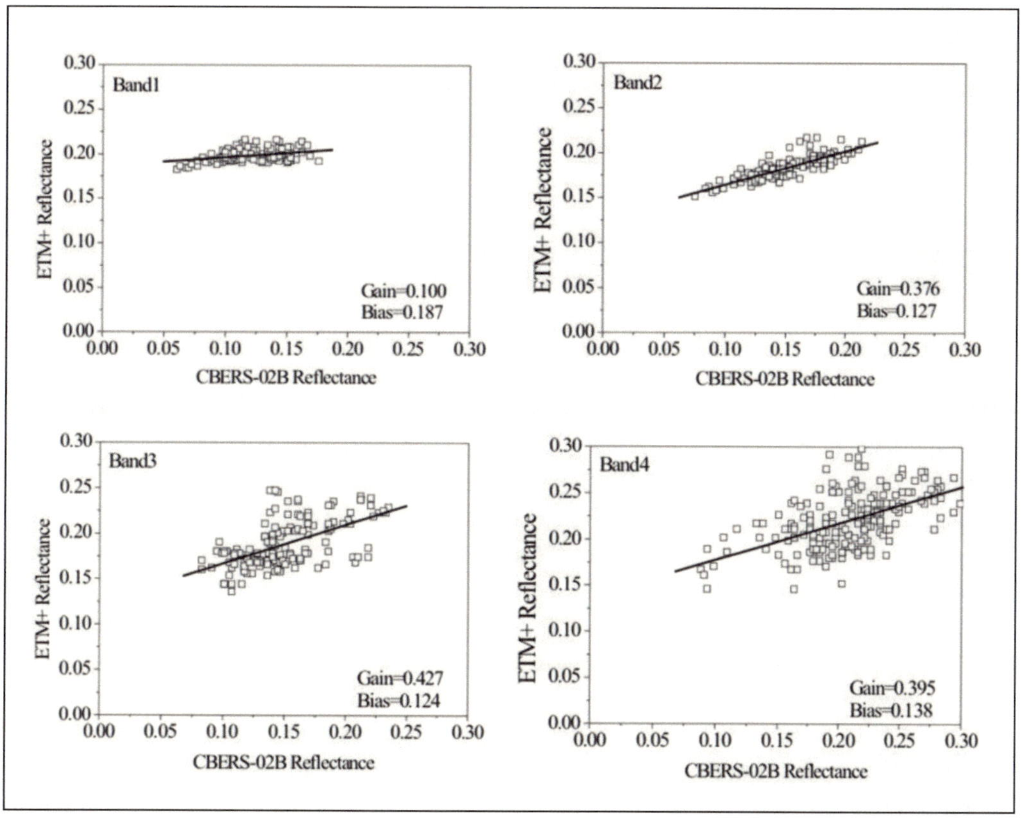

Figure 7. Scatter plots of corresponding bands for scanned pixels around P1 (in F. Chen, et al., 2010)

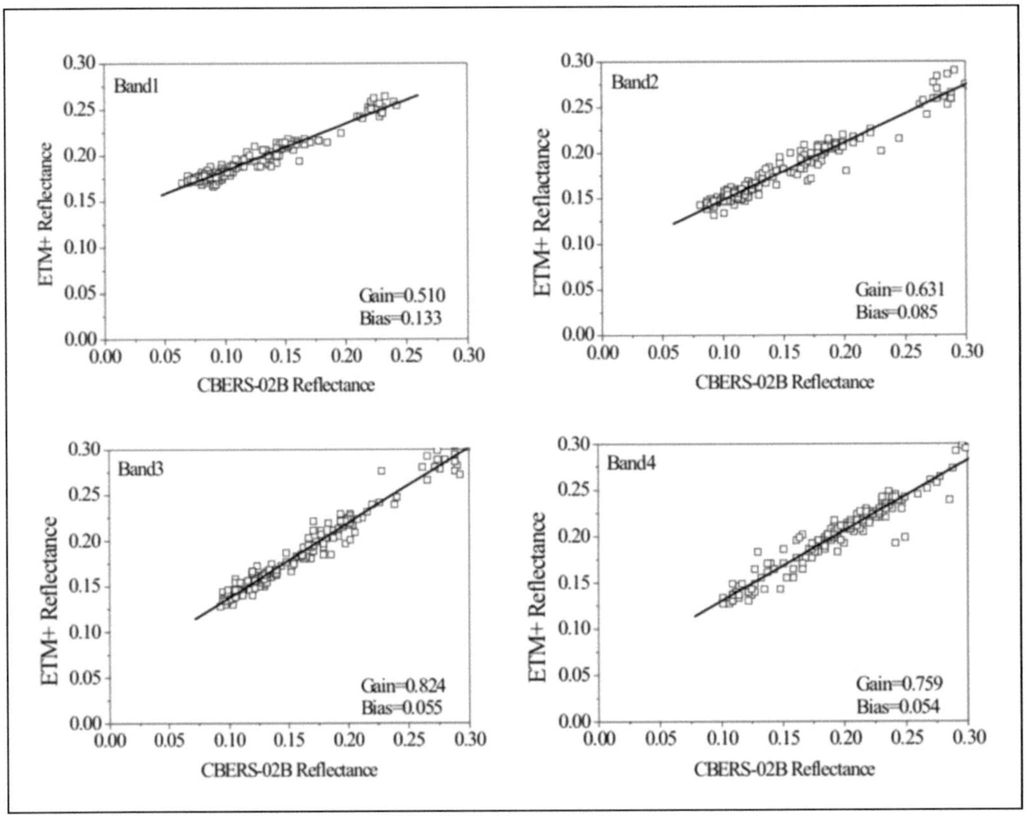

Figure 8. Scatter plots of corresponding bands for scanned pixels around P2 (F. Chen, et al., 2010)

MODIS is another data resource considered as the fill image. Landsat 7 ETM+ bands and the corresponding bands of MODIS are shown in Table 1. Roy et al (2008) indicated the possibility that recovering the SLC-off ETM+ image by means of a semi-physical fusion approach, when the MODIS BRDF/Albedo land surface characterization product was used as auxiliary data. Detailed analysis demonstrated the major advantages of this fusion method, the simplicity for application and the ability in accommodating for temporal variations due to surface change (Roy et al., 2008). The main disadvantages of this method are related to the requirement on adequate data co-registration, computation of geometry and the obvious scale discrepancy between MODIS BRDF/Albedo product and the Landsat 7 ETM+ data. Nevertheless, MODIS provides one more chance for recovering the SLC-off ETM+ image, mainly due to the abundant images it provides. Therefore, further researches are required to tackle the associated issues, then to make the full advantages of MODIS.

Band number of ETM+	Band wavelength(nm)	Band number of MODIS	Band wavelength(nm)
1	450-520	3	459-479
2	530-610	4	545-565
3	630-690	1	620-670
4	780-900	2	841-876
5	1550-1750	6	1628-1652
7	2090-2350	7	2105-2155

Table 1. The multispectral bands of Landsat 7 ETM+ and the corresponding ones of MODIS

2.7. Integrated method

According to previous comparisons, each method has its own relative advantages and disadvantages, compared with other ones. For example, geostatistical method is generally superior to several methods based on the linear relationship (e.g. GLHM, LLHM and AWLHM), but it consumes much more time. Mean while, data obtained by other sensors instead of ETM+ may provide useful auxiliary information for recovering the SLC-off ETM+ image, but the differences between these sensors and ETM+ should be considered, which are related to sensor geometry, spatial resolution, band settings, and so on. Pringle et al (2009) proposed a hybrid technique which incorporates the simple ones with the geostatistical method. For example, after implementing the LLHM the rest un-scanned pixels in the SLC-off ETM+ image can be estimated by means of kriging or cokriging (Pringle et al., 2009).

2.8. Recovering the thermal band of SLC-off ETM+ image

Currently, there have been few researches done to resolve the SLC-off thermal band image, although it had been used widely, as shown in Section 1. A method called the modified AWLHM (see Fig.9)was proposed to fill the gaps in the thermal band of SLC-off ETM+ image, while data obtained by other sensors are used as fill image (here is CBERS).The experiment shows the possibility that using the modified AWLHM method and suitable band combinations to recover the thermal band of SLC-off ETM+ image. While giving the priority to the accuracy, it is more rational and practicable to get brightness temperature directly than to inverse brightness temperature from the recovered thermal band. Based on the detailed analysis on the validation results, we can assume that it is practicable to implement the recovered thermal band in the study of urban thermal environment, with certainty to some extent. However, further researches need to be done to enable more scientific use of the thermal band of SLC-off ETM+ data.

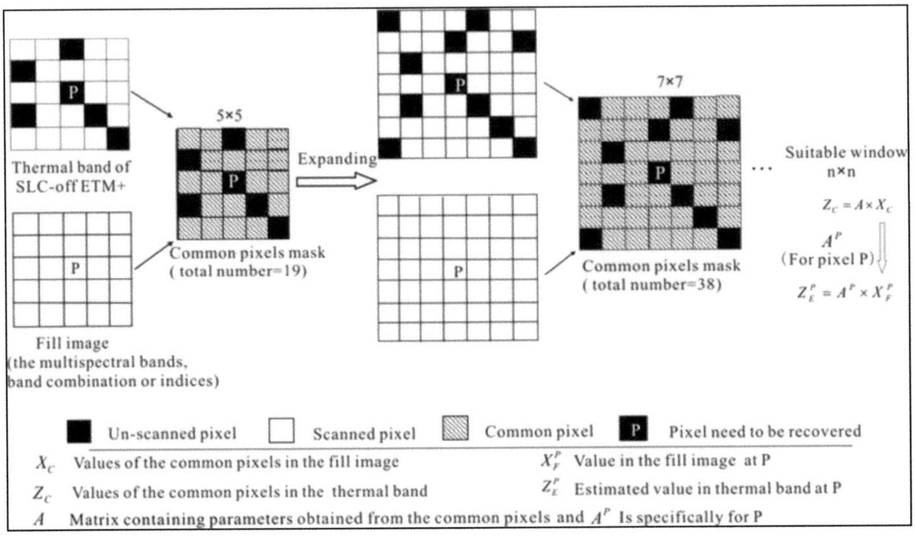

Figure 9. Schematic diagram of the modified AWLHM method for thermal band (in F. Chen, et al., 2011a)

3. Experiments and applications

The possible usage of the recovered ETM+ images either the multispectral bands or the thermal band is an important issue when talking about recovering the SLC-off ETM+ image. However, few researches associated have discussed the possible application of the recovered images. For example, Boloorani et al (2008b) and J. Chen et al (2011) demonstrated the possibility of applying the recovered multispectral bands in land cover/use classification, although they just conducted these studies based on the simulated data. F. Chen et al (2010) recovered two SLC-off ETM+ images acquired at different times and demonstrated the usage of the recovered images in mapping urban impervious surface. The possible usage of the recovered thermal band in urban thermal environment study was discussed (F. Chen et al., 2011a), while its application has also been illustrated (F. Chen et al., 2011b).

Fig.10 shows two recovered ETM+ images for Xiamen Island, locating in Fujian Province, China, which is highly urbanized. Urban impervious surface modelled from these recovered images indicates that similar estimation accuracy was obtained at the filled pixels and scanned ones, as shown in Fig.11 (F. Chen et al, 2010).

Fig.12 shows the simulated results of recovering the SLC-off thermal band. The recovered results are visually acceptable, even in high-contrast areas. Furthermore, the validation reveals that unbiased estimation can be obtained through our recovering procedure at most of the un-scanned pixels (about 80%) in the thermal band (Chen et al, 2011). According to these findings, we confidently assume that the recovered thermal band can be applied in the issues associated with urban thermal environment. Several recovered thermal bands were applied in urban thermal environment studies (F. Chen et al., 2011b). Fig.13 demonstrates the land surface temperature results obtained from four recovered SLC-off thermal bands.

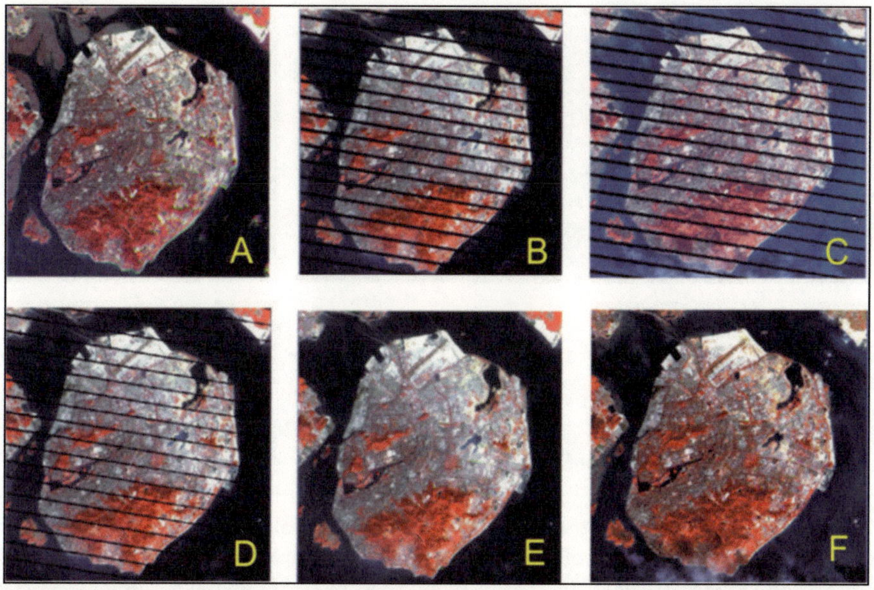

Figure 10. RGB colour composite of the recovered and original ETM+ images and CBERS-02B ((A) CBERS-02B; (B) original ETM+021; (C) original ETM+309; (D) recovered ETM+309 using ETM+ 021 as auxiliary data; (E) recovered ETM+021 using CBERS-02B as auxiliary data; (F) recovered ETM+309 using CBERS-02B as auxiliary data) (in F. Chen, et al., 2010)

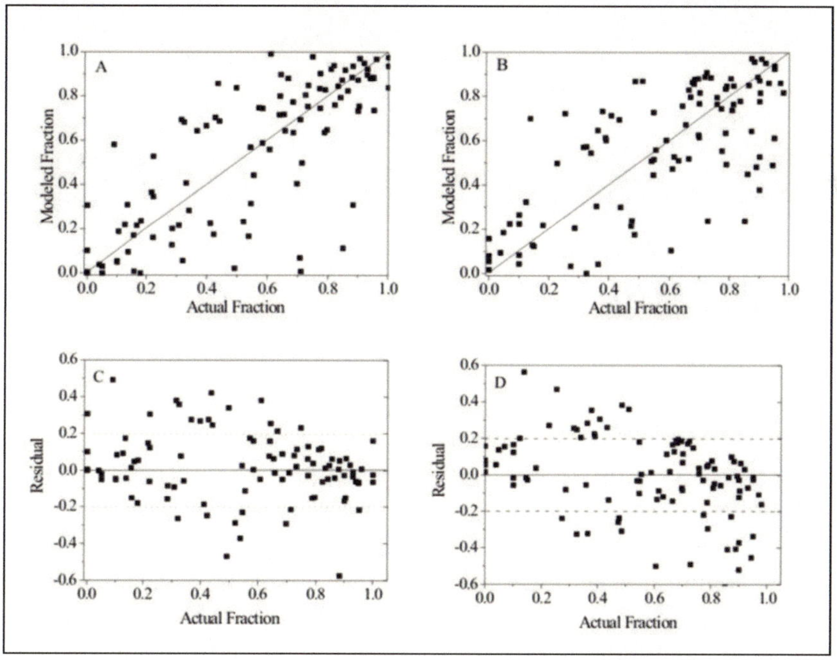

Figure 11. Results of UIS estimation accuracy assessment for recovered ETM+ 021: (A) accuracy assessment for filled pixels; (B) accuracy assessment for scanned pixels; (C) residual analysis for filled pixels; (D) residual analysis for scanned pixels (in F. Chen, et al., 2010)

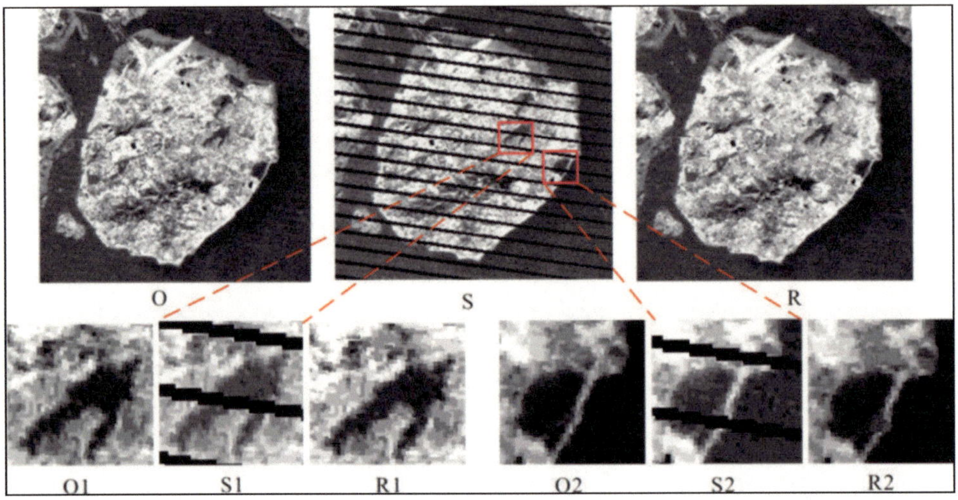

Figure 12. Simulated experiment on recovering the SLC-off thermal band (O): the original one acquired on January 2, 2002, (S): the simulated one obtained by using the gap mask of another SLC-off ETM+ image (acquired on January 21, 2009), (R): the recovered results based on the modified AWLHM method. Additionally, (O1), (S1), (R1), (O2), (S2) and (R2) are extracted parts for illustration (in F. Chen, et al., 2011a)

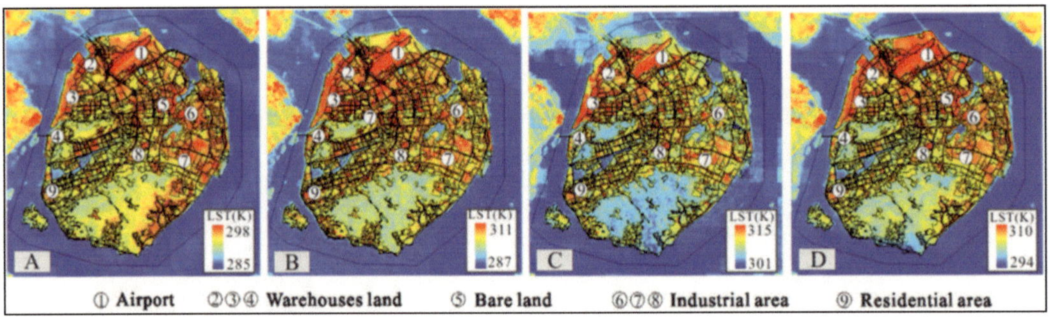

Figure 13. Spatial distribution of LST over Xiamen Island at different times (A, B, C and D are for 21 January, 11 April, 16 July and 5 November, 2009 respectively), and the overlying layer is the detailed land use map digitized manually from the sharpened IKONOS image (in F. Chen, et al., 2012b)

4. Discussion and conclusion

Since the launch of its first satellite in 1972, Landsat mission has continuously and consistently collected images of Earth with global coverage, due to the continuous series (see Fig.1). The moderate spatial resolution of the Landsat sensors is important for scientists or common users, because it is either coarse enough for observing global environment or detailed enough for monitoring human-scale processes. This specifically spatial resolution is sensitive to both natural and human changes, although abundant information is missing for some individual objects. The special characteristics, both data archive with long history and suitable spatial resolution, make the Landsat an important tool, which gives scientist the ability to assess environment changes happened or is happing at local, regional and global scales. Therefore, as NASA administrator Dr. James Fletcher predicted in 1975, if one space age development would save the world, it would be Landsat and its successor satellites (*http://landsat.gsfc.nasa.gov/about/*).

In addition, based on the free data policy announced in 2008, all new and archived Landsat data held by the USGS have been made freely obtainable over the internet for any user (Woodcock, et al., 2008). In the short time since this policy was put into effect, significant benefits are already being realized within the Landsat data user community (Loveland & Dwyer, 2012). So, it is highly possible that Landsat data will experience more widespread usage especially for long-term and large-area environmental issues. Furthermore, the subsequent Landsat satellites (e.g. Landsat 8, Landsat 9, and Landsat 10 and so on) make the possibility to be realized. As Loveland & Dwyer states, the next few years are quite possibly going to be Landsat' s 'golden years' and could be the time in which the Landsat program achieves its full potential (Loveland & Dwyer, 2012).

However, the SLC failure of Landsat 7 ETM+ sensor occurred in 2003 may impact the Landsat data archive to some extent, and even results in a data gap period, especially under the condition that Landsat 5 has also suffered problems with its solar array drive sometimes and the failure of its electronic component currently. Therefore, suitable ways are desirable to resolve the SLC-off problem accurately and robustly, and then enable the usage of SLC-off ETM+. Much effort has been done to meet this goal, widely by different institutions and individuals. Currently, methods based on different assumptions have been proposed and demonstrated, some of which were also discussed in this chapter. Generally, for areas with spatially homogeneous property and less temporal fluctuation, most of them can perform well and the un-scanned pixels in the SLC-off ETM+ images are able to be recovered accurately. Meanwhile, in practice, the un-scanned pixels, locating in heterogeneous areas with obvious temporal changes, are difficult to be estimated. Proper selection of the fill images is important for the recovering procedure; nevertheless, the important criteria suggested by USGS & NASA (2004) are difficult to meet usually. In practice, for a specific application, method and recovering procedure should be determined by balancing its performance and efficiency, besides taking into account the availability of the fill image and land surface properties in SLC-off image. In some cases, images available from other sensors may provide valuable auxiliary information for tackling the SLC-off issue, after being properly processed.

It is worth to note here that, much attention should be paid to recover the SLC-off ETM+ images acquired over urban and suburban areas, although few researches have been conducted. Making full use of the recovered SLC-off ETM+ images is desirable for investigating changes in regions, which have experienced rapid urbanization and consequently suffered environmental deterioration at present. This is a very important and valuable issue, especially for many developing countries or regions, for whom financial supports given to afford abundant satellite images are limited. The recovered SLC-off ETM+ images, along with other Landsat data will provide an opportunity for these countries and regions to monitor, study and manage their own urbanized issues.

Author details

Feng Chen, Xiaofeng Zhao and Hong Ye
Key Lab of Urban Environment and Health,
Institute of Urban Environment, CAS, The People's Republic of China

Xiamen Key Lab of Urban Metabolism, The People's Republic of China

Acknowledgement

This work was supported by the Knowledge Innovation Program of Chinese Academy of Sciences, CAS (Grant No. 09L4401D10), the National Science Foundation of China (40901218) and (41101551). Thanks are given to data providers (e.g. CRESDA, USGS and NASA) for providing the images used in this work. The authors would like to acknowledge all who have contributed to this work, practically Dr. Jingzhu Zhao, Dr. Lina Tang and Dr. Quanyi Qiu, with the Institute of Urban Environment, Chinese Academy of Sciences. Many thanks to all authors of whose scientific publications or reports their work has profited in our manuscript.

5. References

Boloorani, A.D.; Erasmi, S. & Kappas, M. (2008a).Multi-source image reconstruction: exploitation of EO-1/ALI in Landsat-7/ETM+ SLC-off gap filling, In: *Image Processing: Algorithms and Systems VI,* J.T.Egiazarian & K.O.Edward, (Ed.), SPIE

Boloorani, A.D.; Erasmi,S. & Kappas, M. (2008b).Multi-Source Remotely Sensed Data Combination: Projection Transformation Gap-Fill Procedure. *Sensors,* Vol. 8, pp.4429-4440

Chen, X.; Zhao, H.; Li, P. & et al. (2006).Remote sensing image-based analysis of the relationship between urban heat island and land use/cover changes. *Remote Sensing Environment,* Vol.104, No.2, pp.133-146

Chen, F.; Tang, L. & Qiu, Q. (2010).Exploitation of CBERS-02B As Auxiliary Data in Recovering the Landsat7 ETM+ SLC-off Image, In: *Proceedings of the 18 International Conference on GeoInformatics,* 18-20 June, Peking University, Beijing, China

Chen, F.; Tang, L. N; Wang, C. P. & et al.(2011a).Recovering of the thermal band of Landsat7 SLC-off ETM+ image using CBERS as auxiliary data. *Advances in Space Research,* Vol.48, No.6, pp.1086-1093

Chen, F.; Zhao, X. F; Ye, H, & et al. (2011b).Exploring the Spatio-temporal Variations of Land Surface Temperature at the Land Use Unit Level. In: *Proceedings of the Third International*

Postgraduate Conference on Infrastructure and Environment (3rd IPCIE), Vol.2, pp.557-563

Chen, J.; Zhu, X. L.; Vogelmann, J. E. & et al. (2011).A simple and effective method for filling gaps in Landsat ETM+ SLC-off images. *Remote Sensing of Environment,* Vol.115, No.4, pp.1053-1064

Gao, F.; Masek, J.; Schwaller, M. & et al. (2006). On the blending of the Landsat and MODIS surface reflectance: Predicting daily Landsat surface reflectance. *IEEE Transactions on Geoscience and Remote Sensing,* Vol.44, pp.2207–2218

Loveland, T.R. & Dwyer, J.L. (2012).Landsat: Building a strong future. *Remote Sensing of Environment, doi:10.1016/j.rse.2011.09.022*

Maxwell, S. K.; Schmidt, G. L. & Storey, J. C. (2007).A multi-scale segmentation approach to filling gaps in Landsat ETM+ SLC-off images. *International Journal of Remote Sensing,* Vol.28, pp.5339–5356

Pringle, M.; Schmidt, M. & Muir, J. (2009). Geostatistical interpolation of SLC-off Landsat ETM+ images. *ISPRS Journal of Photogrammetry and Remote Sensing,* Vol.64,No.6,pp.654-664

Rajasekar, U. & Weng, Q. (2009).Spatio-temporal modelling and analysis of urban heat island by using Landsat TM and ETM+ imagery. *International Journal of Remote Sensing,* Vol. 30, No.13, pp. 3531-3548

Reza, M. & Ali, S. N. (2008).Using IRS Products to Recover Landsat7 ETM+ Defective Images. *American Journal of Applied Sciences,* Vol.5, No .6, pp.618-625

Roy, D. P.; Ju, J.; Lewis, P. & et al. (2008).Multi-temporal MODIS-Landsat data fusion for relative radiometric normalization, gap filling, and prediction of Landsat data. *Remote Sensing of Environment,* Vol.112, pp.3112–3130

Scaramuzza, P. & Micijevic,E.(March 2004).SLC Gap-Filled Products Phase One Methodology

Available from http://landsat.usgs.gov/documents/SLC_Gap_Fill_Methodology.pdf

USGS & NASA. (June 2003). Preliminary Assessment of the Value of Landsat 7 ETM+ Data following Scan Line Corrector Malfunction, Available from www.ga.gov.au/servlet/BigObjFileManager?bigobjid= GA3430

USGS & NASA.(October 2004). SLC-off Gap-Filled Products Gap-fill Algorithm Methodology: Phase 2 Gap-fill Algorithm,Available from

www.ga.gov.au/servlet/BigObjFileManager? bigobjid=GA4861

Wloczyk, C.; Richert, R.; Borg, E. & et al. (2006).Sea and lake surface temperature retrieval from Landsat thermal data in Northern Germany. *International Journal of Remote Sensing,* Vol.27, No.12, pp.2489-2502

Woodcock, C.E.; Richard, A.; Martha, A.; & et al. (2008).Free Access to Landsat Imagery. *Science,* Vol.320, pp.1011

Wulder, M.A.; & Masek, J.G. (2012).Preface to Landsat Legacy Special Issue: Continuing the Landsat Legacy. *Remote Sensing of Environment, doi:10.1016/j.rse.2012.01.009*

Zhang, C.; Li, W. & Travis, D. (2007).Gaps-fill of SLC-off Landsat ETM plus satellite image using a geostatistical approach. *International Journal of Remote Sensing,* Vol.28, pp.5103–5122